A Gathering of Promises

The Battle for Texas's Psychedelic Music, from the 13th Floor Elevators to the Black Angels and Beyond

A Gathering of Promises

The Battle for Texas's Psychedelic Music,
from the 13th Floor Elevators to the Black
Angels and Beyond

Ben Graham

Winchester, UK
Washington, USA

First published by Zero Books, 2015
Zero Books is an imprint of John Hunt Publishing Ltd., Laurel House, Station Approach,
Alresford, Hants, SO24 9JH, UK
office1@jhpbooks.net
www.johnhuntpublishing.com
www.zero-books.net

For distributor details and how to order please visit the 'Ordering' section on our website.

ISBN: 978 1 78279 094 5
Library of Congress Control Number: 2015934814

A CIP catalogue record for this book is available from the British Library.

Design: Stuart Davies

Printed and bound by CPI Group (UK) Ltd, Croydon, CR0 4YY

We operate a distinctive and ethical publishing philosophy in all
areas of our business, from our global network of authors to
production and worldwide distribution.

CONTENTS

Preface

While the original intention of this book was to provide a comprehensive overview of Texan psychedelic music from the 1960s to the present day, I soon realized that it would have to be at least three times as long in order to accomplish this feat. What started out looking like a very narrow and specific geographical subgenre soon proved almost limitless in its scope. It became clear instead that I would need to focus almost entirely on the music of the late 1960s and very early seventies, and as a result there is only the barest mention, if that, of major Texan psychedelic bands of the post-punk era such as the Butthole Surfers, ST37, Charalambides, Bedhead, Tripping Daisy, Lift To Experience, And You Will Know Us By The Trail Of Our Dead, the Mars Volta, Indian Jewelry and so on herein.

In addition to being forced to exclude most post-1973 artists I have also ignored scores of great Texan garage bands and one-single wonders, a swathe of artists that constitutes a whole sub-subgenre in itself. There has also proved no room to cover important groups such as Kenny and the Kasuals and the American Blues from Dallas, Mouse and the Traps from Tyler, Leviathan, Iota and Wailing Wall from El Paso, Space Opera from Fort Worth, Houston's own Josefus and Christopher and many, many others. Maybe next time.

What *A Gathering of Promises* actually developed into is the story of an inter-related family of 1960s-era bands from East Texas; specifically Austin, Houston, San Antonio and Corpus Christi, with the incomparable 13th Floor Elevators at their center. Their collective experience reflects the social and political changes that the whole of America was going through during that turbulent period, and the way that these changes manifested in a Texan context particularly. Although the bands concerned cannot be considered a movement as such, with common aims, objectives, philosophies and viewpoints, nevertheless they were

1

all aware of each other, often played together, dropped acid together and ultimately perceived a similar vision of unbridled possibilities, though even within the same band the exact nature of that vision was often hotly disputed.

The 13th Floor Elevators, Janis Joplin, the Red Crayola, Bubble Puppy, the Moving Sidewalks, the Golden Dawn, the Lost and Found, the Zakary Thaks, Fever Tree, the Children, the Conqueroo, Shiva's Headband, the Wig, Endle St Cloud, Euphoria and Cold Sun are all united by a shared history and lived experience. That is the subject of this book. These artists embarked on a disparate but connected gnostic odyssey from which some of them never returned, while others faded back into the obscurity from whence they came. Decades later, their music is now known and respected around the world and has directly influenced hundreds of younger bands, some of whom have enjoyed far greater material success than the originators. Meanwhile the Texan pioneers have suffered rip-offs, casualties, legal persecution, tragedy, madness and early death beyond even the usual notorious standards of the 1960s music industry. Hence, a Gathering of Promises; a remarkable coming together of huge talent and artistic vision in a specific and frequently hostile time and place, a great flowering that was nipped in the bud and cut short by circumstances, only to be eventually rediscovered by future generations of music enthusiasts.

It goes without saying that this book is by no means an exhaustive account of this scene. It is merely an attempt to provide a historical framework, an initial narrative to which others may care to add further color or corrections. The record reviews worked into the text should also be taken as only my own personal opinion regarding the relative merits, significance and meaning of the songs and albums discussed. Their main purpose is to send you back to the records themselves, to listen again and make up your own mind. I hope that this book is a beginning, rather than an end.

Acknowledgements

In my research I am aware that I am standing on the shoulders of giants. Paul Drummond's *Eye Mind* remains the definitive biography of the 13th Floor Elevators; it has remained on my desk throughout the writing of the present volume, and is recommended to anyone looking for a more detailed account of this remarkable band. Other names that have regularly recurred as I scoured the internet for articles and information have included Margaret Moser, Bill Bentley and the late Patrick 'The Llama' Lundborg. Though I've had no direct contact with any of these people, I acknowledge their invaluable assistance and their years of researching and writing on the Texan psychedelic scene.

Thanks also to Stu Cook, Roky Erickson, Ted Eubanks, Jim Frost, Clementine Hall, George Kinney, Paul Leary, Craig Luckin, Alex Maas, Billy Miller, Spencer Perskin, Rod Prince, Henry Rollins, Will Sheff and Powell St John for their time and generosity in speaking to me and answering my questions. With the exception of song lyrics and reported dialogue, all direct quotations in the text, unless otherwise accredited, are taken from my personal interviews and correspondence with the above. Personal thanks to Lisa Jayne, Dan Spicer, John Doran, Luke Turner, Phil Hebblethwaite, Will Lawrence, Greg Neate, Andrew Paterson, Neil Palmer, Dan Belton, Alan Hay, Gary Goodman, Daniel Shaw, Chris and Sadie Anderson and the late Mick Farren for all their help and encouragement.

Introduction

On an outdoor stage on the banks of the Colorado River, a 63-year-old man is leading his band through a set of churning, rhythmic, hard-edged blues rock. His grey hair cut short and neat, George Emerson Kinney looks every inch the respectable Texas rancher, dressed smart but casual in pressed blue jeans and white shirt. Yet something in the intensity of his performance gives him away. With the sun starting to set behind him, he lets his electric guitar swing round onto his hip and clutches the microphone stand fiercely with both hands. "There comes a time of starvation, and it is true," he howls. "If you believe in elevation it will happen to you."

George Kinney has endured the time of starvation, in terms of appreciation and recognition at least. He wrote and first sang this song, *Starvation*, with his band the Golden Dawn some 47 years ago, long before many in the audience at this, the 2014 Austin Psych Fest, had even been born. Yet it is also true to say that Kinney never stopped believing in elevation; that is, the potential of the entire human race to ascend to a higher level of psychic understanding and spiritual evolution, a belief that inspired both the name and the songs of the Golden Dawn when they formed in Austin in 1967. It was a belief that the Golden Dawn shared with their close comrades, the 13th Floor Elevators (whom Kinney is of course also acknowledging in the lyric), and it would appear that in the 21st Century, long after the original incarnations of both bands disintegrated under pressure and recrimination, things are indeed finally happening, both for them and for many of their psychedelic Texan contemporaries.

The seventh annual Austin Psych Fest is the largest yet, with over 6000 people from all over the world filling the campsite and attending the three-day event, as well as enjoying pre-festival warm-up events in Austin's clubs and bars. The music line-up is as international as the audience, with a broad definition of psychedelic music taking in acts from across North and South America, Europe, Africa, Australia and Japan. In 2014, the festival's superlative reputation attracted the Brian Jonestown Massacre, the Dandy Warhols, Acid Mothers Temple, Loop, the Horrors, Lorelle Meets The Obsolete, Jacco Gardner, Unknown Mortal Orchestra, Terakraft and more than 80 other artists including co-organizers the Black Angels, who more than any other band revived Austin's reputation as a center for psychedelic rock in the 21st Century. The festival also drew music journalists from all over the globe, and reportedly Hedi Slimane, creative director of fashion house Saint Laurent, diligently photographing audience and bands alike while researching his firm's latest line, 2014's 'Psych Rock' collection.

On the surface it might seem surprising that the upsurge in interest in psychedelic music, new and old, should be focused not on San Francisco or London or even Berlin (with the concurrent and related krautrock revival), but Austin, Texas. Yet the location of the world's premiere psych festival is no accident, and the organizers, the bands and the audience are all well aware of the city's rich and noble psychedelic history. What some may be less aware of is the extent to which the Austin establishment of the 1960s despised and persecuted pioneering psychedelic bands like the 13th Floor Elevators and the Golden Dawn, and how by the beginning of the 1970s the Texan psychedelic scene was considered dead and buried, an embarrassment to those who were a part of it, and a flash in the pan misfire before the era of progressive outlaw country that first put Austin on the map, and established its reputation as "the live music capital of the world." For decades it was Willy Nelson, not Roky Erickson, who was the beloved face of the Austin music scene.

"If the Black Angels could go back in time, they couldn't get a gig to save their lives!" laughs Billy Miller, a 13th Floor Elevators fan from the mid-sixties on. "They'd probably get run out of town on a rail by the music scene itself. So things have really changed; they are the music scene there now, and I'm glad to see it."

Though all native Texans, the Black Angels deliberately moved to Austin in order to start a psychedelic rock band, attracted as much by the city's heritage as by its reputation as a major contemporary music center. "When we first started there weren't tons of people doing that kind of sound," recalls singer Alex Maas. "You can't really touch the 13th Floor Elevators. You can get close; I hear a lot of bands now that I'm like, man, that really sounds like the 13th Floor Elevators, it's really good. But it's like saying someone's as good as the Beatles, you know, it's not ever going to happen."

When they co-founded the Reverberation Appreciation Society, the Black Angels began their transition into arguably the most important, powerful and influential band on the Austin scene. Set up to promote shows and release records by like-minded acts, the Society organizes not only the Austin Psych Fest but similar events around the world.

"The Reverberation Appreciation Society is me, Rob Fitzpatrick, Christian Bland and Oswald James," says Maas. "We started this organization and gave it this weird long name to do stuff like the festival, and we wanted to be able to help our friends if they didn't have an outlet for their music. We've met tons of great musicians over the course of our career, and tons that just don't have an outlet, and that was kind of why the society was created. It was to keep the music going, the music that we believed in. So we'll help them find outlets, whether it be stores that will sell their music or a presence online, or just developing the sound of a band."

This helping hand would also soon extend to the older bands that influenced the Black Angels, like the 13th Floor Elevators and the Golden Dawn. "It only makes sense and it's only fair to give back to that community and that ball of energy that we were inspired from originally. Whether that be Roky Erickson or the

Seeds or the Moving Sidewalks or Simeon from the Silver Apples."

Maas also has his own theories about why Texas was such a nexus for first generation psychedelic rock music. "It seems like with any action there's always an equal and opposite reaction," he says. "So if you have a conservative culture you will have a very liberal underground, whether it's powerful or whether it's modest in its approach to how it wants to grow. Austin's always been a kind of liberal town, and I think the conservative culture in Texas has naturally bred this interesting art escape, this opposite effect to escape from that."

Initially however the establishment response to the appearance of drugs, long hair, youth rebellion and talk of peace and love in Austin was far from liberal. The psychedelic freaks in Texas had to fight much harder just to survive than their brethren in California, London or New York, and this is perhaps what gives Texan psychedelia its distinctive punk edge. Unlike many of the Californian bands to whom the term was first applied, like the Grateful Dead or Jefferson Airplane, psyche-delic rock out of Texas is characterized by an aggressive urgency and desperation that has actually helped it to age far better than its more mellow West Coast equivalent.

Christian conservatism and repressive drug laws were countered by a strong belief in the freedom of the individual and a frontier spirit that could apply to mind expansion as much as lighting out for open land. There is much to be said though for the big skies and the sense of space to be found in the Texan desert and hill country, not to mention the visionary qualities of the native peyote plant, used as a shamanic sacrament by gener-ations of native tribes and curious adepts. The active compound in peyote is mescaline, referred to as "Texas Medicine" by Bob Dylan; mescaline was also the drug taken by Aldous Huxley in his celebrated account *The Doors of Perception,* and was used by notorious occultist Aleister Crowley in his proto-psychedelic

Rites of Eleusis performance of 1910. Though LSD became as popular in Texas as anywhere else, an initial grounding in natural psychedelics like peyote helped distinguish the Texan scene from its Californian equivalent, as George Kinney points out.

"LSD can be a very helpful psychedelic experience, but when all is said and done it is an artificial substance," he says. "When one starts to really get 'high' in the psychedelic sense, one begins to distrust such contrived substances. Psilocybin mushrooms and peyote are natural plants and have a long tradition of being used to enhance the awareness of humans. There is a sense of authority and security in ingesting these medicinal plants that is absent from taking LSD. The result is an experience that is both transcendent and natural simultaneously. One can experience the divine aspects of one's nature and still remained meaningfully connected to Mother Nature. The outlook and behavior, especially the music, expressed this distinction. That's why even the most psychedelic voyagers from Texas remained so down home. The main benefit, to me, of psychedelic music was to combine the transcendent elements of intellectual thought with a very physically moving rhythm and sound.

"Texas itself is a very powerful geographic location. The land and the history there is very unique. Texas used to be its own nation and the fierce independence of the citizens is a tangible ambience that pervades all areas of social and community life."

That "fierce independence" is crucial. Despite the often draconian enforcement of law and order, Texan mythology has also always idealized the rebel, the outlaw and the hard-bitten underdog fighting against the greater power. Nowhere is this last case more obviously exemplified than in the Battle of the Alamo, surely the most powerful archetype and central myth in the collective Texan psyche. Perhaps the brave heroes of the Texas Revolution, who died defending the Alamo Mission in San Antonio against impossible odds, set a precedent that Texas's 1960s psychedelic revolutionaries were already unconsciously following. And if Lubbock's martyred icon of early rock 'n' roll, Buddy Holly, had already captured the essence of the psychedelic experience in his song *Slippin' and Slidin'* (as Jason Pierce of Spiritualized has suggested), then perhaps his El Paso contemporary Bobby Fuller had already written the whole story of Texan rock, psychedelic or otherwise, when he penned his classic *I Fought The Law (And The Law Won)*, shortly before his own premature and still-mysterious demise.

Certainly, Texas's outlaw tradition and proximity to the Mexican border gave it a certain primacy in the American marijuana trade, which in turn meant that Texans had a greater connection and interaction with their fellow heads on both coasts that did any other southern state. Unlike in New York and San Francisco though, Texan psychedelia developed from first principles, and in this sense was truly gnostic, stemming from direct personal experience of acid and peyote rather than being filtered through the media or fashion. Also, Texan psychedelic bands were under far less pressure to temper their vision and make it commercial; being so far from the major centers of the music industry, chances are they were never going to make it anyway. Almost all of the records discussed in this book were released on small local independent labels, that didn't have a clue about this strange new music, but the kids seemed to dig it so what the hell, they thought, let's put it out anyway and hope it will sell.

And ultimately perhaps, the simple truth is that Texans just don't do things by half measures. If they're going to rock, they're going to rock hard; if they're going to drop acid, they might just take enough acid to kill a buffalo. And if they're going to make weird and freaky music, then it's going to be the weirdest and freakiest music you ever heard in your life. Enjoy.

PART I

RIGHT TRACK NOW

Chapter 1

When 18-year-old Rayward Powell St John arrived in Austin in the fall of 1959 as a freshman at the University of Texas, the city was almost unrecognizable from the high-tech metropolis it would one day become. The computing and dot com boom that would transform Austin's fortunes during the eighties and nineties was still the stuff of pulp science fiction, and the city that would come to describe itself as "the live music capital of the world" was still a relatively quiet, conservative community with a population of roughly 180,000; 20,000 of which were students.

"Austin was a beautiful city, a big town," Powell remembers. "And I was right in the middle of it, enrolled in a major university and living on my own. The living on my own part was the best part of all."

Powell St John had been born in nearby Houston in 1940, but had grown up in Laredo, close to the Mexican border. His father had owned a farm, and his earliest memories were of exploring the territory, roaming in the desert and along the banks of the Rio Grande River. When Powell was ten years old his father sold the farm and returned to his original career of teaching; the family moved to town, and Powell began attending Laredo's Martin High School, where his father now taught English and Algebra.

While some high schools gain prestige for their academic scores and others are known for the success of their sports teams, Martin's claim to fame was its first-rate school band, and potential players were recruited early. Although he had no experience as a musician, and didn't come from a particularly musical family, Powell had grown up avidly listening to the country music played constantly on the radio in rural Texas during the 1940s: Bob Wills and his Texas Playboys, Kitty Wells, Ernest Tubb and Hank Williams, whose 78 single *Jambalaya* was the first record he owned. Once he'd got used to living in town the idea of playing music himself began to appeal, and when the

Martin band director came to his grade school with a selection of instruments for the kids to try out on, Powell immediately put himself forward, settling on the flute. After about a year in the Martin school band however, Powell was forced to give up his first instrument when he began to suffer from horrendous ear infections that left him writhing on the floor, screaming in agony. It was discovered that he had unusually large Eustachian tubes, and doctors theorized that playing the flute was actually blasting the infection out of his throat and up into his ears. Powell quit the school band and the flute, but he was determined to keep on playing music.

Given his condition and the doctors' diagnosis, it's perhaps unusual that Powell selected another wind instrument to replace the flute, but it was one that would remain his axe of choice throughout his life; the harmonica. He bought his first harp from the Laredo Woolworth's, having spotted it in the shop window on the way back from the Saturday morning picture show. On the back seat of the bus home, he mastered the Stephen Foster tune *Uncle Ned*, and with no apparent aggravation to his ears either, although those of the other passengers may not have been so lucky.

Powell soon convinced his parents to upgrade his dime store mouth organ for a chromatic harmonica that had all the notes on it, and set to learning his chops with a vengeance. But there were few accessible influences or inspirations for a lonely young harmonica player to turn to; on the radio, his role models were more or less limited to ensemble players the Harmonicats, or the likes of John Sebastian (father of the future folk-rocker and singer-songwriter of the same name, himself no mean blues harpist) and Larry Adler, who played backed by a full symphony orchestra. Powell turned instead to jazz musicians for ideas, gamely attempting to apply to his harmonica the innovations that players like Sidney Bechet and Coleman Hawkins were bringing to the saxophone. Unaware at the time of pioneering blues harmonica players like Sonny Boy Williamson II and Little Walter, Powell mostly resigned himself to simply wandering around his backyard, blowing *Ruby* to accompany his dreams.

Powell had no thought of becoming a musician when he first arrived in Austin; enrolled in the Art Department and the Reserve Officers' Training Corps, he had vague hopes of becoming a painter or of pursuing a career in the army. But although Austin was still relatively small, compared to Laredo it seemed like the big city, and Powell soon found that his horizons were being widened by life at the University of Texas, generally known as UT.

"Laredo was a border town of about 6500, known as the Gateway to Mexico," he says. "Coming from that environment I was very callow and clueless. Austin seemed big to me then."

Austin of course was also the state capital, and as such was a hotbed of lawyers, politicians and campaigners, best captured in local author Billy Lee Brammer's classic 1961 novel, *The Gay Place*. One of the first radicalizing influences on Powell was the student Civil Rights movement, or more specifically, the staunch resistance it encountered from the authorities and the establishment.

"For my part I was very naïve, and coming from a community where I was a member of a minority group the correctness of the Civil Rights Movement seemed like a no-brainer," he says. "Therefore I was taken aback by the controversy swirling around the issue. That was my introduction to Austin conservatism, and it was an eye opener."

Although UT was one of the first southern universities to admit blacks, albeit as recently as 1956, in 1960 its dorms were still segregated, and its 200 African-American students were excluded from varsity athletics, drama productions, student employment and the University Long Horn Band, among other activities. Powell would soon realize that this casually institutionalized racism was typical of a pervading atmosphere of repressive conservatism and paranoia.

"While I felt free and liberated, the town was a very conservative place," he says. "The University tried to make up for the lack of parental control by providing a strongly paternal atmosphere and closely monitoring the activities of the student body." According to Powell, the University's conservatism was at least partly down to its reliance on certain Dallas billionaires for endowments. "They were very concerned about the Civil Rights Movement for one thing, lest it be a destabilizing influence. And when drugs came to Austin the reaction of the authorities was nothing short of hysterical, and the tension ratcheted up dramatically."

Nevertheless, Austin's reputation as a beacon of free-thinking liberalism compared to the rest of Texas was already in existence, though at this stage it was based on a small minority of left-wing students, artists, folk musicians and bohemian holdovers from a previous era. "UT was a major university and there were forward-thinking individuals and cutting edge work going on there," Powell admits. "It seemed to me that there was a tension between new attitudes, social movements and outside ideas, and the conventional and conservative ideas of the establishment."

Powell's introduction to Austin's limited counter-culture came via Ramsey Wiggins, his roommate when he was finally able to live off campus at the beginning of his second year. Up to this point Powell had been working hard and trying to fit in, but had remained socially isolated; Ramsey was an equally scholarly young man, but also a member of the Austin Unitarian Youth Group. He began inviting Powell to some of the group's social functions and parties.

Unlikely as it may seem, Austin's Unitarian Youth Group were considered by some to be the hip kids in town. They were young intellectuals and aesthetes with strongly held left-wing beliefs, the sons and daughters of liberal Democrats and veterans of the Labor Movement who had been brought up to believe in peace, social justice and equality. They also held a passion for art and music, and folk music in particular.

At the very beginning of the 1960s, the folk music revival, which would soon claim Bob Dylan as its Messiah and then its Judas, was in full hootenanny swing. It had yet to really penetrate the mainstream however, and remained largely the preserve of the socially-concerned, college-educated elite. While their younger brothers and sisters were listening to Elvis Presley, Little Richard and Buddy Holly, these liberal folkniks upheld a sometimes spurious but always well-meant cult of authenticity, and sought out the unsung originators of the blues and folk music the more celebrated rock 'n' rollers expanded upon, or commercially exploited and diluted, depending on your point of view. The more committed and thoughtful would also risk their educations, careers and in many cases their lives to support the African-American struggle for equal rights, as well as workers' rights and the peace movement. They spoke out against the spiraling nuclear arms race, were environmentally concerned, and were generally the originators of what would become known as the 1960s counter-culture. For these young people folk music was inextricably bound up with notions of political struggle and the voices of oppressed people around the world, and Texas and the other southern states were on the front-line of the battle for Civil Rights. Though already an instinctive egalitarian, Powell was relieved of much of his small-town naivety by the Unitarians and their liberal allies.

"These people showed me a lot about life, and the way things work in the real world," he recalled to the website *It's Psychedelic Baby* in 2011. "Whereas a year before I had been a spit and polish ROTC cadet passing in review every Thursday, I was now marching in a protest line trying to bring racial integration to the movie houses just across the street from the UT campus." As a result of the protests, the State and Paramount movie theaters both agreed to integrate in September 1961, and University housing was finally integrated in 1964. However, as late as the fall of 1963 Austin's 24,413 African-American residents were still barred from over half of the city's white-owned restaurants, hotels, motels, business schools and bowling alleys, and discrimination in housing and employment was sadly commonplace.

Simultaneous with Powell's political awakening was his introduction to folk music. Ramsey Wiggins' teenage younger brother, Lanny, was an accomplished singer, guitarist and banjo player, who scoffed when Powell told him that he didn't know any folk songs. "Do you know *The Ballad of Jesse James*?" he asked, almost rhetorically as the song was a part of most every Texan childhood. "Sure," said Powell, for whom it also held a special personal resonance, as he was brought up with the cherished and oft-repeated legend that his family was actually related to the famous outlaw. "Well, that's folk music," Lanny replied, and began playing the song, encouraging Powell to join in on harmonica. Powell had found his métier, and the two became a folk duo: the Waller Creek Boys.

The Waller Creek Boys were named after an urban watershed that meanders through downtown Austin and makes its way towards the university, becoming an area of shady, wooded parkland where students would traditionally gather to relax before or after classes. In 1969 it would be the scene of violent confrontation between student protesters and the authorities, when 40 trees were cut down to make way for an expansion of the University Football Stadium, and later fell into disrepair. In 1961 however the name still evoked a laid-back, urban-pastoral vibe, and associated the duo with a particular social scene among the students.

The Waller Creek Boys performed at student parties, summer picnics and anywhere that people were prepared to listen; one regular haunt was the weekly Folk Sing held every Wednesday evening in the UT Student Union, organized by Stephanie Chernikowski. Starting in early 1962, this was an informal gathering where anyone could get up and sing or play a song to their peers. Though small and unambitious to begin with, the Folk Sing would prove a vital cultural catalyst, and as the folk scene became increasingly hip and received attention in the mainstream press attendance snowballed. Starting with an initial group of a dozen or so amateur musicians, at its peak the Folk Sing would see nearly a hundred music fans and general non-conformists, including many younger kids who were members of the Folk Music Club at Austin High School, crammed into the student cafeteria, known as the Chuck Wagon. A more selective and low-key hangout was the backyard of a rundown apartment complex where a number of older artists, musicians and leftover beatniks lived, a building that Powell soon nicknamed the Ghetto.

The Ghetto was former officers' quarters, built during World War II and, like many such buildings, sold to the public once the war was over. A two-story structure that had been converted into apartments, it was located at the end of a gravel drive somewhat off the street and behind another house, hence its unconventional address: 2812 ½ Nueces Street. Through the late fifties and into the sixties, this building was home to a collection of poets, writers and artists who made up Austin's somewhat belated Beat Generation.

"Let me stress, these were not sumptuous accommodations," says Powell, who says that when he later moved into the building he paid sixty dollars a month, utilities included; cheap even for 1962 (other accounts put the monthly rent as low as thirty dollars). Because of both the low rent and the privacy afforded by being off the street, the building attracted individuals from throughout Austin's small but active bohemian community, and a younger crowd soon moved in as the beats moved on. It also became a place where like-minded spirits knew they could hang out and socialize without being threatened or ostracized by the straight majority.

"It was an island of hipness in a sea of conformity," Powell remembers. "Being poor and feeling marginalized and under-appreciated by the dominant paradigm, we tended to hang together, fearing that if we didn't we would hang separately. For that reason the place was called the Ghetto, in reference to the Warsaw Ghetto where another group of people had been brutalized."

Though the Austin authorities were convinced that the Ghetto was a viper's nest of subversive intentions, in reality it was just a rundown party space, where individuals of a liberal and pacifist bent would gather to drink beer and play music. There were two apartments on the ground floor and three above, one of which was a small studio apartment over a garage. This was taken by the first of Powell's circle to move into the building, long before he gave it its distinctive nickname; a musician named John Clay.

Though not widely known, Clay was a hugely influential figure in the early Austin music scene. A singer-songwriter and banjo player, he was often known as John the Dishwasher, from his job at a North Austin coffee house. Long and lean with close-cropped blonde hair, Clay was also a Linguistics student and a familiar sight around the UT campus, always dressed in blue jeans and a white t-shirt (before such a look became the unremarkable norm) and carrying a banjo.

"The first time I became aware of John was one day when I was in line at the cafeteria in the UT Student Union," Powell recalls. "A rather unusual individual was in line behind me, pushing a food tray with one hand and clutching a banjo with the other. It was early for dinner and some of the dinner offerings had not yet emerged from the kitchen. As we approached the cashiers' station and I was paying for my food this person leaned over and addressed the lady taking the money. Stabbing with his finger, gesticulating and struggling to form his question and get the words out he said, 'How, how, how long for the hamburger?' That was my first experience of John Clay."

Clay's stammer mirrored a corresponding lack of physical co-ordination, which hampered his banjo playing and made many see him as a gawky clown. The banjo was not taken seriously as an instrument anyway, unless one could play with showboating, rapid-fire dexterity like Earl Scruggs. "Many times when he would attempt to play a song he would get into it about halfway then make a mistake and stop," Powell remembers of Clay. "He would then start the song again from the beginning. As one can imagine, this made it very frustrating for an audience to listen to John's performances."

Clay's major gift though was as a narrative poet and songwriter, capable of crafting song lyrics that were by turns droll and amusing or thoughtful and sensitive. Many told long stories packed with historic and social detail. "I credit two individuals with giving me the idea that I could write songs," Powell states: "John Clay and Bob Dylan."

Dylan of course was in the ascendant nationally, his first few albums proving that it was possible to write new songs within the folk tradition, and with a unique individual voice that seemed both ancient and modern. But Clay was proof that one could be a songwriter closer to home too. "He was much further along in his study of traditional music than I was, and his study was more detailed," Powell admits. But nevertheless, Clay's songwriting was something that Powell could aspire to, and soon Powell's own original compositions began appearing in the Waller Creek Boys' sets, alongside Lanny Wiggins' vast store of traditional material.

Alongside the Civil Rights crowd, the art students and the folk music aficionados, another group that contributed to the small but lively counter-culture in Austin at this time was centered on the alternative student magazine, the *Texas Ranger*. In stark contrast to the straight-laced official campus newspaper, *The Daily Texan*, the *Texas Ranger* was satirical and irreverent in its intent, and was renowned beyond the university campus, winning several national awards for best college humor magazine. The unpaid staff and hangers-on around the magazine were a hip and hard-drinking bunch who styled themselves 'the Rangeroos,' and included some of the future founders of the 1960s underground comix phenomenon. Artist Jack Jackson (AKA Jaxon) and writer Dave Moriarty shared an apartment above Powell St John at the Ghetto, and from 1962 the *Texas Ranger* was edited by a rangy 22-year-old graduate student and cartoonist named Gilbert Shelton. Shelton's most important contribution to the magazine was the ground-breaking superhero parody *Wonder Wart-Hog*, which began that year and would soon gain fame and notoriety around the world. The strip's vicious parodies and deconstructions of everything that crew-cut America held to be right and true, along with its visceral, grungy and apparently careless art style, set the tone not only for the tiny Austin underground but for the wave of street hippy and even punk culture to come.

These people were the natural audience for the Waller Creek Boys, an anti-establishment, post-beatnik social circle that valued honesty and authenticity above all else, and were quick to ridicule anything that reeked of humbug, pretension or hypocrisy. They were angry about injustice, in love with art and music, and in unqualified revolt against the bland, status-seeking conformity they'd been all but smothered by all their lives. But although they had the attitude down, the Waller Creek Boys were nothing particularly special musically, as Powell would be the first to admit. All this would change however when they recruited a new singer; a first-year UT student by the name of Janis Joplin.

Chapter 2

Janis Lyn Joplin was born in Port Arthur, a Bible Belt oil town right in the south-eastern corner of Texas, close to the Louisiana border, on January 19th 1943. From the start of the forties till the end of the sixties, Port Arthur produced and exported more petroleum than anywhere else in the world. The intercoastal canal linked the town to the Gulf of Mexico, twenty miles away, and great tankers would travel inland to service the massive oil refineries where Janis's father, Seth, worked at a packaging plant for the Texaco oil company, producing metal cans.

Janis adored her father as a secret intellectual, a quiet, gentle man whose work was hard but frustratingly unchallenging. A college-trained engineer whose inner life was nurtured by books and philosophy, he used his engineering skills to design and build home-made playground equipment for his children, but could also be withdrawn and emotionally cold, a solitary drinker who felt defeated and betrayed by life; "the Great Saturday Night Swindle," as he described it to his daughter. By contrast Janis's mother Dorothy was a determined, independent and strong-willed woman who dominated the Joplin household, radiating a clear sense of morality (she was a Sunday school teacher at the First Christian Church) and adhering to a rigid code of what was considered respectable and proper. To some degree this was a matter of self-preservation; both Janis's parents had come from poor backgrounds but were upwardly mobile, and on settling in Port Arthur had just about managed to be accepted into the lower middle classes. Seth was the breadwinner, but Dorothy knew that keeping up appearances was just as important in maintaining their status as money.

Janis's mother hadn't always been so staid. As a young woman in the 1930s, Dorothy East had been most modern and liberated, shocking her family by cutting her hair into a bob, dressing in flapper fashion and smoking cigarettes, while frequenting dance clubs and reading Russian novels. Dorothy had also been a singer, with a soprano voice that had been promising enough to win her a scholarship to Fort Worth's Texas Christian University. But lack of money and disillusionment with the limited teaching on offer led her to drop out and find work in a department store, eventually rising to head of her section.

Dorothy continued to sing at home and in church, and by the time Janis was about five years old it was apparent that she had inherited at least some of her mother's talent. Dorothy bought a second-hand upright piano and taught Janis to play, singing along with her in the evenings. But Seth hated the repetitive, frustrating noise of a child learning her scales, and within a few months Dorothy underwent a thyroid operation that damaged her vocal chords and ruined her singing voice. The piano became a cruel reminder of what she had lost, and with Seth's encouragement was swiftly sold.

An only child until she was six, when she was joined by a sister, Laura, and later her brother Michael, Janis was precocious, doted upon, and made to feel like a little star. An intelligent, creative kid who learned to read early, she made up stories and poems from day one, and also invented plays which she performed in the Joplins' back yard with her friends. Mainly though she drew and painted, and throughout her childhood and teenage years it seemed as though art was her true vocation. Janis had a natural gift for color and composition that was nurtured and encouraged by her parents, as was pretty much everything she did early on. And although she was always somewhat timid, nervous and inward-looking, in the first decade or so of her life Janis was generally happy and well-liked; which is to say, she fitted in.

Although the oil boom had made Port Arthur the fifth largest city in Texas by the time of Janis's birth, it was still in many ways a typical American small town of the Post-War period, where conformity and a steady adherence to the ordinary and unremarkable were the qualities prized above all else. It was a thriving center of industry, part of the 'Golden Triangle' along with nearby Beaumont and Orange, where the refineries burned all night, lighting up the dark sky that stretched forever across the flat, featureless plains. By day the air was filled with constant choking smog, and the rotten egg stench of sulphur.

Nevertheless, if you worked hard you could do well, which invariably meant buying a decent house with a big lawn, a couple of cars and a new TV. Port Arthur was also well-provided for in terms of schools, libraries and health care; but the amenities and cultural life one might expect from a major city remained absent. The only bookstore in town was strictly Christian, the cinemas were popcorn drive-ins, theater the tamest amateur dramatics, and music pretty much the church or a De Souza driven marching band. As for museums and art galleries, forget about it.

What Port Arthur did have however was a rowdy downtown drinking scene and red light district, with funky beer bars, gambling dens, thirty-two whorehouses and a steady stream of customers among the hard-drinking oil men and sailors on shore leave. Throughout the fifties business was taken care of by a mob family from New Orleans, who also kept the Port Arthur police department tightly in their pocket. And like the police, all of Port Arthur's respectable citizens turned a blind eye to the sleaziness downtown, as well as the poverty and lack of opportunities in the strictly segregated black and Cajun parts of the city, which they nevertheless were forced to pass through in order to get to the lakeside beach.

It's easy to sneer at such bourgeois collective neurosis now; indeed, the hypocrisy and injustice of the situation was absolutely clear to Janis and her friends as they entered their teenage years. But the longing to be respectable, to conform, to be clean-living and pure of heart never quite left Janis, and it's important to realize that, for all her later rebellion, she believed in and internalized these values very early on. It didn't take her long to break with them spectacularly, but she was torn and tormented by them throughout her entire life. Her example may have liberated millions of similarly repressed girls and boys around the world, but however natural Janis made it look, it was far from easy, and cost her dearly. Eventually of course, it cost her her life.

This extreme need to fit in and be liked became apparent when Janis began attending school, as she joined one group and society after another, volunteered at the town library, sang in the church choir, and contributed to the school literary magazine, not to mention attending regular games of bridge at the Ladies Aid Society. She joined the Glee Club, the Future Nurses of America, the Future Teachers of America, and even the Slide Rule Club. But Janis had one fatal flaw in the eyes of Port Arthur society; she was just too smart for her own good.

In a town where culture and the arts were implicitly mistrusted, creative intelligence in a child was also to be viewed with suspicion. It was fine enough so long as it meant getting good grades in her classes, which she was certainly capable of doing; not so fine when the education system failed to challenge her sufficiently, and left her bored and looking for other stimuli. Not so fine either when she started asking too many damn fool questions, or loudly sharing opinions that differed radically from the way a nice girl in 1950s Texas was supposed to think.

One example occurred when Janis was 14 years old. The hot topic of racial segregation, and the integration of black students into the white school system that was just beginning in the southern states, was raised in a Current Affairs class. While each of her classmates argued in favor of continued segregation, Janis stood up passionately for equality and justice. She was yelled down and taunted as a "nigger lover" by several of her class-mates for the rest of the year. Meanwhile her teachers and her friends' parents noted that this formerly quiet and conscientious little girl had developed into quite the troublemaker, and a potential bad influence upon her peers.

It was true enough that Janis was changing. Both physically and psychologically, she had outgrown the role of timid, studious child and was searching for a new role for herself as a teenager. Initially she withdrew into a cocoon of depression and self-consciousness, a common reaction to the sudden shameful self-awareness of adolescence. Her pretty blonde hair darkened to a workaday brown, and while Janis remained relatively flat-chested the chubbiness that was considered cute when she was a little girl was now spoken of as a weight problem (though photos from this period hardly show Janis as being obese). More seriously, her skin erupted with boils, spots and acne so severe they required painful dermabrasion treatment. Everyone started saying she was ugly, and Janis stopped even trying to be pretty, at least by the Southern Belle standards of her time and place; she refused to wear make-up or style her hair, and her new look was somewhere between scruffy tomboy and a self-conscious imitation of the gum-popping 'bad girls' she saw on the arms of the duck-tailed thugs down at the drive-in or the 7-11.

Janis didn't drop out to hang around with the rockers, wasters and tearaways on street corners though; she was still too smart for that, and her rebellion took a more individual form, which just made it harder for the authorities to deal with. She had a few close friends her age, fellow misfits including Jack Smith, who she'd known since Grade School, Tary Owens, and girlfriends Karleen Bennett and the slightly older Patti Skaff. But she soon took up with a small gang of boys in the school year above her, who were not so much juvenile delinquents as junior beatniks; intellectual jazz lovers and wild card bookworms whose tastes ran to the esoteric, the forbidden and the surreal.

Initially this group congregated around the incongruous institution of the Port Arthur Little Theater, run by the mother of one of the boys, Grant Lyons, where Janis volunteered as a set painter the summer after ninth grade. They were the typical bright kids who rebel against authority, which in their case took the form of driving across the state line to go bar-hopping in the freer, funkier, Cajun communities over in Louisiana; climbing bridges and water towers at night, or getting drunk on the beach while reading Kerouac's *On the Road* and Allen Ginsberg's *Howl*, both newly published. Among this group were the jazz-loving Jim Langdon, who played trombone in the school band, and Dave Moriarty, a hip intellectual who edited the high school paper. Both would continue to play an important part in Janis's life beyond the confines of Thomas Jefferson High School.

In young boys, a bit of wildness was allowed, even encouraged as a healthy corrective to too much interest in books and music; it proved you weren't no mama's boy. But in a girl, well, that was different. What was she doing hanging round with these older guys anyway? Why the hell didn't she take more care over her appearance, and keep her mouth shut, 'stead of shooting off about race and freedom, and swearing and cussing like a cowboy? Janis could have had a tolerable time of it at high school by fading into the background like plain, homely girls were supposed to. But she was brought up to be the star, the center of attention; no way was the world going to push her to one side.

Instead Janis exaggerated her supposed faults, and created a cartoon character persona for herself that would develop into the hippie rock goddess of the San Francisco scene a few years down the line. Inspired by the beat characters she read about in Jack Kerouac's books, this Janis was loud, outrageous, crazy-tough, cynical, worldly-wise and sexually experienced. Never mind that she was still a virgin, and that inside she was still withdrawn, shy, confused and often desperately sad; she became Crazy Janis, with her deliberately annoying high-pitched cackle of a laugh, crashing every party going and shouting *fuck you, baby* if you don't like it.

Love her or hate her, you couldn't ignore her, and well, most people in Port Arthur hated her. But among the few that loved her, she was still willing to do just about anything to gain acceptance. She was ready to be the butt of any joke, to clown around or just be 'one of the boys'; whatever it took to be liked, to be noticed and to be part of what was happening.

As for sexual relationships, for a certain kind of boy Janis was certainly considered fun to have around, but that was as far as it went. Though she was labelled a slut by classmates and teachers alike, and played up to the stereotype in public, Janis was more naively innocent about sex than most of her peers, and hung onto her virginity till after she left school; longer than most of the conformist cheerleaders and potential prom queens in her year. Rumors flew that the novels she was reading, which included *Lady Chatterley's Lover* and *From Here to Eternity*, were pornography, and the boys assumed that she was easy and slept around just because of her appearance and attitude. More than one would drunkenly hit on her after their respectable, regular girlfriends had gone home, and the stories about her just got worse and more sordid after she refused to put out.

Janis's classmates spat at her and called her "pig"; her teachers wrote letters home to her mother, asking why Janis couldn't be more average, more ordinary. She was getting good grades, and her artistic talent was obvious for all to see, but she was still considered shameful, disgraceful. Her mother agreed, alienated and traumatized by this apparently complete personality change in her formerly perfect daughter. She too urged Janis to be more like everyone else, and had blazing rows with her over behavior and dress.

No doubt in her way Dorothy Joplin just wanted to protect her daughter from the crushing weight of social disapproval. There was also the possibility of actual physical harm from those who disapproved of her, and the very real dangers of teenage drinking and underage sex. But it's hard to sympathize when her parents started to regard even her painting as a sign of bohemian decadence, forbidding her to do nude studies and insisting that she concentrate on landscapes instead.

Port Arthur's prejudices against Janis Joplin were seemingly confirmed when, a week after her seventeenth birthday, Janis snuck off to New Orleans for the weekend. She'd asked her parents for permission but they'd refused, so Janis resorted to the time-honored trick of saying she was staying over at her friend Karleen's house, then borrowed her father's car (she'd got her driving license aged fifteen) to make the 520-mile round trip journey to the jazz capital of the world. Accompanied by Jim Langdon and a couple of other older guys, Janis spent the Saturday night roaming around, soaking up the scene and taking in some legendary New Orleans jazz. They drove back exhausted the next morning, but their car broke down following a minor collision with a stationary vehicle. They were picked up by the cops, who told the three older boys that technically they could be charged under the Mann Act with transporting a minor across a state line, implying statutory rape. There had been no sexual element to the escapade at all, but you wouldn't have known from the gossip that was all over Port Arthur by lunchtime. If any conformation were needed that Janis was a whore, this was it, case closed.

It was around this same time that Janis first discovered that she could sing. As in Austin, the folk music revival had hit Port Arthur, and the hip kids moved on from modern jazz to listening to and collecting folk records. Janis was no exception, and she began singing along with her discs using her remarkable skill as a mimic, previously employed solely for comic effect. Once she'd mastered the earthy growl of Odetta she moved on to the high, pure tones of Jean Ritchie, then practiced switching between the two.

Janis tried out her Odetta voice at a party, showing up the other kids in their poor attempts at one of her songs. She excitedly called Jim Langdon the next day, telling him she'd suddenly discovered she could sing. Langdon wasn't particularly impressed; he was the serious musician, while Janis's role in the gang was as the resident painter. Indeed, Janis still showed no overt musical ambition; she sang drunkenly along with the others and sometimes used her Odetta voice, but her paintings were the main thing. And on graduating from Thomas Jefferson High in the spring of 1960 she immediately enrolled as an art student, at Lamar State College of Technology in nearby Beaumont.

Lamar though turned out to be little better than high school; in fact, it was almost the same as high school, being just one town over and suffused with the same provincial attitudes. Many of the same kids who had tormented her at Thomas Jefferson had also gone on to Lamar and were found waiting, giggling and gossiping, right there in the Student Union. However she was also reunited with Jim Langdon, Tary Owens and Jack Smith, and Lamar had some positive experiences for her, though they had little to do with her coursework at what was essentially a vocational technical college, not an art school. She dropped out after the first semester, and struck a deal to take typing and keypunch operating courses at Port Arthur Business College, where her mother now worked as a registrar. Once she'd passed her secretarial exam, in the summer of 1961, she was to be allowed to move to Los Angeles, under the watchful eye of her mother's two sisters, Mimi and Barbara.

Living with conventional Mimi first, and then with the more liberated Barbara, Janis soon found a job as a telephone keypunch operator and moved into her own place, a slum apartment on Venice Beach. Venice was then still notorious as LA's beatnik district, but its fifties glory days were long past and it was now part squalid drug ghetto, part tourist trap. Nevertheless, Janis loved the relaxed, racially-integrated atmosphere, hanging out with poets, artists and musicians and even singing occasionally at the still-hip Gas House café. She also had her first serious sexual experiences with partners of both sexes. But after a few months

Janis decided to do the whole beat trip and hitch-hike the 400 miles to North Beach, San Francisco, where she hung around the famous City Lights bookstore and met its legendary proprietor, the beat poet and publisher Lawrence Ferlinghetti.

Janis returned to Port Arthur and her parents' home in time for Christmas, and on New Year's Eve Jim Langdon took her to a private jazz club in Beaumont, where Janis sat in with the band for one number. The musicians weren't keen on her raucous, Bessie Smith-influenced performance, and the audience response was pretty lukewarm too. But Janis continued to sing in public, and through the early part of 1962 made several open mic appearances at Beaumont's Halfway House and Houston's Purple Onion, and even demo-ed a radio jingle for a local bank, though her vocal was never used.

In what would become a familiar pattern of rebellious excess followed by a chastened regression to the norm, Janis re-enrolled at Lamar and worked part-time as a bowling alley waitress. Living at home with her parents again, she tried her best to meet them halfway, dressing relatively conservatively and attending church. But her evenings were often spent drinking on the beach with Jack Smith, moving from beer to Thunderbird wine and then on to Bourbon. As she drank, Janis would confide her struggle to be feminine and good and to control the wild demon within. But pretty soon the wild demon would win out again, and what remained of the old gang resumed their mad drives across the state line into Louisiana.

As well as blues and Cajun dance bands, the bars in Louisiana had liquor licenses, whereas in the Golden Triangle it was strictly beer only. Furthermore the legal drinking age was 18, compared to 21 in Texas. Janis would flirt with the roughnecks in the dodgiest dive bars, leading them on and getting them to buy her drinks all night, before splitting suddenly with her Texan friends, including Patti Skaff, Jack Smith and Jim Langdon; they'd claim it took four or five of them to make sure they got out alive.

It was after one such rout in a Louisiana bar that, driving back, the gang overshot Beaumont and Port Arthur completely, and carried on through Texas until, at 5.30 in the morning, they hit Austin. To be precise, they hit the Ghetto, and bundled into the fag end of a typical weekend party. Dave Moriarty was already living and studying there, and Jack Smith had visited and had talked up the city, or the campus scene anyway, as a bohemian promised land, full of kids like them who, you know, read books and listened to folk music; all the things that were decidedly beyond the pale in Port Arthur. Her expectations raised, Janis walked in, and was confronted by John Clay, sat on top of the fridge with a bottle of wine between his legs, singing and playing the banjo. Janis clapped her hands in excitement.

"I love it!" she cried. "I'm going to stay!"

Chapter 3

Powell St John was sat in the Chuck Wagon, nursing a lunchtime coffee and thinking about life, when he saw his friend and fellow art student, Tommy Stopher, walk into the cafeteria. It was fall, 1962, and the start of a new college year; Powell's fourth at UT. He had not seen Tommy Stopher for a while, but at that moment he was more struck by the young woman at Tommy's side. She was wearing a form-fitting black dress, with long, lank hair hanging way down her back. She was also barefoot and, to Powell's mind, extremely attractive. He was glad when Tommy immediately came over; Powell got to his feet and waited attentively to be introduced.

"Powell, I'd like you to meet Janis. She's a friend of mine from Port Arthur, and a vocalist of great talent." Now Powell was both attracted and intrigued; before he'd even heard her sing a note, he was planning a way to get Janis to join up with the Waller Creek Boys. They were already pretty popular on campus, playing at the Wednesday night folk sings right there in the Chuck Wagon, as well as at informal get- togethers at the Ghetto and other places. But a girl singer like Janis could increase their appeal no end. Especially if, as Tommy Stopher suggested, her voice was even halfway decent.

Janis had also enrolled as an art student at UT, persuading her parents to give her one last chance at getting her act together. From 1960 onwards, every freak in Texas had begun heading to Austin, attracted by the promise of a bohemian sanctuary where like-minded souls read and discussed books, and lived and breathed music. Sure, the freaks were still massively out-numbered by the straights; even on the university campus, there were maybe only a couple of hundred free-thinking liberals who could loosely be termed hip, in amongst 20,000 or so squares in their black leather loafers and crew cuts, and elaborate 'bubblehead' hairdos for the girls who for the most part still dressed like their mothers. But a couple of hundred in Austin was a darn sight better than twenty or so in Beaumont, or a dozen at best in Port Arthur.

Most of those Port Arthur hipsters had also shipped out to Austin, while Tommy Stopher and his brother Henry, known to all and sundry as Wali, both hailed from Beaumont; Janis had known them when she was studying at Lamar. They actually had an apartment at the Ghetto, as did other members of Janis's old gang; Dave Moriarty, Tary Owens and Jack Smith. Janis herself was prevented from moving into the building by the university regulations requiring first-year students to live on campus, especially female ones. Nevertheless, the bohemian warren and crash pad was her natural home from home, and the place where she would spend most of the rest of the year - drinking, smoking, arguing, enthusing, balling and, eventually, making music.

Fellow student Clementine Tausch recalled the first time she heard Janis sing. "She dragged a reel to reel tape recorder into one of the Ghetto apartments and asked all of us there to listen to it," she recalled to *Psych Trail Mix* fanzine. "She insisted on leaving the building while we listened, and warned us that we had better tell her the truth about her voice; no matter how harsh, she wanted to hear what we thought."

Clementine had enrolled as an Education major in 1961, at the grand old age of 22, and was already a divorcee with two young children. She knew a fair bit more about real life than most of the young kids at UT, but at this stage she knew next to nothing about blues music. Janis's tape, which featured raw, earthy renditions of a number of Bessie Smith songs, blew her away. She had never heard anything so powerful and emotional, and certainly not from a young white girl like Janis. Powell, Ramsey Wiggins and Wali Stopher, who were also present, were more familiar with this kind of music, but they were equally impressed. There was no doubt in their minds that Janis had got it; she was the real deal.

Nevertheless, Janis was still shy about singing in public. It was an odd contradiction; the persona she presented to Austin was of a loud, ballsy, hell-raising 'jive chick' who drank and cussed and didn't give a damn about anyone or anything. But the insecurity and lack of self-confidence was just below the surface, and liable to break through at any moment. "Don't shit me man; don't tell me shit you don't mean," she repeated, as Clementine, Powell and the gang enthused wildly over the performance they'd just heard on her tape. Janis and Powell began a love affair, but it took over a month before he was able to convince her to sing in public with the Waller Creek Boys.

Although her first live performance in Austin was at a loose, late-night Ghetto jam session, Janis soon became an official member of the Waller Creek Boys, alongside Powell and Lanny Wiggins. They were too hip to change their name; now Janis really was just one of the boys. But she was also the undoubted star of their regular Folk Sing spots, and as Powell predicted their audience numbers swelled once Janis joined. In fact so many people were coming down that it was becoming obvious the group needed a bigger venue at which to play. That place turned out to be a working-class beer joint and country music venue in an old converted gas station on the outskirts of town, named after its larger-than-life proprietor: Threadgill's.

Nowadays Threadgill's is an Austin institution, a popular down-home restaurant, watering hole and live music center. But back in 1962 the original roadhouse was the city's best-kept secret, despite having been a bar and music venue for nearly thirty years. Precious few changes had been made in that time and the gas pumps were still standing, gathering dust outside the former filling station on North Lamar Boulevard, the old Dallas Highway. The clientele hadn't changed much either, and for years no UT student would dream of setting foot in such a place, let alone a collection of long-hairs, beards and wastrels such as the Waller Creek Boys and their following.

Some inroads into this defiantly working-class subculture were made in 1959 when a bluegrass band made up of assistant professors and graduate students began playing there regularly. Moreover, the very unspoilt authenticity that this genuine, undiluted rural country music bar promised made it irresistible to the ardent song collectors and amateur field musicologists of the Ghetto, Powell St John among them. "To me, Threadgill's represented an opportunity to hear and maybe even play along with musicians that were playing the very type of music that interested me the most," he says. In fact, Powell now claims that he felt more at home at Threadgill's than anywhere else; that it provided him with the white, working-class environment he'd never had, growing up in 90% Hispanic Laredo and then finding himself isolated among the middle-class campus scene. "My parents were both from a small village in East Texas where gringos ruled," he claims. "I often wondered what it would be like to be part of such a community. Threadgill's gave me that community."

It was a community watched over by the stern but mostly benevolent eye of Kenneth Threadgill himself; a silver-haired, barrel-chested tower of a man in black spectacles and a tight white apron, who kept the jukebox stacked with Jimmy Rodgers songs and nothing else. It's fair to say that Kenneth Threadgill knew what he liked; and, thankfully, he liked the Waller Creek Boys, he liked Powell and, especially, he liked Janis Joplin. The rowdy girl with the big voice stunned the locals into appreciative silence when she sang, and Threadgill took a fatherly, protective interest in her. He and his wife both looked forward to her visits, and treated her as if she was their own daughter.

Yet as Powell's comments above suggest, Threadgill's was still very much a whites-only venue; no black person would even think of going to such an obviously redneck haunt. The liberal Folk Sing crowd may have marched and protested to integrate Austin's restaurants and cinemas, but they were prepared to turn a blind eye to the segregation in their favorite authentic working-class country music bar. Powell says he never felt that Kenneth Threadgill himself was a racist, just that he was born into a prejudiced culture, and ran a business that catered to that community; and indeed, while he tolerated the long-haired liberals and folk singers once a week, it was the good ol' boys that made his bread and butter. Racist material was still apparent among the posters and decorations on the bar walls however, and when UT music major and regular Folk Sing performer Ed Guinn, who just happened to be half black, half Mexican, asked to come down to Threadgill's to play with the rest of the crowd, Kenneth Threadgill apparently made it clear to John Clay that his friend wouldn't be welcome.

Ultimately, Threadgill's wouldn't be integrated until 1966; the man responsible was legendary Texan blues singer Mance Lipscomb, then 71 years old, who was idolized by student folk aficionados and working-class music fans alike. His reputation was such that Kenneth Threadgill was prepared to take a stand on his behalf, telling his regulars that a black man was playing there that night, and that he didn't want any trouble. He didn't get any.

Not only had Tommy Stopher introduced Janis to Powell St John, her first serious musical collaborator, but he was also indirectly responsible for getting her to focus all of her energies on music. Tommy was a seriously gifted painter, and it was after seeing his work that Janis decided that she was never going to be a truly great artist. She was good, but good wasn't enough for Janis Joplin; she needed a field where she could be the best, at least among her peers. When she decided to give up on painting, that field was music.

"Janis had studied American roots music in much greater depth than I had, knew many more songs, and performed them with great power and authority," Powell says. "Few have heard Janis sing Appalachian mountain ballads, but I'd say she was the equal of anyone performing the music at that time." He was also impressed with how hip she seemed; she had led the beatnik life in San Francisco and LA that he had only read about and aspired to. While the Ghetto crowd considered themselves outlaws, in many ways they were fairly naïve and buttoned down. They were serious musicologists and artists whose drugs of choice remained beer and liquor, and Janis was fully capable of shocking them with her behavior.

"Janis bought to the Ghetto the first joint I ever saw," Powell recalls. "She said it had come to her in the mail, sent by a friend in a garishly decorated envelope with stars and bomb bursts on it and an arrow pointing to one corner of the envelope with a caption reading something like 'Hey, look inside at what's in here!' In those innocent days one could receive a joint in the mail like this."

One reason nobody brought drugs to the Ghetto, according to Powell, was that they just didn't have the contacts; nobody knew how to get them. The other was that the place was under constant surveillance by the authorities. No-one was quite sure why; it was just felt that these shifty, scruffily-dressed characters must be troublemakers, and someone should keep an eye on them. It's true that many had been involved in peaceful political protests, against segregation and other issues, but the worst most of them did was to get drunk and play loud (acoustic) music.

"We were innocent liberals and pacifists but we had reason to be concerned about the attention we were getting," recalls Powell, who moved into an apartment in the Ghetto during that term. "The Austin police department sent a spy to infiltrate our social scene to try and get some dirt on us. There exists a document which the spy produced where this individual (we have never found the person's identity) speculates about the regulars who frequented the Ghetto. There was no proof provided for any of the allegations, of course; there couldn't be, as they were pure fantasy, produced by someone completely clueless as to what he or she was witnessing. But the police and the Office of the Dean of Student Affairs took it seriously. That's how I made it on to the Dean's list of possible troublemakers; although never in my entire university career did I make any trouble."

Incredibly, the notoriety of the Ghetto even caught the attention of the national US Justice Department. "One day I answered a knock at my door and there stood a fellow in a business suit who identified himself as an agent of the FBI," Powell remembers. "He said he was investigating a former roommate of mine, in the military at the time and under consideration to receive a security clearance. He said he wanted to ask me a few questions about this person, his character etc., to ascertain whether or not he should be given such a clearance. All of this seemed perfectly legitimate and although I was suspicious (because of my aversion to authority figures) I invited him in and we chatted for about half an hour.

"Subsequently I learnt from some of my friends that they too had been visited by the FBI, but the questions they got were nothing to do with a soldier being considered for security clearance. Rather, they were asked about the Ghetto. The questions were things like, 'How many people live at the Ghetto? What are they like? What are their meetings like and who are their speakers? To whom do they report?' My friends were puzzled by all this because they knew that the Ghetto was a rundown apartment building where people gathered to drink beer and play music. It was a party venue, not any kind of subversive anti-American cell bent on destruction. My friends told them as much. I later asked my former roommate about the incident and he said that he knew nothing about any security clearance, and so far as he knew he was never under consideration for one. Still, the surveillance continued."

This was of course the height of the Cold War, with the Cuban Missile Crisis of October 1961 bringing the world to within a hair's breadth of all-out atomic war. The McCarthy era of anti-communist witch hunts were only a few years past, and participants in the first folk music revival of the 1940s, such as the popular left-wing folk group the Weavers, had been among those investigated and black-listed. As late as March 1961, the Weavers' Pete Seeger was convicted of Contempt of Congress relating to the McCarthy hearings, and only escaped a ten-year prison sentence on appeal. Beat poet Allen Ginsberg was another early counter-culture figure harassed by the FBI which, under the control of the maniacal J Edgar Hoover, was instrumental in leading the witch hunt against perceived subversives, communists and radicals.

In the early fifties, President Truman expressed concern that Hoover was turning the FBI into his own private police force, even an American Gestapo. Yet Hoover remained in charge of the FBI until his death in 1972, and during the last decade or so of his life the former gang-buster turned fervent anti-communist initiated the infamous COINTELPRO campaign, an undercover department of smears, rumor-mongering and dirty tricks designed to undermine supposedly dangerous, anti-American groups. Those targeted included Civil Rights leaders, anti-war protesters, the Black Panthers, underground magazines, and film stars and rock musicians perceived as being sympathetic to these causes.

In this light, the FBI monitoring of the Ghetto during the early sixties doesn't seem so weird, and nor does the residents extreme caution regarding the use of dope. But the furtive, subterranean drug scene was about to explode dramatically into the open, in glorious, shameless Technicolor.

Chapter 4

"That was a damned risky thing to do," John Clay commented, of Janis Joplin bringing grass into the Ghetto, at a time when possession of a single joint could lead to a ten-year prison sentence. But while marijuana use was just beginning to take hold on the scene, one psychedelic was widely available and completely legal: peyote. This unassuming cactus, lacking the dangerous spines of its fellows, is native to the Texas desert and contains high levels of the psychoactive alkaloid mescaline. *Lophophora Williamsii*, to give the plant its Latin name, is a powerful hallucinogen that has been used by First Nation peoples for thousands of years as part of the sacred rituals of the Native American Church.

As a child, Powell St John had seen the American Indians gathering peyote every spring in his hometown of Laredo. They would either seek permission from the local ranchers to gather the plants in the wild, or would buy it legally from the local cactus nursery. "The proprietor would collect specimens in the field and plant them in beds at the nursery," Powell notes. "The tops of the plant (the buds) would be removed and dried. These would be sold. Meanwhile the plants were still in the ground, unharmed by the amputation of their tops and within a year or so would have grown new tops and be ready for harvest again. At that time all this was perfectly legal."

In fact, peyote was legal in Texas, but not so in other states. In California in 1960, prior to being exposed to LSD and forming the Merry Pranksters, Ken Kesey and his friends were ordering peyote plants through the mail from Powell St John's local cactus farm, Morris Orchids of Laredo, Texas. Powell himself first tried peyote in 1962, having read about Aldous Huxley's experience with the drug in the author's seminal psychedelic primer, *The Doors of Perception* (1954). He took the drug not for kicks, but in the sincere hope that the insights he gained while under the influence would make him a better artist. In Austin at that time, peyote was never viewed as a recreational drug, if only because of the unpleasant physical sickness that invariably precedes the psychedelic experience.

"Armed with the facts and with an open heart I chopped up a head of peyote (green part only) into a bowl of lime Jell-O and proceeded to eat it," Powell told *Psych Trail Mix* fanzine. After the initial nausea, Powell found himself transported out of his body to a place of pure white light and "an overwhelming sense of peace and love. I was at one with the cosmos and in the cosmic sense everything was perfect and right. It was the most profound spiritual experience I ever had."

The use of peyote in native rituals was part of the study of anthropology majors at UT, and generations of Texan bohemians and spiritual seekers had also partaken of the drug. Rumor has it that Chet Helms introduced the sacrament to the folk music and Civil Rights scene, via his anthropology student roommate, prior to dropping out of UT in 1962. A keen organizer of folk gigs and political benefit events, Helms was one of the first Austinites to head west to San Francisco, where he would be one of the founders of that city's world-famous counter-cultural scene later in the decade.

Another UT student with a keen interest in both peyote and folk music was Tommy Hall, although the Civil Rights movement left him cold, to say the least. "Tommy was opinionated, smugly confident, and politically conservative," Powell remembers. "But we were both Bob Dylan fans, and I liked him right away. Some people considered him to be 'full of it,' but I found him to be a very interesting character."

James Thomas Hall was born in Memphis on September 21st 1942, the son of a doctor and nurse couple. When his parents divorced, Tommy stayed with his mother, Margaret Perkins, known to all as Perky, while his father moved to Lubbock, Texas, married another nurse and had two further children. While

Tommy was growing up in fairly stringent financial circumstances, his father accumulated a list of wealthy patients and was living the high life himself. His new family lived on a ranch with a swimming pool, and when Tommy visited he felt resentful and angry, as though he were an interloper in his father's house; literally the poor relation.

As well as being extremely sensitive, the young Tommy had a high IQ which was nurtured and encouraged by his mother. They would collect rocks and fossils together, and she introduced him to a wide range of classical music. He was raised in the Presbyterian Church and devoured science-fiction novels and magazines. These were soon supplemented by an interest in nineteenth-century German philosophy, from Hegel to Nietzsche; two writers who in their different ways would greatly influence his thinking throughout the rest of his life.

Hall arrived at UT in 1961, majoring in Philosophy, and initially at least he seemed caught between two worlds. He was very interested in folk music, and became a regular attendee at the Chuck Wagon Folk Sings, but he had no interest in the left-wing politics that were taken for granted, though hotly debated, among the scene's adherents.

"He had slicked back medium-length hair, a messy beard, wore corduroys and brown shoes with white socks," remembered Clementine Tausch, who first met Hall at the Chuck Wagon. "He was reserved but occasionally came out with some pronouncement that sounded arrogant. For months, I did not like him."

Hall was a member of both the Student Republican Society and the newly-founded Young Americans for Freedom. This latter group is generally characterized as being ultra-right wing, but while the YAF was fervently anti-communist and pro-free market its resistance to big government and commitment to individual freedom also attracted many who would later characterize themselves as libertarians. Indeed, the growing dissent between the conservative and libertarian factions within the YAF led to a schism and the founding of the American Libertarian Party by disgruntled ex YAF-ers in 1971. The YAF was also against racial segregation during the 1960s, and called for an end to the military draft during the Vietnam War. The Libertarian wing within the YAF even argued for American withdrawal from Vietnam, along with the legalization of drugs; positions which brought them closer to their left-wing opponents than to their fellow conservatives.

Hall's politics were very much of this libertarian streak, and would inform all of his later work and statements. Furthermore this libertarianism, later informed and tempered by LSD's revelations of universal oneness and unconditional love, but essentially unchanged, would remain the underlying philosophy of much of the Texan psychedelic movement to come.

And while Hall was mistrusted because of his square appearance and supposedly right-wing beliefs, no-one could deny that he knew plenty about music, and had an impressively large record collection. It was this collection, and his willingness to lend key albums and rare 78s out to those who were interested, that allowed him a grudging free pass into the folk scene's inner circle.

Mixing with the Ghetto crowd, Hall's appearance gradually began to loosen up. Clementine Tausch remembers how he grew his hair and let it fall naturally around his face, Beatles style, but well before the Beatles hit America. He also shaved his beard and adopted a more casual, beatnik style of dress, sometimes wearing old Edwardian suits. Clementine gradually found him more attractive, and the pair began dating, attending the Folk Sing sessions together, where Tommy decided to try to learn a musical instrument, so that he could join in with the regular jam sessions. After trying and failing to master the mandolin, he fell back on the most primitive, down-home American instrument of all: the jug.

Jug bands had been popular in Hall's native Memphis since at least the 1920s, and could be found all across the south during the pre-war period, developing in parallel to the blues and jazz performers of the day. In particular, Will Shade's Memphis Jug Band were successful recording artists between 1927 and 1934, and were hugely influential at the time, arguably as important a prototype for the later skiffle and rock 'n' roll bands as were the electric blues combos. Indeed, the Grateful Dead would later cover the Memphis Jug Band song, 'Stealin', Stealin'' for their first single. The jug player would be just one element in a usually African-American group of musicians who through necessity would fashion their own instruments. These might include homemade guitars and improvised percussion, washtub bass, spoons, washboard and kazoo. In this line-up, the jug would play the part of the trombone or tuba, accentuating the rhythm with low, vibrating parps. The jug would generally be a large earthenware model with a narrow top, which the player would blow into from a distance of about an inch, using the jug's interior as a resonating chamber.

Hall very soon developed his own distinct style on the jug. Not content to be merely a rhythm player, he began vocalizing lead lines inspired by modern jazz artists like Ornette Coleman and John Coltrane. His long, oscillating breaths would create an eerie effect like the wind blowing through an old abandoned house, and had a divisive impact on fellow musicians and audiences alike. Many found it intrusive and non-musical, while others found it fascinating and unique. Certainly, Tommy Hall had found an instrument that suited his personality to a tee.

Tommy and Clementine grew closer when she agreed to coach him in Freshman English, a compulsory course in the first year which Tommy was failing, though in a way that only demonstrated his particular genius. "Freshman English is a required subject, and he had managed to avoid it before he met me," Clementine recalls. "Once we came to know each other, he decided he would try to pass it with my help. I worked for hours coaching him. The absolute hardest thing for him to do was to write essays that contained a certain number of words. He told me that a 1000-word essay on a subject that required only 500 words, or a 500-word essay that required 1000 words, were both impossible tasks."

Clementine and Tommy had been a couple for some time before they first tried peyote. They put up with the extreme sickness and nausea for the psychedelic revelations that followed, but pretty soon they started trying to think of a way to avoid the initial illness.

"We boiled the peyote buttons down until they were a paste, then we inserted the paste into large gel capsules, and then we shellacked the capsules before swallowing them," Clementine says. "The idea was that the capsules would not dissolve in the stomach, but would wait until they reached the intestine, at which point we would get high without any nausea. This process worked beautifully, and we never experienced any ill effects from ingesting the shellac; there was so little of it on the capsules. I have fond memories of sitting around a kitchen table with Powell and Tommy, filling and shellacking those capsules, laughing the whole time."

One member of the Ghetto scene who tried peyote and definitely didn't enjoy it was Janis Joplin. "Tommy, Powell St John and I thought the misery of severe nausea well worth the results of taking peyote," Clementine says. "Janis mostly just got sick." Despite being credited with introducing grass to the ghetto, Janis was not by nature inclined towards psychedelics, and had no wish to explore inner space or to confront her personal demons. Possibly she realized that the risk was too great; that her demons were more powerful than most, and could easily overpower her. Instead, her tastes leant more towards body drugs, and those that promised an escape from reality into sweet oblivion; alcohol, speed, and prescription downers like Seconal.

Janis was having a rough time of university life anyway. While most of the bohemian Ghetto crowd kept their heads down and tried to stay as anonymous as possible, she just couldn't help but attract attention. Barefoot and bra-less, she was profiled in the official university paper, *The Daily Texan*, as the campus freak, the symbolic representative of all that was weird and non-conformist among the student body. And while the caricature was mostly good-natured, she would also become the obvious scapegoat for all those who resented the emerging counter-culture as feckless and decadent, lazy, dangerous and downright un-American.

The turning point came when Janis was nominated for 'Ugliest Man on Campus' in 1962. This was a regular contest in which male jocks from different fraternities would dress up as grotesquely as possible during several weeks in October. There are those who maintain that Janis nominated herself; others who insist her name was put forward by her friends at the *Texas Ranger*, as a subversive joke that she was fully aware of. But whether she was initially in on it or not, the prank snowballed to the extent that Janis's feelings and self-esteem took a serious bruising. She was always the first one to laugh at herself, but no-one wants to feel like they are no more than a joke to their peers. Especially not a young girl with an already fragile ego, who, many say, was already suffering from depression during her first year at university.

The break came just after Janis's mid-term exams. Chet Helms returned to Austin on one of his periodic visits from San Francisco, and hung out with the Ghetto crowd over the Christmas period. Come January, he convinced Janis to drop out and hitch-hike back to San Francisco with him. Partly she just wanted to "get the fuck out of Texas," but Chet also told her that she had the raw talent and authenticity to really make it in San Francisco; that she was wasting her time in a relative backwater like Austin.

Certainly, it was obvious to all that an era was coming to an end. The Ghetto was increasingly under surveillance by the authorities, and was subject to continual harassment, such as the city health authorities blasting the occupants with roach powder from a truck while they were all sat out in the courtyard. Janis for one got the message. In January 1963, after a failed attempt to persuade Powell St John and Lanny Wiggins to come with her, Janis Joplin left Austin and the Waller Creek Boys behind, and lit out for the West Coast.

PART II

THE KINGDOM OF HEAVEN IS WITHIN

Chapter 5

As the Austin folk scene gathered momentum and spread from the university to the coffee houses and clubs downtown, two local high school kids started to be regular faces at the gigs. Sitting listening intently on the sidewalk outside when they weren't allowed in, George Kinney and Roger 'Roky' Erickson may have been only 15 years old but they were already enthusiastic rock 'n' roll fans and budding musicians, drawn to folk music as a potential vehicle for original songwriting.

Austin had a handful of local rock 'n' roll bands (kid bands, the university crowd called them) but they just played covers of standards and the hits of the day, often instrumental surf tunes like the Ventures' *Walk, Don't Run*. Roky and George were aspiring songwriters as well as musicians, but it was unheard of in 1962 for a couple of 15-year-old rockers to try to compose their own material. Nevertheless, the pair could often be found busking on the sidewalk outside the folk clubs for spare change, playing blues or folk standards they'd picked up from older musicians like Jerry Jeff Walker, Carolyn Hester and Townes Van Zandt.

George Kinney was born on 20th December 1946; Roger Kynard Erickson followed just under seven months later, on 15th July 1947. The Ericksons had moved to Austin from Dallas after the war, when Roger Erickson senior enrolled as an architecture student at UT under the Veterans' program, purchased some land on the edge of town, and designed and built the family house. Nearby, the Kinneys were an old Austin family, as proved by their address: Kinney Lane.

"My mother was a theatrical director at the only theater in Austin at the time, and my dad was an actor," George Kinney explains. "They met at the University of Texas. We lived in the 'Kinney Home,' a 200-year-old limestone mansion in South Austin, built by my forebears back before the Texas Revolution.

My family raised horses in the hill country one generation before I was born."

Roky's mother, Evelyn Erickson, was a talented singer and performer who soon enrolled in the UT theater group, which further bonded the Ericksons and Kinneys. "My mom and dad were the belles of the ball in the Austin drama scene and I was raised among actors, writers and directors, often celebrating almost any occasion at our big house," George Kinney continues. "I had my first singing gig at the tender age of four, singing cowboy songs standing on a barstool to reach the mic."

George and Roky grew up together, and were permanently in and out of each other's homes. Roky had two younger brothers, Mikel and Donny, born in 1950 and 1951 respectively, but he remained the favored eldest son, by all accounts spoiled rotten by his mother. His father meanwhile was increasingly absent, working long hours at the office as his architecture practice grew more successful. His specialty was designing swimming pools, a relatively glamorous line of work which drew the family into some pretty fancy social circles.

Attending conventions and throwing lavish parties at home, Evelyn was a natural, if brittle, hostess and social butterfly, and Roky learnt to turn on the charm and play the part expected of him. Roger meanwhile worked hard and put away the booze. "Mom's a neurotic and dad's an alcoholic," was Roky's succinct summary of the family situation at the time, one that also reflected his notably dark and sophisticated childhood sense of humor. And at the age of 12 Roky took a perhaps symbolic dive into the family's own swimming pool (designed by dad) and broke his leg.

"It was supposedly called a musical household but it was kind of an unsolved, America's most interpretive guidance help mystery," Roky told *The Quietus* website in 2009. "They just wanted me to play music. I just had one guitar, a little tiny guitar. Most of the time all my studies were real kind of groovy; I really had to stick with it, but somehow I got it and I didn't really have to do it, I guess. I just went wow, oh my god... I just got it, you know?"

Evelyn had encouraged Roky to perform in public almost before he could walk or talk, pushing him into acting, singing and playing music throughout his childhood. By the time of his accident however, Roky had fallen completely under the spell of rock 'n' roll music. Elvis, Little Richard, Chuck Berry and Texas's own Buddy Holly were blasting out over the airwaves from the mid-fifties onwards, firing up a generation of rebellious kids, usually amid much parental disapproval. But if rock 'n' roll was what got Roky going, then Evelyn was behind him all the way, and for Christmas 1958 she personally bought all her sons electric guitars and amplifiers.

George had also got the rock 'n' roll bug, and spent many afternoons round at the Ericksons' house, listening to 45s and trying to figure out the songs. They were soon joined by another school friend, John Kearney, whose family had moved from Houston to Austin in 1959. Kearney's mother began teaching music at Porter Junior High, where John Kearney found himself a classmate of George and Roky. Being the new kid who arrived with his mom as the new teacher, Kearney was something of an awkward outsider and misfit, but coming from a musical family he was already a fairly accomplished drummer and, like Roky, attended St David's Episcopal Church in downtown Austin.

Roky's mother in particular was heavily involved with the church. The congregation provided friendship and guidance outside of her often stressful home life, and she ardently attended the regular prayer group meetings. Roky had gone to church with her every Sunday from the age of five onwards, and was an altar boy and a member of the junior choir. John Kearney, also an altar boy, recalls how Roky was known for bringing his guitar to the church youth group, though it didn't seem at this stage as if he had any serious musical ambitions beyond entertaining people and making them happy.

Aside from music, Roky's other main passion was horror movies. He would sneak into the local cinemas, underage and unaccompanied, to watch and re-watch endless 1950s horror B-movies and shockers. Kearney recalls staying up late watching Dracula movies on TV with Roky until inevitably Roky's father would wander in during the early hours, drunk and disoriented. When Roky and George would bunk off school to practice their screams at an old abandoned house, Roky was influenced as much by the scream queens of these horror movies as by Little Richard or James Brown.

Inevitably, George and Roky soon formed their own band. They were known as the Fugitives, and were backed by school friends Bill Hallmark on bass and Gary Pounds on drums. They added the emerging British Invasion sounds of the Beatles and the Rolling Stones to their rock 'n' roll cover repertoire, and although their performances never went beyond the garage, it was obvious that Roky was a natural performer. A born enter-tainer and a gifted mimic with a powerful singing voice, even aged 15, he could do uncanny impersonations of Buddy Holly, Mick Jagger, Little Richard or James Brown, switching styles at the drop of a hat. His specialty however, was that blood-curdling scream; a raw battle cry of liberation and excitement that thrilled and chilled in equal measure.

By this time George, Roky and John had all graduated to William B Travis High School in South Austin, and while George and Roky were messing around in the garage with the Fugitives, Kearney had been head-hunted to join one of the top local high school bands. A mutual school friend, Jimmy Bird, invited Kearney to jam with him and a boy from the year above, John Shropshire, who was already a semi-pro singer-guitarist with his group the Spades. As it happened, the Spades had just lost their drummer and had a full sheet of bookings, so the 15-year-old Kearney quickly joined Shropshire in the band with cousins Jack

Roundtree (lead guitar) and Ernie Culley (bass).

The Spades played fraternity parties most weekends, and also hustled for club gigs in town. These were few and far between, as in early sixties Austin there were no real rock 'n' roll clubs. The band were underage and their Beatles, Stones and Chuck Berry covers wouldn't have fitted in either at the folk music coffee houses or the sophisticated jazz and supper clubs that then dominated the city's nightlife. The exception was the Jade Room, a club that was unusual in that it had recently started allowing teenagers in, although you couldn't order alcohol at the bar unless you were over 21. Dressed in smart, matching, maroon blazers, the Spades soon wrangled a Thursday night residency, and gradually the fraternity students who had enjoyed their shows at the weekends started coming down to the club, displacing the older clientele.

In the wake of the Beatles, rock 'n' roll bands were starting to be hip and popular, and in Austin, as elsewhere, the local scene began to expand. Bands like the Deeds and the Babycakes were also playing regularly, and the Spades got their first out-of-town bookings. They also began thinking about writing their own material. This was another sea-change initiated by the Beatles; before Lennon and McCartney there was a pretty strict divide between the performing singers and musicians in a band and the professional songwriters that wrote for them. Obviously there were exceptions, like the Beach Boys' Brian Wilson, but certainly at a local and high school level, bands just weren't expected to write their own material. Now though, even the Spades were trying to come up with original songs, with a view to releasing a single on a local label that would then hopefully get them better bookings and publicity via local radio and newspapers. Back in his South Austin bedroom, Roky Erickson was also applying himself to the craft of writing commercial rock 'n' roll songs. Dissecting his influences like a horror-movie mad scientist, determined to understand what made them vital and alive, he soon distilled their essence into two songs he thought were strong enough to be performed live: *We Sell Soul* and *You're Gonna Miss Me.*

In a way, the whole story of Texan psychedelic music peaks right here. As early as 1963, the defining song of the whole movement, perhaps of the whole garage-psych genre, in or out of the Lone Star State, had already been written. The fact that it was written by a 15-year-old schoolboy who had never yet smoked dope, much less taken acid, who was only beginning to furtively explore the illicit pleasures of alcohol and cigarettes even, should not detract from the status of *You're Gonna Miss Me* as a psychedelic classic.

Just as it wasn't inspired by drugs, the song was not influenced by any kind of esoteric literature, and contains no deep hidden meanings. It seems fairly certain though that Roky was addressing *You're Gonna Miss Me* to his mother. Compared to the attention that was lavished on him as a child, Roky felt neglected as a teenager; moreover, his rebellious ways naturally provoked arguments. By the age of 14 he was already dealing with this situation by absenting himself from it, spending days or weeks at a time at the houses of friends or older acquaintances, usually musicians he'd met on the Austin folk/blues scene.

The lyrics are disguised as a put-down to a lover, addressed to "girl," "baby" and "child." But Roky had barely dated a girlfriend at 15, let alone lived with one, which is the scenario described in the song. Instead, it is his mother who "didn't realize," who will "wake up one morning as the sun greets the dawn" to find Roky gone: "I'm not coming home." "How can you say you miss my loving, when you never needed it?" runs the song's most cutting line; yet one can more easily imagine this line being delivered by the mother to the wayward son, who is now regretting the severing of all ties.

On the other hand, Roky was also merely synthesizing his influences, and it's likely he didn't put too much conscious thought or autobiography into the words. Bobby Darin's 1958 composition, *Early in the Morning*, covered simultaneously on a single by Buddy Holly, has the chorus "You're gonna miss me, early in the morning, one of these days." Roky simply amped-up the punk kiss-off implicit in the sentiment; he didn't care if you missed him or not, too bad, loser, he was gone. Beg, plead and cry all you like; you missed your chance, he just wasn't coming back.

You're Gonna Miss Me wasn't a psychedelic classic yet, however; it was merely a powerful, primitive rock 'n' roll song, or possibly an early example of folk-rock, as Roky's writing seems as influenced by the strummed acoustic dirges and talking blues of the folk scene as the jump-jive, rhythmic imperative of early rock 'n' roll. With the same repetitive four-chord sequence running through most of the song, verses and chorus, it suddenly shifts into a menacing minor key for the middle eight, before returning to the four-chord round for the ride home.

It's this very simplicity though, the almost hypnotic repetitiveness, that makes the song potentially psychedelic, long before the concept of psychedelic rock had even been thought of. Pounding and trance-like at the same time, it also only really works when Roky is singing it. It's his feral growl and desperate screams that give the song its rock 'n' roll energy; sung normally, prettily, it could easily just be a rather sub-standard folk ballad. As it is, the song has a passive-aggressive tension that reflects its author's developing personality, and in this way it's similar to John Lennon's early Beatles compositions; the minimal chord changes and arrogantly lazy structure, the tendency to prefer a modal drone over a lively, McCartney-esque melody. But all these qualities are also pure Roky. Like Lennon, his lyrics are sensitive, wounded, inward-looking and self-regarding, but cloaked in a defensive toughness (which, again like Lennon, he would eventually outgrow).

You're Gonna Miss Me is the song of a spoilt child with a sense of disappointed entitlement, not striking out violently but shuffling moodily around in a carefully contrived sulk. And who but Roky would have written that dramatic shift to a minor key, crafting a passage of horror-movie tension unheard of in most popular songs of the day? Most rock, pop and folk used dynamic key changes either to liven up the dance floor or to cause listeners' hearts to soar, whether in the service of teenage infatuation or political idealism. Here, the effect is one of distinct psychological unease, coupled with a thrilling theatricality; elements that would further make it a perfect fit for the acid-tripping space cadets it would later enrapture.

Both Roky and George left home when they were 17, in 1964, and rented apartments on the same street in Austin. George worked as a night watchman to pay the rent, and attended school during the day, writing poetry in his spare time. Roky stayed up all night playing his guitar and smoking marijuana, which had started to become available around the bohemian coffeehouse circuit, and paid his way by working part-time at his father's architecture firm. Technically he was still going to school too, but his attendance was becoming erratic and his studies were starting to slip.

Still, Roky did put in a memorable school appearance at the end of that term. May 1965 marked the annual high school talent contest; the Spades were to headline, having released their first single the previous month. *I Need a Girl* was a John Shropshire composition, backed by a version of the popular Bobby Freeman rave-up, *Do You Want to Dance*; it was released on the Zero label, set up especially by their booking agent, Gary McCaskill. But following the Spades' professional, well-received set, the compere announced a surprise act: Roky Erickson, on guitar, harmonica and vocals, backed by drummer Joe Bierbower.

Though Roky's one-song performance, possibly a Howlin' Wolf number according to John Kearney's recollections, was shockingly rough and shambolic, it was also undeniably spell-binding. What impressed was Roky's powerful singing; raw and confident, with a soulfulness that belied his tender years, and his ferocious harmonica playing. The members of the Spades were impressed enough that, when lead guitarist Jack Roundtree announced that he was leaving to get married a few weeks later, John Shropshire suggested that Kearney's little friend with the big voice might like to join up as well.

Roky had already put together a band called the Roulettes, with Joe Bierbower and guitarist Gary McFarland, but the Spades were a big deal locally. He accepted their offer, and brought with him a repertoire of James Brown and Little Richard numbers, as well as his own songs, *We Sell Soul* and *You're Gonna Miss Me*. Roky didn't try to introduce his compositions into the Spades' sets immediately, but kept them in reserve until he had his feet under the table. While all the band members took turns at singing and had their specialty numbers, they knew full well that in Roky's powerful vocals they had a devastating secret weapon. Roky soon took over as lead singer, and with the Spades already planning another single on Gary McCaskill's Zero label, Roky's songs were the prime candidates to be recorded.

Chapter 6

Back at UT, Tommy Hall's ravenous intellect was refusing to adhere to any one discipline. Growing ever more interested in the arts, he began writing poetry, possibly inspired by his girlfriend Clementine Tausch, who had switched her major from Education to English and had begun writing a novel. The pair also found time to attend a Music Appreciation course taught by departing music professor John Swanee that was so popular it ran on Saturday mornings at 7.30am. Devouring mystical authors like Gurdjieff and Ouspensky, Hall still sought to place his ideas in a scientific framework, and feeling that he'd learnt all he could from his Philosophy course he changed his major to Psychology, specializing in Psychochemotherapy.

This now obscure term referred to early psychopharmacology and the study of psychiatric or psychoactive drugs in treating mental illness, which was considered as a biochemical disorder. The use of laboratory-mixed antidepressant and antipsychotic drugs had exploded during the 1950s, joining the existing medically-sanctioned stimulants and sedatives; generally derived from opiates, barbiturates or amphetamines, and often available over the counter or on prescription from your local chemist. Hall's interest however was less in the use of drugs to cure illness or stabilize imbalances, but to access hitherto unrealized potentialities within the human mind.

It was under the auspices of UT's Psychochemotherapy department that Hall first tried LSD, probably sometime during 1964. At this point LSD was still legal and wasn't widely available as a street drug, certainly not in Austin. Scientists and doctors were still experimenting with the substance for possible medical and therapeutic use, while the US government and military were also interested in the potential of LSD and other drugs as instruments of mind control, interrogation and torture. This shady chapter in US government history was the responsibility of the CIA's top secret MKULTRA project, now known to have carried out secret LSD tests on military personnel and civilians alike, usually without the subject's permission or even knowledge. Throughout the 1950s and early sixties, surreptitious dosing by authorized government bodies resulted in several reported cases of insanity and suicide; yet as all official records were destroyed in the early seventies, we may never know the true damage caused. Several sources have referred casually to clinical LSD trials being carried out at UT, and although again no official records of such tests exist, the University of Texas has been linked to the MKULTRA project in subsequent investigations.

"As to Tommy's LSD experiment in connection with the psychology department, neither he nor anyone else I knew figured out what that was about," says Clementine, who distinctly remembers reading an article on the tests in a campus magazine at the time. Ken Kesey and Grateful Dead lyricist Robert Hunter both volunteered for what turned out to be MKULTRA-sponsored LSD tests while at Sanford University during the early 1960s, conducted at the nearby Menlo Park Veterans Hospital, and Tommy Hall may well be another counter-culture figure who was first initiated into LSD by the CIA. One thing that is certain is that Hall found the experience of taking LSD in a clinical setting extremely uncomfortable. Knowing that you were being observed and tested while in a vulnerable state was a sure-fire way to induce paranoia, compounded by realizing that your responses were only confirming 'Their' theories. Yet the drug itself was fascinating. The doctors and scientists saw LSD as a psychomimetic, in that its effect appeared to simulate schizophrenia or psychosis. But Hall, primed by peyote and grounded as he was in the writings of Huxley, Gurdjieff and Ouspensky, realized that LSD could be a tool for freeing the mind from the shackles of the ego and the filters that the conscious mind places on our perception.

LSD was not in fact a psychomimetic but a psychedelic - the term coined by British psychiatrist Humphrey Osmond in a letter to Aldous Huxley in 1956 and unveiled to the New York Academy of Sciences the following year. The term conflates the Greek *Psyche*, meaning soul, with *Delos*, to reveal; literally, soul-revealing. The experience of ego death allowed one to see the universe through the eyes of a child, but with an expanded intellect that suddenly realized an infinity of previously unnoticed connections and synchronicities. For some, this experience could be terrifying and could result in a catastrophic loss of self-belief and self-confidence. For others it was a fast track to enlightenment; the ultimate modern, labor-saving device, doing away with time-consuming decades of meditation, fasting and study, and delivering instant satori, and without all the mess and nausea of peyote either.

"I knew it to be an experience that really traumatized Tommy," says Clementine of the clinical tests. "When it came to turning on to LSD regularly with others he made absolutely sure that all present were protected from any unpleasant outside events and felt completely safe in our home, at least until they were accustomed to caring for themselves."

And indeed, despite his traumatic reaction, Hall continued to use LSD on his own terms, supplied by Chet Helms on his frequent visits back from San Francisco. "He would swoop down to Austin on his way from New York to California and drop off such psychedelics as we were not able to secure for ourselves in the beginning," recalls Clementine. But if Helms was quietly introducing his friends to the new drugs that would soon spark a social revolution, many lay the responsibility for introducing acid into the wider Austin underground squarely at the feet of one man: Texan novelist Billy Lee Brammer.

Born in Dallas in 1929, Brammer was already in his mid-thirties when he returned to Austin and began the doomed attempt to follow-up his successful and critically-acclaimed debut novel, *The Gay Place*. Yet he still had a young man's instincts for what was happening in America's subculture, especially where drugs were concerned. "He was the one who first told us about Bob Dylan and the Grateful Dead," recalled fellow Texan author Bud Shrake, who had been given LSD for the first time by Brammer, in Stephen L Davis's book *Texas Literary Outlaws* (Texas Christian University Press, 2004). "He was always plugged in. He always knew what was going on."

While still a college freshman, Brammer had been spellbound by the young Lyndon B Johnson, then a young congressman campaigning to be elected to the senate. The sight of Johnson leaning out of a descending helicopter, whooping and waving an enormous white Stetson at the crowds below, seemed impossibly glamorous to Brammer, especially when Johnson then gave a speech that seared itself into his memory, not so much for the content as for the charisma and intensity of its delivery. Seven years later, Brammer was a struggling writer and journalist in Austin when he heard that Senator Johnson was looking for a "house liberal" for his team in Washington. Brammer took the job, writing speeches, press releases, position papers and even personal correspondence for the Senator, who took the languid intellectual and his young wife under his wing. In turn, Brammer continued to idolize Johnson, who was everything he wasn't; big, bluff, dynamic, a master of *realpolitik* and strategic glad-handing.

Lyndon Johnson would be caricatured in the novel Brammer wrote in those years as Governor Arthur 'Goddamn' Fenstemaker: a manipulative, larger-than-life, dangerously flawed but powerfully charismatic southern politician who dominates the pages of *The Gay Place*, published to great acclaim in 1961. By this time Johnson was vice-president, and in an inevitability that must have surprised no-one except, apparently, Brammer himself, Johnson was not best pleased with his thinly-veiled portrait, and excommunicated the writer from his circle. Struggling with the pressures of finding his first novel acclaimed as a masterpiece, Billy Lee Brammer was back in Dallas and paying the rent with local news work when he found himself in the second press car in Kennedy's motorcade during the President's fateful November 1963 visit to the city; two days later, he was also a witness to the assassination of Lee Harvey Oswald. With Kennedy's death, Johnson was now President and Brammer was commissioned to write a biography of his former boss, friend and hero. Unfortunately, everyone close to Johnson and on his staff was under strict instructions not to co-operate with Brammer in any way, and Billy Lee found he was the only legitimate journalist in the United States denied White House press credentials.

This was the state of play when Brammer and his second wife Dorothy settled back in Austin in the summer of 1964. Billy Lee was still attempting to somehow write the biography, or start another novel, but in reality he was mostly taking large amounts of drugs. He had started using Benzedrine in college, and it became second nature for him to stay up all night writing on speed while working for Johnson in Washington. He was also partial to marijuana, and was a connoisseur of pills of all kinds with an encyclopedic knowledge of their effects, his legendary tolerance surpassing that of the most hardened junkies. He had taken LSD as early as 1963, when his friend and fellow Texan novelist Larry McMurty had introduced him to Ken Kesey, with whom McMurty had studied Creative Writing at Stanford University. Like Brammer, Kesey had just published a successful and highly-acclaimed debut novel, in Kesey's case *One Flew over the Cuckoo's Nest* (1962). Although he had yet to conceive of the Merry Pranksters or purchase his famous bus, Kesey was already accumulating large supplies of acid, and enjoyed nothing more than turning on a wide range of guests at his weekend-long California ranch parties.

Already a veteran drug enthusiast, Brammer took to acid like a fish to a flame, and ensured a ready supply of the potent blue liquid was available at his Austin home. Around the same time his use of speed escalated dramatically when he began injecting crystal meth. "I bounced around the subculture after leaving LBJ, writing unfinished masterpieces by the score, ingesting hogsheads of drugs and acquiring a local image as the best approximation of guru and human wonder around," Brammer wrote in a private letter. Part Scott Fitzgerald, part Neal Cassady, the successful but romantically-flawed novelist bonded with Austin's younger writers, artists and musicians in an exercise in mutual glamour. "He became fascinated by what was going on with young people," his wife Dorothy remembered, speaking to writer Al Reinert in a *Texas Monthly* profile of the writer in 1979, a year after his death. "The whole sixties thing that was just getting started; he could see it coming. He thought it would change the country, and he wanted to be a part of it." Their parties tried to be Austin's equivalent of Kesey's prototype acid tests, but were far more chaotic and disheveled, and without Kesey's high-minded sense of mission.

Tommy Hall was not among those young people won over by Brammer's dissolute ways however. If Brammer was a charmingly amoral Dionysian who believed that all drugs were equal, then Hall was far more partisan and idealistic in his enthusiasms, earnestly evangelical about mind-expanding sacraments like peyote, marijuana and LSD, but abhorring chemical 'uppers' like speed, or downers like heroin or even alcohol. Acid was not, for him, a recreational drug but a highly potent key to universal understanding, one that had inspired him to begin his great work; a vast iconoclastic study fusing science and religion, mysticism and mathematics, poetry and psychology, chemistry and philosophy.

In the summer of 1963 Tommy Hall joined Ghetto refugees such as Tary Owens and Wali Stopher at the Mansion, a large house at 702 West 32nd Street. Prized since the early 1950s for its anonymity, the Ghetto was by mid-1963 too well-known as a hotbed of counter-cultural experimentation to be feasible, and the parties and get-togethers began to move elsewhere. When Tommy moved in the Mansion had already been raided at least once, but the police hadn't found anything beyond home-brewed beer and peyote, which was still legal. Nobody was dumb enough to keep weed on the premises, at least until Tommy arrived. He had become as enthusiastic a consumer and proselytizer for marijuana as he was for peyote and LSD, and seemed happy to just give it away to anyone he thought deserving. His main kick was not money, but the joy of turning people on and, as he saw it, spreading enlightenment.

Many were uncomfortable with Tommy's new drug evangelism, and the fact that he just couldn't stop talking about the positive qualities of dope, acid and mescaline. He was risky to be around, especially when possession of even the tiniest amount of marijuana was a felony that could get you two to ten years in the penitentiary, with life imprisonment a distinct possibility if you were convicted on a second offence. Certainly the freaks were starting to get noticed, and the local cops were itching to bust anyone who looked like they might be a doper.

Hall however was now a man with a clear sense of his own destiny, and this destiny was not to be served by keeping his head down and tending to his own affairs. Feeling that he'd learnt all he could via the established channels, and hardly interested in an official qualification to further his career, he dropped out of UT just before his finals and married Clementine. This was hardly a sign that he was about to settle down and go straight, however; instead, Clementine became an equal partner in Tommy's plans to turn on the world, though perhaps strangely in hindsight she was more reluctant at first to try marijuana than she had been with peyote or LSD.

"Tommy had brought some back from Mexico, where he and friends (including my very conservative brother Ricky and Powell St John) had spent his bachelor party stoned out of their minds," she recalls. "He begged me to smoke some with him on our wedding night. I did and immediately went into a deep sleep!" So much for weed's aphrodisiac qualities; Clementine compares the occasion to her parents' wedding night, when her mother, who was a teetotaler, was convinced by her new husband to take a drink for the first time, and spent the whole night being violently sick.

Soon however the couple began buying marijuana in large quantities. "When it became difficult and/or expensive to procure any, Tommy and I would set out to Mexico in our station wagon and purchase pounds of it and bring it back for distribution to friends," Clementine says. "At that time, Tommy had short hair and I would put my long hair in a very conservative French roll and we would show up at the border to the US looking like a respectable couple. We would arrange for my two children to be asleep on a blanket in the opened-out back of the station wagon, said blanket disguising the marijuana packages. When the border guard would come to my window and ask me if we were bringing back any illegal fruit etc. into the US I would reply that I had purchased some dry beans and I hoped I would be allowed to keep them. This always brought a wave-us-on gesture and smile on the guard's part."

The Halls set up home together in Austin, where they continued to be familiar figures around the UT campus, and their house became a nexus for all-night flights of chemically-assisted conversation and revelation. Their good friend Powell St John was one regular visitor, enjoying their wit and sophistication and Tommy's wide-ranging knowledge which led to many good-natured debates. Powell had also experienced LSD as a positive and liberating force, crediting LSD with helping him to not only write songs but also freeing him to make significant strides in his graphic art.

Following Janis Joplin's departure for San Francisco at the beginning of 1963, the Waller Creek Boys had limped along without her for a while, but the magic had obviously gone. Lanny Wiggins had married and became a much more serious individual, and soon he and Powell drifted off in different directions. The break came when Kenneth Threadgill asked Powell to join his semi-acoustic country band, the Hootenanny Hoots, along with guitarist and songwriter Bill Neely. They toured around Texas playing for beer and tips, and were sponsored by Lone Star Beer, who gave them all matching western shirts with the brand embroidered on the back. It was a fun gig, and Powell learnt a lot about music and playing and people. But as far as his newly acid-inspired song-writing was concerned, it was something of a retrogressive step.

"It was the mid-1960s," he admits. "The British Invasion was under way. The Beatles, the Stones, Yardbirds, Moody Blues and all the rest were on the radio constantly and the folk scene was winding down. People were ready to listen to rock 'n' roll."

Powell was also coming to realize that most of the old blues players that the white, middle-class students on the folk scene idolized, including his great mentor, Mance Lipscomb, already played electric instruments when performing in their own communities. It was only when they had a well-paid folk gig with the college audience that they broke out the acoustic guitars and gave the kids the down-home, 'authentic' experience they seemed to expect. "By this time I was trying my hand at song writing and the power of electric music appealed to me," Powell told *It's Psychedelic Baby*. "My thinking was that the sheer volume I could achieve electrically would compel people to listen to my message, whether they wanted to hear it or not."

By 1965, Tommy Hall was thinking much the same thing. He and Powell were both obsessive Dylan fans, but Hall had been disappointed by the left-wing protest songs that dominated Dylan's first few albums. He was much more heartened by the direction begun on 1964's *Another Side of Bob Dylan*, and continued on 1965's *Bringing It All Back Home*. Dylan was turning inward, documenting his own intuitive stream of consciousness on songs like *Chimes of Freedom* and *Mr. Tambourine Man*. The intricate, surreal and multi-layered imagery of these pieces convinced Tommy Hall, and many others, that Dylan was also initiated into the LSD experience. The fact that he was finding an enthusiastic audience for these complex, illusive creations was enough to convince Tommy that a rock 'n' roll band was the most suitable vehicle for his own vision. Now he just needed to find that band.

Chapter 7

"When Tommy announced to the community that he was planning to start a rock 'n' roll band, I took the news with a grain of salt and no small measure of skepticism," Powell St John recalls. "Tommy had no experience with electric music, much less organizing and leading a band. I dare say that most of us were dubious at best. The real shocker however was Tommy's reason for starting a band. He intended to use the band format to proselytize for the acceptance and general use of psychedelic drugs! This led many of us to think that perhaps Tommy had lost his mind. I thought he was doomed. If he did not succeed his already shaky reputation in the community would be shot. If he did succeed I gave him maybe six months before he would be rounded up and sent to prison for a long, long time."

'Turn-On Tommy' as the once strait-laced Hall had become known may have seemed crazy, but he was also a man for his times. By 1965, psychedelics were out of the bag in Austin, and the folkies and beatniks were seriously investigating the transformative possibilities of rock 'n' roll, or at least electric folkrock. When Dylan played the inaugural date of his first full electric tour at Austin Municipal Auditorium on September 24th 1965 he later commented that the Austin audience "got it" in contrast to the booing and bewilderment he encountered elsewhere on the tour. This is hardly surprising, as the acid-fried audience members, including St John, Hall, George Kinney and Roky Erickson, were already clued in to the advantages of combining meaningful lyrics with volume, electricity and mind-expanding drugs. Austin was just waiting for the rest of the world to catch up.

Meanwhile, more new arrivals continued to make the Austin scene. 20-year-old William Royce Scaggs was born in Ohio, but had attended a private school in Dallas called St Marks, where he gained the nickname 'Boz' and met a fellow aspiring blues singer and guitarist named Steve Miller. Miller already had a school band, the Marksmen, and Scaggs joined on guitar before hooking up with Miller again at the University of Wisconsin, playing as the Ardells and the Fabulous Knight Trains. Scaggs dropped out after a year and joined the US army; stationed in San Antonio, he began heading up to Austin at the weekends. After getting his discharge in 1964 he joined the UT extension school, and wasted no time in forming a new band he called the Wigs.

To be wiggy was to be cool, but the name was also a sly nod to the fact that crew-cut army recruits would often don long-haired wigs when they ventured into town to check out the hip clubs and bars. "Basically it was an R&B sort of thing and it was the cleanest, most proficient R&B I'd ever heard," Scaggs later recalled to *Dark Star* magazine. "They were really deep into it; amazing blues artists. They'd studied it, gotten down every chop and lick, and then they got started in on their own style."

The other members of the Wigs were John 'Toad' Andrews on guitar, Bob Arthur on bass and George Rains on drums. Andrews was a blues prodigy who was one of the first white musicians to go over to East Austin to play at all-black clubs like Charlie's Playhouse. He gained his nickname of Toad from jumping off the makeshift stages at frat parties and hopping around on the floor playing his guitar with his teeth, a gimmick he'd learnt from black R&B players long before any white teenagers had heard of Jimi Hendrix.

After exhausting the Austin frat party circuit, Boz Scaggs heard that London was mad for Texas blues artists like Jimmy Reed and Bobby 'Blue' Bland, and decided that the Wigs should try their luck over there. Andrews and Rains were unable to make the commitment, but Boz and Bob Arthur headed across the Atlantic with another local guitarist, Benny Rowe, to relocate the Wigs to the swinging center of the mid-sixties music scene. Unfortunately, while it was true that in England American blues musicians were accorded a degree of respect and reverence they rarely enjoyed at home, London at the beginning of 1965 was already in the throes of its own highly-competitive blues boom. By the time John Andrews was able to join them in March, the Wigs were washing dishes and unable to get work permits. The band split, with Boz Scaggs busking around northern Europe solo, and eventually cutting a debut album in Sweden.

By mid-1965 Andrews, Arthur and Rowe all wound up back in Austin, where Benny Rowe formed a new version of the Wigs, renamed first the Whigs, then just the Wig. He brought in keyboard player Billy Wilmot, who he'd previously played with in the Intruders, and Billy recommended his friend John Richardson, formerly guitarist in the Twilighters. The band was completed by bassist Jess Yaryan and Rusty Weir, the singing drummer from popular high school band the Deeds. Meanwhile, John Andrews and Bob Arthur teamed up with drummer Darryl Rutherford to form a British Invasion-influenced blues-rock band called the Chelsea.

George Kinney had watched his best friend Roky's swift rise, from the ashes of their garage band the Fugitives to lead singer with the wildly-acclaimed Spades, with a mixture of admiration and envy. So when the Chelsea advertised for a vocalist, he went along to audition, and got the gig. "Those guys were way ahead of me at the time," he says now. "I'm glad they liked my singing or I would never have had a chance with them. It was a really good covers band. I'm surprised we didn't get rich and famous."

The Chelsea's storming sets of songs by the Beatles, the Rolling Stones, the Yardbirds and Dylan soon gained them an impressive reputation on the frat party circuit. They also attracted the attention of the older student crowd, who were starting to get over their folkie snobbery regarding electric rock 'n' roll music. Powell St John began playing harmonica with the Chelsea, using them as a testing ground for his ideas about forming a rock band.

"We played frat gigs and clubs in Austin, Houston and San

Antonio," Kinney recalled. "I was Austin's version of a younger, Texas-styled Mick Jagger; at least in my own mind."

"We were called the Chelsea and dressed like English guys and smoked English cigarettes trying to pass ourselves off as Englishmen at sorority gigs," was John Andrews' more sober summation of the band when talking to Bill Bentley for an *Austin Chronicle* interview in 2005. The Chelsea found their feet at a club called the Clown's Den, on San Jacinto and 18th Street. "We got a two-track recorder and went down to the 11th Door and recorded some songs, but it was all blues and there really wasn't a market for it. So we had our photo taken and ran an ad in the Texan that said 'Just back from European tour' and the Clown's Den was packed."

While George was wowing sorority girls as frontman with the Chelsea, Roky Erickson was making some serious waves with the Spades. The band had played what they thought was a disastrous gig at a city-wide battle of the bands at the Palmer Auditorium, where on a big stage with no monitors none of the band could hear what each other was playing. But Roky delivered such a full-on blistering performance that, even though they lost the contest to the Babycakes, their bookings tripled overnight, and they became the most sought-after rock 'n' roll band on the Austin circuit.

"By the time school starts back up, Roky's musical career is looking up," John Kearney told interviewer Andrew Brown in 2003. "It becomes obvious at that point to him, and everyone else, that he has a career in music, and that's the point that it's building to." Indeed, by late 1965 the Spades were packing out the Jade Room every Thursday night, and so when the authorities at William B Travis High School insisted that Roky cut his hair he refused, and dropped out a few months shy of graduating.

In November 1965 the Spades went into TNT Studios in San Antonio to record their second single; both Roky Erickson compositions, though for some reason the song-writing credits would read "Emil Schwartze." A primitive early incarnation of *You're Gonna Miss Me* was backed by *We Sell Soul*, a slow-burning R&B groove with a semi-spoken opening verse in which Roky tries to rouse the audience, gospel preacher style. Yet by the time the single was released, Roky's whirlwind ride with the Spades was almost over.

That summer, Tommy and Clementine Hall had combined a peyote buying trip with a two-week beach vacation on Padre Island, the long, narrow barrier island along the South Texas coast, facing into the Gulf of Mexico. Just as they were about to return home they ran into a pair of teenagers from Austin, one of whom, Stacy Sutherland, recognized Hall as a cat he'd bought weed from when he was still in high school. Both were spending the summer playing in a surf-oriented rock 'n' roll band in the resort town of Port Aransas, on Mustang Island to the north. After getting wasted with the Halls on Romilar cough syrup and Acapulco Gold, they persuaded the couple to stick around and come up to watch them play.

The band were called the Lingsmen, and as well as Stacy Sutherland on guitar and John Ike Walton on drums, they featured Benny Thurman on bass and violin, and vocalist Max Range. With the exception of the Austin-born Thurman they came from Kerrville, a rural small town in the hill country a hundred miles west of Austin, and although they were friends and all experienced musicians in their different ways, they had invented the band on the spot in order to secure a summer residency at a club in Port Aransas called the Dunes.

22-year-old Benny Thurman had never actually played the bass guitar before the Lingsmen were formed; he was a classically-trained violinist, an ex-marine and a country and western fan who didn't actually know or like rock music. The band's first choice for bassist, Ronnie Leatherman, couldn't make the gig as he was still in school in Kerrville, but he came down for two weeks to give Benny a crash course on the instrument.

Stacy Sutherland and Max Range had played together since they were both 16, in high school rock 'n' roll bands the Traditions and the Signatures, and had even backed up San Antonio's Doug Sahm in the early stages of his career, playing a number of shows with him around the region. Even as a teenager, Sutherland cut a dark, brooding presence, and was continually torn between a strict Baptist upbringing that appealed to his introverted, troubled soul, and a predilection for the rock 'n' roll life, with all of the hell-raising and chemical abandon that entailed. In Sutherland's inner life he was literally walking between God and his angels on one hand, and Satan and his minions on the other. He seems to have felt that he was damned from birth, and if drugs like peyote and marijuana didn't offer salvation, he used them to try and gain some kind of understanding of the supernatural forces that were controlling his destiny. All of this came out in his guitar playing; by turns haunting and savage, tender and tormented, born deep in the blues and the western twang, but ringing out with its own eerie, sorrowful yearning.

Tall and rangy, 22-year-old John Ike Walton was the straight man of the bunch, though he was as keen as Stacy on roaring round the streets of Kerrville on a motorcycle after midnight, playing cat and mouse with the local cops. His father owned property near the Gulf of Mexico and had struck oil there, which was how John Ike had managed to kit out the Lingsmen with brand new state-of-the-art equipment for their hastily-arranged residency. And although they were faking it at first, they got good, quick. They mixed up British Invasion covers with surf songs, rock 'n' roll, and blues and country interludes, when Benny would whip out his fiddle to blast through *Orange Blossom Special*.

The Halls were impressed, as much by the audience numbers and excited reception the Lingsmen were getting as by their music, which was still almost entirely covers. They kept in contact when the Halls returned to Austin, and Tommy and Clementine debated whether, with a few crucial changes, the Lingsmen could be the band they were looking for, to spread Tommy's message of LSD enlightenment to the world.

Encouraged by his old Port Arthur buddy Jim Langdon, now covering the local music scene for his Nightbeat column in the *Austin Statesman*, Tary Owens was the first of the college crowd to check out the Spades at the Jade Room, and was instantly impressed with their phenomenal vocalist. The next week, he brought down Powell St John, Tommy and Clementine Hall to see the band. It was obvious to them that while the Spades were okay, Roky was in a different class. "The kid was electrifying," Powell St John remembers. "There was no doubt this 18-year-old was a genuine prodigy. He had all the chops; I think he was born with them. Suddenly Tommy's dream of putting together a band didn't seem so far-fetched after all."

Meanwhile the Lingsmen had returned to Kerrville in a hurry, after John Ike found himself talking to a major narcotics cop at the Dunes bar. Max Range stayed down in Port Aransas, quickly hiring a new backing band, but Stacy, John Ike and Benny were at a loose end. They were perfectly happy to accept Tommy Hall's invitation to check out this band the Spades in Austin, especially when he told them that they had an incredible singer, possibly ripe for poaching.

They met at the Halls' house first, and browsed through Tommy's incredible record collection while listening to him rap. Before they went to the Jade Room, Tommy gave them all LSD; the first time any of the youngsters had tried the stuff. Roky would recall how they seemed to all have auras around their heads as they walked in, and were impossible to miss from the stage. Afterwards, Roky came back to the Halls' place, where the Lingsmen had their equipment set up, and the trio essentially auditioned for Roky, with Tommy Hall joining in on the jug and the guitar sound augmented by a swirling echo chamber. It was like nothing Roky had ever heard before, and he was blown away. Although he had some misgivings about letting down John Kearney, Roky recognized that the Spades were strictly little league compared to these guys and immediately threw in his lot with the as-yet-unnamed new band. They went into intensive closed rehearsals for two weeks, with the intention of moving smoothly into the Spades' Jade Room slot at the beginning of December. It seems that it was Clementine Hall who came up with the new band's moniker, sat in bed working on her novel while the band were gathered in the couple's lounge, trying to come up with a name. Tommy came in and asked her if she had any ideas.

"I chose Elevators because Tommy and I admired black rhythm and blues bands who had similar short and inspiring names," she explains. "Tommy presented this name to the band and then came back to me saying they loved it but it was too short. So I came up with Thirteenth Floor because one, 13 was my lucky number and two, there were at the time no 13th floors in any public buildings; they were considered unlucky by a then-superstitious public. I later realized that the 13th letter of the alphabet was M, which could be said to stand for marijuana."

The name also fitted Tommy Hall's intentions for the new band perfectly; that they would be 'elevators,' lifting minds and souls to new levels of consciousness and understanding, and once it was in place everything seemed to happen incredibly quickly. Just three weeks after giving them their first review, on November 30th Jim Langdon announced in his Nightbeat column that Roky had left the Spades. Their single, *You're Gonna Miss Me* had just been released, but now there was no band to promote it. The Spades had been on the verge of breaking up anyway, with high school ending and bassist Ernie Culley going off to college, and so they gracefully surrendered their residency to Roky's new band. On December 8th the 13th Floor Elevators made their Jade Room debut.

"Oddly enough, those first couple of gigs, they weren't that well received," John Kearney told Andrew Brown. "I remember one person turning to me and saying, listen to that shit. Bring back the Spades."

Seen from the perspective of the slightly older, more sophisticated student set, Powell St John's recollection is decidedly more positive. "The crowd was large, and there was an air of anticipation tinged with skepticism," he says. "Many were still doubtful about the enterprise. But the skepticism vanished as the Elevators performed song after stunning song, covers and originals all as good as anything we had heard on record or in live performance. I think it safe to say that by the end of the evening all those in attendance were Elevators fans."

Certainly the Elevators lacked the tightness of Roky's former group, inevitable after only two weeks' rehearsal, and insisted on playing at a deafening volume that further muddied their sound. Yet there was to be no going back to the days of the Spades. Though initially playing many of the same songs as their predecessors, the 13th Floor Elevators were definitely something new. It was December 1965, and the era of Texan Psychedelic Rock had begun.

Chapter 8

Tommy Hall's central idea was that the 13th Floor Elevators should 'play the acid.' This would require them to all take the drug together before every performance, to become of group mind, and then to somehow pass on the experience to the audience in the form of a 'contact high,' whether the crowd was tripping or not. To this end the band all ritually took LSD together at their first proper rehearsal at the Halls' house where, under Tommy's guidance, they had an intense but largely positive experience. The exception was drummer John Ike Walton, who found he was unable to keep time under the influence of the drug, and later became convinced that he was dying. In the Halls' back yard, he thought that Tommy and Clementine were Adam and Eve, and that they were all passing through the Garden of Eden on their way to Heaven, or Hell. While Roky just zoned out, Stacey passed through the death-and-rebirth experience into a completely clear state of mind, and Benny ended the night climbing up a tree and talking to a bluebird, John Ike swore never to take acid ever again.

The rest of the band did their best to keep to the Tommy Hall Schedule, as it became known, but there were disturbing consequences almost from the beginning. The brooding, hellfire-obsessed Stacy had a bad trip, to say the least, as early as the Elevators' third gig at the Jade Room. The venue's main prop was a large papier-mâché Chinese dragon, and Stacey became convinced that he was dying, and that the dragon was Satan come for his soul. He high-tailed it down the street, only for Tommy to come after him and convince him that if he was dying and damned anyway, he might as well finish the set.

On another occasion, Roky went back to his parents' house while still tripping after an early rehearsal, and his mother apparently thought that he was having some kind of psychotic episode and rushed him to the hospital. The Halls claim that he was sectioned and given shock therapy while high, which marked the beginning of his lifelong mental illness, and that Tommy and Tary Owens had to break in and get him out. On the other hand, Evelyn Erickson denies that this ever happened, and it certainly seems out of character for a woman who all her life distrusted conventional medicine, and who would rather turn to the power of prayer for healing, whether it be for Roky's broken leg after his childhood swimming pool plunge or his later schizophrenic behavior, than trust the advice of doctors and hospitals.

Austin didn't know how to deal with the new drugs, and it's hardly surprising that the rock 'n' roll kids at the Jade Room were bemused by the Elevators' early gigs, as they had no frame of reference yet for what the group were doing. Playing in a mainstream venue to a mostly underage audience, the Elevators couldn't yet come right out with their full psychedelic agenda, and must have just seemed like a loud, weird dance band that weren't quite right. Clementine Hall however remembers their early audiences as being mostly enthusiastic and respectful.

"There was such a mix of college frat boys, jazz musicians, hippies, older drinkers, cowboys and everything else I can think of, so it was, to me, surprising how well everyone got along," she says. "I can remember one performance given at a frat dance in the very earliest days. There was a very odd phenomenon: we noticed that the kids were not dancing, but were standing in an orderly manner up front and watching us closely. At one point, they began, first a few of them and then all of them, rubbing the back of their necks. We did not attribute this to neck strain from standing too close to the stage, because even those pretty far away were doing it.

"Tommy talked about this with us after the concert. He said that my mother (a bit of a scholar), who had had many a religious discussion with him long before we formed the Elevators, had talked about the three categories of experience (likened to the Trinity) that a Christian can have: one, the Father experience, two, the Son experience, and three, the Holy Ghost experience. She had defined the three experiences to him; most importantly, she had said that the Holy Ghost experience was when a group or crowd of people suddenly and unexpectedly (and apparently independently of each other) all made the same gesture or action. This action was caused by a shared spiritual experience. He said that he believed that what we had witnessed was a Holy Ghost manifestation, and that he thought the kids were rubbing their cerebral cortexes because they were having a spiritual insight of some sort. He later jokingly referred to the event as being 'goosed by the cosmos.'"

As 1965 spun into 1966, the Elevators were much more in their element playing for the UT hipsters at parties organized by the *Texas Ranger* magazine. There, Tommy would preface their performances with a short speech that acted as a bold and blatant mission statement, before playing to an audience at least as stoned as they were, tripping on acid, grass, peyote or some combination of the three. But the Elevators weren't the only weird and wired rock 'n' roll band emerging on the UT campus. St John and the Conqueroo were originally an acoustic folk duo of Powell St John and Tary Owens, not dissimilar to the original Waller Creek Boys. Tary had named them after the Afro-American myth figure of High John the Conqueror, also known as St John the Conqueroo, who in turn lends his name to the supposedly magical herb John the Conqueror Root. In folklore, John the Conqueror was an African Prince sold into slavery and transported to America, where he escaped thanks to his cunning and magical powers. On the one hand he represented an arche-typal Trickster figure, supposedly the model for Uncle Remus's Br'er Rabbit; on the other, he was a kind of Afro-American equiv-alent of the British King Arthur, a great emancipator and folk hero who never truly died but would one day return to lead his people to salvation. He was also an incarnation of the West African Yoruba deity Elugua.

As for the herb, John the Conqueror Root is used for sex magic and luck in gambling; in the Muddy Waters song of the same name, the hero rubs the root in the courtroom in order to stay out of jail. He also mentions "John the Conqueroo" as a sexual talisman in his hit version of *Hoochie Coochie Man* (originally recorded by Willie Dixon). Like the folk hero, the root is an important part of African-American Hoodoo culture, and is a key ingredient in a Mojo Hand, a small bag of magical totems worn as an amulet for protection or the casting of spells. From Hoodoo the character made a natural transition into the mythology of the blues.

Tary Owens was becoming more deeply involved in his work as a blues and cultural archivist and couldn't commit to the duo, but Powell retained the name for an ad-hoc band he put together with guitarist Charlie Prichard, bassist Ed Guinn and drummer Tom Bright. Born in San Antonio in 1945, Prichard was already a blues and folk scholar who had released one single in 1964 with his San Antonio jug band Tom Swift and his Electric Grandmother, whose lead vocalist was the original Cosmic Cowboy, the soon-to-be successful country singer-songwriter Michael Martin Murphey. Guinn meanwhile was the biracial music major who had been warned away from Threadgill's, a 300lb classically trained clarinet player with a huge afro who was the first black player in UT's recently desegregated Longhorn Band. He was also known for riding his motor scooter around campus, along walkways and hallways, and rejoiced in the now-dated nickname 'Superspade.'

As St John and the Conqueroo played more of the *Ranger* parties and ventured into the Austin club scene, their diverse musical influences made for an interesting brew. Ed Guinn was into Stockhausen, while Charlie Prichard wanted to sound like Blind Willie Johnson: "I wanted to be black and he wanted to be well educated or whatever," Prichard later recalled to *Terrascope* magazine. St John and the Conqueroo would play blues, folk and soul, and R&B standards like *In the Midnight Hour* and *Mustang Sally*, but jammed on them until they became extended, freeform psychedelic improvisations.

Guinn played clarinet and occasionally keyboards as well as bass, and was possessed of a powerful blues voice that was soulful and chilling in equal measures. Powell also sang, and played harmonica and kazoo, while Prichard contributed particularly blistering, wailing lead guitar that fused blues with classical melodies, and improvisations based on contemporary modal jazz. There were also many guest players sitting in, which at different times included Wali Stopher, Bill Carr, Minor Wilson and a young singer-guitarist named Bob Brown, who was still at high school. Tommy Hall even jammed on jug with the Conqueroo occasionally, prior to forming the Elevators.

"The Conqueroo were actually before the Elevators," notes Billy Miller, then an Austin teenager and rock 'n' roll fan; "they were very beatnik subversive underground, definitely. The folk scene had that sort of aura about it, but beatniks didn't play rock 'n' roll. And the Conqueroo sort of got by by being real blues savvy, and sort of passing as an underground blues band."

The Conqueroo's subversive moves included being the first rock or folk act to play over in black East Austin, at Ira Littlefield's IL club, where the all-black audience was mightily suspicious of this inter-racial, proto-hippy folk-rock band, not to mention the crowds of white UT students they brought with them. But they were tolerated so long as they packed the place out and the beer kept selling, and other adventurous rockers followed them, including the soon-to-form Shiva's Headband and Billy Miller's Amethyst. The Conqueroo also played the former Clown's Den on San Jacinto, just down the block from the Jade Rooms where the Elevators debuted, which had been renamed the Library, and then the Fred. This blues and folk club was gamely adapting to the weird changes initiated by Dylan's becoming a plugged-in, polka-dotted electric surrealist, and saw

St John and the Conqueroo backed by Austin's first psychedelic lightshow, the Jomo Disaster.

Jomo Disaster was founded by Houston White, Gary Scanlon, Travis Rivers and Steve Porterfield; four Austinites who had travelled to San Francisco and New York during 1965, and had seen the early psychedelic lightshows in those cities in full effect. On returning home, they decided to set up their own Texan equivalent. As it happened, Steve Porterfield and Travis Rivers soon returned to California, joining Texans like Chet Helms who were vital catalysts for the San Francisco scene during the Summer of Love and beyond. But Houston White and Gary Scanlon stuck around, and by the beginning of 1966 the Jomo Disaster Lightshow was illuminating Austin in a manner never seen before.

White and Scanlon were part of the same Ghetto / *Texas Ranger* group as St John and the Conqueroo, so it was natural that they should initially go out together. They soon found that psychedelic lights and projections could serve a more practical purpose in Austin than just creating a trippy atmosphere, particularly in a rough and rowdy hangout like the Fred. "There were fist fights every night and belligerent drunks were the norm," Powell told *Terrascope*. "This was how we found out that a strobe light could bamboozle a drunken redneck to the point that he couldn't throw an effective punch, and would sometimes even nauseate him to the point of regurgitating his beer."

The Conqueroo later lived and rehearsed at Billy Lee Brammer's Caswell House on the corner of 15th Street and West Avenue, known as The Castle. The other tenants included *Ranger* cartoonists Gilbert Shelton, Jim Franklin and Joe Brown; Shelton would base his legendary comic book creation the Fabulous Furry Freak Brothers on this scene, with Freewheelin' Franklin inheriting Jim's surname, but most everything else from Joe Brown, while the Conqueroo's large, afro-sporting guitarist Charlie Prichard became the model for the hapless Fat Freddy

Freekowtski.

Meanwhile the Elevators had begun writing new material, fusing Tommy Hall's convoluted, esoteric poetry to music written by the band. They had begun using noise and feedback as a separate element in their playing and composition, facing their amplifiers towards each other to create what they referred to as "the third voice." Although Tommy Hall remained the Svengali figure and mastermind behind the band's development, and John Ike Walton considered himself *de facto* band leader (they were still using the Lingsmen's equipment that he'd paid for), by the end of 1965 they'd also acquired a manager-cum-booking agent in the form of 21-year-old folk singer Jim Stalarow.

Stalarow was something of an eccentric figure himself, and was happy to follow Tommy Hall's suggestion of printing up business cards for the band, describing them as purveyors of Psychedelic Rock; in 1965, the first known use of the term. "We meant more than metaphysical, which could describe something outside of normal experiences but which might be had without the use of mind-altering drugs," says Clementine Hall, of her and Tommy's original use of the term. "Once mind-altering drugs were used, the experience could be called psychedelic, and a psychedelic experience could not be had without those drugs. Psychedelic was used for all sorts of experiences, but not usually used with regard to music. I think we pretty much came up with that association, but I am not positive." Jim Langdon would quote the phrase in the heading of a review of the Elevators for his Nightbeat column on February 10th 1966, the first recorded use of the term "psychedelic rock" in print.

The business cards were designed by local artist John Cleveland, who also supplied the band with their distinctive eye in the pyramid logo, based of course on the dollar bill but with many ambiguous and occult associations, not least the notion of the third eye or ajna chakra that the Elevators hoped to awaken. The third eye also symbolizes the pineal gland, believed to naturally secrete the powerful psychedelic DMT at birth and death. "Consult your pineal gland" would become a popular saying in Discordianism, the counter-cultural, anarchistic pseudo-religion founded in Dallas in 1965 by Greg Hill and Kerry Thornley, which would also become associated with the eye in the pyramid design.

Jim Stalarow's other major contribution was bringing Houston talent scout Gordon Bynum to see the Elevators at the Jade Room. Bynum was impressed enough to book the Elevators into Walt Andrus' Studios in Houston at the beginning of January, to record a single: a new version of *You're Gonna Miss Me*, backed by a re-working of a song Stacy Sutherland had written for the Lingsmen, *Tried to Hide*. The band (with the exception of John Ike Walton) all took acid the night before the recording, and Bynum set up his own label to release the record, the name of which, Contact, was highly appropriate.

You're Gonna Miss Me by the 13th Floor Elevators was released on Contact on January 17th 1966. It was a local hit, and the Elevators were drawing crowds of 500+ every week that they played. But they were also attracting the attention of the authorities. The Lingsmen had come close to being busted for pot in Port Aransas, and the Austin police had been advised to keep an eye on Stacy and John Ike. When a small amount of weed was found in their hotel room (they'd initially stayed at the North Lamar Hotel in Austin while rehearsing intensively for the Elevators debut gig, rather than commute from Kerrville), the manager called the police. He identified not only Stacy and John Ike but "Roger 'Rocky' Erickson, George E Kinney and J Thomas Hall, members of a small local jazz band playing in the Austin area, who are believed to be using and trafficking marijuana."

The heat was not slow in coming down. On January 27th the Vice Squad raided the Halls' home. They found Tommy, Roky and Stacy all tripping on mescaline, with John Ike sober and Clementine, also straight, taking care of her children. Locating two pounds of marijuana in the garage, they arrested all the young men present. Clementine called her father to collect the children, and then made sure that she was arrested too, in order that she could accompany Tommy to the station to make sure he wasn't brutalized. Tragically, the police found a bag of syringes and needles in the bedroom that had belonged to Clementine's first husband, who had been treated for tuberculosis. The police called Clementine's mother and told her that her daughter had been arrested for heroin possession; she had a heart attack as a result, and died just a few days later.

Immediately the police went to Roky's old apartment and searched that too. He had just moved out but the police still had his former address, and found more grass on the premises. It seems plausible that this was planted, as Roky had cleaned the place thoroughly before leaving. Nonetheless, all five were charged with possessing marijuana, and the bust made a sensational story on the local TV news, sending further waves of paranoia and fear rippling through the nocturnal underground that the Elevators had suddenly exposed to the light.

Much to John Ike's chagrin (he'd paid for it), the band's van was also confiscated, and to add insult to injury was later spotted being used by the police as an undercover surveillance vehicle. Their bail conditions forbade the Elevators to leave Texas, and they lost their spot at the Jade Room to the Wig. Yet their local popularity remained undiminished. Their debut at a new club, the New Orleans, was broadcast live on KAZZ-FM, and perversely their outlaw status won them new respect from the rednecks who had previously baited them as long-haired hippies. Even their cover songs furthered their rebel mythology, including the likes of Bo Diddley's *Before You Accuse Me* and the Animals' *We Gotta Get Out of this Place*.

To avoid further police hassle, rehearsals moved to a ranch on the outskirts of town owned by John Ike's family, notable for having a ship's steering wheel mounted in the driveway. Though the band now had to be somewhat cautious about smoking dope, their LSD ingestion continued unabated, and one band member or another could often be found stood at "the steering wheel of the world," guiding the planet carefully towards the sunrise.

Billy Miller: "The Elevators shows were not like any other shows. The closest I could compare it to would be that it had the vibes of a subversive SDS rally. The only other band that I saw that had that sort of vibration was the Velvet Underground. And it wasn't like the Elevators or the Velvet Underground were political either, but they were really subversive. And the Elevators, in their own way, they were more hardcore than anyone. It was like being in some subversive dark underground beatnik den, as opposed to some rock 'n' roll type thing; it didn't have the rock 'n' roll band type of vibration. It was something so underground and subversive. It was like the first beatnik rock 'n' roll, you could say.

"The Elevators themselves were almost looked upon as some kind of an educational experiment. The police were not really hounding them at all, at first, and the local citizenry, for the most part, they considered them crazy, but the attitude for the most part was they're our crazies. Or they may have considered them outlaws, but they're our outlaws. And they were looked upon like NASA, the Moon Program. The headquarters was there in Houston of the Space Exploration Program, and Texans were kind of proud, and they considered the Elevators a type of version of astronauts. And so they actually had a lot of clout, and it seemed like the narcs and the police and people like that were actually kind of fascinated with them at first.

"And then there was some kind of shift, a political shift, and I think it was because they were playing in nightclubs and places where they really had no business playing. Places where kids were going. I think when the Elevators became popular with kids, that was what made the police declare open season on them. These little teen clubs and places where they played, they really had no business playing places like that. If they wanted to stay out of trouble they could have just stuck with the university crowd. And then left Austin and not gone back there."

PART III

ROLLERCOASTER

Chapter 9

When Janis Joplin left Austin for San Francisco in January of 1963, she didn't immediately find the success and acceptance that she was hoping for. It had started promisingly enough; after hitching cross-country for three days straight, she and Chet Helms had gone straight to Coffee and Confusion, an old-style beat-folk coffee bar in North Beach that ran a 'non-stop hootenanny' at which performers were unpaid, and strictly forbidden from soliciting donations from the audience. But apparently Janis's half-dozen country, blues and gospel tunes (sung *a cappella* bar the odd strum of her autoharp), got such a rapturous reception from the assembled folkniks that the proprietor broke with tradition for the first time, and allowed a hat to be passed. Depending on which source you believe, Janis earned anything from fourteen to sixty dollars that night.

The nearby Coffee Gallery became Janis's regular haunt, however, where she performed alongside other budding folk and blues musicians who would soon become mainstays of the California rock scene. After living in Texas the sense of freedom in San Francisco seemed intoxicating; it was more or less possible to get by without money, and Janis crashed in the basement of a communal house on Sacramento Street, salvaged discarded food from the street markets or the docks, and ate at church soup kitchens. You could dress as raggedy and weird as you wanted and nobody cared; if you sang or played music you were instantly accepted into this freewheeling community where ideas, energy and escaping the rat race were more important than 'making it' or worrying about the future.

These notions had existed in Austin too, of course, but in San Francisco there were so many more freaks, and there was a sense that they belonged to some kind of half-recognized bohemian tradition. Moreover this funky, sprawling city, facing west onto the great Pacific Ocean, somehow felt that much more open, optimistic and full of possibilities. In Austin, the hipster community was like the Alamo, heroically holding out while under siege by overwhelming opposition. In San Francisco, they felt more like pioneers, carving out a bold if precarious new lifestyle at the end of the western trail.

The west was still wild however, and San Francisco had its dangers, especially for a young woman as brazen, outspoken and unconventional as Janis. She was barred from the Coffee Gallery after she rejected the advances of a particularly influential player within the local folk scene, and was beaten up by a motorcycle gang after leaving a lesbian bar. She attracted some record company interest and the odd high-profile gig, such as performing, unbilled, at the 1963 Monterey Folk Festival, but none of them came to anything, possibly because the San Francisco folk scene still preferred its female singers to be willowy, pure-voiced Joan Baez types, romantic pre-Raphaelite maidens in gossamer gowns.

Most damaging of all though was Janis's predilection for hard liquor and shooting speed, bad habits which were condoned and even encouraged by the more extreme and edgy West Coast bohemia she found herself in. She was drinking heavily from the moment she arrived, and at some point began injecting Methedrine, possibly when she spent the summer of 1964 in New York. Certainly not long after she got back she began dealing as well, and early in 1965 was so strung out, hallucinating and paranoid that she attempted to check herself into the San Francisco General Hospital as a mental patient. She was turned away, and began using heroin instead, as a way to numb the pain of the speed comedown.

In May 1965, mentally shattered, physically emaciated and at the end of her wits, Janis came home to Port Arthur. She came back not only to recover her health and her sanity, but also to get married. She had met a guy who seemed like a perfect romantic gentleman; handsome, smartly-dressed, well-mannered, charming and to all appearances absolutely besotted with her. Unfortunately he was also a sociopathic con-artist and a compulsive liar, who was even more deeply into speed than Janis was; and he was already married.

While waiting for her bigamous fiancée to join her, Janis moved back in with her parents and made another of her periodic attempts to go straight. She stopped drinking, re-enrolled yet again at Lamar College, scraped her hair back into a bun and wore demure, conservative dresses, with long sleeves to hide the track marks on her arms. Eventually the fiancée turned up and duly charmed Seth and Dorothy Joplin, formally asking Seth for his daughter's hand in marriage. But he did suggest they hold off publically announcing the engagement until he had sorted out one or two minor details. He then split, never to return. For a while he stayed in touch, sending letters to Janis and her family and calling Janis on the phone. But when he failed to visit her over the Christmas holidays, everybody gradually began waking up to the fact that the wedding was off.

By this time Janis had tentatively started singing again. Though she initially avoided her old Austin crowd, she had kept in touch with friends from Port Arthur like Jim Langdon, who after many attempts convinced her to get up and sing at the Halfway House coffee bar in Beaumont at Thanksgiving. He gave her a respectful and encouraging write-up in his Nightbeat column, and this led to a handful of low-key performances in Houston. In mid-December, not long after the 13th Floor Elevators had played their debut show at the Jade Room, Janis returned to Austin for a guest spot at the popular blues club, the Eleventh Door. Powell St John remembered seeing her set, and being shocked at how staid and prim she looked, like a school-mistress. Her voice however was intact, and more fierce and bluesy than ever.

With Janis at the Eleventh Door, the 13th Floor Elevators at the New Orleans Club, the Wig at the Jade Rooms, St John and The

Conqueroo at the IL Club and the Chelsea at the Fred, Austin in the early part of 1966 was starting to get lively. The different threads of the underground were starting to coalesce, as art students, rock 'n' roll kids, beer-drinking cowboys and intro-spective peyote eaters all mixed and mingled, and country, blues and folk, rock 'n' roll and R&B all went into the same pot. Collaborations naturally followed. Tommy Hall asked his close friend Powell St John to write some songs for the Elevators, knowing that he was an early initiate into peyote and LSD, as well as an experienced songwriter. Roky Erickson met Janis Joplin at a party, and Roky immortalized the moment in the line "I've seen your face before, I've known you all my life." He then gave this to Clementine Hall, who wrote the remaining lyrics for what became one of the 13th Floor Elevators' best-loved songs, *Splash 1*.

The show that in most peoples' memories really captures this sense of great potential beginning to bloom was a benefit concert for the blues musician Teodar Jackson at the Methodist Student Centre on March 12th 1966. Teodar Jackson was a blind fiddler from rural Gonzales County who often played alongside Mance Lipscomb; he had become seriously ill and was in urgent need of money to pay his medical bills. Tary Owens had become aware of Jackson's plight while in the process of documenting local blues musicians on his reel-to-reel tape recorder, as part of his work as UT's official folklore archivist. And though Jackson sadly died within two months of the benefit show, on May 1st at Austin's Brackenridge Hospital at the age of 62, the funds raised did at least ensure his final days were relatively comfortable and dignified.

The concert featured the 13th Floor Elevators, Janis Joplin, organizer Tary Owens, Powell St John, Kenneth Threadgill, Bill Neely, John Clay, Mance Lipscomb and Robert Shaw. Despite being very much a blues event, the concert is also said to have featured Austin's first psychedelic lightshow, created by future

Vulcan Gas Company lighting genius Roger Baker using a bubble machine. In fact, Houston White's Jomo Disaster lightshow were already active and had actually backed the Elevators at a show in Kerrville the previous night. Dressed in a severe black dress and accompanying herself on acoustic guitar, Janis sang the blues-folk standards *Codeine, Going Down to Brownsville* and *I Ain't Gotta Worry*, plus (according to some) Ray Charles' *Drown in My Own Tears* and as an encore her own composition *Turtle Blues*. Jim Langdon naturally described her set as the most exciting portion of the program, and wrote that she "literally electrified her audience with her powerful, soul-searching blues presentation." This in a concert that he also noted "featured perhaps the finest package of blues talent ever assembled under any one roof in Austin."

The Elevators meanwhile arrived at the venue just before they were due to take the stage, and left immediately afterwards. Since they'd been busted they didn't want to stick around anywhere long enough for the cops to catch on, and their sudden appearances and disappearances only furthered their enigmatic outlaw legend. However, Tommy Hall did arrive early enough to catch Janis's set, and was impressed enough to ask her to consider joining the band as a second vocalist. Janis for her part watched the Elevators' set and was equally impressed by Roky's fiery, soulful hard-rock singing, which many felt was a great influence upon her own subsequent style. Despite rumors though Janis never sang with the Elevators, and the possibility of her joining them as a second singer remained unfulfilled. It seems unlikely that Janis would have considered such a move at this stage anyway; she was still trying to go straight, terrified by the fact that she'd nearly destroyed herself with drugs in San Francisco. She was wary of the music scene as a whole because of the temptation of drugs, and with the notoriety of their recent bust still hanging over them and their open and continuous use of acid both onstage and off, the 13th Floor Elevators were surely the last group Janis would have considered joining.

Remaining resolutely on the folk-blues circuit, Janis continued to perform sporadically at the Eleventh Door club and elsewhere, including the Barrelhouse Blues Festival at the Union Auditorium on May 5th. As her health and confidence improved she began to loosen up and became more like her old self again. That month she quit college at Lamar and moved from Port Arthur to Austin, a sign that she was serious about resuming her singing career. However, at the end of that month she abruptly returned to San Francisco, this time for good.

Travis Rivers had come back from the West Coast with an open offer from Chet Helms for Janis to audition for a new band he was managing called Big Brother and the Holding Company. He convinced Janis that the heavy drug scene that had ensnared her before was all over, and there was a new wave of electric folk-rock bands that she really needed to be a part of. Travis took her down to the Fred to see the Chelsea, who by then were playing a heavily blues-based set, closer to the band members' true passions than British Invasion covers. Eventually Janis was won over. "Yes, that's what I want to do," she admitted. She conveyed her decision to her closest friends: Jim Langdon, who wasn't thrilled that she was walking out on her existing commitments, and Powell St John, who gave her a song he'd just written as a farewell gift. That song was *Bye Bye Baby*. Janis and Travis left in a car-load of freaks on May 30th.

Though the Elevators were still forbidden to leave Texas under their bail conditions, they too were itching to spread their wings. By now playing regularly in Houston and Dallas, they made two appearances on the local music TV show *Sumpin' Else* and for about a month actually relocated to Dallas, attempting to open their own venue in a derelict grocery store on North Collett Street. This was bankrolled by Emma Walton, John Ike's mother, who was starting to take a managerial interest in the band following Tommy's sacking of Jim Stalarow. The 13th Floor Club never happened, but John Ike continued pushing for his mother to manage the band, which deepened the rift between him and Tommy Hall. As the sole non-drug-taker, John Ike saw himself as the only responsible band member. He never bought into Tommy's acid enlightenment philosophy, and as far as he was concerned was the only one looking out for their career. To this end, he personally copyrighted the name 13th Floor Elevators and refused to have any more to do with Gordon Bynum and Contact Records.

Part of the problem was that Contact was unable to meet the demand for *You're Gonna Miss Me*, which was now getting radio play and selling nationwide. Unfortunately, almost all of those sales were bootleg copies, pressed up by local distributors; a not uncommon practice in the music industry of the time. The Elevators had a potential hit on their hands, but in Dallas they subsisted on a diet of acid, pot and powdered soup sachets from vending machines. They also became known for drinking Romilar cough syrup and Listerine mouthwash to get high, exhibiting a dedication to achieving altered states that aroused a mixture of dismay and shocked respect in their peers. More seriously, Benny and Stacy were now injecting speed, partly in order to aid their performances but also to counter-balance the dissociative effects of LSD.

Benny in particular was becoming increasingly estranged from the rest of the band. He had his own religious interpretation of the acid experience which clashed with Hall's pseudo-scientific mysticism. While Stacy and John Ike had their Kerrville background in common, and the childlike Roky was increasingly close to Tommy and Clementine, the three of them forming an odd family unit, Benny was out on his own. He had missed the big bust, a piece of good luck which excluded him from the outlaw camaraderie of the band, but in fact was deteriorating the fastest from constant drug use, shaving his head and freaking out on stage.

In May 1966, the Elevators were invited into the offices of Houston record label International Artists, who were interested in re-issuing *You're Gonna Miss Me* nationwide. At this stage they didn't sign to the label as an act for anything beyond the one 45, but the deal also included rights to an album's worth of songs the Elevators had recorded at Walt Andrus's Houston studios in February. Apparently on reading the contract, Benny didn't say anything but whipped out his fiddle and, like a Texan Harpo Marx, played a suitably withering response.

International Artists was anything but international and cared little for art. Started by producer Fred Carroll as a label for the Houston band the Coastliners, in late 1965 Carroll sold the name to lawyers Bill Dillard and Noble Ginther, music publisher Ken Skinner and studio boss Lester Martin. None of them knew anything about the music industry, but they figured there was money to be made. Looking around for a local record that they could make into a hit, it didn't take them long to pick up on *You're Gonna Miss Me*. In an uncredited 1977 interview, Stacy Sutherland alleged that Gordon Bynum simply sold the Elevators' Contact contract to International Artists behind the band's backs. "We'd signed a release to *You're Gonna Miss Me* to a fellow named Gordon Bynum who was an independent record producer here in Houston," he said. "We were already getting calls from major labels and we wanted to negotiate, but he jumped up, freaked out and sold that record to International Artists, which was two lawyers and Lelan Rogers that had never been in the record business before."

As IA began repressing *You're Gonna Miss Me* for national distribution, Benny Thurman left the 13th Floor Elevators. His replacement was Stacy's old Kerrville school buddy Ronnie Leatherman; the original choice for bass player in the Lingsmen, who had taught Benny how to play his instrument in the first place. By this time the band were back at the Jade Room, the New Orleans having decided that hosting live rock 'n' roll bands was too much trouble, and on June 29th Benny played with the Elevators for the last time in the first set, then handed over to Ronnie for the second.

By July, International Artists were convinced enough of the Elevators' potential to sign them to a more long-term contract. Lelan Rogers, brother of country singer Kenny, had been hired as IA's 'national promotion man' specifically for *You're Gonna Miss Me*. He was the one man in the company who knew how to do his job, and the single became a major hit on several California radio stations as a result of his efforts. When John Ike was told that the band was number one in Sacramento, he was ready to sign to the label that had made this possible, but Tommy Hall needed to know that the record company understood the sacred nature of the Elevators' quest. He singled out Nobel Ginther to be initiated, on the basis that he was a local boy who had gone to school in River Oaks with Elevators soundman Sandy Lockett. Tommy gave Ginther acid and played Dylan's *Blonde On Blonde* album to him repeatedly until the bewildered lawyer begged him to turn it off, all the while explaining the intricacies of his Gurdjieff and Korzybski-derived philosophy of enlightenment through chemistry. It seems Tommy was satisfied that Ginther understood, as he came away happy to sign a contract.

In retrospect, at least, some of the other band members were less happy. "We hired a lawyer to check the contracts out," Stacy Sutherland remembered in 1977. "But the company got a hold of him and told him to tell us they were standard contracts, and the next thing we know we're in lock, stock and barrel and he owns part of us, our own lawyer! They'd bought him out right in the middle of the negotiations." Roky initially refused to sign, likening the deal to handing Einstein's theory of relativity to a cop.

On the 8th of August, the band's trial for possession of marijuana finally came to court. Although scheduled for 'hanging judge' Mace Thurman, who was particularly fearsome when it came to drugs cases, the hearing was brought forward and the case was heard by the elderly Judge Woods, who did not normally deal with criminal cases and was obviously unfamiliar with the matter at hand. The charges against John Ike and Clementine were immediately dismissed for lack of evidence, and Roky got off on a technicality, as the search warrant for his apartment had the wrong address on it. As for Tommy and Stacy, when Judge Woods read that a small amount of marijuana had been tested as evidence he understood it to mean that only a small amount had been seized, rather than the two pounds of grass that was actually the case. Seeing before him two white, educated young men, rather than the poor blacks usually busted for drugs at this time, he decided to be lenient in what was, after all, a first offence. They were given two years' probation, with their A&R man Lelan Rogers named as the responsible citizen who would make sure they kept their noses clean.

It was an amazing result, as everyone was convinced that the Elevators were going to be locked away forever. Increasingly, people around the band were starting to attribute magical powers to them; it seemed they just couldn't be busted. More prosaically, it seems the district attorney's wife was a member of Evelyn Erickson's prayer group, who may have got her husband to change the date of the trial to a time when Judge Thurman would be on holiday. In any case, the 13th Floor Elevators were now free men, although Tommy and Stacy's probation conditions forbade them from entering any establishment where intoxicating beverages were sold, ruling out most bars and clubs; a tough restriction for any working band. But with their record company contact essentially acting as their probation officer, they were in the best possible position to get around these details, even if it inevitably tightened the company's grip on them. Immediately after the trial, they applied successfully to have their probation shifted to San Francisco.

Powell St John was also seriously thinking of quitting Austin.

When The Elevators were initially arrested, many thought it was the prelude to the 'big bust' that would round up all the undesirables in town. Rumors of a mass arrest circulated every week, and such a plan was in fact being mooted by the police department. Powell was fully aware that his name was on the list and that he was under surveillance. He had noted how the police, the FBI and the University authorities had observed and harassed the Ghetto; now he was aware of an unmarked car following him everywhere he went. This encroaching atmosphere of doom and paranoia wasn't helped by a beating he suffered at the hands of a group of rednecks around this time.

The final straw happened on the 1st of August 1966, with the notorious Whitman killings. Charles Whitman, a 25-year-old former engineering student and US marine, climbed to the top of the 307-foot university tower and began shooting students and citizens in the streets around the campus, seemingly at random. Armed with a sawn-off shotgun and a selection of high-powered rifles, his range extended to a quarter of a mile. He murdered sixteen people and wounded 32 others in the first mass shooting of its kind in America.

Powell had just finished rehearsing with the Conqueroo and had gone over to black East Austin to get a ticket for a James Brown concert that night. "Little did I know at the time that I was within range of this former Eagle Scout and marine sharpshooter," Powell told *Terrascope*, and in fact Whitman shot a cyclist who was riding down the same street. The good folk of Texas were advancing on the tower with deer rifles in hand, ready to take the assassin down; meanwhile, at the ticket outlet, a crowd of black Austinites gathered round the radio, waiting anxiously for the latest news on the shootings. They knew that if the sniper turned out to be black, their whole community would suffer reprisals. Powell for his part was equally fearful lest the killer turn out to have long hair and a beard.

"We were saved when it turned out that the guy was white

and had a crew cut," Powell recalled. "About three weeks later I left Austin for Mexico, vowing never to return."

Chapter 10

The Whitman killings were not just a local tragedy; at the time they seemed like a symbolically senseless act that ushered in a new era of chaos and uncertainty. "He was our initiation into a terrible time," one Austin shopkeeper was quoted as saying after the massacre, and indeed Whitman was the first of the lone gunmen, killing randomly and without warning or reason, that would become almost commonplace thirty or forty years later, especially on the campuses of America's colleges and schools. "The center was not holding," Joan Didion wrote in *Slouching towards Bethlehem*, her essay on the San Francisco counter-culture, referencing Yeats' famous poem, *The Second Coming*. And if some rough beast was indeed slouching towards San Francisco to be born, then it was surely Texas that it was slouching out of.

In 1966 it was less than three years since the President had been cut down in Dallas, a shocking act of unexplained violence that had reverberated around the world. But political assassinations at least had precedent, and could in some ways be understood. After Charles Whitman, no-one was safe. To be shot down in the public streets, on a warm summer's day, for no reason and without even seeing your assailant was incomprehensible; and Whitman was a clean-cut, all-American boy, one of our own. What, then, of the newly alienated children of America, who were experimenting with mind-altering drugs, dressing in strange clothes, listening to weird, atonal music that espoused relativity and revolution, and were running away to San Francisco to live lives of mendicant squalor and poverty? For many, these were signs of the coming apocalypse as sure as the assassination of the President, the escalation of the war in Vietnam and the continual threat of atomic extinction. Didion's controversial 1967 essay portrayed the hippy children as tragically naive, near-illiterate orphans led astray by sinister, unseen pied pipers; descending into a nihilistic cul-de-sac of shallow, live-for-the-moment philosophies, dangerous political rabble-rousing and damaging, indiscriminate chemical abuse.

There may have been some truth in Didion's portrayal of the Haight-Ashbury hippies; many of the original pioneers felt that by mid-1967 the original scene had already been irredeemably soured. These early adopters of the sixties counterculture preferred to be known as freaks, reserving 'hippies' for those suburban, weekend bohemians lured in by the simplistic media portrayal of the culture; those who, as Tommy Hall wrote, "for the sake of appearances take on the superficial aspects of the quest." And despite Didion's scathing commentary, the majority of the original freaks were driven by idealism and utopianism, a love of art, music and sensuality unencumbered by senseless shame and guilt, and a perhaps overly-romantic but nonetheless sincere desire for freedom. To again quote Tommy Hall, they were on "a quest for pure sanity," as opposed to the blatant insanity of the mainstream society they'd been born into. A society driven by war, fear, a capitalistic work ethic and oppressive religion, hung up on consumerism and status symbols, hooked on caffeine, alcohol and prescription pills, and riddled with racism, resentment, violence and greed. Surely there was a better way? Perhaps by sloughing off all the mindlessly adhered-to trappings of modern suburbanite society, the young could return to some state of prelapsarian innocence and start again, building loving, peaceful communities of their own where sex, drugs and rock 'n' roll would be seen not as sins, but as primary sources of joy and nourishment.

All of these impulses came together on October 16th 1965, at a dance at the Longshoreman's Hall on San Francisco's Fishermen's Wharf, advertised as 'A Tribute to Dr. Strange.' The venue was consciously chosen for its association with left-wing, working-class radicalism, and numbers were swelled by an anti-war demonstration that had marched on the Oakland induction center that day. The mood inside however was anything but worthy and austere. Bill Ham's pioneering psychedelic lightshow recreated the cosmic universe of the Steve Ditko-drawn comic book character being surreally lauded, while loud electric folk-rock from the Charlatans, the Marbles, the Great Society and the Jefferson Airplane vibrated in the marijuana and incense-scented air.

The impact was not so much from the music and the lights though as from the sheer numbers present; over a thousand, many in thrift-store fancy dress. All suddenly realized that there were far more freaks and hipsters in town than they'd previously thought; that far from being marginalized outsiders they were a real community, with the power and possibility that entailed. Also hugely important was the fact that people were actually dancing to rock bands. Though the psychedelic nightclub the Matrix had opened two months earlier and had the Jefferson Airplane as its house band, dancing there was strictly forbidden by city ordinance, as it was anywhere except for a licensed dancehall.

The Dr. Strange Tribute had been organized by the Family Dog, a bunch of entrepreneurial weirdoes connected to the rock band the Charlatans, who had been running a kind of hip western theme bar, powered by Owsley acid, out in Virginia City called the Red Dog Saloon. After a handful of further dances at the Longshoreman's Hall the Family Dog were shut down by the city, and began looking around for a possible venue that already had a dance permit. They opened negotiations with the Fillmore Auditorium, a theater in the city's black neighborhood that hosted R&B acts like Bobby Bland and the Temptations, but were beaten to the punch by a 34-year-old promoter named Bill Graham.

Born Wolodia Grajonca, Graham was a Berlin Jew who had narrowly escaped the Holocaust and had grown up tough via orphanages in Germany, France and the Bronx. Having arrived in San Francisco in the early sixties, he'd become an unlikely ally of the San Francisco Mime Troupe and had organized a series of benefits for them, the second of which was held at the Fillmore on December 10th 1965. Seeing the potential in the emerging San Francisco rock scene, Graham secured a three-year lease on the Fillmore, and to all intents and purposes shouldered the Family Dog out of the picture. At the end of 1965 the original collective broke up, but before leaving for Mexico in February 1966 Dog co-founder Luria Castell sold the Family Dog name to an enthusiastic small-time dope dealer who'd been helping out at their events; Chet Helms.

Helms had come a long way since 1964, when he'd been just as strung out on speed as Janis. After breaking his addiction he'd discovered an old ballroom in the basement of a communal house on 1090 Page Street, and began organizing informal jam sessions there. These became so popular with musicians and spectators alike that they evolved into paying parties, and after buying the name from Castell, Helms founded Family Dog Productions and came to an arrangement with Bill Graham whereby they would both book rock shows at the Fillmore on alternate weekends. Helms had a street-level connection with the scene and an empathy with the music that Graham lacked, and initially the New York businessman could see the benefits of having the Texan freak on board. Within a few months however Graham may have felt that he'd learnt as much as he needed, and the clash of styles and personalities became too much for both parties. Helms was happy for the kids to smoke dope at gigs; Graham certainly wasn't. Graham would cut a deal with a band that ensured a decent profit for all concerned; Helms would promise them more money but then find that he couldn't pay at the end of the night. The final break came after the Family Dog put on the Paul Butterfield Blues Band for three nights, and made over $18,000. The next morning Bill Graham had locked the band into an exclusive two-year contract that forbade them from playing for any other San Francisco promoters, including

Helms' Family Dog.

That April Helms took over the top two floors of an old 1930s ballroom on the corner of Sutter and Van Ness, in San Francisco's Polk Gulch neighborhood, and renamed it the Avalon. With its art deco elegance and sprung dancefloor, the 500-capacity Avalon Ballroom had a readymade, funky style in tune with the Edwardian chic beloved of the San Francisco counter-culture. Helms had become a major player in the San Francisco music business, but crucially without losing any of his freak credibility. In Joan Didion's essay and elsewhere, Helms is portrayed as the King of the Hippies, a long-haired, bearded, voluble sage, somewhat in love with his own mythology. "Chet was one of the greatest raconteurs I ever met," confirms Clementine Hall, though she emphasizes his soft, humble and self-effacing manner. "He always wore a long black coat and a black Amish-looking hat, had long flowing white hair and beard and carried himself like an aristocratic priest." Where others in the culture distrusted the media, Helms was always happy to talk to reporters and TV crews, offering them perfect off-beat soundbites and nuggets of pseudo-oriental wisdom. Though genuine and altruistic rather than money-driven, Helms realized the value of publicity, and wanted the scene to grow and prosper while remaining true to its roots. It was on this understanding that he managed the rise of a fledgling SF acid-rock band known as Big Brother and the Holding Company, while realizing that the one thing they needed to achieve true greatness was a decent lead singer. Happily, he knew just the girl.

Big Brother and the Holding Company had evolved out of the jam sessions Helms had organized at 1090 Page Street. Featuring guitarists James Gurley and Sam Andrews, bassist Peter Albin and drummer Dave Getz, they had played their debut show at the Open Theater in Berkeley in December 1965. Gigs at the Matrix and the Fillmore followed, displaying a raw, sloppy punk energy that made even the early Jefferson Airplane and Grateful

Dead seem relatively slick in comparison. Playing rough and fast and inspired by speed, acid and free jazz, in many ways Big Brother were the first San Francisco street band, as opposed to semi-professional folk musicians turned pseudo-psychedelic. Their star was Detroit-born James Gurley, a freeform punk-mystic who was regarded by many as the greatest psychedelic guitarist of his day. As a child, Gurley had lost his teeth and most of his hair while acting as a human battering ram in his father's daredevil carnival sideshow act. With Gurley hurtling off on manic, 45-minute, two-note guitar solos, and their outrageous, establishment-baiting name, Big Brother and the Holding Company were a self-described 'freak rock band' with little musical knowledge but a thirst for experimentation. And under Helms' management, they were the house band at the Avalon from its opening.

When Janis auditioned for Big Brother at the beginning of June she was terrified and struggled to keep up and find space for herself in their avalanche of noise, feedback and tumbling drums. Yet they undoubtedly had a strange but powerful chemistry together. Where they bonded was in their shared rawness, their commitment to feel and authenticity over hitting the right note every time. Janis's folk-blues background necessarily tempered and tamed the all-out wildness of the early Big Brother; having any kind of lead singer required more structure, more control than Big Brother was used to. But it didn't take long for Janis to move and swing right along with them. Though at first she only sang lead on about a third of the songs, being relegated to tambourine-shaking backing singer on the rest, Janis soon took on more prominence as the band adapted their set to her voice.

Having initially lived with Travis Rivers, who asked her to marry him, Janis soon moved in with Big Brother and their wives and girlfriends in a communal house in Lagunitas, across the bay in secluded Marin County. The move allowed the band to practice together all day and every day, but Janis was acutely aware that she was the only one in the household who wasn't part of a couple. Drugs were also a constant temptation, and Sam Andrews' girlfriend, Speedfreak Rita, more than lived up to her name. Janis soon began injecting meth again, along with Rita and James Gurley's glamorous boho wife Nancy; the women endlessly stringing beads together in speed-fuelled parody/ acceptance of clichéd feminine archetypes.

Influenced very much by Nancy Gurley's style, Janis began making herself over into the hippy goddess of the San Francisco counter-culture. At the same time, it seemed as if she was trying to forget and disown her Texas past. After all, what had the state ever given her but grief and heartache? Port Arthur had hated her just for being herself. Now she could truly be who she was, she thought, as she put on another disguise, this one all beads and feathers, freedom and spontaneity and unbridled excess. Janis Joplin, the star, the legend, was born fully-formed in San Francisco in 1966, and anything before that was, well, somebody else's story. Never mind that it was Austin that first encouraged her to sing, that gave her a creative, supportive community to belong to. That was yesterday, and Janis was about living in the now. Not that she ever really forgot her old friends or those who helped her out; but to Janis, Texas was mostly bad memories. San Francisco was where it was happening; what was the point in looking back?

Maybe this explains why Janis seemed to suddenly turn against Chet Helms, resulting in the band firing him as their manager. Janis had seriously considered leaving Big Brother on several occasions, as other bands made overtures towards her, and Elektra Records tried to poach her for a supergroup to be put together by house producer Paul Rothschild, featuring Janis alongside Taj Mahal and others. Chet Helms refused to stand in her way, which just made the insecure Janis feel that she wasn't valued enough. Perhaps to deflect attention away from her disloyalty, she insisted that Chet was putting too much time and energy into running the Avalon to be managing Big Brother as well. The band were also riled at Chet for turning down a deal from New York's Mainstream Records on their behalf; label owner Bob Shad had expected Helms to conspire with him to rip Big Brother off and lock them into a lousy contract, and Chet had righteously kicked him out the door. The band however felt they should at least have been told about the offer, especially because they figured that once they had a record contract Janis would be forced to stay with them.

Chet Helms accepted the band's decision to fire him with equanimity. They'd only ever had a verbal contract, and he made no effort to reclaim any of the money he'd invested in them, or to make a claim against future earnings. He would continue to book them at the Avalon, later introducing them on stage at what became their big breakthrough show, the Monterey Rock Festival in June 1967. Before then however, in the midst of a disastrous residency at the Mother Blues Club in Chicago, far from home, managerless and broke, the band accepted Mainstream's offer, signed an ill-advised five-year contract with the label and rush-recorded what would become their debut LP.

Initially however Mainstream only seemed interested in putting out the tracks as singles. First off in October 1966 was Peter Albin's *Blindman* backed by a cover of Moondog's *All is Loneliness*, which gained only local airplay and barely any sales. *Down on Me / Call on Me* came out in March 1967 and did somewhat better, apparently charting in Detroit at #29; when it was reissued in September 1968, it hit number 43 nationwide. *Bye Bye Baby* backed by *Intruder* (August 1967), and *Women is Losers* backed by Albin's *Light is Faster than Sound* (November 1967, with Janis's name highlighted on the disc) were both flops. The final Mainstream single, consisting of a couple of outtakes from the album sessions, was *Coo Coo / The Last Time*, released in February 1968 and finally reaching number 84 that November, by which time Columbia Records had already made the band stars.

The album, *Big Brother and the Holding Company*, wasn't actually released until September 1967, when Mainstream decided to capitalize on the band's sensational show at Monterey. Despite the engineers carefully omitting any hint of the volume and distortion Big Brother would use onstage, and all of the songs being cut back to radio-friendly single length, the LP stands up remarkably well for late 1966, when held against the roughly contemporary debuts by the Jefferson Airplane or Love. Unfortunately it would sound dated and quaint by the fall of 1967, by which time those bands and others were in full psychedelic flight. The songs on the first Big Brother album are essentially pre-psychedelic; heavy blues and folk-rock that only hint at the raga-like freeform extemporizing that they were developing onstage.

The record opens with a sensitive, confident reading of Powell St John's *Bye, Bye Baby*, and whether Powell wrote the song with Janis in mind or not, its bittersweet beauty has grown with the years, as we wonder which of the song's two protagonists has really been "left to face it all alone." The band play with a touching, old-time-y swing and Gurley's lead guitar is soulful and restrained. His own song *Easy Rider* continues the light, country feel, almost a sardonic talking blues with Janis on harmony vocal and the snapping R&B rhythm appropriated by the Rolling Stones on a song like *Off the Hook*. Joplin's own *Intruder* nails that early San Francisco sound, the swirling, biting blues-folk, with just a hint of acid in the dense interplay of liquid mercury guitars, sounding very much like something off the October 1967 debut album by Country Joe and the Fish, whose singer, Joe McDonald, Janis would live with during the early months of 1967. *Light is Faster than Sound* and *Blindman*, both by Peter Albin, merge the folk-rock of early Airplane with the baroque, frenetic garage rock of LA neighbors Love, Janis's harmony on the latter giving the chorus the feel of a more rough-edged Mamas and Papas.

Janis and Sam Andrews duet on the blues ballad *Call on Me*, before Janis's *Women is Losers* which sounds relatively tame and damped-down in its studio incarnation. *Down on Me* also sounds positively embryonic compared to the epoch-defining performance Janis would deliver at Monterey, and as for the light relief of Albin's well-realized garage rocker *Caterpillar*, one can't help wondering how much influence it may have had on the young Jonathan Richman. The droning, fuzz-baked duet of *All is Loneliness* closes the original album, and while it's fine as far as it goes, it frustrates because you sense just how much more haunting and far out it could have been given a producer who would've allowed the band their head. Typically, the best track was left off the initial Mainstream release; *Coo Coo* finds Janis in raw, harrowing vocal form, as though with the archetypal hellhounds on her trail, and demonstrates just how much she'd been holding back through the rest of the sessions. Gurley too turns in some fine, spiked, neo-gothic guitar licks. *The Last Time* isn't quite as strong, but its desperate blues rush, with Janis on lead vocal, should still have displaced one of the lesser songs that did make the album cut.

With more sympathetic production, Big Brother's debut could have been a seminal collision of early San Francisco psych and Texan blues. As it was, it was merely a pretty good album, and by the time of its release, too little, too late. Nevertheless, by 1967 Janis Joplin was well on her way to both stardom and tragedy, all of which is well-documented and falls largely outside the remit of this book. We leave her then on the cusp of greatness, and turn instead back to another bunch of Texan freaks, also charging up Interstate 10 in search of the Californian dream.

Chapter 11

Having been dumped by Janis, Travis Rivers next found himself acting as the West Coast connection for the Elevators. Following their court case he immediately arranged their first San Francisco shows, booking them not into the Avalon as one would expect, but at the Fillmore on the 26th and 27th of August 1967. However, another California contact and would-be manager, who Clementine Hall remembers only as "Jim," had booked the Elevators to play at the Longshoreman's Hall on Fisherman's Wharf opening for Them on August 24th, just two days ahead of the Fillmore weekend. Along with the fact that they swiftly secured two nights at the Avalon for the weekend after, this *faux pas* was enough to infuriate Bill Graham, who naturally assumed he had the 13th Floor Elevators under exclusive contract. As soon as they arrived, Tommy, Clementine and Roky were hauled into Graham's office for his standard "You'll never work in this town again" speech.

"He believed that we had deliberately screwed him," Clementine Hall remembers. "He shouted at us and said he could destroy us. I remember particularly his stating: 'I'm an old street fighter from New York; you do NOT want to mess with me. You will cancel your booking with the Avalon immediately or you will never play the Fillmore.' It took all of Roky's charm and Tommy's wit to talk Bill around to letting us have one night at each venue."

In the end the Elevators played both nights at the Avalon but only one at the Fillmore, with Country Joe and the Fish making their unbilled Fillmore debut as Saturday night's headliners. As for the Longshoreman's Hall date, Clementine remembers it clearly. "The main thing that stands out for me is the fact that the place was *packed* with young people, particularly young girls, and that the security staff were carrying them out on stretchers as they fainted in the audience," she says. *"You're Gonna Miss Me* was number one on the charts at the time, and was being played constantly on the radio; it obviously brought in a lot of teens.

"Most of all, I remember that Stacy was absolutely shocked and upset about the reaction. He had never ever performed before such young girls, had never, in Texas, experienced that sort of carry-on (or carry-out, to be correct!). He kept saying, 'This is wrong. It's just *wrong!* I don't want us to be popular, to be seen as teen idols, I don't want to be *this kind* of popular!' He craved recognition as a serious musician and he craved it from other serious musicians. I got the impression that for Stacy, the situation was bordering on *satanic.* He was very sensitive to evil, and often perceived it in places where we did not. He wanted the others to turn around and go back to Texas.

"For Tommy, the teen reaction was to be avoided because it trivialized the music of the Elevators, not because it was unholy. Tommy's desire was to reach spiritually minded people who could advance themselves through the use of music. I do not recall the reaction of the other members of the band. I doubt, knowing them, that they were much concerned at all."

The Elevators had arrived in San Francisco with a hit single on their hands, a fact which was both a blessing and a curse. As Clementine recalled, International Artists' reissue of *You're Gonna Miss Me* had hit number one in San Francisco and was never off the radio. It would reach number 14 on KIST in Santa Barbara on August 13th, and in October would peak nationally at number 55 on the Billboard Hot 100. This obviously gave the band a higher profile, but it also flagged them up as a pop act, rather than the Texan wing of the psychedelic underground. To make matters worse, the band all had close-cropped hair from their recent court appearances, and unlike Janis they would never swap their jeans and work shirts for the beads, bangles, velvet and paisley that were *de rigeur* in the streets and ballrooms of Haight-Ashbury.

After the show at the Longshoreman's Hall, the Elevators

collectively went to see the Yardbirds play at the Carousel Ballroom, but left all their equipment in their unguarded van outside the venue. They came out of the gig to find that it had all been stolen. With the crucial Fillmore show the very next evening, new amplifiers, guitars and drums all had to be hastily acquired. International Artists were supposed to pay for this, but in 1977 Stacy Sutherland insisted this was not the case. "They never would come through when we had our equipment stolen," he said. "We went for nearly a year without any equipment to play on. We had to rent equipment to play on."

On September 2nd and 3rd the band finally played at the Avalon Ballroom, with Chet Helms organizing an all-Texan line-up: the Sir Douglas Quintet opened, and an unbilled John Clay played a solo acoustic set before the Elevators came on. This may have been a mistake, as Jack Jackson recalled to Paul Drummond in *Eye Mind*. "John Clay, this crazy banjo player, tall, skinny guy, he would honk and spit in a handkerchief and stick it back in his pocket and continue. He came on before they did, and that horrified the hippies because here's this hick…"

Jackson also suggested that the jug-playing put the San Francisco audience off; firstly because it was so constant and frenetic, upsetting the laid-back, mellow vibes they were hoping for, and secondly because it compounded the image of the Elevators as some hick parody of a freak-rock band straight from the Beverley Hillbillies, in their quaint rustic work clothes, refusing to communicate with the audience and blasting away with their loud-but-tight psychedelic rock 'n' roll, as opposed to the deliberately loose and meandering folk-rock of the Bay Area bands.

Clementine Hall admits that The Elevators had "a rather stiff stage presence, which contrasted sharply with the flamboyant appearance of the bands the Avalon patrons were accustomed to… I think they were perceived as cowboys without cowboy hats." Ten years later the 13th Floor Elevators would have been called punk, and 15 years after that grunge, although they wouldn't have fitted in with those scenes exactly either. They were strange and unique, experimenting and trying to go as far out with their music as possible, while still staying true to their essential natures. But unfortunately in San Francisco psychedelia was already being codified as a fashion, with strict rules forming about just who did and didn't belong. The beautiful people of the Haight were like the beautiful people of any time and place; at their worst they could be snobbish, superficial and self-absorbed.

Many Texans were equally scornful of the San Francisco scene however, feeling that the likes of the Charlatans and Jefferson Airplane were sloppy and poor musicians by the standards of the tight, well-drilled groups on the Austin and Houston club circuit. "They sort of struck me as amateurs in every sense of the word," Stacy Sutherland said in 1977 of the early Jefferson Airplane, and voiced his disappointment with the vaunted San Francisco scene in general. "We were really interested in the culture and all, to see it all, and there were a lot of really groovy people and everything, but it was just different. Although they had been into drugs possibly considerably longer, they weren't more spiritually sincere or more advanced necessarily than Texas."

The group that the Elevators bonded most closely with was, perhaps surprisingly, the Grateful Dead. "They were probably the most sincerely involved with acid at that time, when we were out there, than any band we met," Stacy recalled admiringly. "They'd been living in the mountains and taking acid with spiritual sincerity. They did free concerts and benefits, and had a true concern for people and the scene itself."

Members of the Dead attended the Avalon shows, and introduced themselves afterwards; later, when Big Brother returned from Chicago, Janis took the Elevators to a party with the Dead, where they all got high in purpose-built treehouses atop giant redwoods. "The Dead had taken over a former girls' camp and were living there communally," Clementine Hall recalls. "They had a large tree house which sat near the tops of some giant redwood trees, and it was there that we sat for hours with them and their entourage, smoking marijuana and exchanging stories. In all the time I had been smoking marijuana, I'd never been able to shake my paranoia about police appearing suddenly (especially after the terrifying arrest in Texas), *until that night.* I knew that we would have more than enough time to dispose of anything we wished long before any cop could reach us, even if a cop wished to reach us up there. I could have stayed up in those trees forever. I was blissfully happy."

For their part, the Grateful Dead couldn't believe that the Elevators actually played gigs on acid, and were somewhat awestruck by the far-out Texans. The Elevators certainly had respect and credibility where it counted, and it's highly probable they would have won over San Francisco eventually, if only they could have kept it together. As it was, they decided that if they couldn't make it immediately as an underground band in San Francisco, then the only thing to do was to capitalize on their new-found position as budding pop stars. They embarked on a relentless and grueling tour of obscure Bay Area teen clubs, church socials, dances and roller derbies throughout September, often playing two or three shows a night and driving for several hours between venues, still tripping. Taking acid for every show was difficult when playing two or more consecutive nights, as LSD won't always work without a break between trips. But playing several gigs in one night enabled them to get the maximum performance time out of each dose.

Unfortunately, Roky for one was starting to show the strain. Along with the demanding schedule of shows and the unstinting regimen of drugs, he was also being called up by the draft board. Tommy took it upon himself to make sure that Roky seemed a most unsuitable candidate to be shipped out to fight in Vietnam, and before his first hearing, in early September, he dosed him up with Asthmador, an over-the-counter asthma medication often abused as a hallucinogenic. The fact that it was easily obtainable over-rode its reputation as an unpleasant and dangerous experience, and it could be bought as a powder or as cigarettes, in packaging oddly similar to the color scheme of the Elevators' debut album. Smoke too many, or scoop the powder into gelatin capsules and swallow, and you're off on a trip that even seasoned psychonauts describe as a rough ride and not for the faint-hearted. No wonder, as Asthmador's main ingredients were the witch-herb cum poison belladonna (deadly nightshade) and datura stramonium AKA loco weed.

Tommy would have seen it as almost blasphemous to abuse LSD or peyote for the purpose of fooling the draft board, but Asthmador, which did not give the user any special insights or mystic understanding, was fit for the job. The fact that it was difficult to tell whether the symptoms, which included disorientation, confusion, high temperature, loss of co-ordination and ability to communicate, as well as vivid and usually unpleasant hallucinations, were caused by a drug made it even more ideal. Unfortunately, the stuff seems to have worked too well, and pushed Roky over the edge. He was told to report to the hospital for medical tests, and ended up being confined in the mental unit on more than one occasion.

In a disturbing sign of things to come, Roky was also picked up while walking down the street, his erratic behavior causing the police to demand to see his ID, and when he couldn't provide any they took him to the hospital. Not for the first or last time, Tommy and Elevators soundman Sandy Lockett had to break him out before insulin therapy or, worse, ECT were applied. Soon Roky became isolated from his friends and even his other bandmates, as Tommy and Clementine took charge of him and kept the troubled singer in seclusion for his own good. Some thought that the pair were manipulating Roky, and that their continued insistence on LSD as the sacrament of their quasi-mystical philosophy amounted almost to brainwashing. Jack Jackson claimed he was turned away when he went to visit Roky at the Halls' Haight-Ashbury apartment, and muttered about the pair getting into the voodoo wizard trip, with Tommy wearing robes and gowns and brandishing a magical staff. Yet Roky obviously needed taking care of, and there's no doubt that for all their weird ways, Tommy and Clementine genuinely loved Roky, as did almost everyone who knew him.

Stacy Sutherland felt that it was in San Francisco that things really started going wrong with the band, and that they started losing touch with reality and with each other. John Ike and Ronnie Leatherman, along with Elevators roadie Cecil Morris, had moved into a house in Larkspur, San Pablo across the Golden Gate Bridge from the city. Stacy meanwhile was living in a Texan commune close to the Avalon. They only saw Roky and Tommy at shows, where they were increasingly concerned at the singer's deterioration. On more than one occasion Roky would freeze up on stage, unable to remember the complex lyrics Tommy had written for him. The Halls would arrive with Roky at the last minute in their broken down car, and then spirit him away just as quickly at the end of the night.

Stacy felt that Roky continued to take acid, even after he started to become mentally ill, because he felt obliged to continue on with their sacred mission. "We thought that bad trips were caused by doubts and inner fears, fear of ourselves," Stacy said in 1977. "So you tried to overcome it, just bow down and keep going. But finally I noticed that even when people weren't on bad trips they were still on bad trips. They were so high they were spaced out to the point where they didn't need acid and they were still flipped."

International Artists were demanding that the band return to Texas to record an album while *You're Gonna Miss Me* was still hot. Most urgently they wanted a follow-up single, and were threatening to release the Elevators' version of Buddy Holly's *I'm*

Gonna Love You Too from the Contact sessions, which Tommy for one certainly didn't approve. Instead, they flew to Houston and recorded *Reverberation (Doubt)* and *Kingdom of Heaven* on September 20th while high on DMT, with engineer Bob Sullivan. On September 23rd the Elevators played a radio promotion show at 7am on a ferry in the San Francisco Bay, and then flew to LA to appear on the nationally-syndicated music show, *Where the Action Is*, hosted by Dick Clark. They mimed beside a swimming pool, Roky's eyes blurred pinpricks and the whole band incongruous and unsmiling in their heavy coats and work clothes amid the hand-jiving, clean-cut teenage audience. That night they played two club shows, as usual in different towns, miles apart. On September 30th and October 1st they were back at the Avalon, headlining over Quicksilver Messenger Service.

On October 8th they drove overnight all the way from San Francisco to Dallas to record their debut album. They arrived at 1.30pm the next day, and were in Summit Sound Studio at 2am, with Lelan Rogers producing and Bob Sullivan once more acting as engineer. First of all they all got stoned and dropped acid. Then Tommy went onto the studio roof to do his yodeling vocal warm-ups, and at 3am was questioned by police for meditating on a tree stump in the studio's vacant parking lot. In the remaining three hours they recorded the bulk of the album, playing live at full volume. They got most of the basic instrumentals down in one take, and then overdubbed vocals and jug. The next day they spent five hours recording *Don't Fall Down*, which they'd written on the way from San Francisco to Dallas, basing the music on Roky's old Spades song, *We Sell Soul*.

On Sunday 16th October, the 13th Floor Elevators appeared at the Avalon as unbilled special guests supporting Big Brother and the Holding Company, the second and final time that they shared a stage with Janis. Also on the bill were the Sir Douglas Quintet and an SF supergroup called the New Peanut Butter Sandwich, featuring members of the Grateful Dead, Quicksilver

Messenger Service and Big Brother. *Reverberation (Doubt)* was released on October 28th and reached number 129 on the national charts; the Elevators promoted it with an infamous appearance on *American Bandstand*. After miming *You're Gonna Miss Me*, the band were engaged in banter by host Dick Clark, who asked Tommy Hall "Who is the head man of the group?" to which Hall replied "Well, we're all heads," to the glee of dopers and nascent hippies across the nation.

The band were back at the Avalon on November 11th and 12th, supported by Moby Grape; on the second night Tommy and Roky forgot to turn up, then wandered in halfway through and watched from the audience before realizing they were meant to be onstage. In December their debut album, *The Psychedelic Sounds of the 13th Floor Elevators*, finally hit the shops, in theory anyway. Distribution was patchy, and promotion non-existent. There was a launch party though, on a houseboat in San Francisco Bay. The boat was a floating acid lab, belonging to two LSD chemists-cum-dealers. By this time the band's former bassist Benny Thurman was also in San Francisco; he had become a psychedelic preacher, high on speed and LSD and playing his fiddle on street corners, then preaching dementedly from his incredible customized Bible. He was invited to the album launch and on the boat laid down on a sheet of freshly impregnated blotter acid, literally soaking up the vibes.

At the end of 1966 the band went home to Texas for Christmas, all except for Clementine, who didn't want to take her son Roland out of school. They intended to return; San Francisco was starting to accept them, and the international media was starting to notice the wild scenes going on in the city. Bands were starting to sign big-money record deals, and in 1967 the San Francisco Sound would take over the world. But by then the Elevators were stuck between floors; unable to make it to the next level commercially, they were also too far gone to come back down.

Chapter 12

If the 13th Floor Elevators' debut album was a commercial failure, then it was largely down to International Artists' complete lack of promotion or advertising. Supposedly the company was in fact fearful of promoting a band that were so blatantly linked with the drug culture, and actually tried to suppress the album rather than sell it. And as with Big Brother and the Holding Company's debut, studio engineers baulked at the amount of distortion and reverb the Elevators used live and substantially toned down this aspect of the sound in the recording, also remixing the results without the band's knowledge. More seriously, the album was poorly mastered and pressed, resulting in a weak, murky sound that dissuaded many listeners and reviewers from paying close attention to the songs.

On the plus side, John Cleveland's primitivist, hypnotic and decidedly trippy sleeve art was incredibly eye-catching and a perfect representation of the music within, even if *Rag* reviewer Bob Simmons did joke that - given its December release date - the green and red color scheme made it look like a Christmas album. The rear was dominated by an adaptation of the eye-and-pyramid design Cleveland had originally adopted for the Elevators' business cards, dividing two contrasting sets of sleeve notes, one by Lelan Rogers and one by Tommy Hall. Rogers provides a fairly standard list of thanks to supporters within the business, peppered by a warm, laconic sense of humor; his notes end with thanks to "the many DJs whom we have never met personally but who kept asking what is that funny little noise in that record?"

Tommy Hall's notes are something else entirely, being a serious, almost academic summary of the album's concept. Namedropping Aristotle and Einstein, Hall cryptically discusses how important it is that man see the connections between all things, enabling him to "restructure his thinking and change his language, so that his thoughts bear more relation to his life and his problems." While celebrating the fact that "recently it has become possible for man to chemically alter his mental state and thus alter his point of view," Hall judiciously stops short of mentioning LSD or any other drug by name. Instead, he couches his philosophy in terms of semantics and "the quest for pure sanity."

Hall's sleeve notes do however capture what is often the first and most coherent epiphany experienced while on acid; the interconnectedness of all the ideas and concepts one had previously kept compartmentalized, the realization of complete relativity and the way that the microcosm perfectly reflects the macrocosm. Hall takes this a step further, emphasizing how this awareness of connections, "with perfect cross references," empowers one to have instant, instinctively correct reactions to almost any situation. This is the classic beat notion of spontaneity being next to godliness, as expressed in Kerouac's spontaneous composition and the ideal of the Zen Hipster whose conscious and subconscious selves are perfectly integrated, and who because he is at one with himself is also at one with the universe, and so can never put a foot wrong. Acting instinctively and bypassing rational thought, he acts with perfect natural timing, mirroring the be-bop rhythms of modern jazz, and so is always moving flawlessly through time and space, and the jeweled Buddha-nature of the universe that appears endlessly fractured but is actually perfectly, indivisibly whole.

Hall then talks us through each song on the album, carefully ordering them into a classic journey of discovery in the mold of Jung or Herman Hesse. By force of will he fits together disparate lyrics written by Roky, Clementine and Powell St John alongside his own creations, persistently relating them to "the new system," "the new direction" and "the quest," in opposition to "the old reasoning," "the old system" and the "old order." In Tommy's Nietzschean world view, LSD is the catalyst for an evolutionary mutation in mankind, and "the new man views the old man in much the same way as the old man views the ape." Thus, in classic messianic cult style, the persecutions and tribulations undergone by the Elevators and their followers merely reinforce their status as visionaries and martyrs of the coming new age.

Unfortunately for Tommy, International Artists ignored his crucial conceptual ordering of the songs and instead ordered them partly randomly and partly according to tried and tested commercial formulae: opening with the hit single, following it with a rocker, then a ballad, and so on. Yet with an acid-informed view of the universe nothing is accidental, and without intending it, IA's ordering of the album works at least as well as a psychedelic guide as Tommy's.

According to Tommy Hall's sleevenotes, the album should begin with a critique of the old order (*You Don't Know, Thru the Rhythm, Monkey Island*), followed by a description of the way forward (*Rollercoaster, Fire Engine*) and then a warning of the pitfalls to avoid on the quest (*Reverberation, Tried to Hide, You're Gonna Miss Me*), before ascending, via the rapture of Splash 1 and the discipline and focus of *Don't Fall Down* to the final revelation that *The Kingdom of Heaven is Within You*. This benign, structured, forward-moving journey is completely disrupted by the album's actual running order; yet this fractured progression, with its disorienting highs and lows, ironically reflects the typical acid trip a whole lot better.

The other irony about *The Psychedelic Sounds* is that for a band who were actively trying to promote and evangelize for LSD use, the Elevators' debut album sounds like a terrifying descent into insanity and drug-damaged hell. It's a thrilling, visceral recreation of a bad trip, the confusion and disorientation punctured by visions and revelations certainly, but at the expense of the complete stripping away of ego, identity and mental certainty. And while Tommy's lyrics are asserting one thing, Roky's unhinged, terrified delivery often seems to suggest the opposite. Yet this tension and ambiguity turns out to be the record's greatest strength.

With the running order as it was released, the album's opener, *You're Gonna Miss Me*, takes on the sense of a prophecy; by the end of this, the "me" that you knew will be gone, perhaps forever. We are headed ultimately not for the Kingdom of Heaven but the lacerating self-criticism of *Tried to Hide*, where everything you thought you knew turns out to be wrong, and you realize you've been living a lie: "When I got near all I saw was fear, and I know that you tried to hide cos you cried and you lied about it." You may come out of this a realer, more genuine person, but can you survive having all of your illusions shattered?

Along with *You're Gonna Miss Me*, *Rollercoaster* also mirrors the initial rush of a trip coming on, using the metaphor of a fairground ride to describe the confusing mix of sensations; ecstatic, frightening and intense all at the same time. John Ike's reverberating cymbal splashes usher in Stacy's snaking oriental guitar lines, brilliantly counter-pointed by some minimal, atonal picking by Roky. Oddly enough, on the first verse it seems as though Roky is singing about Tommy, and Tommy's Svengali-like influence over him, even though Tommy wrote the lyrics: "Once, somewhere, sometime ago, his eyes were clear to see; he put his thoughts into my mind and gave myself to be. He stopped me from living so unsane…"

We're still climbing the mountain, going round in wide circles like the spiral path the shaman follows in ascending to a sacred peak. Roky's vocals are haunted and hesitant, as though method-acting a role from a horror movie or an HP Lovecraft short: he's the shell-shocked narrator who has been through some unspeakable experience, seen things that no man should see; or, possibly, is fighting the effect of some kind of brainwashing. Certainly, by the time the chorus hits: "Come on! And let it happen to you; you've got to open up your mind and let everything come through," we're hardly convinced that joining him in this experience is a good idea.

By the second verse we're off on the winding, speeding trail into the unknown, as Roky describes the trip and how "it slides you through your view" until "you look back to where you thought you'd stayed." Verse three conveys the lasting effects: "After you trip life opens up, you start doing what you want to do." The line "You find out that the world that you once feared gets what it has from you" reflects the idea that much of reality as we know it is our own creation; or rather, what we think of as reality is a simulacra, a model constructed in our minds based on the input of our perceptions, and so each of us quite literally creates the universe anew in each moment, and we are all in greater control of the reality we inhabit than we generally realize. This is the meta-programmer in the nervous system described by Dr John Lilly, or "the master who makes the grass green" in the Zen tradition; converting whirling particles of energy into the impression of solid things, which we then attach concepts and associations to. Through meditation and discipline we can learn to recognize and to some extent control and direct this perception, and by extension reality as we know it. This is the gateway to a magical approach to the universe, and LSD, peyote, DMT etc. are tools for kick-starting the process.

But again, as an advertisement for the benefits of LSD, *Rollercoaster* is a far more terrifying prospect than, say, Jefferson Airplane's *White Rabbit* or the Beatles' *Strawberry Fields Forever*. Even Pink Floyd's damaged seer Syd Barrett sounded as though he was enveloped in childlike wonder, and though the Doors' Jim Morrison explored the dark side of human nature, he always sounded supremely in control. Roky, by contrast, sounds completely crazy, alternately ranting and terrified. It's partly real and partly an act; Roky the horror movie buff and genius vocal interpreter. But you know that whatever he's on, it's freaking him out. There's nothing pastoral, nothing of peace and love and serenity here; no retreat into the comforting imagery of Victorian children's literature, no newspaper taxis or cellophane skies. Instead, there's just the stark, naked, white-light vision of the universe seen uncensored, with the mind's safety filters removed. We may be seeing "with brand new eyes," but like X, the hero of Roger Corman's classic 1963 B-movie *The Man with The X-Ray Eyes*, such complete perception is more than anyone can stand. And bearing in mind that the studio version of *Rollercoaster* is positively neutered compared to the version played live, you can see why so many of San Francisco's Beautiful People didn't take to the Elevators: their trip just sounds like too much of a bummer, and they're seriously harshing on everyone's mellow.

It's not just Roky either; the track is driven by the spellbinding interplay between Stacy's chiming guitar and Tommy's unstable jug-playing. Stacy's ascending modal riffs take you close to the edge, at times Methedrine jagged and weirdly angled like a John Coltrane horn part, while Tommy's constant runs on the jug mirror the racing madness of your thoughts. In this context, *Splash 1* has an almost unbearable pathos; co-composed by Roky and Clementine, it's essentially a perfectly innocent, haltingly beautiful and understated love song. Over a descending sequence of echoing, picked folk guitar chords, Roky sings "I've seen your face before; I've known you all my life." Tommy's interpretation of this song is that it "describes a meeting with a person who radiates the essence of the quest." Yet it's hard not to hear a poignant yearning for the security, certainty and safety that LSD has destroyed. When Roky sings "And now I'm home... to stay," it's as though he's looking for someone to comfort and protect him, and a sanctuary from the terrifying acid visions. But the song seems to belong to an earlier time, and the innocent faith it describes is now irrevocably lost.

Reverberation begins with a hint of feedback (similar to the opening of the Beatles' *I Feel Fine*), before Ronnie Leatherman's pulsing bass dominates another descending chord sequence, with

Roky singing "You finally find your helpless mind is trapped inside your skin" and "You start to fight against the night that screams inside your mind." *Reverberation* is a total bad trip of a track, and a bizarre choice for the band's second single; who was going to play this on the radio in 1966? With its ghostly, high-backing vocals, slightly out of phase, and the haunting jug line, the song is about how your fears and doubts will hold you back, and that the way to best experience LSD is just to go with the flow, accept whatever comes and freak freely. Yet the band can't resist hamming it up and piling on the nightmarish imagery, concluding that the reverberation is "Driving your mind insane, causing your blood to drain; leaving just charred remains." The point may be that if you don't worry about it, then this probably won't happen, but you don't feel inclined to chance it.

Neither is *Don't Fall Down* any more reassuring. The repeated chanting of the title phrase sounds like it's coming from a Greek chorus of sardonic ghouls, taunting you with the knowledge that you're stumbling, incoherent, out of your mind. The song is based on the Spades' *We Sell Soul*, but the contrast between the two is striking. The somewhat corny but genuine energy and urgent tension of the original is replaced by a washed-out, enervated fog that is nevertheless just as genuine and human. The song urges you to keep going for the benefit of a lover who relies upon you, but it sounds almost hopeless; like you're carrying a mortally wounded companion through the Vietnam jungle, both of you bleeding to death, and you keep saying "Just hang on, it'll be okay."

Side two kicks in with the clattering, unearthly roar of *Fire Engine*. This track was originally released as the B-side of *Reverberation,* and one can't help thinking that surely it should have been the A-side. Freaky and nightmarish it may be, but *Fire Engine* is still essentially a souped-up R&B tune with plenty of manic energy, and as such would have been an ideal follow-up to *You're Gonna Miss Me,* and might have secured more airplay and captured the public imagination in a similar way. Roky's soul-chilling, tremulous screams and howls mix with Stacy's clanging guitar and capture perfectly DMT's frightening rush; the jug is kept low in the mix for once, though Tommy does provide the high, ghostly backing vocals that contribute greatly to the song's eerie atmosphere.

"Let me take you to the empty place in my fire engine," Roky sings, though the way he phrases it it's clear that he's actually singing "Let me take you to DMT place." The song was recorded with the band smoking DMT (Dimethyltryptamine), a powerful hallucinogenic that kicks in almost instantly and, while lasting only a brief time, completely takes the user to another dimension where among other things their sense of time is distorted, so that 10 minutes might seem like hours. It is in the DMT dimension that psychonauts often speak of encountering what author and researcher Terence McKenna called "Machine Elves"; sentient, independent alien intelligences whose intentions are ambiguous, but who, like Tommy Hall, seem to be encouraging us to see beyond the illusion of reality to the true nature of the game.

Thru the Rhythm is a swampy, clanking beast of a song; Stacy's dancing guitar riffs are funky, melodic and edgy at the same time, and Tommy's lyrics take on the form of a mystical riddle, suffused with dark, powerful imagery. "Through the rhythm of darkened times, painted black by knowledge crimes and repetition's pointless mime…" Each verse ends with a question: Who am I? Where am I? Where are you? The object is to question everything, from "The books that rehash the same old lies" to "The fool's gold that they pawn off as their prize." To slough off society's conditioning until you discover the true prison-like nature of your surroundings and climb "above the slime," to find your own free essence rather than conforming to the limited, stereotyped identity forced upon you from birth.

A trilogy of songs by Powell St John comes next, though IA credited him as John St Powell on the album sleeve, in a blatant and successful attempt to avoid paying royalties. *You Don't Know* is filled with strongly psychedelic imagery, betraying not only Powell's debt to Bob Dylan but also his visual, painterly approach to his craft and the influence of LSD on his writing. "Your eyes are filled with coral snakes and liquid plastic castles... corny dots and window panes and pink and silver tassels." The Elevators make the song their own, with their trademark tempo shifts and meshing guitar lines, Stacy ringing out over Roky's fuzz. Though written from the fond perspective of an older male to a somewhat immature girlfriend, in an acid context this song represents the often-traumatic moment when you realize that your whole normal way of thinking and behaving is naive, simplistic and false compared to the awakening experience of your true nature.

Kingdom of Heaven again has something of Dylan about it, and follows on perfectly from *You Don't Know*; if you can rise above the shallowness of your old self, and not be crushed by the realization of what a fool you've been, then you're ready to achieve your true God nature. Powell uses the rich imagery of high church religion, incense and candles, stained glass windows, choirs and altars, only to point out that the Kingdom of Heaven isn't to be found in a church or a book, but within your own mind and soul. The Elevators play the song as a slow electric blues, as close as they ever came to the classic San Francisco sound of the Grateful Dead or Jefferson Airplane, with Hall's swooping, plunging backing vocals adding to the stoned, weightless atmosphere.

Monkey Island is a relatively straightforward R&B groover about feeling like an outsider in straight society. "I'm living on Monkey Island, right in the middle of the zoo... pretending I'm a monkey too." Roky's desperate screams reflect the paranoia Powell wrote into the song, and the sense of increasing pressure that eventually caused him to flee to Mexico. "With my paisley tie and my one button suit, I'm about as close as I can get. I guess

I must be doing okay, because they haven't caught me yet." Tommy's jug imitates the chattering of apes, and the hesitancy of Roky's final declaration of how he's "pretending to be a monkey too" breaks down into grunts, hoots and cries, suggesting that the pretense has finally caught up with him and that's he's succumbed and become a monkey like all the rest. The question of where the act ends and reality begins would become an increasingly pertinent one for Roky.

The album ends with Stacy Sutherlands' storming *Tried to Hide*, partially rewritten by Tommy Hall and, as we've seen, ending the album and the trip on a critical, excoriating note. It wouldn't have been quite right after all for a bunch of punks like the Elevators to conclude with the reassuring message of *Kingdom of Heaven*. Instead they go out on the attack, though the version here isn't as powerful as the original recording that was used as the B-side of *You're Gonna Miss Me*, which was faster and featured some blistering harmonica playing from Roky.

We come away from *The Psychedelic Sounds* not so much enlightened as shell-shocked. The veil of illusion has been torn away from our eyes alright, but we're not so sure that we're comfortable with what we're seeing. One thing is for sure; there's no going back, and no place left to hide. To carry on pretending to be a monkey now would be an act of self-deception so great that we'd never be able to live with it. Where other psychedelic proselytizers saw the LSD experience as a return to childhood, for the Elevators it represented childhood's end; a necessary loss of innocence that prepares one for ascending to the next level. Whether we'll be able to get there in one piece is of course quite another matter.

PART IV

EVERYBODY'S HERE

Chapter 13

The 13th Floor Elevators had only been in San Francisco for four months, but Texas had moved on considerably in their absence. In late 1966, while the Elevators were struggling to gain due recognition in California, their influence was belatedly making itself felt across the breadth of the Lone Star State. By 1967, an infrastructure of venues, lightshows, like-minded bands and fellow heads was starting to come together that would in theory allow the Elevators to assume their rightful position as crown princes of a Texan psychedelic movement. The cruel irony was that, by the time the scene they'd instigated was underway, the 13th Floor Elevators were already burnt out, the first casualties of the visionary trail they'd pioneered.

Much like their New York contemporaries the Velvet Underground, or the Sex Pistols in London ten years later, the 13th Floor Elevators were a band whose influence far outweighed their record sales and apparent following. Everywhere they played, audience members experienced an epiphany, and many went on to start Elevators-inspired psychedelic rock bands of their own. Similarly, the bands that played on bills alongside the Elevators often came away shaken to their very foundations, and determined to re-think their musical and lyrical approach based on the Elevators' ground-breaking performances.

Even for those who hadn't seen the Elevators live, the band's mythology was spreading like wildfire across their home state. Here was a bunch of Texan boys who took strange and powerful drugs before every show, and yet somehow couldn't be busted. The legend of the Elevators attributed magical powers to Roky, Tommy and the rest; it was whispered, half-seriously, that no prison cell could hold them because they could walk through walls and turn invisible. Not only did LSD open up their minds to high visionary states, it was said, but they could communicate telepathically and see into the future. Before the days of documentation by the music press, let alone the internet, the Elevators were a contemporary western outlaw myth, the 1960s equivalent of the James Gang or Billy the Kid. They were larger than life, the authorities couldn't catch them, and they could be coming to your town soon.

So powerful was their aura that the earliest example of the Elevators' influence occurred even before the band was formed. When Stacy, John Ike and Benny Thurman were playing as the Lingsmen in Port Aransas in the summer of 1965, they would often gig along the Gulf Coast in nearby Corpus Christi. The large resort town had a particularly exciting local rock scene from the mid-sixties onwards, partly because it had the infrastructure early on that many bigger cities in Texas lacked. The local radio stations competed to present the best homegrown music, with the top station being KEYS 1440. The KEYS Top 30 chart was featured in 'Go', a weekly section of the daily *Corpus Christi Caller*, dedicated to the local teen scene. This also included a column by DJ Charlie Brite (titled, unavoidably, Brite Ideas) that covered the bands in a similar manner to Jim Langdon's Nightbeat column in the *Austin Statesman*.

There was also a TV show, *Teen Time* on Channel 3 every Saturday morning, also hosted by Charlie Brite, which was the Corpus Christi equivalent of *American Bandstand*, and gave airtime to many local groups. Venues like the Carousel Club, the Tiki Teen Club, the Elks Club, the Beach Club and Peppermint Lane all booked rock 'n' roll bands, and down the Gulf Coast, in towns like Port Aransas and Rockport, groups would entertain tourists with covers of the latest hits by the Beatles, the Rolling Stones, the Yardbirds and the Kinks, as well as surf instrumentals in the Ventures mold. This inevitably meant that there was stiff competition among the groups, who soon realized that having your own original material was the way to stand out from the crowd.

"With the local bands, popularity just depended on who had

a record out at the time," recalled Jerry Chandler of Corpus Christi band Four More, in the sleevenotes to Cicadelic Records' 2011 compilation *Revolution! Teen Time in Corpus Christi (1965-1970)*. Four More hit big locally with their Merseybeat-flavored single *Don't Give Up Hope*, backed by the more punky *Problem Child*, in early 1966. Still at high school, they pressed 300 copies on their own Fairchild label, and when they sold out signed a distribution deal with Jack Salyers and Carl Becker at J-Beck Records. J-Beck was the final cog that made the Corpus Christi scene turn over, and produced a run of singles by the hottest local bands that, years later, would become cornerstones of the U.S. 'garage band' collector's market.

Yet Carl Becker and Jack Salyer were essentially just two music fans who both worked as baggage handlers at Corpus Christi Airport and spent all of their extra money on their dream of running a record company. "Those two wanted to be record promoters so bad they could taste it. And they were really great people too, honest to a fault and willing to put everything they had into what they loved," according to Rod Prince, hotshot lead guitarist with the first Corpus Christi band to release a single on J-Beck: the Bad Seeds.

"My dad played a little, by ear, and a one-note man, but there was always music in the house, all sorts of styles," Rod Prince recalls. "Got my first cheap guitar at 13; dreadful action, bloody fingers, heh. But I stayed with it because I loved making music." Prince's father was an aircraft mechanic and the family moved around a lot, so every two or three years Rod would find himself in a new town with a new set of local guitar players to imitate. This rootless childhood must also have encouraged his dedication to learning the guitar, with no permanent friends to distract him from practicing. Being a guitarist also immediately gave him an identity every time he arrived in a new school or neighborhood.

"I did seem to have a gift for it, and I loved playing above all else," Prince says, noting that once he got a decent guitar he made rapid progress, and when the family settled in Corpus Christi he found friends who also played instruments and music soon took over his life. Prince's early influences included Nashville session man Grady Martin, particularly his lead guitar playing on Marty Robbins' 1959 hit *El Paso*, as well as Dick Dale, Chuck Berry and Lonnie Mack, and a mentor who was somewhat closer to home.

"The one player that really shaped me and really had the biggest influence on me was Johnny Reinhart, a local Corpus guitarslinger and the best in town," Prince says. "I'd stand right in front of the stage and watch his every move till he finally started actually taking time to show me what he was doing. An awesome player."

When Reinhart quit the band he was in, the Velvederes, he nominated the young Prince as his replacement. "Rodney the Cub, heh," Prince recalls. "I wasn't remotely good enough for that band, at 15 with no experience to speak of. But the keyboard player Gary Beck spent hour upon hour in the afternoons showing me the songs, and generally turning me into a pro musician."

Prince moved on to other local bands, including a vocal group called the Titans that featured a young drummer named Bobby Donaho. "It was a bunch of guys from the high school choir, and me," Prince laughs. "Bobby sang bass, as well as being a kickass drummer." Then there was the Four Winds, which Prince formed with Velvederes drummer Crans Nichols, bassist Joe Dodd and fellow guitarist Mike Taylor. Though often cited as being a Merseybeat influenced outfit, Prince stresses that they were around before the Beatles broke stateside. "Taylor could do Gene Pitney perfectly," he notes. "So that'll give you an idea of what the Winds were like."

In 1964 Rod Prince and Mike Taylor formed the Bad Seeds, bringing in Bobby Donaho from the Titans on drums and

Taylor's friend Henry Edgington on bass. Prince had met both Taylor and Edgington, who were a few years older than he was, while playing in the Velvederes. "We practiced in my grandparents' living room," Prince chuckles. "I've forgotten how we hooked up with Carl and Jack, but I imagine they approached us at some point, since those two loved music as much as everyone else back then."

Certainly the Bad Seeds quickly became the number one band in Corpus Christi, and in early 1965 J-Beck released their debut single *A Taste of the Same / I'm a King Bee* (J-1002). Written by Mike Taylor, *A Taste of the Same* is considered a garage-punk classic, with Taylor's sardonic whine sliding greasily across Prince's sinister guitar licks. A fusion of surf and folk-rock, swathed in reverb, the track pulses with venom and excitement, and Prince contributes two blistering solos. They followed this with a novelty surf instrumental, *Zilch (parts 1 and 2)*, also on J-Beck (catalogue number J-1003), which the Bad Seeds got to perform on national TV, on Dick Clark's *American Bandstand*. Written by Prince, it's a killer guitar workout and dance number that must surely have been a highlight of the band's live set.

Seemingly unstoppable, early in 1966 the Bad Seeds took part in a Battle of the Bands at Corpus Christi's Carousel Lounge. To everyone's surprise, they only managed second place; the winners were an improbably young new group called the Zakary Thaks. Though the Bad Seeds were not yet done it was a symbolic changing of the guard, and the wild, long-haired Thaks would almost immediately replace them as Corpus Christi's number one teenage rock 'n' roll band.

The Zakary Thaks had evolved out of junior surf band the Marauders, whose initial line-up featured guitarists Glenn Jower and Pete Stinson, bassist Wayne Harrison, drummer Rex Gregory and occasional vocalist Chris Gerniottis. Formed, like the Bad Seeds, in 1964, but all significantly younger, the group members were childhood friends who had grown up around Corpus

Christi's Sherwood Park. Appropriately, considering the future Zakary Thaks' anglophile/mod leanings, all the street names in the neighborhood had a Robin Hood, Merrie Olde England theme: Nottingham Drive, Warwick Drive, Friar Tuck Drive, King Richard Drive, Little John Drive, and so on.

When problems at school caused Rex Gregory to be sent to live with his father in Houston, he was replaced on drums by David Fore. Fore was impressive enough that when Gregory came back to Corpus Christi and wanted to rejoin the Marauders, they were reluctant to kick Fore out. Instead, Gregory replaced Wayne Harrison on bass. Harrison was restricted as to when he could play with the band due to his strict parents, as well as a demanding paper round (no doubt hampered by all those bow and arrow wielding outlaws jumping out of the trees around Sherwood).

Glenn Jower soon left too and was replaced by hotshot Hispanic guitarist John Lopez, at which point the Marauders changed their name to the Riptides. At the beginning of 1966 the Riptides appeared on *Teen Time* alongside another Corpus band called the Last Five, whose standout feature was their amazing drummer, Stan Moore. They persuaded Moore to join them, gave Fore his marching orders, and changed their name to the Zakary Thaks, the name taken apparently from a non-existent group in a British music magazine, with the spelling changed to seem more hip and offbeat. The group's vaguely English-sounding name reflected their love of the British Invasion sound, especially the Rolling Stones and the Yardbirds, and they also had the look down more than any other Texan band, with their long pageboy bobs and mod clothes, bought from Corpus Christi's recently-opened 'Mod Shop.' The band owed so much of their look to the shop, an attempt to cater to the teen crowd by the more established upmarket store S&Q Clothiers, that they eventually recorded a radio ad for it.

Stan Moore was more than just an incredible drummer; he

was a strong-willed and driven individual, who according to Gerniottis was the unofficial leader of the Zakary Thaks. He insisted that they practice constantly, and his perfectionism led to the teenage band developing the tight, high-energy sound that gave them the edge over the local competition. He also came up with the best songs for them to cover, often suggesting B-sides or album tracks that no-one else had yet picked up on, and which the Zakary Thaks could make their own. It didn't hurt either that he came from a relatively wealthy family, and lived in a big house where the band could rehearse. His father, Lester Moore, even invested in the band, paying off studio bills and buying a station wagon to get them to gigs.

While still only in their mid-teens (Chris Gerniottis was a mere fourteen years old at the beginning of 1966) the Zakary Thaks played the Dunes Club in Port Aransas, where the Lingsmen had recently been the house band, and were briefly the house band themselves at a short-lived rival club called the Sugar Shack. And after their triumphant performance at the aforementioned Carousel Club Battle of the Bands, they were snapped up by J-Beck, who in July 1966 released their debut single, the all-time garage classic *Bad Girl*, backed by a version of the Kinks' *I Need You* (J-1006).

Bad Girl is perhaps the ultimate proto-punk song, with Chris Gerniottis' barked, machine gun vocals eschewing any notion of melody, spitting out nasal, barely intelligible rhymes in time with Stan Moore's hurtling drums, in a manner that the Ramones would make their trademark nearly ten years later. Factor in the rattling-thrash guitar riff, the dumb-to-the-point-of-genius chorus ("Bad Girl, Bad Girl, Bad Girl, Oh Yeah") and a flailing, unhinged solo from John Lopez, and you have two minutes, nine seconds of snotty garage-punk perfection.

The two songs were recorded at Jimmy Nicholls' two-track studio in McAllen, down in the Rio Grande Valley. Nicholls owned the Pharaoh label that released many great sides by

McAllen garage bands like the Headstones, the Playboys of Edinburg, the Cavaliers and Christopher and the Souls. The Thaks travelled down with the Bad Seeds, who were still signed to J-Beck and were laying down some demos. Yet the band had already recorded what turned out to be their final single: *All Night Long / Sick and Tired.*

All Night Long remains a confusing and fascinating footnote in Texan psych history, being a lyrical rewrite of the 13th Floor Elevators song, *Tried to Hide*. This was a Stacy Sutherland composition, which the guitarist had originally worked up with the Lingsmen during their Dune Club residency in the summer of 1965. No recording of their original version of the song exists, but after some lyrical alterations by Tommy Hall it was recorded as the B-side of the Elevators' debut single in January 1966, and later re-recorded, in a less frenetic version, for that band's debut album.

The Bad Seeds had obviously learnt the tune from the Lingsmen, having seen them playing around Corpus Christi and Port Aransas many times over the previous summer. "I'd heard them play that tune many times and I liked it a lot," Rod Prince remembers. "I didn't know the words or anything, but the rest of the boys thought it was pretty kickass too, and we played it at practice for grins till Carl and Jack heard it. Then nothing would do but we'd have to work it up and record it."

Bad Seeds drummer Bobby Donaho wrote an entirely new set of lyrics and sang on the track, now titled *All Night Long* and recorded at Gold Star Studios in Houston, within days of the Elevators recording their version across town at Walt Andrus' studio. Despite being a Rod Prince-Bobby Donaho rewrite of a Stacy Sutherland composition, the Bad Seeds' *All Night Long* still bears the writing credit "T. Hall – S. Sutherland," as by then *Tried to Hide* had been registered as such on the Elevators' behalf by Gordon Bynum.

"That whole thing's an embarrassment to me," Prince sighs.

"But we were just kids then. Stacy and John Ike remained good friends of mine always. Fine folks they were and are. Ol' John spent time teaching me five-string banjo at one point, and he's a master player on that instrument for sure."

Granted catalogue number J-1005, The Bad Seeds' version emphasizes the song's roots as a Kinks-derived rave-up, setting it to a stomping, pounding rhythm close to a more technically proficient Dave Clark Five. The lyrical rewrite sets it up as a wounded love song rather than a number about hiding one's dope stash, as Stacy originally conceived it, and Prince plays a typically jaw-dropping solo. The flip is also a pretty decent slice of tight, punkish folk-rock, but the single couldn't revive the Bad Seeds' ailing fortunes, and they split up soon after its release.

Henry Edgington left music and embarked on the course that would eventually see him becoming an evangelical preacher, while Mike Taylor was retained by J-Beck as a writer/producer, working closely with the label's new rising stars, the Zakary Thaks. But Rod Prince and Bobby Donaho continued playing, adding bassist Steve Lohse and a couple of freaky characters recently arrived in Corpus by way of San Antonio; Roy Cox and David Frazier.

At just eighteen, Roy Cox was already a respected player in SA; his band, the Mysterions, had a local hit in 1965 with their single *Is It a Lie / Why Should I Love You*, both songs written by Cox, who also sang and played guitar. They later changed their name to the Chessmen, before Cox quit and headed over to Corpus Christi. There for some reason he adopted the pseudonym of Scotty Dacherelli, and spoke in an English accent for the whole time he lived there. His friend David Frazier meanwhile had the longest hair anyone had ever seen in Corpus, hanging right down his back, and suffered regular harassment as a result.

With Frazier on vocals and Cox on organ, the New Seeds struggled to germinate in Corpus Christi and after six months a version of the band with Prince, Donaho, Frazier, Cox switched to bass and Ronnie Huth on keyboards headed out to Los Angeles to try to make it there. It didn't happen, and the band swiftly broke up, with Cox and Frazier returning to San Antonio, while Bobby Donaho and Rod Prince stayed on. Their long partnership finally ended in mid-1967, when Donaho joined the Mike Nesmith-managed Penny Arkade. Prince returned to Texas, figuring his rock 'n' roll career was all over. But in fact, the best was yet to come.

Chapter 14

Even more so than Corpus Christi, and certainly more than Austin, where university frat parties were most bands' main earners, the Houston music scene was dictated by its many 'teen clubs', and the bands they favored. The Teen Clubs generally operated a membership scheme, only open to kids aged between 15 and 20; no alcohol was ever served, and local police officers would generally be in attendance. Nevertheless, these venues offered a genuinely exciting night out, and an opportunity to see some of the greatest rock 'n' roll bands of the day, with touring acts frequently appearing on the teen club stages alongside local talent.

The first Houston teen club of note was La Maison, opened in 1964 as La Maison du Café, a folk club on San Jacinto and Wichita run by George Massey. In mid-1965 Massey went into partnership with Jerry Clark, a cameraman on the *Larry Kane Show*, which ran for two hours every Saturday afternoon on KRTK (Channel 13), between 1959 and 1971. Like *Teen Time* in Corpus Christi or *Sump'n Else* in Dallas, this was Houston's TV equivalent of *American Bandstand*, and Clark convinced Massey to start booking the local rock 'n' roll acts that were proving so popular on the show at La Maison. The club moved to an old church on Bagby and McGowen, changing its name to La Maison Au Go Go where, as the name suggests, it was also the first Houston club to feature go-go dancers, perhaps inspired by the teenage groovers who were a major attraction on the *Larry Kane Show*.

Proclaiming itself "Houston's only Go-Go for young people" and "Open 8 days a week," the house band at the re-launched La Maison Au Go Go were Houston folk-rockers the Baroque Brothers, soon to alternate with a Brit Invasion-influenced combo called the Six Pents. Late in 1965 La Maison moved again, go-go dancers and all, to a derelict supermarket on 1420 Richmond

Street, where the 13th Floor Elevators played some legendary early shows. But by mid-1966 it was back at the old church at 319 McGowen, where it struggled on till the end of the year, its reputation severely damaged following a scandal when Jerry Clark was charged with statutory rape, though he was later acquitted.

Beside the Baroque Brothers and the Six Pents (who later changed their name to the Sixpentz), two other important bands that started out playing at La Maison were the Misfits and Euphoria. The Misfits had been formed in 1965 by Pete Black (vocals/guitar), Jim Frost (guitar), James Harrell (bass), and Mickey Bishop (drums), while their 'fifth member' was the artist George Banks, an older friend who acted as their informal manager. They were originally the relief band at La Maison when the Baroque Brothers had other engagements, but their horizons were broadened when George Banks took Pete Black and James Harrell to see the debut performance by the 13th Floor Elevators at Austin's Jade Room. Later on John Kearney from the Spades briefly joined the Misfits on drums, and when the 13th Floor Elevators played La Maison alongside the Misfits early in 1966, the two groups became close friends. By now the regular house band at La Maison, the Misfits' sets increasingly leaned towards Elevators-inspired psychedelic rock.

Euphoria was also hugely influential on the Misfits and on the Houston scene in general during the summer of 1966. This group had moved to Houston from Los Angeles and had a convoluted history. Singer/guitarist Wesley Watt and drummer Dave Potter were originally members of Cleveland band the Amazing Bushmen. The Bushmen had moved to LA, where they were joined by bassist and songwriter Bill Lincoln, who had previously been in the Strangers alongside future Walker Brothers Scott Engel and John Maus. After the Bushmen split, Watt and Lincoln stuck together as a songwriting team, recording several singles with studio-based, near-fictional bands (the War Babies,

Nobody Cares, the Word), before forming Euphoria Mark I with Dave Potter and guitarist Douglas Czinki. They fell apart when Bill Lincoln married an English girl and moved to Salford in the UK, and Watt put together Euphoria Mark II, retaining Potter and adding bassist Pat Connolly, who had been an original member of the Surfaris, co-writing and playing on their classic hit song *Wipeout*.

The trio moved to Houston, where they made quite an impression during their four-month existence. Scott Holtzman in the Houston Post described Euphoria as playing the purest form of psychedelic music he had ever heard live, calling them "strong leaders of the [psychedelic] trend." "Euphoria… were definitely psychedelic progenitors of surf music," the Red Crayola's Mayo Thompson told Richie Unterberger in 1996. "Incredible guitar playing… what you saw with Hendrix, the same principle, taken to its highest expression."

Also loosely managed by George Banks, this line-up of Euphoria recorded its lone single at Andrus Studios. *Hungry Women / No Me Tomorrow* was released on Bob Shad's Mainstream Records, the same label that originally signed Big Brother and the Holding Company, in the fall of 1966. The 45 was a flop, yet both songs are fully-formed psychedelic classics, astonishingly sophisticated and ahead of their time. Euphoria certainly show a heavy Byrds influence, but the folk-rock shades even deeper into psychedelia, suggesting a close familiarity with the Beatles' *Revolver* (which can only just have been released when the single was recorded) and those perennial Texan favorites, the Jeff Beck era Yardbirds. *Hungry Women* marries a chiming raga-rock riff to a speeding, nimble rhythm section and Watt's pleading, McGuinn-like vocals narrating a cryptic, murky scenario: "the cops carried me down the stairs and I looked up to see your glare… Crazy hungry woman there are too many of you." Chemically-assisted perspectives on morality and behavior are hinted at in lines like "my mind's been blown I can't think to say" and "you want to be evil because it's fun."

The complex arrangements extend to disorienting multi-part vocals and unsettling harmonies, as well as constantly shifting time signatures. Once again, it's hard to think of anyone who was making records as astonishing and deeply trippy as this in 1966. "Too much for you," high ghostly voices repeat, before the song breaks down to a half-spoken "I don't mind... waiting in line" and then takes off again for a final run at the stratosphere. The brooding *No Me Tomorrow* is more conventional folk-rock, though highly accomplished, but concludes with an astonishing final forty seconds of electrifying modal jazz in an *Eight Miles High* vein. Apparently a whole albums' worth of material was taped at Andrus Studio but remains unreleased, though a handful of further tracks have since turned up on compilations.

By the time their single was released however Euphoria's time as a Texan band was up, and they had already moved back to LA, taking George Banks and the Misfits with them (minus Jim Frost, who was married and already had a young child). Neither band found success in California; the Misfits to all intents and purposes came to an end with no gigs forthcoming, and Pete Black and James Harrell actually joined the live line-up of Euphoria on more than one occasion while in LA. Despite their record deal however they too struggled to find work. Euphoria Mark II imploded in a morass of drugs and recrimination, not helped by the fact that Wesley Watts and Dave Potter were both married men, trying to have separate family lives alongside their musical careers.

Back in Houston, the action was already shifting away from La Maison to the Catacombs, which opened at the beginning of 1966 at 3003 South Post Oak Road. Although the dress code specified "school clothing," the Catacombs was a pretty hip space, with low ceilings and black walls painted in fluorescent designs, and two rooms with a stage in each. Support bands would play in the back room, then the headline act would start immediately afterwards on the main stage. The Catacombs was managed with great personal energy by Bob Cope, and owned by Ames Productions, the company founded by brothers Richard and Steve Ames. With money from the local oil industry (their family owned Ames Oil and Gas), they not only bought into the Catacombs, but managed several local bands and ran their own record label, Tantara. While older brother Richard looked after business, Steve Ames was a musician and songwriter himself and played keyboards with Neal Ford and the Fanatics, who during the latter part of 1966 were not only the house band at the Catacombs but the most popular band in Houston. By this time however, Ames, who had only one kidney, had already retired from stage work, finding that the late nights and travelling were seriously affecting his health.

Formed at the end of 1964 by singer Neal Ford, at age 20 already a veteran of several teen-pop singles with the Ramadas and the VIPs, the Fanatics mixed hard-edged, Kinks-and-Stones-derived rock with solid R&B, folk-rock and novelty pop. Though hardly psychedelic (Ford absolutely forbade any use of drugs or even alcohol when the band was working) they were no strangers to fuzz, driving Hammond organ and the odd weirdly menacing chord sequence or guitar riff. Yet this was always combined with an adherence to old-fashioned showmanship that demanded smartly matching outfits and corny synchronized onstage routines such as the band all crouching down in a line and rowing across the stage with their guitars.

The original line-up featured Ford alongside guitarists Johnny 'String' Stringfellow and Jon 'Big Jon' Pereles, plus WT 'Dub' Johnson on bass, John 'Baby John' Cravey on drums and Dennis Senter on keyboards, who didn't last long enough to acquire a nickname. After the Fanatics' debut single in January 1965, *I Will Not Be Lonely* (a garage classic) he was replaced by Steve Ames, with brother Richard coming in as the band's manager. At the beginning of 1966 the Ames brothers established Tantara Records in order to release The Fanatics' second single, the moody, psych-tinged folk-rock of *Bitter Bells*.

Steve Ames stayed with the Fanatics through the summer of 1966, a time when the band's profile rose steadily, with local airplay, appearances on the *Larry Kane Show* and increasingly well-attended shows, including opening slots for the Beach Boys and the Lovin' Spoonful. They were regularly mobbed by screaming girls, and gigs often deteriorated into near-riots as the local kids decided to re-enact the scenes of Beatlemania they'd seen in the newsreels with the Fab Four's closest local equivalent. In June the Fanatics released a cover of *All I Have to Do is Dream* on Tantara, but shortly afterwards Ames left to concentrate on management and production. He was replaced on keys by 18-year-old Lanier Greig; a far flashier player whose frenetic organ runs became characteristic of the classic Fanatics line-up.

The band's fourth single, *I Will If You Want To* (September 1966) had a brooding majesty that was distinctly psychedelic, with John Stringfellow's greasy slide guitar echoing over the spare, rolling rhythm, and Greig's understated keys descending into an aural abyss of loss and despair on the bridge. The Fanatics' profile was boosted still further when Ames signed them nationwide to Nashville's Hickory label, who released the bizarre, cod-gothic single *Shame on You* in January 1967. It was the flip, *Gonna Be My Girl*, however that became a number one single on both of Houston's major radio stations, resulting in the Fanatics requiring a police escort whenever they played a show in town. In February 1967 they were clear winners of a *Houston Post* Battle of the Bands, yet to tell the truth their star was already on the wane, as Hickory guided them in a middle-of-the-road direction increasingly at odds with the times, and Ames Productions focused their attention on another of their small stable of acts: the Moving Sidewalks.

The Sidewalks' story begins at Houston's Robert E Lee High School, where one Billy Gibbons played in bluesy covers bands from the age of 14 on: the Saints, the Ten Blue Flames and ultimately the Coachmen, AKA the Coachmen V. Gibbons was born on December 16th 1949 in the relatively affluent Houston neighborhood of Tanglewood. His father, Frederick Royal Gibbons, was a concert pianist and conductor who had worked for MGM Studios in Hollywood, but young Billy was more interested in the black R&B music he heard blasting out of Houston's big tower radio stations, not to mention the flashy personality jocks who hosted the shows. By early 1966 The Coachmen V consisted of Gibbons on lead guitar and vocals, plus rhythm guitarist Bob Bolton, bassist Mike Frazier, keyboard player Kelly Parker and drummer Dan Mitchell.

This was the line-up that went into Gold Star Studios on April 22nd 1966 to record the two original songs they'd worked up between them: Dan Mitchell's *Stay Away* and a Billy Gibbons original named *99th Floor*. *Stay Away* was certainly a groovy little number, but *99th Floor* was the one that really caught the ear and the imagination. Named in sincere tribute to the 13th Floor Elevators, the song was powered along by Kelly Parker's keyboards, riding over a two-chord guitar part not entirely dissimilar to *You're Gonna Miss Me*. There was even a hint of Tommy Hall's jug-enhanced scat warbling in the original demo, with Billy Gibbons singing about how "we got on the elevator and then we shut the door; and we won't stop until we get to the 99th Floor," before launching into a Roky-alike scream and harmonica break.

After listening to the recordings over and over however, the band knew that they weren't up to scratch. They just sounded far too tame; the result of a bunch of inexperienced kids going into a big studio for the first time, with an engineer (Bob Lurie) more used to recording folk and country, and determined to avoid any hint of distortion or feedback. It was at this point that the Coachmen approached Ames Productions. They'd known Steve Ames since July 1965, when the Coachmen V had opened for

Neal Ford and the Fanatics; nearly a year later he was still playing keyboards in that band, but was seriously thinking about moving into production. Working with the Coachmen would give him valuable experience, and accordingly Ames went into Doyle Jones Studio with them on the 19th of May to recut the tracks. Once again though, the sessions were unsatisfactory.

Nevertheless there was something about the Coachmen and *99th Floor* in particular that had real potential, and Ames resolved to keep working with them. The band was evolving all the time, and Bob Bolton was kicked out as Billy Gibbons envisaged a more stripped-back, bare-bones unit, with himself as the only guitarist. After briefly toying with the name the Missing Links, they officially became the Moving Sidewalks in June 1966, the name inspired by the automated walkways at Dallas's Love Field Airport, as well as the 13th Floor Elevators and the increasingly freaky, psychedelic spin that British bands like the Beatles and the Stones were putting on Billy Gibbons' beloved rhythm and blues.

By August 1966 Steve Ames had left the Fanatics and was able to take a more serious interest in the Moving Sidewalks, attending their rehearsals and arranging one last, make-or-break attempt to properly record *99th Floor*. He approached the man who had somehow managed to at least partially capture the essence of the 13th Floor Elevators' sound on record; Walt Andrus. On October 4th 1966, Ames and the band went into Andrus Studios in Houston to cut the definitive version of *99th Floor*.

Hard and heavy, and drenched in fuzz and menace, the song seemed a sure-fire winner. Ames arranged an audition for the band with Mainstream Records, who had just released the Euphoria single and were considering signing other Houston bands. The label hedged their bets, taking out an option on the Moving Sidewalks' material, but shortly afterwards keyboard player Kelly Parker left the band and the Moving Sidewalks continued to play around Houston as a trio for the rest of the year, waiting for Mainstream to make up its mind.

It was around this same time that what was left of the Misfits returned to Houston, in a state of some disarray. Nevertheless, George Banks, Pete Black and James Harrell reunited with Jimmy Frost, found a new drummer in Micky Bishop's younger brother Steve, and started playing under a new name: the Lost and Found.

Unfortunately the Lost and Found were initially notorious not for their music, but for being the first band in Texas to be busted for possession of LSD; even though the drug was still legal in the state at the time. James Harrell, Pete Black, George Banks and Steve Bishop were arrested along with six other youngsters when they were apparently found in possession of "50 pills and capsules, suspected of containing LSD," and a pound of marijuana, according to a November 30th report in the *Brownwood Bulletin*. Eight of the ten arrested were charged with seven counts based on possession or use of marijuana, and five counts of possessing LSD, "based on Texas dangerous drug statutes." Acid had been banned in California the previous month but was still legal in Texas, and it seemed that Houston police intended to use the bust to make the case for a similar ban in their home state. The article quotes the head of the Houston Narcotics Bureau, Captain Jack Renois, as saying that if the LSD charges were followed through it would be "more or less a test case," while District Attorney Carol Vance admits that this was the first occasion of anyone being charged with possession of LSD in Texas; hardly surprising, when the drug was still perfectly legal. If tests confirmed that the pills contained LSD, then the prosecutors intended to "prove" through "expert medical testimony" that the hallucinogen should be classified as a dangerous drug.

The timing couldn't be worse for the four (identified in the

Brownwood Bulletin as "members of a rock 'n' roll group"), as they were about to begin a residency at a newly-opened Houston teen club, the Living Eye. This was run by old-school songwriter Jimmy Duncan (known for writing Bobby Helms' number one country hit, *My Special Angel*, plus equally saccharine songs for Fabian and Ricky Nelson), but nevertheless cultivated a distinctly psychedelic image from the outset, with a huge pulsing eyeball decorating the club's low ceiling. The opening night in November 1966 was promoted by flyers and a radio ad, voiced by the Houston Post's Scott Holtzman through layers of sepulchral reverb, which proclaimed "If you're 21, you're too old; if you're 14, you're too young. If you're in between; take a fantastic voyage into the heart of an android."

Perhaps unsurprisingly the test case failed, and the charges were thrown out of court, though the four were all still placed on ten years' probation. It's popularly thought that the name change from the Misfits to the Lost and Found was to escape the scandal of the drug bust, but George Banks insists it was more to do with the changes the band went through in Los Angeles. Playing with and as Euphoria had expanded Black and Harrell's horizons, and when they were reunited with Jimmy Frost after a long absence it was obvious they weren't the same band anymore. They were Lost and Found.

Banks also rejects suggestions that the band signed to International Artists just because it was run by two lawyers who could help them get out of the drug charges. The connection more likely came about through the band's friendship with the 13th Floor Elevators, who recommended them to their label when they were looking around for other bands to sign. IA was based right there in Houston and was a natural fit, so with yet another new drummer on board (Steve Webb), the Lost and Found resumed their residency at the Living Eye. But it would be August 1967 before they recorded their debut album for the label, by which time IA had already followed up the Elevators'

Psychedelic Sounds with the debut from another controversial Houston group: the bizarre and legendary Red Crayola.

Chapter 15

On the very weekend of the Charles Whitman killings, on August 1st 1966, the Zakary Thaks travelled to Austin to take part in a battle of the bands. They didn't win (that honor went to soul group the Mustangs), but the Thaks still saw it as a big break, a pivotal show where everything really seemed to come together for them. They actually came third in the contest, with second place going to the Wig.

In the Elevators' absence, the Wig were probably Austin's number one rock 'n' roll band, and were moving ahead in great strides. They had been taken under the wing of KOW DJ Paul Harrison, who acted as their manager, soundman and producer. The Wig rehearsed in his living room, and he provided them with high quality PA equipment, while as a guitar player himself he had a definite idea of how the group should sound. The result was a killer live act, and the Wig was making good money as the house band at the Jade Room through the latter part of 1966. Nevertheless, they still wanted to get their sound down on record.

A first experimental foray down to Austin Custom Records on Hancock Drive resulted in an acetate single, with cover songs on both sides; *Searching* and *You're So Fine*. The Wig would also recall a couple of trips down to Andrus Studio in Houston, once on their own and once with Lelan Rogers, but claim neither session resulted in anything worthwhile. They finally put out their debut single in November 1966, as the sole release on Paul Harrison's Goyle Records: *Drive It Home* backed with *To Have Never Loved At All. Drive It Home* is a wild, stomping rocker that fuses punk and R&B in a tight, relentless groove that never lets up but just whips harder and harder. Yet it was the moody ballad *To Have Never Loved At All* that got constant airplay on KOW, eventually hitting number one on the station's charts.

The band was mobbed by screaming girls at a show in

Victoria, where their long hair incited scenes similar to Beatlemania as the teenage fans chased them around the building. This show also led to a brief stint as the backing band for bill-topper Freddie Cannon, known for hits like *Tallahassee Lassie* and *Palisades Park*. With their own set including such crowd-pleasing staples as *Everybody Needs Somebody to Love, In the Midnight Hour, Hey Joe, Louie Louie* and so on, the Wig attracted a more mainstream audience than the Elevators; fraternity members and air force guys who were turned off by Tommy Hall's jug playing and that band's general weirdness.

The band leader, main songwriter and lead singer of the Wig was Rusty Weir, who as a drummer made up in brute force what he lacked in finesse and precision, playing so hard that the other members would be constantly showered in his broken sticks. His composition *Crackin' Up* was the Wig's second single in May 1967; a heavy garage classic, drenched in fuzz and raw, soulful psychodrama energy. There's a definite psychedelic edge to this single, with its echoing backing vocals, sudden time changes, distorted lead vocals and Johnny Richardson's crazed lead guitar bucking like a wild horse over pulsing organ and pounding drums. The flip, *Bluescene*, was a groovy instrumental jam, highlighting the dueling lead guitars of Richardson and Rowe, and credited to the anagrammatic 'W Theig.'

While the Wig were keeping things rocking at the Jade Room, St John and the Conqueroo had shortened their name following the departure of Powell St John, and had grown into Austin's number one underground band. Bill Carr had replaced Powell as singer and harmonica player, alongside bassist Ed Guinn, lead guitarist Charlie Prichard, drummer Tom Bright and rhythm guitarist Bob Brown. Though still in his teens, Brown was developing into a notable songwriter, and his laid-back, country-tinged compositions won increasing space in the Conqueroo's repertoire. With Gilbert Shelton designing their posters and the Jomo Disaster providing their psychedelic lightshow, the

Conqueroo continued to pack out the (admittedly tiny) IL Club and the Fred with their freewheeling mixture of folk, rock, jazz and rhythm & blues, and also established a residency at the Pussycat Club in San Antonio. By the end of 1966 however the Conqueroo and their associates were thinking bigger than playing small folk and blues clubs. They felt that if they could establish a strong collective identity they could book other freak bands, from Texas and beyond, and bring together the disparate strains of Austin's underground culture under one roof, without acquiescing to the demands and the control of the beer joints and nightclubs. The Teodar Jackson Benefit in March, when the Elevators had played alongside Janis Joplin and the cream of Austin's blues and folk scene, showed that it could be done. But the group also looked to the Elevators' success in San Francisco, and that city's thriving psychedelic ballroom scene, supported by striking and innovative posters, lightshows and an underground press. Austin certainly had the raw talent to manage a similar scene of its own; rather than let it all drain away to the West Coast, why not make it happen right there in River City?

Given the disdain of the authorities, the police and the local rednecks for anything perceived as subversive or anti-American, however, it was a risky proposition. Even the university was refusing to bend with the prevailing wind, as in December 1966 Frank Erwin was elected chair of the UT Board of Regents, the body that established university policy, holding the position until 1971 despite increasing resentment from students and faculty alike. Erwin was a staunch ally of Lyndon B Johnson and a leading figure on the conservative wing of the Democratic Party, serving as chairman of the State Executive Committee. At UT, Erwin was a dictatorial figure who brooked no opposition, and first caused controversy as a board member in 1964 when he fired the university comptroller, granting the Board the ability to award all building contracts, which his opponents alleged went to his political allies rather than contractors selected on merit. He was also an ardent segregationist, and is said to have worked doggedly behind the scenes to dismiss professors suspected of harboring left-wing sympathies. He was equally zealous in his persecution of the emerging student counterculture, political or otherwise. But there were signs that the tide was starting to turn in the underground's favor, as Fall 1966 saw the first issue of *The Rag*, an alternative, counter-cultural newspaper with strong SDS sympathies. *The Rag* favorably covered local rock music and psychedelic experimentation, and sought to explicitly link it to radical, left-wing politics and protest against the Vietnam War.

Students for a Democratic Society (SDS) were a radical national student organization that was the most visible face of the 1960s 'New Left' in America. Originating in the Civil Rights movement of the early sixties, they soon rejected both conventional party politics and old guard communism in favor of direct action and "participatory democracy," calling for an end to the war in Vietnam, solidarity with the Black Panthers and ultimately the dismantling of the existing establishment power structure. The chapter at UT was one of the largest and most vocal in the country, thanks in no small part to the campaigning of SDS pioneer Jeff Shero, later known as Jeff Nightbyrd, a UT student who was part of the original Ghetto crowd and a Folk Sing regular. Shero was elected to the National Council of SDS in 1963, and though seen at first as a naïve Midwestern farmboy by the East Coast intellectuals then in charge, he was pivotal in moving SDS away from moderate party politics towards a more radical, free-wheeling approach.

Shero built the Austin chapter rapidly by registering every alienated person on Campus that he could, building up a non-traditional cross-section of integrationists, peace protesters, early environmentalists, bohemian artists, writers and musicians, bikers and general rebels who hated the fraternity- and sorority-run social scene. Though lacking a conventional political education, this motley crew, who soon numbered more than 200, bonded through actions such as an anti-war sit-in on Lyndon B Johnson's ranch. Shero, who in 1965 became national vice-president of SDS, noted that Texans tended to be less uptight and less academic than their East Coast peers, but they also had more to lose, as most did not come from left-wing families. He became associated with the phenomenon of 'Prairie Power,' which advocated a decentralized, anarcho-syndicalist form of organization that put a radical spin on traditional Texan self-determination.

The impetus for *The Rag* came when a right-wing student, John Economidy, was elected editor of the official UT campus paper, *The Daily Texan*. The paper had a history of crusading for liberal causes, going against the grain of the Austin establishment. But Economidy explicitly set out to change all that, boasting that he was the only alternative to "another female editor" and essentially turning *The Daily Texan* into a mouthpiece for the university establishment. Among those particularly incensed by this were SDS members Thorne Dreyer and Carol Neiman, with Dreyer describing Economidy as "a veritable fascist... his campaign platform was essentially to kill all the commies and uncover all the dope on campus."

Dreyer and Neiman had spent the summer of 1966 at an SDS project in Haight-Ashbury, where they met Michael Kleinsman of Michigan's *Paper*, one of the first underground newspapers and the first to come out of a university community, as well as Max Sherr of the *Berkeley Barb*. They returned inspired to create Austin's own underground paper, one that would serve not only as an alternative to Economidy's *Daily Texan*, but which would hopefully unite Austin's diverse community of radicals, bohemians and teenage rebels, sweetening the SDS/New Left political line with irreverent Texas humor and psychedelic artwork. "The Austin radical scene has the strongest sense of community of any I have come in contact with," Dreyer wrote in his letter to the newly-formed Underground Press Syndicate, announcing the arrival of *The Rag*. "Hippies and politicos merge."

The first issue hit the streets on October 10th. One SDS member, George Vizard, caused a scandal by selling copies of the paper on UT's West Mall, in violation of campus ordinance. His sales pitch apparently involved shouting "Commie propaganda; get it while it's hot! Page six is soaked in LSD; it's a cheap trip! Read about the freaks!" This in a town where even suggesting that the Russians were people too, and didn't necessarily deserve to be nuked out of existence, could earn you a severe beating. Vizard faced up to campus security, claiming he was a non-student and so didn't have to abide by their rules, and supposedly sold 1500 copies of the paper through sheer bravado. *The Rag* was an instant hit.

It's probably not coincidental that *The Rag* also chose the West Mall as the location for their 'Gentle Thursday' happening, announced in the October 31st edition. The brainchild of Jeff Shero, it was described as "a celebration of our belief that there is nothing wrong with fun," and participants were invited to simply do as they pleased; suggestions included bringing a dog or a baby to campus with them, dressing in bright colors, having a picnic on the lawn, reading poetry, exhibiting paintings, flying a kite or presenting your math professor with a bunch of flowers. Yet this seemingly innocuous event was deliberately timed to coincide with an annual invite-only fraternity costume party; the sort of status-reinforcing frat event that had caused Janis Joplin such misery. According to Austin folklorist Glenn W Jones, participation in Gentle Thursday "signaled an ideological solidarity with radical politics and bohemian values which were in opposition to dominant structure." Or as one student put it, "you have to understand that until that moment, people didn't just do things like sit down on the West Mall and talk to each other."

As well as sitting on the grass and talking, people played folk music and bongo drums, flew kites, shared food and chalked peace signs and flowers on the sidewalk, while a fighter plane mounted outside the Reserve Officers Training Corps building was anonymously graffitied. The event was a huge success, and inspired similar campus gatherings around the country; *The Rag* followed it up with 'Flipped Out Week' in April 1967, which coincided with Austin's spring mobilization against the war. Later Austin love-ins and free festivals were all a direct outgrowth of the original Gentle Thursday.

The Rag actively promoted local psychedelic rock and folk bands, recognizing Austin's music scene as its greatest strength and an important community-building tool. It shouldn't necessarily be assumed however that the bands always shared their political sympathies.

"Tommy and I lost interest in the SDS civil rights people because, although we agreed with their cause, we found them to be just as wrong-headed in their attitudes and actions as the juvenile delinquents of the decade before," says Clementine Hall. "By that I mean that every time we were around the SDS's members and someone ran in shouting about a possible demonstration to take place, they would all get extremely worked-up about the news and would run around gleefully, behaving as though a 'rumble' had been announced. Their demeanor was often violent and they appeared to be relishing the possibility of a violent confrontation; not my or Tommy's scene at all."

Certainly *The Rag* made no pretense at objectivity, and unapologetically wrote and reported from a radical left-wing, revolutionary, anti-establishment point of view. It made the news as well as covering it; organizing protests, attending the protests, and then writing about the experience afterwards. The paper was seen as unique among the underground press in springing directly from an existing counterculture, as opposed to trying to create one according to the top-down vision of some self-appointed radical elite. *The Rag* was run democratically, with editors renamed as 'funnels' and the staff all contributing ideas and deciding the editorial direction. As such there was no hard party-line, and the common ground among *The Rag* staff, the Austin SDS and the wider bohemian scene was an irreverent, instinctive anarchism that was uniquely Texan. For instance, *The Rag* was the only underground paper to have a regular column on motorcycles, 'The Bent Spokesman,' and was noted for its psychedelic artwork and pioneering cartoons. Jack Jackson, Gilbert Shelton and Jim Franklin were all regular contributors, as the freak flag was passed on to *The Rag* from *The Ranger*. Shelton debuted his "Furry Freak Brothers" strip in *The Rag* in May 1968, while Jim Franklin introduced his soon-to-be famous armadillos on the paper's pages. *The Rag* so upset the Austin establishment that Frank Erwin banned it from being sold on the UT campus in 1969, leading to a four-year legal battle that went all the way to the Supreme Court (and concluded in *The Rag*'s favor).

At the same time as *The Rag* was becoming the public face of the Austin freak community, the Jomo Disaster's Gary Scanlon and Houston White teamed up with Elevators/Conqueroo soundman Sandy Lockett to put together their own music promotion venture. Taking the name of Charlie Prichard's defunct jug band, they called themselves The Electric Grandmother, and their first show was a triumphant homecoming for the 13th Floor Elevators at the Doris Miller Auditorium on January 7th 1967. A nondescript-looking municipal hall on the outskirts of East Austin, the Doris Miller Auditorium nevertheless held over 2000 people, and was well away from the established club and bar circuit. There was an art nouveau poster by Mark Weakley, lights by the Jomo Disaster and support from the Conqueroo, who also returned to jam with The Elevators after that band's headlining set. The show was a sell-out and augured well for an anti-establishment, psychedelic DIY culture in Austin that could operate as a genuine alternative to the mainstream. The same line-up filled the much larger Austin City Coliseum on February 10th, supporting the release of the Elevators' new single, *Levitation / Before You Accuse Me*, which IA had sneaked out, with typical lack of fanfare, a few days earlier. The single would peak at number 20 on Austin's KNOW radio station in March, but failed to chart anywhere else in the country. In between, The Electric Grandmother had also promoted a *Rag* benefit at the Methodist Student Centre on February 1st, with the Conqueroo headlining (backed, as always, by the Jomo Disaster lightshow) and support from the Chelsea.

This would turn out to be one of the Chelsea's final shows, as George Kinney increasingly realized that they had slipped behind the times. He desperately wanted to write and play his own original material, and although the Chelsea were all excellent musicians, they played largely the same cover songs as every other band in town, and so could never generate the same authentic excitement and shock of the new as the 13th Floor Elevators. Upon their return from San Francisco, Tommy Hall and Roky Erickson had actually moved in with George, his wife Dana and their newborn baby; John Kearney and his wife Susie also shared the Kinneys' large house. George was the only one working to pay the rent, but his ongoing, friendly rivalry with his childhood pal Roky was undoubtedly one of the spurs that drove him to quit the Chelsea, and accept an invitation from his old school friends Jimmy Bird, Bill Hallmark and Tommy Ramsey, who had 'turned on' and wanted a singer and lyricist for a freaky new rock group they were putting together.

Bill Hallmark had played bass in the Fugitives with George and Roky, and guitarist Jimmy Bird was the guy who had introduced John Kearney to John Shropshire, and so got him the gig in the Spades. Tommy Ramsey was on lead guitar, and with George on vocals it was natural that Kearney should be their first choice for a drummer. The new band was called the Power Plant, an obvious allusion to sacred herbs and consciousness-altering plants such as marijuana, peyote and psilocybin mushrooms. This indicated their outlaw status and psychedelic direction from the start; the Power Plant would be the Elevators' natural allies in the sacred quest, and certainly not just another rock 'n' roll dance band.

Yet despite the success of *The Rag* and the Electric Grandmother shows, early 1967 was still a particularly risky time to join the quest. Although Tommy and Roky were living with the Kinneys in Austin, the other Elevators had retreated to the Sutherland family ranch outside Kerrville, where the band rehearsed, as the heat in Austin was just too heavy for them to stay in town. The Power Plant meanwhile began rehearsing at Jimmy Bird's dad's taxidermy shop, on an abandoned acreage outside of the city limits.

"Privacy was essential," Kinney wrote in 2006, on the *Texas Psychedelic Ranch* website. "The law in Austin, shall we say, highly disapproved of our music and our lifestyles. Possession of even a small amount of marijuana could land you in prison for many, many years; even life imprisonment was a legal option for judges in some cases. To be a young, long-haired hippy musician in those days was like wearing a sign around your neck saying arrest me, I am likely in possession of pot."

The cops weren't the only antagonists that the new generation of long-haired and freaky-looking musicians had to worry about either. "At that time in Austin most of the youth were mama's boy frat rats, stuck-up sorority chicks or more-or-less ignorant rednecks," George explained. But if these street toughs thought that the Power Plant and the 13th Floor Elevator members were effete aesthetes and peaceniks who wouldn't fight back, they were in for a surprise. "The difference with my band and most of the others, however, is that we had been raised in South Austin, and fighting was second nature to us," Kinney continued. "You can imagine the surprise a group of would-be redneck aggressors experienced when upon attacking us they often found themselves bleeding on the ground, watching us leave with their former girlfriends. It was dangerous fun, but the fun ended there."

The outlaw lifestyle soon became too much for John Kearney; when his wife Susie became pregnant he decided that he needed to find a full-time, steady job, and was replaced on drums by Kerrville boy Bobby Rector. A further complication was that George's wife Dana and Roky Erickson were childhood sweethearts, and with them all now living under the same roof, old feelings started to reawaken. Dana would soon leave George for Roky, even as the friendship between the two bands secured the Power Plant a recording contract with International Artists. But not before they changed their somewhat risky name.

"The name the Power Plant, to me, was an open invitation to trouble," George says. "It was clever, but too dangerous to my view." Bill Hallmark and Tom Ramsey suggested the Golden Dawn, which many have assumed was taken from the occult secret society of which Aleister Crowley was a member. Apparently though, this wasn't the case. "At the time of naming the band I had read Crowley, but dismissed his general premise as restrictive and non-organic, not enough love-based thinking for me," George explains. "So the band was not named after his group. Still, the concept of the idea of a golden dawn, a new era of human development that was within our grasp, was appealing to me, so I went with it."

More than any other Austin musician, George Kinney would follow Tommy Hall's philosophical lead, embracing the ideas of Gurdjieff and Ouspensky and actually reading the books for himself, tracing their ideas back to Plato and Aristotle and embarking on his own self-taught course of esoteric knowledge. When in 2013 I asked him to clarify the nature of the sacred quest that he felt the Elevators and the Golden Dawn were undertaking, George responded thus: "The sacred quest, of course, is

Jung's Hero's Journey, but modified to account for the outrageous social realities of the 1960s. Human beings are not yet fully evolved. Although there is little evidence that we are evolving physically, the evolution of our psychology is the next level or modality of our evolution.

"We are, as such, self-evolving models. That is, it is within our potential evolutionary scope to evolve our consciousness, our awareness; our fundamental sense of identity. By doing so, we will grasp and fulfil our most beneficial evolutionary potential and continue along our journey to whatever abilities and forms are best for our species. The most comprehensive universe is a quantum field of all possibilities, the world of potentia. By expanding our awareness we can connect with the higher aspects of our nature, our souls, such that our individual wills become resonators with the will of absolute consciousness, the ground of all being: God."

Chapter 16

Born in Houston in February 1944, Mayo Thompson had come up through the folk singer scene, performing solo early on at La Maison and the Jester Folk Club, as well as on a couple of occasions with a comedy act called the Seventy-three Balalaikas. Enrolling at Houston's University of St Thomas to study Art History and Philosophy, he met Frederick Barthelme, then known as Rick, at the college's arthouse film club. Barthelme was about to be kicked off the Architecture degree course at the University of Houston, having decided that he really wanted to be an artist; this was somewhat embarrassing, as Barthelme's father was a successful architect and a professor of architecture at the university. On the other hand, his older brother Donald had been a journalist on the *Houston Post* before becoming director of the city's Contemporary Arts Museum; Donald Barthleme had also begun publishing short stories in the *New Yorker* magazine and other places, and was already developing the reputation that would see him acclaimed as one of the greats of American post-modernist literature.

In mid-1966 Thompson and Barthelme decided to form a band. Neither were musicians, but as Barthelme later wrote, "the deal was to participate in the party and do something surprising while you were at it." The pair soon recruited St Thomas philosophy major Steve Cunningham, and at some point the band may also have included Cunningham's friend Bonnie Emerson and one Danny Schact. They settled however as a trio, with Mayo Thompson on guitar and vocals, Steve Cunningham on bass and Rick Barthelme on drums. Barthelme named them the Red Crayola; possibly in tribute to Mayo's mother Hazel Cunningham, a much admired art teacher who let the band rehearse at her home. The name also reflected the joyfully primitive, unfettered creativity and childlike sense of exploration that the group would cultivate.

Initially however, the Red Crayola were merely an inept covers band, playing the likes of *Hey Joe, Louie Louie* and *House of the Rising Sun* as the resident band at an obscure club called simply Love, on the corner of Richmond and Shepherd, run by their friend Mark Froman. But the Red Crayola were also very much a part of the Houston art scene, performing at gallery openings and happenings, making short films, and generally operating in a far broader cultural milieu than that of frat parties, teen clubs and mastering the latest Beatles tunes.

"Because we couldn't play all that well, we had to do something else, something more interesting," Barthelme wrote. "And since we were art-inclined, we went that route, leaning on every possible art idea at every turn. Soon we were making 'free music,' playing long improvised pieces heavily invested in feedback, random acts of auditory aggression, utterances of all kinds. We began to have big ideas about ways to listen to music, and what 'music' was."

Drawing on the inspiration of La Monte Young, Albert Ayler, the Fugs, John Cage, Dadaism and Yoko Ono's work with the Fluxus group, within a few months the Red Crayola's sets were entirely self-written, mixing surreal songs with improvisations in which boundaries between band and audience were swiftly broken down. In one sense, they saw themselves as a parody of hippy culture and psychedelic rock; Mayo Thompson placed them in the tradition of outsider artists like Texas's own Legendary Stardust Cowboy, or satirists like Stan Freiberg and Spike Jones, whose sonic experimentation and use of studio sound effects, in lampooning 'bad' music on their records, often bordered on the avant-garde. Rick Barthelme sympathized with this point of view too, early on deciding to wear many belts onstage and adopting the nickname 'Belto': "a cruel parody of another drummer of the moment."

But the Red Crayola's attitude was also that of classic art school punk rockers. "We set out from the beginning to mark our

difference from everybody," Mayo Thompson told Richie
Unterberger. "We wanted to eliminate everybody, and we
wanted to tighten the logic. We wanted to say, is there logic in
pop music? And, if there is, if there's a claim for a certain kind of
progressive logic or certain kind of developmental logic, well,
let's see where it goes. So our strategy was totally informed to
some extent by art and avant-garde traditions and those kinds of
things. But our aim was to shut everybody else up. 'Cause we
hated everything everybody did, just about, with the exception
of a few things."

Those "few things" included the early work of Country Joe
and the Fish, as well as avant-folk guitarist John Fahey and
progressive songwriter Van Dyke Parks. They were also
informed by the likes of the Beatles, Dylan and the Stones, but
saw no point in repeating what had already been done. "Partly,
the logic was a certain kind of extremism, let's say, in relation to
the previous standards," Thompson said. "We were not hippies;
we weren't involved in the worldview that informed counter-
culture. For us all these kinds of things, these interests and
considerations, came out of a general impetus to make art in
general."

Many were completely bemused by the Red Crayola's performances. Mayo noted that during the 1960s, and perhaps
especially in Texas, people expected a high quality of
musicianship, even in 'alternative' music, which the Red Crayola
had no ability or intention to deliver. "People looked at what we
were doing as unorthodox in some sort of sense, as neither the
mainstream nor the counterculture," he said, adding that they
were seen as even weirder than "professional weirdoes" like
Frank Zappa, Captain Beefheart or the Velvet Underground. In
turn, they saw these acts as essentially sell-outs, trying to have
their cake and eat it by playing experimental music within
conventional rock structures. "We said fuck the framework,
listen to this, motherfucker," Rick Barthelme later wrote. "And

then busted your eardrum." But in spite, or perhaps because of their unique, out-there status, the Red Crayola developed a following of friends and acquaintances who became regular participants in their extended improvisations and performance pieces. The band named this group The Familiar Ugly, and they became an expected part of the Red Crayola's sets.

Lelan Rogers first encountered the Red Crayola during a shopping trip in Houston with his wife, towards the end of 1966. KNUZ-FM were hosting a battle of the bands contest in a small marquee set up outside the Gulfgate Shopping Mall, and as the Rogers passed by the Red Crayola were up there playing. Rogers took it as a brilliant scam; three people on stage with four or five instruments, which they obviously didn't know how to play, just making noises but, crucially, getting a wildly enthusiastic response from the crowd, who were mostly aged between 13 and 15. But what really impressed Rogers was that there were many older folk watching who didn't get it, but still wanted to be in on it. "The older crowd, twenty-five to eighty, wanted to be part of what the youth were enjoying," he told Jon Savage in the sleevenotes to 1980's *Epitaph for a Legend* compilation. "I was watching the faces of the crowd, and I figured anybody that was able to put on a crowd like that, there's got to be a market."

The audience's reaction in some ways recalls the celebrated short story *The Balloon*, published in 1968 by Rick Barthelme's older brother Donald. In the story, an unnamed artist inflates a giant balloon above Manhattan, as "a spontaneous autobiographical disclosure" inspired by a personal loneliness that he doesn't expect anyone else to recognize in the work itself. "There were no situations," he writes, "simply the balloon hanging there." Yet people react in different ways, with "daring children" leaping and playing on the balloon, literally enjoying it on a surface level, while adults find it "interesting" and at first earnestly debate its meaning, but this soon subsides: "we have learned not to insist on meanings, and they are rarely even looked for now." Many are immediately hostile to the balloon's apparent purposelessness and the fact that it exists without reason or invitation, while others project their fantasies and desires upon it. Critics engage with the amorphous mass, and like the Red Crayola, "It was suggested that what was admired about the balloon was finally this: that it was not limited, or defined." But soon criticism, analysis and hostility give way to a practical, even commercial exploitation of the balloon's presence; writing messages or hanging lanterns on its underside, for instance. Similarly, Lelan Rogers didn't know what the Red Crayola meant, but his experience with the 13th Floor Elevators had taught him one thing: crazy sells. He could sense the sea-change happening across the business, and he knew that if the kids dug it, then the grown-ups would eventually fall in line. He determined to take the Red Crayola to International Artists.

If the demand for freaky rock 'n' roll in Texan cities like Houston was broad enough for the avant-garde Red Crayola to enjoy an enthusiastic grass roots following, then at the other extreme it also took in bands whose sound was somewhat more stately and considered, yet still had an uncanny quality that marked them out as intrinsically psychedelic. The Fever Tree were one such group, and while this Houston band's psychedelic phase was relatively brief, it did produce one of the genre's enduring hit singles; though the title of that song, *San Francisco Girls*, only served to further obscure their Texan roots.

The Fever Tree started out as the Bostwick Vines, formed in 1964 by 15-year-old Spring Branch High School-student Michael Knust. An aspiring guitarist, Knust was already good enough to be giving lessons, and having seen the Beatles on the Ed Sullivan show he was already entertaining the idea of putting a rock 'n' roll band together. To this end he persuaded one of his beginner pupils, EE 'Bud' Wolfe, to switch to bass, and taught him that instrument instead. Another guitar teacher, the slightly older Jerry Campbell, joined up on lead guitar, and brought in one of his pupils, Dennis Keller, who was a lousy guitarist but a naturally gifted singer. Campbell's friend John Tuttle on drums completed the initial line-up.

Like the Zakary Thaks, the Bostwick Vines took their name from a magazine advert while desperately searching for a phrase that sounded vaguely English; like the Zakary Thaks, they had no idea what, if anything, their chosen name was meant to mean. With the early Rolling Stones a big influence, the Bostwick Vines would cover the likes of *Satisfaction*, *It's All Over Now* and *Empty Heart* while dressed in modish Beatle Boots and tweed capes. Unfortunately, Jerry Campbell was old enough to be drafted and was sent to Vietnam, so Knust shifted to lead guitar and brought in Don Lampton on keys and rhythm guitar to fill in the gaps. Their first show was on the roof of Mullin's Music Store, close to Spring Branch High School on Houston's Westview Avenue, cunningly timed for just as school was finishing for the day. Knust would later recall that traffic was backed up for miles, while 2000 of the school's 3500 pupils gathered in the parking lot cheering them on until the police broke the gig up.

The Bostwick Vines' period as anglophile Stones copyists was brief however, and their outlook was dramatically changed after seeing both Euphoria and the 13th Floor Elevators play at La Maison Au Go Go in early 1966. They had been alerted to the shows by Scott Holtzman's 'Now Sounds' column in the *Houston Post*; the go-to source not only for finding out what was happening locally, but for tips on all the latest sounds then emerging from England and San Francisco. The members of the Bostwick Vines would follow Holtzman's columns almost religiously, and after having their minds blown by the Elevators and Euphoria, they decided to approach Holtzman in person.

A music columnist for the *Houston Post* since February 1966, Holtzman was also a sometime folk singer himself, cutting two singles with Kay Oslin for International Artists under the collective pseudonym Frankie and Johnny. He and his wife

170

Vivian, a theater director, were also jobbing songwriters, whose creations had been recorded by the New Christy Minstrels among others. And although in 1966 he was a clean-cut, short-haired thirty-something whose 'Now Sounds' head shot gave the impression of a matinee idol from twenty years earlier, Scott Holtzman was well-connected and hip to all the latest trends on the East and West Coasts, as well as what was going on in the local scene. The first to alert *Houston Post* readers to keep an eye out for such hip signifiers as psychedelic poster art, liquid light-shows, flower children and love-ins ("People all come to the park and give flowers away to strangers"), he occasionally got ahead of his provincial readership, as on the 16th of April 1967 when, in a column promoting a forthcoming "Now Sounds Groove-In," he wrote: "I was accused of putting the freaks down last week by calling them freaks. I wasn't. It's a term that's used for Freak-Outs and Love-Ins on the West Coast." He would generally sign off with the snappy catchphrase "Hang ten and a half."

After meeting with the Bostwick Vines, Scott and Vivian Holtzman agreed to take the band on, though some might argue they took them over, gradually becoming their managers, songwriters and producers. Scott Holtzman's first act was to rename them the Fever Tree, a canny decision in 1966 that would align them with the emerging cool psychedelic groups rather than the already fading Anglo fad. His next was to secure them a deal with Mainstream Records, the New York label that had signed Big Brother and the Holding Company and Euphoria, and which had also been courting the Moving Sidewalks.

By early 1967 the Sidewalks had solidified into their classic line-up, with Gibbons and Mitchell joined by Tommy Moore on Hammond B3 organ and the goofily flamboyant Don Summers on bass. They had been waiting four months to find out if Mainstream were going to release their single, *99th Floor*; time spent honing their increasingly powerful live act, a brand of heavy, psychedelic blues-rock defined by the interplay between

Billy Gibbons' mercurial guitar playing and Tommy Moore's low-down funky organ licks. But ultimately Mainstream passed on *99th Floor*, and it was released instead in March 1967 on manager Steve Ames' Tantara label, which he had originally established for the purpose of putting out records by his old band, Neal Ford and the Fanatics. The same month, Mainstream released *Hey Mister* by the Fever Tree.

The contrast between the two songs is interesting. While *99th Floor* is a raw garage rave-up in celebration of passionate teenage sex, *Hey Mister* is a strangely mannered confection in which the singer urges an older man (this is what the appellation "mister" seems to suggest anyway) to stay away from the girl he's after that night, because it's the week that she gets to spend quality time with her sister. Barely two minutes in length, it's an intriguing and unusual choice for a debut single. Dennis Keller's strong, soulful vocals ride a descending chord pattern that dominates your internal jukebox through sheer force of repetition; though lacking any obvious chorus or instrumental hook, it's still catchy as hell. The listener is forced to focus on the lyrics, but the subject matter is obscure; it's obvious that the mister has been cheating and lying, but why does the girl spend this one week with her sister, and why does that mean she'll find out all about his conniving ways? Is it because he came on to the sister as well? Is "spending time with her sister" a euphemism for the girl being on her period? Could there even be darker themes of incest and abuse at work here: is "mister" the girl's father?

Whatever, *Hey Mister* shot to number one in the Houston charts, thanks in part to the smart, confident playing, with Bud Wolfe's bass and Michael Knust's guitar arpeggios interlocking tastefully over John Tuttle's jazzy rhythms. The harpsichord-like keyboards were played by Scott Holtzman's protégé, a young session musician named Rob Landes, after Don Lampton was judged not up to scratch. When Landes was also brought in to play on the follow-up single, *Girl Oh Girl (Don't Push Me)*

(Mainstream 665, May 1967), the writing was on the wall for the hapless Lampton, and Landes officially replaced him soon after. In fact, the changeover was so quick that the rather straight Landes had to be hastily made over as a 'rock star' for his debut gig, with theater director Vivian Holtzman dressing him in old clothes and gluing a false moustache to his face backstage. Unfortunately during the show, as Landes began sweating heavily due to nerves and the heat of the psychedelic lightshow being projected onto him, the fake rock-star moustache began to gradually slip down his face.

Girl Oh Girl, also known as *Girl Don't Push Me*, was an anthemic slab of brooding, southern country soul, with Landes' warm, funky organ sound augmented by stabs of brass. Keller alternates between the moody withdrawal of a young Scott Walker and a hairy-chested, but somehow clean-cut, throaty passion redolent of Neil Diamond. Like *Hey Mister* it was extremely successful in Houston but failed to generate much interest or radio play elsewhere. Both tracks (and their respective B-sides, *I Can Bang Your Drum* and *Steve Lenore*) were written and produced by Scott and Vivian Holtzman, which is perhaps why they sound like the work of a much older band. In fact, Michael Knust was only just about to graduate from high school when *Girl Oh Girl* hit number one on KNUT. Fever Tree (they dropped the definitive article after their first two singles) were now in great demand, and they and the Moving Sidewalks played together often through the summer of 1967, a period when Michael Knust's guitar style began to develop away from the clean, unobtrusive style of the band's early singles towards the innovative use of feedback and sustain that would characterize Fever Tree's debut album. His initial kick in that direction came from seeing Cream live in Los Angeles, shortly after finishing high school, but playing alongside Billy Gibbons night after night surely left its mark too.

The Moving Sidewalks' star was also in the ascendant. *99th*

Floor had hit number one on both KILT and KNUT by the end of April 1967, and the following month the single was re-released nationally on New York's Wand Records. The label also released the Sidewalks' follow-up single, *Need Me / Every Night a New Surprise* (Wand 1167, September 1967). The A-side was an unapologetically commercial Billy Gibbons composition that nevertheless sacrificed none of the Sidewalks' well-honed edge; indeed, with its catchy, needling chorus and tremolo-laden guitar vamps, *Need Me* shows that Michael Knust wasn't the only one to have been influenced by Cream, and also that the early recordings of the Jimi Hendrix Experience had already reached Billy Gibbons' 17-year-old ears. *Every Night a New Surprise* meanwhile was written by Steve Ames while he was still playing in Neal Ford and the Fanatics, and is a more typical organ-led garage rave-up. Although the single didn't match the success of *99th Floor* it still went Top 10 in Houston, and like Fever Tree the Moving Sidewalks spent the remainder of 1967 gigging hard and recording tracks for their debut album. But from this point on, the two bands' destinies would diverge remarkably.

Chapter 17

The fourth and final Electric Grandmother show took place at Houston's Music Theater on February 18th 1967. The 13th Floor Elevators were supported as usual by the Conqueroo, though with a few line-up changes; Bill Carr had been let go and Wali Stopher had come in on keyboards and percussion, while ex-Chelsea drummer Darryl 'Zeke' Rutherford had replaced Tom Bright. International Artists had got involved as co-promoters and had hired Houston's number one DJ, Russ 'Weird Beard' Knight as MC, and the show was plugged heavily on his show on KILT-FM. IA were also recording the show for a potential live album, with Walt Andrus and Frank Davis hired to oversee the process. Unfortunately, things didn't go entirely as planned.

The venue being in the round and featuring a slowly revolving stage didn't help; already tripped-out musicians struggling to focus on the audience really don't need the added distraction of gradually shifting clockwise while playing. There was also no backstage area, and after booking the show International Artists behaved with their usual paranoia, alienating themselves from The Electric Grandmother and keeping the Elevators completely isolated from everyone. IA booked practically a whole floor of Austin's Holiday Inn and hired off-duty police to act as bodyguards and security. The band were locked in their rooms while the cops guarded their doors, then at the last minute they were hustled into a van that supposedly locked from the outside and driven over to the Houston theater.

Far from making them feel safe, having off-duty police officers constantly watching over them just made the band even more paranoid, and the show suffered as a result. Roky kept forgetting lyrics on stage and missing whole verses, while Stacy suffered the mother of all bad acid trips, and had the terrifying experience that would come to be known as the "three visions." Before the show he saw Roky and Tommy turn into wolves, and realized that he and the rest of the band were evil, because they were spreading drugs and Satanism in the world. At the concert, Russ 'Weird Beard' Knight was dressed in a sorcerer's costume, and Stacy decided that he was the devil and that the theater, with its lightshow and revolving stage, was Hell. Three Angels appeared, bathed in light, to judge him and to give him three prophecies. The first was that he would lose his girlfriend of eight years, Laurie Jones; the second was that he would end up in jail. The third prophecy Stacy claimed was too terrible to relate, but it is widely believed that he was warned of his own premature death. He jumped off stage and ran for the door, and the 13th Floor Elevators were forced to play the biggest show of their career without their lead guitarist.

Following this debacle, Sandy Lockett quit working for the Elevators, and The Electric Grandmother was renamed the Vulcan Gas Company. The Elevators themselves were booked into a ridiculous 14-week residency in Houston by International Artists, who remained unwilling or unable to organize a national tour for the band. They wanted them where they could keep a close watch on them; the name of the Living Eye Club, where the residency took place, now seemed ironically appropriate.

Meanwhile, IA were cautiously gauging the potential of their newest signings, the Red Crayola. Initially they had them record a short demo session, just so that the label could hear if they had any songs as well as their live freak-outs. Two tracks from these sessions, *Nickle Niceness* and *Vile Vile Grass*, were later released on the *Epitaph for a Legend* compilation, and showcase Mayo Thompson's vivid, surreal lyrics in a stripped-back, almost acoustic format, while three more numbers would be re-recorded at Andrus Studios for the Red Crayola's debut album.

In some ways, *Parable Of Arable Land* is one of the most psychedelic albums ever recorded; in others, it isn't really psychedelic at all. As Mayo Thompson noted, "we weren't hippies," and while the Red Crayola's debut is certainly one of the most far-out albums of the 1960s, or indeed any decade, it owes little if anything to psychedelic trends or the LSD experience. Instead, it brings concepts and ideas from the classical and artistic avant-garde to bear on primitive Texan garage rock, comparable in some ways to what Frank Zappa's Mothers of Invention or Captain Beefheart's Magic Band were doing, but different in that those groups comprised highly skilled musicians, whereas the Red Crayola were artists and experimental thinkers with only the most rudimentary grasp of their instruments. Even the Velvet Underground sound hopelessly conventional by comparison.

Since he was in Houston anyway, Roky Erickson went along to the album sessions, and wound up playing on two of the album's most popular tracks, contributing keyboards to *Hurricane Fighter Plane* and harmonica to *Transparent Radiation*. Roky's organ playing is the most 'psychedelic' feature of the album, contributing hugely to the sound and appeal of the opening track, *Hurricane Fighter Plane*. The shimmering keyboard sounds, like splashes of light reflected in slowly drifting water, are very different from the R&B derived organ stabs then common in garage or psych rock, and give the track a similar feel to the early Pink Floyd. Yet the Floyd's debut single, *Arnold Layne*, wasn't released in the US until 24th April 1967, a fortnight after the recordings for the Red Crayola album were finished. Pink Floyd's own debut, *The Piper At The Gates Of Dawn*, would not see the light of day until August.

Riding a gloriously primitive, insistent three-note bassline, *Hurricane Fighter Plane* is closest to something from *Black Monk Time*, the 1966 proto-punk classic by the West Germany-based American band the Monks, though it's doubtful that the Red Crayola would have heard this album at the time. Mayo Thompson's surrealist, sexually/chemically loaded lyrics are delivered in a tremulous hiss that's part sneer, part frightened, urgent declaration. He's like a man reporting back from some bizarre parallel reality, knowing that you won't believe him but not caring, because what's he's seen is The Truth.

Roky's echoing harmonica adds a soulful, bluesy edge to the sinister and apocalyptic *Transparent Radiation*, while the brilliant *War Sucks* also has something of the Monks' Cro-Magnon urgency, and its jangling, monomaniacal raga sound and thudding trashcan beat recalls the aforementioned Velvet Underground. Curiously, Mayo's preaching, jabbing vocals even have something of Mick Jagger about them, though without the preening sexuality, as he takes on first the military generals and politicians ("remember what happened to Hansel and Gretel") and then God himself for allowing such atrocities to happen ("Your silence is part of a fad.")

In the sleevenotes to the 1980 International Artists compilation *Epitaph for a Legend*, Lelan Rogers claims that the famous New York DJ Murray the K was sacked for playing *War Sucks* on air. "This country was in a real mess with the war. We put that song *War Sucks* on the album and that was controversial to say the least," he told Jon Savage. "Murray the K, the DJ in New York City at W-NEW got a copy from my promotion man and said 'This is what's happening.' And he promptly got fired. He then started at W-NEW FM and they had figured they didn't want that on AM and they were starting that station so they put it on FM."

In fact, during most of 1966 and 1967, Murray the K was the flagship DJ on New York's WOR-FM, one of the first FM stations, where the former madcap personality jock pioneered the "progressive" FM format of playing long album tracks rather than singles, and breaking new songs that were thought to be important and ground-breaking, if not necessarily commercial. He championed Bob Dylan and 15-year-old Janis Ian, whose controversial single *Society's Child* told of an interracial love affair; he was also a supporter of the 13th Floor Elevators, and agreed to fund an East Coast tour by the band after George Banks got a copy of the album to him via Peter Yarrow of Peter, Paul and

Mary (the tour never happened). So it's highly possible that he may have been playing the Red Crayola on his show, and indeed, that this may have contributed to his being fired by the station. Murray was sacked in October 1967 because he "put himself above the station and its interests," according to WOR-FM general manager Bob Smith, and refused to adhere to the station's playlists or to attend the meetings where the playlists were compiled. *The Village Voice* also reported that Murray continued playing songs that he had been specifically told not to play, and gave as a prime example Dylan's anti-war classic, *With God on Our Side*. This was the beginning of the station's shift back towards a Top 40 format, in which DJs would have no input into the creation of a strict, limited playlist, following the recruitment of notorious station consultant Bill Drake, who seemed to be the main instigator of this sweeping deconstruction of the otherwise successful progressive radio experiment.

The decision to abandon what had proved a popular format seems to have been more political than commercial; with advertisers abandoning the station in droves, WOR-FM started to live up to its name in fanatically supporting American action in Vietnam. Within weeks of Murray's departure, the station was playing Victor Lundberg's almost comically right-wing, patriotic and pro-military hit single *An Open Letter to My Teenage Son* every two hours, accompanied by a pre-recorded announcement stressing its importance. DJ Scott Muni was fired in November for following this track with Joan Baez's *Saigon Bride*, and joined fellow former WOR-FM jock Bill 'Rosko' Mercer at WNEW-FM, which picked up the album-oriented, progressive baton that WOR-FM had so unceremoniously dropped. Murray the K however did not join the WNEW line-up, but moved into TV. Interestingly, an *FM Guide* interview notes that Murray always pronounced WOR-FM "War-FM," leading one to wonder whether his playing of *War Sucks* could be interpreted as a dig at the station itself, as well as the Vietnam conflict they were so keen to promote.

Over on side two of the Red Crayola album we find the surreal, Freudian nursery rhyme of *Pink Stainless Tail*, a charging garage rocker with a pseudo-Turkish interlude that constantly threatens to trip over its feet; the bizarre instrumental title track, which sounds like the workings of some kind of clockwork steampunk perpetual-motion machine (and again, anticipates and exceeds the musique concrete ending of Pink Floyd's *Bike*); and the strange and haunting *Former Reflections Enduring Doubt*, an enigmatic ballad with half-spoken lyrics meditating on some barely communicated loss. Yet the most distinctive features of the album are the "Free Form Freak-Outs" that link each track together, the songs emerging and then disappearing again into the chaos, making the album one seamless piece of sonic madness. The Free Form Freak-Outs were the work of the band's accomplices/fan club The Familiar Ugly, who share joint billing with the Red Crayola on the album sleeve.

The Familiar Ugly's contributions were in fact recorded before the band's, on April Fool's Day 1967, when over fifty people crammed into Andrus Studio to improvise wildly on household percussion, industrial power tools, talking dolls, furniture, bells, bottles and sticks and even a revving motorcycle, as well as guitars, drums, flutes, whistles, kazoos, harmonica, handclaps and human voices. The Red Crayola then returned on April 10th, with Roky Erickson, to record their six songs proper, which were worked into the mix by Walt Andrus and Frank Davis, who also had the task of editing down, and adding subtle effects to, the Familiar Ugly's hours of freaky jamming. While many find the Free Form Freak-Outs boring and irritating distractions from the songs, they remain crucial to the character of the album, and are actually wonderful examples of free music that John Cage would surely have approved of. They maintain a constant tension, a momentum of weird sounds that never disintegrates into aimless repetition.

The album cover features a gorgeous, brightly colored abstract painting by George Banks, while the back contains sleevenotes by one General Fox (a name plucked from the lyrics to *War Sucks*) that bear all the stylistic hallmarks of nominal producer Lelan Rogers, part goofy enthusiasm and part apologetic justification, replete with embarrassing references to "Today's Rebellation Generation." Rick, Steve and Mayo are allowed short statements that could have come straight from the writings of the aforementioned John Cage: "Silence is the conceptual ideology in which sound is published. Music has to do with the publication of choices relevant to production." "There are then, no non-participating agents." "Limited definitions define limit and one can go just so far."

Lelan Rogers would estimate that *The Parable Of Arable Land* sold between thirty and forty thousand, 22,000 of those in New York on the back of Murray the K's patronage. Its reputation would however grow over the years, particularly in the UK. And as the second album release on International Artists after the Elevators' debut, it confirmed IA as a label dedicated to pushing the weirdest freaks around, and even as champions of the musical avant-garde, when in fact it was run by a couple of very straight lawyers who just didn't have a clue what they were doing.

Meanwhile, the 13th Floor Elevators were rapidly disintegrating. Their main problem was that, like other International Artists acts, they were forbidden to book their own shows and could only play gigs that IA organized or approved. Yet IA was either unwilling or unable to organize a national tour, and in a state of enforced inertia, with pressure from the authorities bearing down on them, the band's own energies began to tear them apart. They had engaged a lawyer, Jack McClennan, to try to bring their chaotic affairs into some kind of order, and to renegotiate their draconian contracts, but the only result was that the Elevators became entangled in a complex web of lawsuits on top of their other difficulties. IA was desperate for a second album from the band, and had booked them into Andrus Studio in August; when legal action derailed the sessions, the Lost And Found were rushed in to make use of the studio time instead.

The resulting Lost And Found album, *Everybody's Here*, does sound somewhat rushed; the band's live sound was also apparently somewhat tamed, either in the recording or the mix. But while somewhat thin and two-dimensional, it's still a fine collection of jangling, psychedelic folk-rock, poised midway between Houston and LA. Unlike the earthier, hard-rocking Elevators, or the experimental art music of the Red Crayola, the Lost And Found album has a jet set feel that marks them out as a nightclub band, their brand of groovy psych perfectly suited for the dancefloor and colored walls of the Living Eye Club. Lelan Rogers is credited as producer as usual, but as his sleevenotes consist of fulsome praise for engineer Frank Davis, and Davis's name and picture are included on the back sleeve as though he were a part of the band, it's fair to assume he contributed considerably to the finished product.

Forever Lasting Plastic Words opens the album on a weary, reflective note, its descending folky guitar clusters suggesting the Byrds with a Texan country-blues twang; Pete Harrell's vocals even have the same nasal, blocked-nose quality as Roger McGuinn. Jimmy Frost contributes the title track, a dream-like Dylan pastiche with sly, druggy lyrics ("You are a head of your times") and trippy, out-of-sync backing vocals, muttered asides, part-reversed exhalations of smoke, and tics obviously designed to mess with your head while stoned. "It's alright now, everybody's here; it's alright now, 'cause I ain't even there!" These two songs were also issued as a single ahead of the album's release.

There Would Be No Doubt picks up the pace, again sounding very much like early Byrds but with added Texan psychedelic touches, including drummer Steve Webb contributing a very credible Roky-like scream. This is followed by an intriguing version of the Elevators' *Don't Fall Down*, which is less desperate and sinister than the original, almost convincing as a conventional love song in sentiment, despite the bizarre squeaked backing vocals on the chorus and the unsettling reversed drumming. Following the languorous instrumental *Zig Zag Blues*, dedicated to the makers of the titular cigarette papers, *Let Me Be* is an album highlight, its clanging chords ushering in a racing plea for tolerance and personal freedom, driven along by James Harrell's bubbling bass, and jug-playing unashamedly in the manner of Tommy Hall. It's tempting to read lyrics like "Let me be like I want to be, let me see like I want to see" as a response to the band's earlier LSD bust; yet the track is the second contribution by Jim Frost, who wasn't involved in that particular fracas. Interestingly, this and Frost's other sole writing credit, *Everybody's Here*, are the most explicitly druggy songs on the record.

I Realize is another standout, a fast rocker that combines a fiery R&B groove with urgent, possibly acid-inspired vocals ("I found out what it's all about; I realized by the look in my eyes, that's where it's at") and a soaring, harmonized folk-rock chorus. Another of Steve Webb's Roky-like screams ushers in a rave-up of an instrumental break and a funky, scatted coda. The slow, raunchy *2 Stroke Blues* is less successful, with Webb now overplaying his Roky impersonations, but *I'm So Hip to Pain* has an off-kilter, almost Syd Barrett-like lurch, two spacious, surging instrumental breaks, and an odd chorus of "Rain, Rain, Rain." Perhaps best of all is the closing instrumental jam, *Living Eye*, "dedicated to the Living Eye teen club, Houston, Texas," which finally allows the band to get some raw fuzz into their sound, clearly nodding to the Byrds' *Eight Miles High* and the Yardbirds' take on *Smokestack Lightning* along the way but showcasing their own individual talents as they do so, Frost's lead guitar in particular untethered and rutting furiously at last.

The Lost And Found, the Red Crayola, the Golden Dawn, the Zakary Thaks, Fever Tree and the Moving Sidewalks were all now proving that the 13th Floor Elevators' weirdness was contagious. All displayed a distinctly Texan brand of psychedelia that was harder, tougher and stranger than its Californian or British counterparts. While many of these groups would be short-lived, others would proliferate in their wake, sprouting like peyote cacti, prickly, thick-skinned and dangerously mind-altering, in the un-nurturing soil of their repressive home state.

PART V

EVOLUTION

Chapter 18

Like the Lost and Found, the Golden Dawn also recorded their debut album during the summer of 1967. Pieced together in several sessions over the course of about three months, the ten songs are a strange, appealing mix of primitive rawness and surprising sophistication, absorbing the influence of the English rock bands that George Kinney covered with the Chelsea, the Rolling Stones and the Kinks in particular, and adding a dash of Dylan, more than a spoonful of Texan blues, and a full cornucopia of organic psychedelics. They may have thought that 'Power Plant' was too blatant a band name, but they were happy to use it as an album title, and the true meaning of the phrase was hammered home by a typically colorful and eye-catching George Banks sleeve, depicting swirling cannabis leaves, glowing a fiery red and gold, above fields of yellow mushrooms. The Golden Dawn had no time to be subtle; maybe they realized, even as they were making it, that *Power Plant* would be their one shot at getting their vision across. Indeed, every track screams out with the urgency of their mission; no less than jump-starting evolution, and moving as many as possible on to the next psychological and spiritual level, before it's all too late.

"It is vitally important that through meditation and constant self-examination we conceive clearly and distinctly the proper relationship of the body of man," George Kinney wrote, in sleevenotes that echo the writing of Tommy Hall, but with an even more spiritual tone. "And we must not delay, for even as the body is satiated with the fruits of the earth, so the soul may be starving." Kinney was no puritan, and never for one moment did he suggest that we should abstain from the pleasures of the flesh; all he was saying was that we should feed our head as well, and look to our spiritual development and our greater relationship with the universe, as well as satisfying our immediate physical appetites.

Opening with the sound of wind chimes, apparently tagged onto the song against the band's wishes, *Evolution* rides a fiery guitar riff and a driving beat, before breaking down into a simple, Stones-influenced middle eight of piano and vamping bass that then kicks dramatically into the main riff again. The wind chimes remain prominent throughout, and do distract from a powerful hard rock song that really doesn't need such frills. Kinney's high, reedy vocals are pushed forward in the mix, emphasizing the importance of the lyrics and favoring intensity and emotional commitment over technique. His singing seems designed not to sooth us with melody, but to jar us out of our pleasant, sleepwalking state and to force a reaction, positive or negative, to what he is saying.

Heavily influenced by Gurdjieff, *Evolution* finds the Golden Dawn setting out their stall as musical prophets/guides to our essential psychic and spiritual advancement: "Everything relates if you believe." Yet their music is never weighty, overblown or pretentious, with half the songs coming in at under three minutes, and only *This Way Please* stepping beyond the five minute mark. This melancholy, hallucinatory ballad drifts through spiraling halls of chiming guitars, with Kinney spaced out and sadly reaching back to a lover who is floating away from him, unwilling to cast off her conventional worldview and join him on his trip. "Together we can find a better state of mind," he pleads. "Just open up your eyes; beyond your body there lies another way, another day." As the song progresses, he grows more frustrated and impatient: "Why don't you stand beside me? You know that would delight me, and I would help you understand." But as he fades into the universal flow, still calling out for her to follow, you know that she's stayed behind.

Starvation may be the album's best song, a chugging, bluesy rocker warning of an inevitable "time of starvation" that can nevertheless be overcome if you "believe in elevation." The song makes explicit the Golden Dawn's alliance with Roky's band, agreeing with Tommy Hall that "you've got to reorganize the channels of your thought." Densely packed with basic advice on consciousness expansion, Kinney's writing is more direct than Hall's; less flowery and mystical, but concentrating a very similar message down to a useful essence. *I'll Be Around* has a similar feel, Kinney's voice jumping up an octave on the second part of each verse as he howls his message into the listener's face, judicious use of reverb adding to the intensity. Essentially this is Kinney the prophet in the wilderness, waiting impatiently for the rest of the world to catch up; knowing fervently that he's right, but driven almost to madness by being out alone on the frontier, mocked and hounded by those he's trying to save. His final, broken screams of "Should I wait around for you to call?" are almost chilling in their angry desperation.

Seeing is Believing has a slight country twang, as well as something of the Kinks' suited and booted swagger, as Kinney suggests that in the post-McLuhan, psychedelic era, the title phrase is an outdated cliché that just isn't true anymore. *My Time* addresses the generation gap via the album's hardest fuzz-drenched rocker, with Bobby Rector on exemplary form on the drums and Tommy Ramsey contributing some scorching lead guitar. After such savagery, the melodic folk-rock of *A Nice Surprise* reassures any acid-tripping listeners that "There's nothing bad around; nothing here can hurt you, don't let it bring you down," while advising them to "listen to the music of the day" and telling them not to relate "Something new" to "something in your past," as "that is what will hang you up so fast."

The album concludes with a trio of love songs, grounding us back in personal relationships, while also focusing on the fact that Love in the larger sense must remain the guiding principle in our psychological evolution. And though they may focus on boy meets girl, boy tries hard not to lose girl, they all maintain a deeply psychedelic sound, suggesting many deeper levels of meaning. The Kinks-like *Every Day* is notable for an early example of a backwards-recorded guitar solo, while *Tell Me Why* is packed with reversed tapes and sound effects in a miniature of studio experimentation comparable to The Beatles' best contemporary work, yet on a fraction of the time and budget. Finally, *Reaching Out to You* conflates romantic love with personal evolution, as both involve the shedding of old skins, old identities, and the courage to move on to a different, but hopefully better, plane of existence.

Though suffering from a somewhat thin sound, like the Lost and Found's *Everybody's Here*, *Power Plant* by the Golden Dawn has belatedly come to be recognized as a psychedelic classic. The songs are strong and the message sincere, while Walt Andrus' and Frank Davis's production is largely sympathetic, augmenting the tracks with subtle yet effective sounds and treatments, avant-garde for their day and remaining tasteful rather than dated nearly fifty years on. Unfortunately, International Artists denied the record any chance to get the contemporary reception it deserved when they delayed its release by almost a year, so as not to clash with what they saw as their flagship release, the 13th Floor Elevators second album. When *Power Plant* was finally released, with typical lack of promotion from IA, the Golden Dawn were derided as Elevators copyists by those who chose to review the record, such as *The Rag*, and were ignored by many more who felt their particular brand of psychedelic garage-folk-rock was already passé.

But even the Elevators were struggling through 1967. On April 13th they put on their own show at the Doris Miller Auditorium, under the auspices of fictional promoters the Smoldering Banana Peel, supported by the Wig and the Gentle Debacle lightshow. This was a blatant and only partially successful attempt to recreate the vibe of the Electric Grandmother concerts; the Electric Grandmother in turn were now trading as the Vulcan Gas Company, and put on their first shows under this name at the same venue on April 22nd and May 6th, both featuring the Conqueroo supported by San Antonio band Rachel's Children, and the Jomo Disaster lightshow. Rumors that the Elevators were splitting up grew increasingly frequent; one or more members failed to turn up to gigs so often that their booking agents, Talent of Texas, would put them on with a British Invasion covers band called Bryan's Blokes, who knew enough Elevators material for one or more of their number to step in and play with the headliners if necessary. It got to the point where they could, and would, cover for the whole band, and posters would desperately advertise "The Original Elevators" to distinguish a hopefully intact, authentic line-up from the Bryan's Blokes version.

Behind the scenes, the major faultline was the widening split between Tommy Hall and John Ike. None of the band had any money, but Tommy was able to cadge handouts from IA to continue supplying them all with acid; meanwhile, he was shutting himself away to work obsessively on the songs for the next album, co-writing exclusively with Roky, then bringing the songs to Stacy to work up for the band. John Ike meanwhile had much to be angry about; despite the fact that his mother had invested thousands of dollars in the Elevators neither of them had any say in their direction, and had never seen a single cent back from gigs or record sales. He hated Tommy's LSD regime, didn't think much of his new songs, and had always despised what he saw as the gimmicky jug sound. As he legally owned the rights to the band's name, he hatched a desperate plan to return to San Francisco without Tommy or Roky, get a new singer and relaunch the 13th Floor Elevators on the West Coast.

Ronnie Leatherman sided with his rhythm section buddy, but Stacy was undecided until the law made up his mind for him. He was caught with a drunken friend in a car with marijuana seeds on the floor, which was considered a violation of his probation. The actual arrest happened onstage, at the end of the Elevators' residency at the Living Eye in Houston. On Friday 26th May the Vice Squad jumped onstage in the middle of *Fire Engine*, handcuffed Stacy and led him away through the crowd, nearly provoking a riot. Of course Stacy was tripping, and once they had him in the car the cops told him they were going to take him out beyond the city limits to shoot him, and then claim self-defense. Stacy did his best not to freak out as the car hit the highway towards the edge of town, before finally turning back towards the station.

Ultimately, the situation led to International Artists gaining even more control over the band; they paid Stacy's bail, putting him even more in their debt, and because he was forbidden to leave Texas he was obliged to stay with Tommy and Roky. But John Ike and Ronnie had decidedly had enough, and while legal negotiations proceeded, the Elevators held open auditions for a new rhythm section. In this state of disarray the band could only watch as the psychedelic movement that they had single-handedly kicked off in Austin blossomed around them. The pioneers that had fought for this freedom found they were left out in the cold.

Certainly the Elevators were a glaring omission from the line-up for Austin's first Love-In, held at Zilker Park on September 24th, though the fact that no International Artists acts made the bill suggests that the company's infamous policy of barring its artists from soliciting or accepting outside bookings was in full effect. Instead, the event showcased a new generation of Austin psychedelic bands, with Circus Maximus, Shiva's Headband, the Thingies and Black Lace joining the Conqueroo and, unbilled, the Wig, who opened the day's proceedings.

Circus Maximus had actually formed in Austin, at the Clown's Den open mic night back in 1965, under the name of the Lost Sea Dreamers; the acronymic possibilities of the name were entirely intentional. Jerry Jeff Walker, Bob Bruno and Pete Troutner were three Houston-based folk singers who decided to pool their talents and headed out to Walker's native New York where, augmented by Gary White on bass and Dave Scherstrom on drums, they played regularly at the Nite Owl Café and eventually secured a deal with Vanguard Records. Vanguard weren't happy about the drug connotations of the band's name, and insisted they change it. By this time they were the house band at the new upmarket, avant-garde psychedelic nightclub the Electric Circus, which hosted contemporary classical performances alongside the cream of the new psychedelic rock bands, plus state-of-the-art projections and lightshows. Doubtless this inspired their new name, but Bob Bruno also later wrote that "The Clown's Den came to mind, as well as 'the first clown of the Circus Maximus,' from a Houston experience when I had helped Pete through the window of one of our friends, January, who had inadvertently locked herself out, being incapacitated by her drug experience."

In New York, Circus Maximus had an intriguing association with the electronic composer Morton Subotnick. Subotnick was artistic director of the Electric Circus club, and Circus Maximus often came onstage to a recording of one of his compositions. Subotnick also produced the club's *Electric Christmas* event at Carnegie Hall in December 1967, where Circus Maximus and Subotnick appeared alongside the city's innovative early music ensemble, the New York Pro Musica. "I was directed to compose and arrange a piece by Guillaume de Machaut called *La Douce Dame Jolie*, and turn it into a modern pop piece to be the center of the show," Bruno recalled.

Circus Maximus released their self-titled debut album on Vanguard in the fall of 1967. For the most part it contained accomplished folk rock, heavily influenced by the Byrds and mixing jangling 12-string guitar with jazz rhythms and electric solos. Sometimes smooth, sometimes veering towards punk, the album has elements of psychedelia and social protest but became best known for Bob Bruno's uncharacteristic soft rock/jazz fusion epic *Wind*, a staple of progressive FM radio during the latter part of 1967, and an underground hit. A second album, *Return to Neverland*, followed in the summer of 1968, but by the time of its release Circus Maximus had already broken up. Bruno and Walker were obviously heading in different musical directions, and while Bob Bruno continued to use the band name to pursue a more jazz-oriented direction, in 1968 Jerry Jeff Walker kickstarted a successful solo career by writing and recording the instant standard *Mr. Bojangles*. In the early seventies he settled in Austin and became a leading figure in the progressive country scene.

Shiva's Headband meanwhile were a new band formed by 24-year-old classical violinist Spencer Malcolm Perskin, alongside his wife Susan plus Bob Tom Reed (guitar), Kenny Parker (bass) and Jerry Barnett (drums). Something of a musical child prodigy, Perskin had been accepted as a special music student at Dallas's Southern Methodist University at the age of nine, and studied classical violin part-time there for eight years. Moving to Denton to complete his education at the University of North Texas, he played at the local folk club, where he met future stars of progressive country Michael Martin Murphey and Steven Fromholz, as well as Shiva's future manager Eddie Wilson. He also had a fortuitous encounter with Doug Sahm of the Sir Douglas Quintet, and a famous friend.

"My wife and I had just moved to Denton, and I went over to a friend's house and I didn't know who Doug was, I didn't know anything about the pop music world real much," Perskin says. "I just saw this bunch of Mexicans and a cowboy, and it turned out that was Doug and his band. But then he actually came over with Bob Dylan, they were really close, and I think he was the one that encouraged me. They actually came over and stuck a tape of *She's about a Mover* on the tape player, and then I plugged in a tape of a bizarre thing I had done also, just completely crazy stuff, you know. Plus I was on a ridiculously potent dose of LSD at the time, so I was off the planet anyway."

Sahm and Dylan encouraged Perskin to move out of the folk and classical bag he was in and to start an electric rock 'n' roll band, a plan he put into action shortly after he was kicked out of University. "I got thrown out of college for using obscenity in poetry and my civil rights work that I was involved in, the integration movement and stuff like that," Spencer says. "I could have just stayed in Denton there if I hadn't of got thrown out of an apartment for having a black student friend come study with me one day. But that's how things were." He and Susan moved to Austin and set about starting both a family and a band; with the exception of "three or four private shows," the Love-In was their first public gig.

"Doug was the one who kind of encouraged me to get a guitar and everything, but when I got all the equipment I just kind of forgot about getting a lead guitar, and by default I started playing the violin as a rock instrument," Perskin says. "We actually got fronted by the father of the fellow that was trying out on bass, who took too much acid and got caught riding naked. Anyway we went through a process where his dad wound up being the one that kind of helped us buy some equipment." Shiva's Headband represented the new Austin sound, a fusion of country, blues, folk and acid rock that would soon eclipse the primal garage rock of the Elevators, the Wig and the Golden Dawn. Although they took their cues from the Grateful Dead and, closer to home, the Conqueroo, unlike those bands Shiva's Headband didn't rely on elongated jams based on existing tunes. They wrote and performed their own material from day one which, Spencer claims, "was considered almost outrageous by our musician friends, and there was zero tolerance for us at the few bars around town." Ultimately, Shiva's Headband would be vitally important in changing that situation, and giving Austin its eventual reputation as a global music center.

In contrast, the Thingies were something of a fly-by-night

phenomenon. Vocalist Phil Weaver, guitarist John Dalton, bassist Larry Miller, drummer Gordon Marcellus and organist Ernie Swisher were from Topeka in Kansas, though Phil Weaver had grown up in Waco, and Larry Miller had led an itinerant childhood as an Air Force brat, and had gone to school in Abilene, Texas. Miller also joined the Air Force after school, which was how he came to be stationed in Topeka, and it was here in 1963 that he formed the surf band TR4. The following year they changed their name to the Coachmen, and in mid-1965 they changed again, to the Horrible Evil Thingies (taken from a line from the Beatles film, *Help!*).

With that name swiftly shortened to the Thingies, and band leader and songwriter Miller the only surviving member of the original TR4, they recorded a single for the local Casino label, *It's a Long Way Down* backed by *Merry-Go-Round of Life*. A minor hit in Kansas, the single boosted the band's reputation to the point where they were able to headline the 3500-seater Topeka Auditorium, though their set mostly consisted of the usual mix of Stones, Kinks and Yardbirds covers. This all changed when they saw the West Coast Pop Art Experimental Band at the Topeka Tiki Club in early 1967. The Thingies stage show became heavily psychedelic, incorporating a lightshow, smoke bombs, psychedelic stage clothing and more original material that was increasingly far out.

In June 1967 the Thingies relocated to Miami for the summer, where they became the house band at a 3000-capacity nightclub called The World. Rumors of an impending drugs bust caused the band to leave in a hurry, intending to head directly for San Francisco; however, a stopover in Texas to visit Phil Weaver's hometown of Waco led to an unbelievable streak of luck that was to change their plans dramatically. First, they ended up staying in Waco for a full fortnight when a local motel not only let them stay for free, but gave them free rehearsal space. With their stage show honed and polished as a result, they decided to head up to

Austin and walked straight into the Matchbox club, where owner Bill Simonson immediately offered them a regular gig and a management contract, purely on the basis of their outlandish appearance. Simonson had set up his own psychedelic promotions company called the Owl, and was co-promoter of the Zilker Park Love-In with the Vulcan Gas Company; hence the Thingies were added to the bill, only a few days after they had arrived in town. In December 1967 they recorded the brilliant droning psych of *Mass Confusion,* backed by the equally wild *Rainy Sunday Morning,* as a single for Austin label Sonobeat, but split soon after.

To avoid trouble, the Love-In was also co-sponsored by the Austin Police Department, and although the Vulcan had organized the event, paid for the permits and commissioned the poster, Simonson persuaded artist Tony Bell to use an owl as the main part of the design, thus effectively using it to promote his rival venture. The Owl never took off however, and the success of the Love-In was only an overture to the Vulcan Gas Company opening its own venue at 316 Congress Avenue, on the weekend of the 27th and 28th of October 1967. The Conqueroo and Shiva's Headband were the house bands and with a spectacular lightshow, run by Don Hyde, Roger Baker and Steve Plasky, the Vulcan would swiftly come to dominate the music scene in Austin, and across Texas, for the rest of the decade and beyond.

Chapter 19

Though the Zakary Thaks effectively displaced the Bad Seeds as the number one band in Corpus Christi and on J-Beck, they continued to regard the older group with nothing but respect and admiration. Indeed, after the Bad Seeds' split, singer-guitarist Mike Taylor was retained by J-Beck as a writer/producer, and came to be considered the unofficial sixth member of the Zakary Thaks. "He was a mentor as far as if we were not sounding right, he would let us know and it would be in a way that only he could hear, you know?" Thaks frontman Chris Gerniottis recalled in an interview with Peter Buesnel on the *Sherwood Forest Gang* website. "We trusted him enough. He was like the uncle that looked out for us and even though we surpassed the Bad Seeds as far as stature goes, we still in the back of our minds thought of Michael Taylor as the Bad Seeds guy and that was our first idol group. So we always listened to him. He was a character and he was funny as hell. He always kept us laughing."

Mike Taylor also launched a short-lived solo career on J-Beck, as 'The Fabulous Michael.' His three singles all featured the Zakary Thaks as his backing band, starting with *I'm Nobody's Man / My Last Day* (J-1007) in September 1966. Posing moodily but uncomfortably in his publicity photos, his receding hairline greatly in evidence, Michael specialized in innocuous folk-pop ballads, pitched somewhere between the Everly Brothers, Bob Lind and Gene Pitney. *My Last Day* at least had a certain melodramatic intensity, and follow-up single *Gotta Make My Heart Turn Away* (J-1008, February 1967) had some pleasing romantic troubadour flourishes, as well as Thaks drummer Stan Moore layering on some warm organ tones. But the flip, *People Sec. IV,* was an incomprehensible slice of mawkish drivel; when *Gotta Make My Heart Turn Away* was reissued on Roulette a month or so later, it was replaced with the bland white soul of *I'd*

Only Laugh, but still went nowhere. In mid-1967 Mike Taylor quietly retired The Fabulous Michael, and returned to a backroom role with the Zakary Thaks.

After the Thaks' debut single, *Bad Girl*, shot to number one in Corpus Christi, it was picked up for national distribution by Mercury Records. Mercury took out a full-page ad in Billboard to announce their new signings, but unfortunately by the time they actually released the single in November 1966 its momentum had been lost. Part of the problem was that the band members were all still under age, so it took six months for Mercury to sort out the legal contracts. Back on J-Beck, the band went to Doyle Jones Studio in Houston, where they were presented with the luxury of an eight-track recording desk and a couple of days in which to stretch out and experiment. The result was their second single, *Face to Face / Weekday Blues* (J-1009) which was actually the band's biggest seller, although it only made number two in the local charts in March 1967.

Riding a brilliant, slip-sliding two-note guitar riff that John Lopez was apparently still working out when they recorded it, *Face to Face* is a far more developed song than *Bad Girl* while losing none of its predecessor's energy and magic. Chris Gerniottis proves that he can actually sing, or at least declaim tunefully in an appealing pop-punk nasal fashion, and the song speeds through its edgy twists and turns like a souped-up ghost-train ride. While the track is obviously influenced by Jeff Beck-era Yardbirds, who the Thaks opened for in Corpus Christi on October 30th 1966 (actually Beck's last gig with the band), the Thaks make it entirely their own; the bottom end has more fuzz than a national police convention, and Lopez twists the riff into a magnificent, wailing, near-modal solo.

Although the Zakary Thaks never broke out of South Texas, they were treated as superstars in their hometown, even when still at school. Girls in the years below them fought over their old exercise books, and while the band never became millionaires, J-

Beck records looked after them reasonably well for a small label in the mid-sixties. Chris Gerniottis remembers there being a checking account in the band's name from which they paid themselves a weekly wage, sharing out cheques between them on the way to school on a Monday morning. For a while in 1967 they were earning $150 per week each, enough so that Gerniottis could save up for a second-hand Pontiac Le Mans when he turned sixteen.

The band's local star status never made them exempt from the usual rules and petty hassles for kids their age, however. In particular, the Zakary Thaks ran into trouble over their long hair, which resulted in all the members, bar Chris, being kicked out of high school before graduating. The Corpus Christi Independent School District had strict hair length codes, but Gerniottis managed to get around this by having his Beatles bob cut just short enough in term time so that he could slick it down with VO-5 and then grow it out during the summer.

All the musicians and hip kids in Corpus Christi would get their hair cut by Tracy Herrin, the only barber who would cut long hair, and who could be trusted not to give you a crew cut. He was so cool that for many years he also operated a record shop out of the back of his barbers. Long hair in Texas was still a big deal however, and the Zakary Thaks were targeted by outraged rednecks on a weekly if not daily basis. When playing outside of Corpus, they would also get grief from racists who objected to the presence of the Hispanic John Lopez in the otherwise white band.

The Thaks' third single was due to be a Rod Prince/Mike Taylor composition, *Passage to India*. Prince had finally returned to Corpus Christi after the break-up of the New Seeds and several months in Los Angeles. Although he had no intention of starting a new band, he got back together informally with his old Bad Seeds partner to write a few songs, the strongest of which were the aforementioned *Passage to India*, with its eastern-flavored guitar riff, and a track called *A Gathering of Promises*. Pete Stinson in particular liked *Passage to India* and the Zakary Thaks duly recorded the song, but J-Beck turned it down in favor of a Mike Taylor solo composition, *Please*. If the incense-choked raga-psych of *Passage to India* was a long way from the Thaks' punk roots, then *Please* sounded more suited to The Fabulous Michael, smoothing out many of the band's rough edges in what nevertheless remains a catchy slice of jangly, harmonizing power pop. Flipside *Won't Come Back* has more of their old energy, including a racing John Lopez solo, but it still lacks the magic spark of *Bad Girl* and *Face to Face*.

The harmonies on *Please* were apparently instigated by the new partner in J-Beck Records, Lofton Klein. At this point Carl Becker was branching out on his own, leaving J-Beck to his partner and brother-in-law Jack Salyers, and Lofton Klein gradually moved into Becker's role. A founding member of the Pozo Seco Singers (alongside Mike Taylor's sister Susan and future country star Don Williams), Lofton Klein had sung backing vocals on all of The Fabulous Michael's singles, and now the harmony-loving Klein also took over management of the Thaks. It was at his suggestion that the band recorded radio jingles for the Mod Shop and Jaxx Beer, but his most enduring legacy was his decision to make a 16mm film of the band running through a representative portion of their live set in the studio. While Chris Gerniottis is adamant that the film, like the band's records, doesn't come anywhere near capturing the full power of the band onstage, it remains a valuable and unique document of a teenage garage band in mid-sixties Texas, performing at their peak.

Although not seen in the film, the Zakary Thaks often covered 13th Floor Elevators songs live, including *You're Gonna Miss Me*, *Levitation* and, perhaps surprisingly, *Slip Inside This House*. For these numbers they were usually joined onstage by a guest jug player, Gordon Nost. The Thaks supported the Elevators on several occasions, and looked on them with awe; if they were allowed to write and record more of their own material, the Thaks may well have produced more classic garage-psych in the Elevators mold. Instead the final single by the Zakary Thaks' original line-up once again featured two Mike Taylor compositions. The baroque oddity *Mirror of Yesterday* found the once proudly-primitive garage band bolstered by horns and strings, on a confection that wouldn't sound out of place on an album by the Left Banke or the early Bee Gees. Chris Gerniottis makes a decent stab of playing the tremulous troubadour, and the song is an agreeable enough pastiche, but the overall ruffled shirt and crushed velvet ambience only further confused the band's hardcore fans. The B-side, *Can You Hear Your Daddy's Footsteps*, is a grandstanding folk-rock sermon which, despite some rather confusing imagery in the opening lines ("Can you hear your father's footsteps baby, banging on the door?"), has some wild, dirty guitar playing and retains much of the band's old aggression in a more sophisticated vessel, like drinking rough Texas moonshine from a china cup.

"Each one got worse as far as I was concerned," Chris Gerniottis later admitted of the band's singles. "For instance, *Please*, because we had not written it, it wasn't really a true reflection of what I felt we were as a band... It's Mike Taylor's song. It's not, you know, the Thaks. When we'd write songs it would be as a group. For all practical purposes, *Face To Face* was written by the group... *Bad Girl* was like the one true picture of what the Zakary Thaks were as a group. That literally was written by all five of us in one afternoon."

As for *Mirror of Yesterday*, Gerniottis simply said "it wasn't us." "I felt it was trying to sound too much like *Eleanor Rigby*. Too many violins and stuff. We couldn't come close to making it sound like that live. The other side, *Can You Hear Your Daddy's Footsteps*, we really spent a lot of time on that record, but that wasn't the Thaks either, you know? As far as I'm concerned, the

Thaks were represented by the first two records and the flip side of *Please, Won't Come Back*. But after that they went downhill because it wasn't the group. It was somebody else writing for the group and every time that happens, not every time, but most of the time, it just doesn't come off well."

The Zakary Thaks mark one came to an end on New Year's Eve 1967. Influenced by the 13th Floor Elevators' newly-released second album, and having opened for bands like Jefferson Airplane, Stinson, Lopez and Moore wanted the group to pursue a more psychedelic direction, while Gerniottis and bassist Rex Gregory disagreed and wanted to stick to their high-energy roots. As a result they were asked to leave the band, with Stan Moore apparently feeling that Gerniottis's style wasn't right for the new material they were developing.

As it happened, Chris Gerniottis was able to go straight into another Corpus Christi band, the Liberty Bell, whose singer Ronnie Tanner had just been drafted. Gerniottis joined lead guitarist Al Hunt, rhythm guitarist Richard Painter, drummer Carl Aeby and original Marauders bassist Wayne Harrison in the band, who had already enjoyed local success in 1967 with three singles on Carl Becker's new label, Cee Bee. The first had been a rough and ready cover of the Yardbirds' song *The Nazz are Blue*, backed by Willie Dixon's blues standard *Big Boss Man*. The second, their best, paired Al Hunt's moody *For What You Lack*, notable for its gothic, choral backing vocals and an oozing solo full of creepy restraint and sustained distortion, with Ronnie Tanner's driving, dramatic *That's How It Will Be*. Tanner also wrote their third single, the jangling *Something for Me*, backed by the self-explanatory *Al's Blues*.

It had been Carl Becker who had paired the band, originally called the Zulus, with singer Ronnie Tanner, as well as suggesting the name change to the Liberty Bell, in imitation of the similarly patriotically named Paul Revere and the Raiders. They were the flagship band for his Cee Bee label, which he'd launched in mid-

1967 after leaving J-Beck. After putting them together with Gerniottis however, he licensed them to Houston soul label Back Beat records, resulting in the 1968 single *Thoughts and Visions / Look for Tomorrow*. Both tracks were written and sung by Gerniottis, with the A-side a blustering ballad with a passing resemblance to the Small Faces' *My Way of Giving*, but enlivened by Al Hunt's innovative guitar technique, like a Texan Jeff Beck and Jimmy Page rolled into one.

Another Gerniottis composition featured on the B-side of the Liberty Bell's fifth and final single. *Recognition* was a questing, jazz-inflected, minor-key melodrama comparable to the work of Arthur Lee's Love; after a typically brilliant Al Hunt solo, it ends in unsettling, reverberating idiot groans from Gerniottis, as though he knew their efforts would only be doomed to obscurity. One of the Liberty Bell's finest moments, it was unfortunately paired with the disastrous *Naw Naw Naw*, a cover song forced upon the band by the record company that was barely a Liberty Bell recording at all. The band was already breaking up, and bassist Wayne Harrison and drummer Carl Aeby had already departed for college. Carl Becker brought in the Zakary Thaks' Stan Moore and Rex Gregory to replace them, while Al Hunt's guitar playing is forceful but uninspired by his standards.

Naw Naw Naw was written by R&B legend Andre Williams, who had brought the band to Back Beat and also produced the session, though it seems he was only nominally present. "I remember him passing out in the control booth," Gerniottis said. "He had some kind of drug problem and kind of bottomed out. He just kind of had some personal problems and the record was so flat... it was the wrong concept." Gerniottis does his best, but he's far from suited to the material, and the song drags. It flopped, and the band called it a day.

It's a great shame, as the Liberty Bell were one of the great lost Texan rock bands, with a magical chemistry and a potential that was never fully realized. Some of their best material even went unreleased at the time. Al Hunt's *I Can See*, with Ronnie Tanner on vocals, is a raw and powerful garage rocker, while *Reality is the Only Answer* and *Eveline Kaye* date from their later psychedelic era, with Chris Gerniottis upfront. *Reality* in particular is a storming piece of acid psychosis, defined by Hunt's chopping, pinching, cascading echoplex guitar and Gerniottis's mad preacher vocals. Dedicated to Hunt's mother, *Eveline Kaye* is a gentle, eastern-flavored ballad that showcases the softer, subtler, but no less impressive side of the guitarist's playing.

While Gerniottis was singing for the Liberty Bell, Pete Stinson, John Lopez and Stan Moore had kept the Zakary Thaks going, with the addition of new singer John Kenney and a female flautist whose name has been unchivalrously forgotten. They were pushing in a more sprawling, psychedelic direction influenced by Jefferson Airplane and Traffic, but their Corpus fans had difficulty adjusting to this new approach, and the line-up faltered after just three months when Stinson joined the Navy, and Kenney and the flute player also left. Bringing bassist Rex Gregory back into the fold, Lopez and Moore continued throughout 1968 as a three-piece, playing the Vulcan Gas Company in Austin and releasing a further single, *My Door / Green Crystal Ties* on their own Thak Records.

My Door certainly bears the influence of the ascendant San Francisco Sound, yet it's still unmistakably the Zakary Thaks, with John Lopez's rude, slashing guitar giving the track a blazing Texan edge despite the sneer-free harmonized vocals. *Green Crystal Ties* meanwhile is a fuzz-heavy tangle of thrilling garage psych, kicking and straining against the tight bounds of its own limitations. In 1969, following the demise of the Liberty Bell, Gerniottis re-joined the Thaks, and the band found themselves on Cee Bee Records for their sixth and final single, *Outprint / Everybody Wants To Be Somebody*. *Outprint* is poppy blues-rock, with just a hint of psychedelia in John Lopez's guitar solo, while the flip is swaggering, chest-beating country-rock, somewhere between the Who and Creedence Clearwater Revival.

The reunion lasted barely six months before Chris Gerniottis left the Zakary Thaks again. The band opened for Steppenwolf in Fort Worth in April 1969, and were booed off the stage; Gerniottis read the writing on the wall, and left to form the short-lived Kubla Khan, who released one obscure single, a cover of Elton John's *Bad Side of the Moon*, before the seventies dawned. Chris Gerniottis was still only eighteen, but his once-promising music career had stalled indefinitely. He decided to go to college in Houston, setting the course for his eventual career as a teacher, back in the same high school that once threatened to kick him out for his long hair.

The summer of 1971 found Gerniottis, on college vacation, hooking up one more time with Stan Moore and John Lopez under the Zakary Thaks name. Recruiting bassist Tom Engle and keyboard player Mike Gregory from Kubla Khan, they got a gig as the house band at Corpus Christi's Rogues Club, but the terms of their engagement demanded strictly Top 40 covers, and none of their own material. Apparently they were still a tight, powerful band, but no-one much cared anymore; it was clear the Zakary Thaks' glory days were long gone, and after that summer they went their separate ways.

Meanwhile back in the summer of 1967, Rod Prince was at his parents' house in Mathis, just north of Corpus Christi, wondering what to do with the rest of his life. Suddenly the phone rang. It was Roy Cox, who had returned to San Antonio after the New Seeds had broken up. Having heard that Prince was back in town, the ambitious Cox wasn't about to let the finest lead guitarist he'd ever played with slip through his fingers. And though Prince figured he was done with rock 'n' roll, Cox managed to convince him that potentially they could pull together a really top-flight rock band who could be serious contenders. Prince, for his part, had long had a vision of a rock band that featured two dueling lead guitars, an idea that Cox was entirely in sympathy with. Somewhat fearing that he was letting his heart overrule his head, Rod Prince joined Roy Cox in San Antonio for several months of poverty and couch-surfing as they sought out the players for their new outfit.

First on board was muscular, 6' 3" drummer Clayton Pulley, who in turn brought in fellow Austinite Todd Potter. Potter was Pulley's physical opposite, a wiry, diminutive guitar player who was still at high school, but nevertheless was able to match Rod Prince riff for riff. With Cox on bass, Prince and Potter clicked instantly, and began to work up the twin lead guitar sound in Prince's head. Adding singer and saxophonist Danny Segovia, they initially adopted the unwieldy moniker Willowdale Handcar, taken from a book by Edward Gorey and one of several names that Rod Prince and Bobby Donaho had played under while struggling out in LA. Rehearsals took place at San Antonio's Pusi-Kat club, and early demo recordings included Prince's two co-writes with Mike Taylor, *Passage to India* and *A Gathering of Promises*.

Danny Segovia was ousted when Prince, Potter and Cox decided to handle vocals between them, putting an emphasis on harmony singing that, together with the twin lead guitars, made his saxophone seem like so much superfluous clutter. Clayton Pulley also left, to be replaced by new drummer Craig Root. And at some point in early 1968 the band decided on a new name, the first evidence of which was a week of ads in the *San Antonio Express* from March 9th onwards, proclaiming simply "The Bubble Puppy is Coming." At the end of that week of teasers Bubble Puppy finally arrived, playing their debut show proper on March 15th 1968, opening for the Who at the San Antonio Municipal Auditorium; a plum gig they secured by letting the Who use their rehearsal space at the Pusi-Kat while they were in town. A week later on March 23rd, "the exciting new Bubble Puppy" were to be found opening for popular local band Lord August and his Visions of Lite at the Pusi-Kat Club. And although their name is generally thought to be inspired by "Centrifugal Bumble-Puppy," an invented, futuristic children's game alluded to in Aldous Huxley's *Brave New World*, a real game called Bubble Puppy apparently already existed. I found reference to it in a Belleville, Kansas newspaper from 1952, two years before *Brave New World* was published; frustratingly, no details of what the game involved were revealed.

Chapter 20

While Rod Prince and Roy Cox were putting together Willowdale Handcar/Bubble Puppy in the late summer of 1967, they also made ends meet by filling in as members of the Laughing Kind. Indeed it seems like almost every San Antonio musician of the 1960s played at some point in the Laughing Kind, which was initially put together by singer Max Range when the Lingsmen hurriedly quit their 1965 residency at Port Aransas's Dunes Club. Lingsmen Stacy Sutherland, John Ike Walton and Benny Thurman went on to form the 13th Floor Elevators and never looked back, but their Kerrville buddy Max was left holding the baby down in Port Aransas and was desperately in need of a new backing band. He immediately put through a call to San Antonio group the Loose Ends, who arrived in Port Aransas just in time to see the Lingsmen packing away their gear and departing. Rechristened by Max, the Loose Ends became the first incarnation of the Laughing Kind.

Consisting of brothers Bob and Dan Galindo on guitar and bass respectively, second guitarist Bill King and drummer Buddy Toscano, this line-up was only ever intended to be a temporary emergency measure. The Galindo brothers soon quit, returning to San Antonio to join the Serfs, and then the Zilches, who eventually became the Virgil Foxx Group (stealing their name from the flamboyant organ player). Many line-ups of the Laughing Kind followed, including one based on Roy Cox's old band the Mysterions, before the summer of 1967 found Max and Bill King joined by lead guitarist Chris Holzhaus, bassist Mike Marechal and drummer Sam Allen; Rod Prince and Roy Cox stepped in when Holzhaus and Marechal left midway through the season.

Mike Marechal and Sam Allen had been the rhythm section in San Antonio band the Stoics, formed in early 1965 with singer Al Acosta and guitarists Bill Ash and Roy Quillan. The Stoics were strongly associated with local tough-ass motorcycle gang the Capinch, who acted as bodyguards for them onstage; Capinch leader Johnny Cutrer was given a writing credit on the B-side of The Stoics' sole single, as he fronted the cash to pay for it. That song was the punk classic *Hate*, paired with Roy Quillan's equally great *Enough of What I Need* (which was actually based around the same three chords as the flip). The seven-inch was released in an edition of 150 on the Stoics' own Brams label in January 1967, but less than a month later the band split over musical differences, with Marechal and Allen joining the Laughing Kind along with Chris Holzhaus from the Stoics SA rivals, the Argyles.

Fronted by singer-guitarist Steve Perron, the Argyles also started in spring 1965 with Perron and Holzhaus joined by organist Lou Cabaza, Benny Treiber on bass and Steve Anderson on drums. The original line-up released two singles in early 1967, all cover songs: *White Lightnin' / Farmer John* and *Still in Love with You Baby / Turn on Your Love Light*. When Chris Holzhaus then left for the Laughing Kind he was replaced by Bill Ash from the Stoics, and Andy Zsuch replaced Steve Anderson on drums. The Argyles soon began to move in a more psychedelic direction, and in March 1967 they took the bold step of starting their own psychedelic nightclub, the first of its kind in San Antonio, named the Mind's Eye.

A pre-opening night article in the *San Antonio Express* credits Steve Perron and Benny Treiber as the brains behind the club, and makes much of its garish décor, describing the fluorescent orange, black-lit tunnel leading to the club proper, the op art patterns on the walls "ranging from a violent pink to an explosive purple" and the battery of lights, oil projections, strobes and "surrealistic movies" that would combine to bamboozle the club's patrons, who 21-year-old Perron envisaged as "people who are out of their teens but still like music with a beat and a place that's different."

Of course Perron and Treiber also saw the club as somewhere for their band to play regularly, and although the *Express* article still describes the pair as members of the Argyles, when they took on the position of house band at their new psychedelic club the group decided to become known as the Mind's Eye too. They soon released a single under that name, the faux-psych classic *Help, I'm Lost* on Jox, backed by the Argyles' previous A-side, *Still in Love with You Baby*. Written by Steve Perron and classically trained keyboard player Lou Cabaza, the Doors-like track combines prominent organ with scraping cello to emulate a full string section, some raga-like guitar work from Ash, and Perron's strident vocal, declaiming about an angel's song, the devil's touch, love, rain and the nature of reality. Lost? Me too.

Located at 1234 Austin Highway, the Mind's Eye club opened on the weekend of March 10th and 11th 1967, with headlining sets from the rapidly disintegrating 13th Floor Elevators (described in the *San Antonio Express* piece as "A West Coast Group"). Lou Cabaza remembers hanging out at the club the afternoon before the opening, awaiting the arrival of the legendary Austin band that had been such a profound influence on them. Suddenly the door flew open and a bedraggled character stumbled through, fell to the floor and looked up at them while on all fours. "Is this the Mind's Eye?" the unidentified Elevator apparently gasped. The Mind's Eye Club lasted till June, when it was closed down for problems with fights and drug use on the premises; the Mind's Eye band, now with female co-vocalist Cassell Webb, headed for Los Angeles, on the basis of a loose connection with Texan Monkee Mike Nesmith, hoping for a break out west.

Meanwhile, the 13th Floor Elevators were looking for a new rhythm section. Long-disgruntled drummer John Ike Walton was given $300 and released from his contract with International Artists in return for surrendering his rights to the band's name. He departed for San Francisco along with Elevators bassist

Ronnie Leatherman and guitarist Johnny Richardson from the Wig, who had also just split up. He hoped to follow up old contacts and put together a new band out there, but things didn't work out, and he was soon back in Austin, pursuing further legal action against the Elevators and their label.

Danny Thomas was a 19-year-old drummer attending Trinity University in San Antonio when his roommate invited him to the Elevators' show at the Doris Miller Auditorium in April 1967. Born in Charlotte, North Carolina, he had drummed and toured extensively with R&B bands the Caravelles and the Soul Brothers before going to college. Not being particularly interested in psychedelic rock, he hadn't yet checked out the Elevators, but he knew a guy who was a big fan. Danny Galindo had seen the 13th Floor Elevators many times, since first hearing *You're Gonna Miss Me* on the radio, shortly after he left the Laughing Kind. He and Thomas had jammed together often at pizza joints around San Antonio, and so he joined Danny Thomas and his roommate Charlie Booker, an old friend of Stacy Sutherland's from Kerrville, for the drive up to Austin for the gig.

Both Galindo and Thomas thought the show was great, but more importantly, either on the way to the gig or afterwards, they ended up getting stoned and jamming with Stacy Sutherland for several hours, and exchanged phone numbers. The three of them connected so well musically that when John Ike and Ronnie left the Elevators, Stacy pushed for them to join up full-time, over many better-established musicians. There were no formal auditions; Lelan Rogers called up the boys and asked them to come in to International Artists and sign a contract. Then it was straight into intensive rehearsals in Kerrville for the Elevators' second album. The result was their magnificent grand folly, *Easter Everywhere*.

The album opens with what is perhaps the Elevators' finest song, and is certainly Tommy Hall's magnum opus; the eight-minute-long *Slip Inside This House*. Based upon a chord sequence created by Roky Erickson, who thought it sounded like Beethoven, and perfectly augmented by Stacy's serious, elegiac guitar licks, *Slip Inside This House* is modelled on Dylan's hallucinatory, high watermark epics of a year or so earlier, such as *Gates of Eden* or *Like a Rolling Stone*. The verses just keep on coming, each one more densely packed with layers of meaning and powerful poetic imagery than the last. The result is a bombardment upon the senses, even a Rimbaudian derangement of them; and yet the aim is not simply to dazzle, but to communicate on all levels, intellectual, emotional, instinctive and associative all at once. Tommy Hall's poetry is like a kind of pre-internet hypertext; every other phrase could be a link that takes you to a far longer text, leading the listener potentially to a lifetime of reading. There are a multitude of references that, if decoded, direct one to esoteric, mystical and scientific theories, volumes and treatises that are nevertheless all connected in Hall's grand system, into a multi-layered exposition of universal wisdom.

It would be presumptuous of me to attempt to fully explain the meaning of every line of *Slip Inside This House*. Tommy Hall's epic lyric is an occult text in the true meaning of the word, the message of which must to some degree always remain hidden and obscured; nevertheless, once a few key phrases are understood, the general message of the song is easily apparent.

The opening line, "Bedouin tribes ascending" could set one off on the wrong foot unless one realizes that "Bedouin" is simply a word meaning nomad or wanderer; rather than implying any specific mythological or tribal context, this simply establishes the theme of motion, of always moving on and never staying in one place. "From the egg into the flower" suggests the idea of the Cosmic Egg, or World Egg, a near-universal myth symbol that in modern cosmology is often used to represent the singularity; Georges Lemaitre's "primeval atom," the state of potentia that existed before the Big Bang. Seen in this context the universe, created in the Big Bang, is the flower, growing ever outwards; although it should be noted that in the song the flower doesn't grow from the egg, but rather the wandering tribes ascend from egg to flower.

Nevertheless, we've established a theme of continual motion and change being the driving force of the universe and all creation, which Hall solidifies into the image of a continually flowing river; always changing, yet always the same. If you tread water you will find your "limbs begin dissolving," but if you can find a way to go with the flow and let go of attachments, tapping into the "river power" of "the stream that clears your head," then like Noah in his Ark you will survive and prosper while others drown. "True conception, knowing why, brings even more than meets the eye," hints at hermetic knowledge; we can exist, and feel, and know, "in this dark we call creation," but with an effort we can awake to "the high baptismal glow" where the possibilities are literally endless. "There is no season when you are grown; you are always risen from the seeds you've sown." Once you've ascended to the higher level, you will not wax and wane, you will be in a perpetual state of bliss and wisdom, as shown by the many examples and models in many different traditions. You merely have to choose the one that works for you, putting your own metaphor on the eternal truth of the river of life, flowing ever upward. And just as the myths suggest, when you open your heart it will be filled with all the knowledge and love that you can possibly hold.

The song then advises us to live in the moment, and to head off black moods and depression by lifting your mind into the ever-shifting dance of existence; to let go of the past ("sweep the shadows from your awning") and to go with the flow. "Shrink the fourfold circumstance" remains mysterious, yet surely relates somehow to the limitations of material reality. Instead of surrendering to these we should follow the light of higher worlds, leaving behind our "shell of foam" like "twice-born gypsies," shedding our attachment and moving on, both within this life and also beyond it.

"Four and twenty birds of Maya baked into an atom you polarized into existence, magnet heart from red to blue," is not only a pun on the "four and twenty blackbirds" of the nursery rhyme, but also a reference to the Hindu belief that Pradhana, the eternal essence of material nature that existed before creation, equivalent to the Cosmic Egg mentioned earlier, was comprised of 24 elements. Time, or the Will of God, was the 25th element that set it all in motion and created the material universe, which Hindus nevertheless believe is illusory, and named Maya. This belief has parallels in quantum physics; a quite separate fact is that there are also 24 chemical elements that make up the human body. The magnet heart shifting from red to blue suggests the scientific terms 'redshift' and 'blueshift.' Put simply, a redshift is when electromagnetic radiation increases in wavelength, to a lower frequency, and blueshift is when it decreases in wavelength to a higher frequency. Cosmological redshift is due to the expansion of the universe, and occurs when an object is moving further away; a blueshift indicates it is getting closer, as for example the Andromeda Galaxy is moving closer to our own Milky Way. Yet all this is only how it appears from our own limited perspective: "To such extent the realm of dark within the picture it seems true; but slip inside the house and then decide."

The next verse describes Kundalini yoga, and the way that, once awakened, the lightning travels along our spine through the seven chakras, before ultimately awakening our pineal gland, or third eye. This is the way to achieve personal enlightenment, so that you are no longer at the mercy of man-made gods, but can control and direct your own reality. Once you join the elite brotherhood of those so illuminated, you will trust in the eternal song of the spheres; you will become one of the "three-eyed men," higher not only than the one-eyed men who think they rule (in the kingdom of the blind?) but also those two-eyed men who understand the mystery enough to wield occult power and influence. The three-eyed men are not even concerned with trivial power games, they can go where they will; they are, ultimately, only passing through this plane of existence.

So what, ultimately, is this house we should slip inside? The seven chakras are often referred to as houses; also, our mortal existence and our physical body are merely temporary houses that we stay in for a while, before passing on. Equally, other levels of knowledge and existence can be accessed in this life; they too are houses that we can slip inside of as we pass by. As outlaws and heretics, the Elevators were at this stage literally holed up in safe houses, like the early persecuted Christians; the listener can slip inside their house for a while, and be enlightened. But ultimately the message is that we should not, indeed cannot, stay in any one house for too long. Change or transformation is the only true reality.

Clementine Hall has a more mundane explanation for the song's title. "Tommy and I had a favorite outing," she says. "We would drive through the more affluent neighborhoods of whatever city we were in and look at the architecture; both of us admired fine architecture. On one such occasion, I asked Tommy to stop in front of a particular house, so I could 'slip inside this house.' I used those exact words. Tommy immediately got out his ever-present little spiral notebook and asked me to repeat what I'd just said. He then asked me what I meant by the words and I told him they referred to something I had done ever since I was a little child: mentally walking around the inside of the house and picturing myself living in it. He wrote this down in his notebook. He often stopped me when I was speaking and wrote down my comments, later using them or parts of them in lyrics. I used to write poems myself, and I had a habit of speaking in metaphors (still do), and Tommy often told me he thought I was the most intelligent person he knew. To be perfectly honest, I know that I am nowhere near Tommy's league. I consider him a genius, if a genius is one whose insights are effortless (and I do think that is the definition of a genius)."

It may seem excessive to dwell in such depth on one song, but in truth *Slip Inside This House* towers above the other material on *Easter Everywhere*, just as it would dominate any album that it was featured on. The only other track on the LP that is in the same ballpark is the closing number; *Postures (Leave Your Body Behind)*. This is in some ways a sequel to the opening piece, bringing us full circle. Over a sophisticated, loose R&B groove that highlights the skill of the band's new rhythm section, Roky regales us with instructions of how to keep climbing, referencing the soul music tropes of "keeping on" and getting higher, but in this case using them to describe ascension to a higher level of consciousness and being.

Tommy Hall was concerned that the counter-culture was failing to follow its highest aspirations, and was slacking on the self-actualization trip, returning to the comfortable hypocrisies of straight thought and existence, or "creeping back from the affair." This song was to urge them back onto The Quest: "Live the love, it gives its return; the higher you're living now the purer it burns." He constantly urges the listener to remember that we are beings of pure energy, that we are self-directed, and that we have a choice to follow our higher or our lower instincts.

"You raise your sense income and your level of being by finer and finer and finer agreeing," is practical advice for the resolution of difficulties, that Tommy tried to practice in everyday life; the idea that we should look for our common ground in any disagreement and try to expand upon that, rather than focus on our differences. The song ends with a six-line quotation from the book *The Secret of the Golden Flower*, a Chinese Taoist meditation guide probably from the 12th Century, translated in the 1920s by Jung's colleague Richard Wilhelm, which was a major influence on Tommy's thinking at this time. The final line, "The love you feel is love you hear" has a positive resonance similar to the couplet with which Paul McCartney, in 1969, would close *The End*, the last song the Beatles ever recorded together: "the love you take is equal to the love you make."

Unfortunately, the remainder of *Easter Everywhere* fails to provide a coherent journey between these two points. Despite their diligent writing regime, Tommy Hall and Roky Erickson just weren't able to come up with an album's worth of new, original material amid the chaos of their lives at the time. Thus the ten songs on the album include two from an earlier recording session, still featuring the rhythm section of John Ike and Ronnie Leatherman (*She Lives (In A Time Of Her Own)* and *Levitation*) plus writing contributions from Stacy Sutherland (*Nobody To Love*), Powell St John (*Slide Machine*) and Clementine Hall (*I Had To Tell You*) and even a Bob Dylan cover (*It's All Over Now, Baby Blue*). The remaining Hall-Erickson compositions are a pair of beautiful cosmic love songs; *Earthquake*, which celebrates physical love, and *Dust*, which is more spiritual, suggesting that love will endure as a positive force even after the physical relationship has ended; that love in fact is an eternal force, stronger than death.

These are all great songs in their own right. Powell's *Slide Machine* is a haunting homesick lament from his Mexican travels, the title referring to the mechanical devices used to clear rocks and other debris from the roads, and not, as many thought, a syringe used for injecting heroin. The song does however contain coded references to marijuana: "My woman here she's got a dozen names; she's sought by soldiers and they try to keep her tame." He's stuck down south, haunted by the old gods of Mexico, broke and lonesome, "trying to get back to you." The Elevators perfectly capture the song's mix of magic, sorrow and the sense of ominous thunder clouds gathering over blank desert landscapes. Stacy's full, echoing guitar lines ring and moan over Dan Galindo's bubbling bass, and Roky's vocals ache with loss and wonder.

She Lives (In A Time Of Her Own) was recorded in the same session as the *Levitation* single, and unmistakably features John Ike on drums and Ronnie Leatherman on bass. It seems to be not about a real woman, but about the eternal 'other,' traditionally characterized as feminine. This could be considered as our own inner voice or the guidance of the Goddess, or even the voice that we hear speaking to us via peyote, LSD, DMT or psilocybin mushrooms. Particularly notable are the soft, droning backing vocals on the chorus, surely influenced by the band's time in San Francisco; though this is compensated for by the tough Texas boogie of the guitars. Stacy Sutherland takes lead vocal on his own composition *Nobody to Love*, a deeply personal song about his recent break-up with his long-term girlfriend Laurie; the first of the three tragedies foretold by the angels in his terrifying LSD vision in Houston. Stacy's voice is appropriately muffled and haunting, while his stinging, burning guitar playing speaks for itself, chasing round in ever-decreasing circles of pain, regret and self-admonition, an emotional agony which Tommy's blithely burbling jug almost seems to mock. Rise above it and look to the future, it seems to say; but Stacy's tormented blues prove it's not that easy, nor indeed should it be.

The first side of the album closes with Dylan's *(It's All Over Now) Baby Blue*. It seems perverse, at this late stage, for the band to put a cover song on an album that was supposed to be their great lyrical statement. The obvious assumption is that they had just run out of material; yet given the obvious Dylan influence of *Slip Inside This House*, *Baby Blue* is in a way an appropriate choice. Often interpreted as another of Dylan's great kiss-off songs to a lover, and a song about moving on, the Elevators reclaim it as a profound drug song. In their hands, *(It's All Over Now) Baby Blue* is unmistakably about the transformation engendered by powerful psychedelics, and the notion that once you've been through the trip, your old life, with all its comfortable assumptions and half-baked certainties, is irrevocably over and you have to start anew. The song in fact relates to Tommy's statements on the first album sleeve about the dissolution of the old order and the old ways of thinking, and how those on the Quest must always look forward. It also features possibly Stacy Sutherland's finest guitar solo, a masterpiece of dissolving, spiraling echoplex-inflected curved lines, snaking together like infinite, and impossibly complex fractal patterns.

Side two kicks off with the powerful, heavy dirge of *Earthquake*, on which Tommy insisted on recording a huge reverberating steel sheet to simulate the sound of thunder, though this isn't audible in the final mix. Roky's occasionally mumbled, breathy vocals and the long, sustained notes of guitar distortion suggest that the band may have been listening to Hendrix before recording the song. *Dust* is a fragile, near-acoustic ballad before the classic garage-rocker *Levitation*. With music by Stacy Sutherland, and John Ike and Ronnie Leatherman on drums and bass, the song has a hard-driving rhythm, peppered with plenty of cymbal splashes, that roots it in the rock 'n' roll of 1965/66 that the Elevators by now had largely moved on from.

Even more of a welcome throwback is Clementine Hall and Roky Erickson's *I Had to Tell You*. The high, pure, almost Joan Baez-like tones of Clementine's backing vocals, along with Roky's harmonica playing, make this acoustic ballad a powerful reminder of the folk songs of 1963; only a few years gone, but already a far more innocent time. Like her earlier *Splash 1* it seems a poignant yearning for the certainties and security that had been lost in the chaotic upheaval of the times.

Although she and Tommy had effectively separated when the Elevators had returned to Austin from San Francisco, Clementine was still an integral part of the making of *Easter Everywhere*. "Tommy had me flown to Texas at the request of Roky and Stacy (as well as for his own sake) and I stayed with Tommy and the others, and was present at every rehearsal out at Stacy's family cabin, and was also present at the recording sessions," she says now. "I wrote *I Had to Tell You* at that time. I had an almost prophetic vision of Roky and the psychological problems he would experience in later years. I tried to write it as if it were my own experience, but Tommy said that one line which originally went 'I can hear my voice echoing your voice, softly,' would be more powerful for a male (Roky) to sing if I reversed it to 'I can hear your voice echoing my voice, softly.' I agreed, and changed the line. On that song, there was only one line that could be considered a quote from Roky, and that's the line, 'Don't you even think about it, I'm feeling fine.' Whenever anyone voiced concern about something to Roky, he would respond, 'Don't you *even* think about it,' reassuringly. He was very sensitive to the distress of others and frequently made what I call 'comforting noises.' Very very sweet young man."

Easter Everywhere is a great album, but not the grand coherent statement it was intended to be. Instead it's the sound of a once unified band breaking down into its separate parts, much like the later Beatles LPs. Two different rhythm sections feature on the record; Stacy seems increasingly a separate force, his playing standing mysteriously apart throughout. Even Tommy Hall's focus seems split between his cosmic vision and his floundering relationship with Clementine. And while Roky is in fine voice, you sense his growing discomfort with the wordy intellectualism of Tommy's lyrics.

George Banks' striking cover shows a blazing sun that represented the crown chakra, while on the rear sleeve an 18th Century Indian painting maps out all seven chakras on the figure of a meditating yogi. There are also individual photos of all five band members; no longer are the Elevators a mysterious, unified force, but separate human beings, all looking in different directions. There's Roky, wide-eyed and curly-haired, looking up and smiling softly into the distance. Stacy, in profile like a prison mugshot, bathed in demonic red light, facing left, brooding and alone. Galindo and Thomas, on the other side, are rock n' roll journeymen, both dealing with the job at hand. And Tommy, looking directly at the camera, has a finger to his lips: here is the secret. Don't tell.

If Hall was the Head of the band, then Roky was the Heart, and during recording at Andrus Studio their positions became more and more entrenched. For Roky, performing was about emotion; for Tommy, it was about getting an intellectual message across. They actually came to blows on the subject, and both temporarily quit the band during the fraught, month-long sessions, which inevitably were fuelled by constant LSD use. The album was never finished to the satisfaction of all parties; the tapes were simply sent for mastering when the time and the money ran out.

Tommy Hall intended the title *Easter Everywhere* to suggest the coming universal Christ Consciousness. It was an optimistic statement of rebirth and resurrection, of man being absolved of sin and finally realizing his own God-nature. Unfortunately, Easter is also a time of crucifixion. In the immediate future, as the authorities came down on the 13th Floor Elevators like the vengeful Roman Empire, and whatever magical luck they'd possessed as a band seemed to forsake them, the album's title would come to seem like a grim prophecy indeed.

Chapter 21

If the 13th Floor Elevators were struggling to make that difficult second album then the Red Crayola had a slightly different problem. They had no trouble producing a worthy follow-up to their debut; they were just having great difficulty finding an audience, or anyone at their record company, who would accept what they gave them. As a result, the Red Crayola actually produced three equally brilliant candidates for their second LP, but only one of them would actually be released; moreover, the band would be torn apart in the process.

On the back of the uncategorizable genius of *The Parable Of Arable Land*, which supposedly sold 30,000 copies in New York and San Francisco, barely a thousand anywhere else, the Red Crayola decided not to bother with touring and went straight back into the studio. They were much more interested in the opportunity of producing new music in a professional environment than they were in attempting to compete on a live circuit that would surely have rejected them anyway. But perhaps the Red Crayola over-estimated the license they'd been granted, as after hearing the tapes for the band's intended second album, to be titled *Coconut Hotel*, International Artists turned down the recordings.

The label may not have had a clue about the new psychedelic and experimental music that they were half-heartedly promoting, but nevertheless you can see their point; even by the Red Crayola's standards, *Coconut Hotel* is willfully uncommercial. It is also brilliant. Properly a work of the contemporary classical avant-garde, the record dispenses with The Familiar Ugly and their Free-Form Freak-outs; it also abandons any attempt at pop or rock song structures, and with one semi-exception does without vocals at all. Most notoriously, the album contains 36 "one-second pieces" that are more or less exactly that; brief musical sound fragments (clonks, sqounks, crashes, bleats, burps

222

and bashes) with delays of varying duration between them.

As musical entertainment, these pieces are a one-shot joke that soon wears thin; the best that can be said for them is that by their nature they are at least over fairly quickly. But they make a clear statement that on this album musical entertainment is not really the point. This is a conceptual record (distinctly different to a concept album in the rock sense) that is primarily about artistic musical ideas, and the process of carrying them out. And when one's expectations are duly adjusted, it's also highly listenable.

Opener *Boards* is a six-and-a-half-minute drone for organ and guitar that possesses both tension and beauty; there is a definite progression of sounds as well as a thrilling sense of space and strangeness. Yet it is not so far out; in rock terms alone, it recalls the floating, free-form passages of Pink Floyd's *Interstellar Overdrive* and anticipates the early electronic experiments of Tangerine Dream. It breaks off sharply, with a jarring edit, before *Water Pour*, in which guitar, bass, and possibly banjo are plucked, scraped and vibrated arrhythmically to the occasional accompaniment of cymbal splashes and, yes, poured water. Next up are all 36 one-second pieces, incorporating piano, strangled saxophone and drum, masterpieces of timing if nothing else, and accumulating into a kind of sustained Dadaist absurdism.

Organ Buildup is just over a minute of a humming organ warming up, accompanied by a brushed snare drum and growing in volume until it suddenly cuts out, and *Vocal* features some wordless, and indeed tuneless, vocal improvising over harp-like guitar pluckings and swanee whistle, with occasional interjections of drum, organ and saxophone. Again, the result is strangely affecting; haunting and womb-like, or conjuring a somehow childlike alien landscape that is not entirely hostile, but not entirely friendly either. *Free Guitar* is a sustained acoustic raga with free jazz overtones, its suppressed violence vaguely reminiscent of some of the Velvet Underground's more experimental passages, and quite thrilling. The album concludes with three short improvisations, two on guitar and one on piano.

The album would have to wait until 1995 for an official release by Drag City Records, but it did circulate privately to some degree at the time, most fortuitously coming to the ears of Professor Kurt Von Meier at UCLA's Art History Department. Von Meier was an iconoclastic and inspirational figure who had written a book on the history of rock 'n' roll and had connections that extended to Andy Warhol and the Velvet Underground over on the East Coast. He was impressed enough to attempt to secure the Red Crayola some festival gigs in California that summer. Sadly, they were turned down by the Monterey Pop Festival, but they were invited to the Angry Arts Festival in Venice, Los Angeles, as well as that year's Berkeley Folk Festival.

Frederick Barthelme would recall that, "at Kurt's house, where we were staying, we encountered some or all of the Doors. Who remembers? Just like in the TV movies, there was acid in the punch." He also adds that "By this time we'd put aside almost all pretense of being a rock band, and were bent on making the toughest music we could, more and more of which was derived from art musicians and run through both a rock grinder and a can't-play-all-that-well grinder. Noise music."

The Angry Arts Festival took place on Thursday 29th June, with the Red Crayola appearing onstage at the Venice Pavilion at some point in the afternoon, "a little earlier than planned," according to the compere. Von Meier introduced them as "a wild group from Houston, Texas, believe it or not," to a smattering of patronizing chuckles from the audience. The laughter soon faded as the Red Crayola proceeded to pulverize the crowd with painful, atonal feedback accompanying free jazz improvisations on distorted electric bass and piercingly high electric guitars. Yet this was no proto-thrash metal assault, and the set soon settled into a mostly low, oscillating drone of strangely brutal beauty. Eschewing drums, or rhythms of any sort, the Red Crayola's half-hour set was an exercise in sound as texture, as environment; uncomfortable at times, perhaps even boring at others, and always demanding, but never one-dimensionally aggressive or confrontational.

The Berkeley Folk Festival began the following day and stretched out until Tuesday over a long Fourth of July weekend. Kurt Von Meier was also on the bill at Berkeley, booked to speak as a folklorist alongside pioneering San Francisco music critic Ralph Gleason, Archie Green, and Phil Spector. The musical fare meanwhile included Doc Watson, the Reverend Gary Davis, James Cotton and younger bucks like Richie Havens, Janis Ian, Country Joe and the Fish, Kaleidoscope and the Steve Miller Blues Band. The Red Crayola were booked to appear at a 'Dance Concert' at the Pawley Ballroom on the Sunday night, alongside Doc Watson, Seattle acid-rockers Crome Syrkus and the Cleanliness and Godliness Skiffle Band, and the early evening session on Monday, appearing below Country Joe and the Fish. There was also a Jubilee Concert at the Hearst Greek Theater on the Tuesday afternoon, featuring all the festival artists, that was broadcast live on San Francisco's KQED radio.

The Red Crayola's Sunday night set was memorable for Steve Cunningham 'playing' a block of ice that was melting onto an amplified aluminum foil sheet. Over this faint but regular rhythm, like a metronome, Thompson and Barthelme improvised trails and blasts of feedback, spare jazz piano and saxophone, various kinds of industrial noise and the abuse of contact microphones attached to parts of their bodies. Another innovation, according to Rick Barthelme, was that they attached heavy copper wires to their electric guitars rather than regular strings. One festival-goer protested that their set was so abrasive and feedback-heavy that it killed their dog.

Nevertheless, the Red Crayola were still allowed to return to the Pauley Ballroom the following evening, when they were accompanied by guitarist John Fahey. One would think this incredible pairing would be cause for celebration, but at the time, this now legendary musician was still all but unknown. Fahey had self-released his debut album, *Blind Joe Death*, in 1959 at the age of 20, paying for the record from his wages as a gas station attendant. But said Maryland gas station was just about the only place the album was available from. Back then he was already an astonishing player, weaving intricate blues madrigals on an open-tuned steel-string guitar, but his following barely extended beyond the folk club aficionados of Maryland and Washington DC.

In 1963 Fahey moved to California and began a Master's degree in Philosophy at Berkeley, but soon switched to the Folklore Studies program at UCLA, writing a thesis on bluesman Charley Patton. At the same time he re-launched the Takoma label he had invented for his so-far sole release, putting out albums by kindred guitarists Robbie Basho and Max Ochs, as well as further releases of his own. But while enjoying increasing recognition, he was scathing about the complacency he saw in the burgeoning West Coast hippy scene, his music obsessively exploring themes of dread, darkness and death rather than positivity, color and light. Fahey's 1966 album, *The San Bernardino Birthday Party And Other Excursions*, incorporated tape loops, backwards recording, editing and overdubbing that took his blues-folk guitar playing into the realms of the experimental and psychedelic, even though Fahey was a hard-drinking conservative who despised drugs and the mystically-inclined, anti-establishment culture that went with them. His experiments were informed more by modern composers like Charles Ives, Stockhausen and Pierre Schaeffer, and his attitude was punk before punk was invented. This position of being simultaneously of the counter-culture and yet antagonistic to it, in some ways ahead of it and contemptuous of its failings, while still enjoying its support, gave him much common ground with the Red Crayola.

Their performance together came just as Fahey had completed his Master's; he had also got married just days earlier. Fahey would in theory be considered a natural fit for the Berkeley Folk Festival, as a blues scholar and guitarist of considerable local renown. The fact that he chose to align himself with the atonal electronic noise of the Red Crayola, rather than any of the more traditional blues artists on the bill, could be considered as typical cussedness, or as a more serious statement of intent. Fahey was declaring himself a member of the avant-garde, rather than some backwoods traditionalist, and this was the direction his subsequent recordings would increasingly take, while never losing their American folk roots. When he was rediscovered in the early 1990s, his champions were post-punk experimentalists like Sonic Youth and Jim O'Rourke, rather than classical guitarists, new age musicians or folk finger-pickers.

Fahey also shared management (Ed Denson's Joyful Wisdom Enterprises) with headliners Country Joe and the Fish, so it was presumably easily arranged that he should sit in with the Red Crayola. If anyone thought that Fahey's presence would guide the Crayola in a more conventional direction than their previous night's performance however, they were grievously mistaken. Fahey improvised a kind of industrial raga over the Red Crayola's pulsing, minimal rhythm, and a nightmarish lament gradually coalesced out of the random feedback and distorted overdriven improvisation. Later the set descends into slapstick, with squeaky toys employed alongside percussive bursts of sound better suited to a *Tom and Jerry* short; but just as the audience are starting to laugh comfortably along, the music once again takes a sinister turn, distorted drones rising up out of nowhere like menacing black thunder clouds.

Following the live radio broadcast of their third and final set of the festival (when the announcer, not realizing the Red Crayola had started their set, chattered inanely over their opening minutes of feedback and improvisation) the Red

Crayola were invited by John Fahey to open for him at his upcoming club date at the New Orleans House. It took only ten minutes for their performance to empty the room; the club's manager reportedly paid them ten dollars to stop playing and get off the stage. Nevertheless, the Red Crayola and the equally confrontational Fahey, famously described by his manager as the only artist he knew whose record sales went down after he made a live appearance, hit it off, and booked time in Berkeley's Sierra Sound Studios to record a long improvised session together.

The Red Crayola and John Fahey recorded four reels of tape; easily enough for an album, but none of it was to ever see the light of day. International Artists were outraged at one of their acts recording an album without their knowledge or permission, and with an artist who was signed to another label at that. Fahey in fact had just signed to Vanguard Records, a label that certainly outranked International Artists should there be any dispute over ownership of the masters. Panicking, IA refused to fly the band back to Texas unless they brought the tapes with them and handed them over.

This was the final straw for Rick Barthelme and Steve Cunningham, who effectively washed their hands of the whole business. They flew back to Houston and delegated Mayo to go down to San Francisco, collect the tapes and deliver them to International Artists. The Red Crayola had fully intended to release an album from the sessions, but the recordings went into the IA vaults and like many of the labels' master tapes effectively disappeared for good. These recordings have never surfaced even on bootlegs, a huge loss to any enthusiast or student of 20th Century experimental music.

The Red Crayola had effectively broken up. None of them wanted anything more to do with International Artists, and Rick Barthelme moved to New York and started writing and making conceptual art, eventually following in the footsteps of his brother Donald by becoming a successful and critically acclaimed novelist and short story writer. Mayo Thompson returned to Los Angeles and for a time worked as a sound man with the experimental rock group the United States of America, at the same time as continuing to pursue his own musical ideas. He also met with Nico, who had just left the Velvet Underground and was about to embark on her solo career. They discussed working together, but decided they were incompatible.

Early in 1968 however International Artists got back in touch with Thompson and told him that the Red Crayola still owed them a second album. Barthelme could not be persuaded to rejoin, but Thompson teamed up again with Steve Cunningham and the pair employed a young drummer called Tommy Smith, no relation to the Texan singer of the same name who was a member of the Laughing Kind, and regrouped as the Red Krayola. The changed spelling was not so much an acknowledgement of their revised line-up, but rather a necessary response to a cease and desist letter from the lawyers of the Crayola Crayon Firm, who had somehow belatedly heard of the band. Another change was that International Artists were no longer using Andrus Studios, but had bought Gold Star Studios in January 1968, renaming it International Artists Studios. As a result, the production genius of Walt Andrus and Frank Davis was absent from the Red Krayola's second album, and Lelan Rogers had also recently departed from International Artists. Rogers was allegedly fired by IA co-owner Nobel Ginther in February 1968 after an argument between the two; supposedly a drunken Ginther had turned up at Gold Star where Rogers had been recording Lightnin' Hopkins' *Freeform Patterns* LP, and Rogers took exception to Ginther's patronizing attitude towards the legendary bluesman.

Produced by the band with Gold Star's resident engineer Jim Duff, *God Bless The Red Krayola And All Who Sail With It* was no after-the-fact embarrassment or contractual obligation, and arguably even surpasses its predecessor. Housed in a strikingly minimal black and white sleeve, in direct contrast to the overwhelming color and complexity of the packaging on *The Parable Of Arable Land*, *God Bless...* also featured a much sparser, stripped-down sound. Gone were the maximalist free-form freak outs of The Familiar Ugly, and the dense, urgent garage rock of songs like *Hurricane Fighter Plane*. In their place were twenty spare, fragile creations that stripped away all the distortion, bombast and special effects of late sixties rock, leaving a sense of space around the musical pieces that presented them as artistic statements, like abstract paintings or installations in a cool, white-walled gallery.

This was an album that didn't need to rely on volume, distortion or sonic gimmickry to create a psychedelic impression. On *God Bless...* the Red Krayola took their music in the opposite direction, crafting short, hesitant numbers that were as inherently odd and off-kilter as anything in Captain Beefheart's holler or Syd Barrett's thousand-yard stare. With its boxy, damped-down sound and Mayo Thompson's plaintive, untrained vocals, some tracks suggest the Velvet Underground's eponymous third album, yet this wasn't released until nearly a year later. Other pieces, more sketches or exercises than songs, are similar to ideas the Residents would explore on their debut album in 1974. A whole decade after it was released, *God Bless...* would find semi-kindred spirits in post-punk outfits like the Fall, Swell Maps, Young Marble Giants and the Raincoats, bands that would either claim the Red Krayola as an influence, or find themselves in coincidentally similar opposing stances to the overblown virtuosity and emotional clichés of the rock mainstream. But even these proudly experimental outsider groups never matched the sheer otherworldly strangeness of *God Bless The Red Krayola And All Who Sail With It*.

The album opens with *Say Hello to Jamie Jones*, a primitive, cryptic nursery rhyme set to a meandering bassline and stamping drums. Named after a member of The Familiar Ugly, the song is as catchy as it is impenetrable. The *a cappella* interlude of *Music* is performed by a female chorus credited as "Mary Sue, Dotty, Pat, Barbara, Elaine, Carolyn and Candy," who harmonies like a seriously stoned Andrews Sisters. Singing "We're gonna have music, won't you sing a little bit, and wink or squint?" the track comes over like a deadpan satirical riposte to their many critics and antagonists who just wished the Red Krayola would play them a recognizable tune.

Certainly, 'music' barely covers *The Shirt*, in which the barest ghost of a song shivers under and over unidentified factory sounds; possibly, given the title, a clothing manufacturing plant. The sound of rivets being hammered home acts as a kind of unstable percussion, jarring the listener out of any kind of reverie. Though Mayo Thompson has consistently and explicitly denied there being any kind of political message in his music, *The Shirt* could be heard as contrasting the romanticism of music with the overpowering reality of capitalist production. Glassy, echoing sounds of an unidentifiable nature add to the musique concrete feel.

Listen to This recalls the one-second pieces from the then-unreleased *Coconut Hotel*, while *Save This House* initially seems a conventional song thanks to Tommy Smith's propulsive, professional drumming and Steve Cunningham's surprisingly tight bass playing. But mistimed harmonies create a disorienting dissonance that amplifies the unresolved, surreal nature of Mayo's lyrics. *Victory Garden* meanwhile may be the Red Krayola's strongest song as such; a heart-breaking, ramshackle ballad that subverts its own sentimental romanticism by being addressed to a protagonist named Adolf. Victory Gardens were plots of vegetables planted to aid the war effort in World War II, and this song could be read as a satire on the nostalgia for such times. With Mayo singing, in high, cracked voice, of "the serious virgin" and "your suit of chrome it shines so bright," the track recalls both the Velvet Underground and Dylan at his most surreal, but without the latter's amphetamine compulsion to color in all the spaces between the notes. Yet the memorable hookline, "Don't say you've said goodbye now" resonates above and beyond any specific intention.

Coconut Hotel is an exercise in surreal vocals and free piano, before *Sheriff Jack* comes over as a kind of cack-handed boogie, starting out conventionally 'good' before swiftly falling apart, constantly slipping in and out of time. Lyrically it's the tale of the lonely, death-haunted Jack, whose girlfriend Susie won't marry him because "she don't feel right about the hangings every night." Opening with a burst of jarring noise, *Free Piece* continues the same arrhythmic flailing, with Thompson and Cunningham riffing disinterestedly on *Say Hello to Jamie Jones* while Smith kicks into a semi-virtuoso drum solo. *Ravi Shankar: Parachutist* is a tense, ominous tale, rather like a punk-noir Syd Barrett, once again featuring harmony vocals from Mary Sue, Dotty and the other girls. The noted Indian sitar master is lost while taking part in a sky-diving contest; "In the air he drew a picture; what he saw I do not know" suggests that Ravi experienced something while falling that made him decide never to return to earth again. The stop-start punk rock of *Dairymaid's Lament* glories in hardcore, lo-fi double-strummed guitar riffing yet is intricately structured in a manner closer to the conservatory than the garage.

The album's second side is relatively more conventional, containing recognizable songs rather than sketches, although it does open with the dissonant chords of *Big*, under which a little girl, one Holly Pritchett, wishes she was "big." Her voice is mixed so low you can hardly hear her. *Leejol* dances through its changes on spindly but precise guitar lines, always balanced precariously above any root note. *Sherlock Holmes* is another standout, its loose, languid narrative oddly anticipating the jazz-prog collective Gong in its sense of naïve freedom, though of course with a Texan punk edge.

This feel continues through *Dirth of Tilth* and *Tina's gone to have a Baby*, songs that sound like nothing else that existed at that time. Any reference points occur only with hindsight; bands like the Fall, Pavement and Guided By Voices, and even these only in passing. *The Jewels of the Madonna*, with its squealing, strangled guitar riffs and Steve Cunningham singing, could be Sonic Youth, while the clanging descent of *Green Of My Pants* and the asylum-friendly *Night Song* exist in a parallel universe where Zappa's Mothers of Invention were rescued from their progressive jazz-rock muso cul-de-sac by the beauty of musical incompetence.

God Bless The Red Krayola And All Who Sail With It was released by international Artists in May 1968. It sold poorly; the label showed no interest in any further material for the band, who once again all went their separate ways. And though Mayo Thompson would resurrect the name years later for future recordings and performances featuring varying line-ups, the Red Krayola's era as Texas's freakiest band was over.

PART VI

DARK SHADOWS

Chapter 22

As 1968 dawned in Texas, it must have seemed in many ways as if the counter-culture was winning. The Vulcan Gas Company had opened in Austin in October 1967, while in Houston, Love Street Light Circus Feel Good Machine was a purpose built psychedelic club and venue, opened by local artist David Addickes on June 3rd 1967. Located in Allen's Landing in the city's downtown area, between the university campus and the banks of the Buffalo Bayou, Love Street Light Circus was on the third floor of an otherwise unimpressive building on 1019 Commerce Street. The main complaint of bands playing there was that they had to lug their equipment up four flights of fire escape to the venue, and then load out the same way.

Addickes had been inspired to create Love Street Light Circus after a visit to San Francisco and the Avalon and Fillmore ballrooms. He ran his own lightshow, which included large wall-size projections that would feature photographs of patrons snapped at the club the night before, a provocative entertainment developed directly from Ken Kesey's Acid Tests, where audience members would have their conversations secretly recorded and then played back over the sound system while they were tripping. The 200-capacity club had tables and chairs around the side walls and a central area known as the Zonk-Out, where the majority of the audience would recline in rows on cushions set against head rests on the floor. A band would play on stage, with go-go dancers off to one side. Like many other Texan rock clubs, Love Street sought to attract a teenage audience and so didn't serve alcohol.

Fever Tree and a particularly confrontational Red Crayola played at the club's opening weekend, and although by the end of the year Addickes had sold the club to retired Air Force Sergeant Cliff Carlin, Love Street Light Circus was successful enough to inspire many imitators; the most blatant of these was the Electric Tangerine Life Machine on 10650 Kirsch. New, self-consciously psychedelic bands like the Elastic Prism and the Starvation Army Band also started springing up to satisfy the growing demand for wild and freaky sounds. Indeed, for many the good times were only just beginning, and there would still be many fine shows and much great music made. But with hindsight, the psychedelic movement's great moment had already passed. The brief burst of innocent, inspired idealism had ended, and the consequences were decidedly mixed. Hard drugs like heroin and speed became more prevalent, while street LSD was adulterated and dubious alternatives like STP and PCP flooded the market. Bastardized chemicals supplied by criminal gangs were swallowed like candy by prematurely jaded school-children, while the psychonauts and cosmic philosophers of only two years earlier either moved on or burnt out. It may have seemed like the party was still in full swing, but long shadows were already lengthening across the Lone Star State and beyond.

One effect of the trend towards heavy acid rock was that many of the original psychedelic club bands, with their more melodic, concise songs, were now considered passé. A classic example was Thursday's Children, formed by keyboard player Charles Helpinstill and guitarist Jan Pedersen at Houston's Rice University in the spring of 1965, out of the pit orchestra at, of all things, a college minstrel show. Both were classically trained, though Helpinstill had played one high school rock 'n' roll show at the age of 14 in 1958, alongside Johnny and Edgar Winter in his native Beaumont.

Helpinstill hooked up with the Norwegian-via-New Orleans Pedersen after discovering that Pedersen could play every Beatles song ever written, and also that their two voices were able to harmonize perfectly on those songs. Originally calling themselves the Druids, they became Thursday's Children with the addition of bassist Pat Sullivan, rhythm guitarist Steve Brown and high school drummer Richard Gollwitzer. Never really psychedelic, they specialized in a sophisticated Beatles/Zombies hybrid that on occasion anticipated the late seventies power pop of Squeeze or Nick Lowe. Pedersen also excelled at Byrdsian folk-rock, which he played on a home-made 12-string guitar. By their own admission they were refiners rather than innovators, but they were also trained musicians, mostly in their early twenties, which gave them a technical edge over the high school garage bands they were competing with in the Houston area.

A residency at La Maison led to a management deal with Gordon Bynum, who also managed the Six Pents and had recently discovered the 13th Floor Elevators. Their debut single *Try, Girl* came out on Houston soul label Paradise, a melodic gem that played to the band's strengths, while the rockier B-side, *You'll Never Be My Girl*, was lifted above the norm by a Beatles-ish bridge. Bynum then took the band to International Artists, for whom they recorded *Air Conditioned Man* (IA-110, October 1966), which openly borrowed from the Kinks' *Well-Respected Man*, with a nod to the Beatles' *Paperback Writer* and a cod-Egyptian oboe solo. Better was the flip, the irresistibly catchy *Dominoes*.

During the summer of 1966 Thursday's Children all moved into a derelict house on the edge of Houston, under the pretense that they were architecture students who wanted to study the building's unique properties. They played gigs to pay the $100 a month rent, ate rarely, and wrote and rehearsed furiously. The result was their excellent third single, *Help, Murder, Police* (IA-115, March 1967). Despite producer Walt Andrus toning down the fuzz guitar, the tough pop chord sequence, harmonized chorus and spiraling lead guitar add up to a strong distinctive track. Overleaf was the equally worthy *You Can Forget about That*, notable for its catchy chorus and Helpinstill's brief, quasi-classical pianoette solo.

Tensions were starting to tug at the band however, not helped by Pedersen's decision to cover the entire first side of the newly-released *Sergeant Pepper's Lonely Hearts Club Band* at teen club shows through the summer of 1967. There was also a growing rift between those of the band who had embraced the growing drug scene and those, like Helpinstill, who very much hadn't. International Artists put them into Andrus Studio to record an album, but lost interest in the project just as the band members, approaching graduation, started worrying about the draft and what they were going to do with the rest of their lives. The only track to emerge from these sessions was the urgent, jazz-tinged *A Part of You*, which tantalizingly hints at what Thursday's Children could have achieved; perhaps Texas's own *Odessey And Oracle*.

Following one further single, the appropriately titled *No More Rock N' Roll* on Rampart Street Records, Thursday's Children split in March 1968. Minus Helpinstill and bassist Pat Sullivan, they briefly regenerated into the more psych-friendly Pointing Hand Group for one single, 1969's *Bus Ride*, before fading into obscurity. Charles Helpinstill would find success as the inventor of the Helpinstill Pick-Up, a magnetic pick-up for amplifying pianos onstage. Founding the internationally successful Helpinstill Company, his clients included Neil Young and Elton John, and he continued as an acclaimed blues pianist under the stage name of Ezra Charles.

Somewhat similar but more obscure is the story of the Lemon Fog. Like the Fever Tree, the band formed at Spring Branch High School, though they were several years younger than Michael Knust. Vocalist Bill Simmons, guitarists Terry Horde and Keith Manlove, bassist Danny Ogg, drummer Chris Lyons and keyboard player Ted Eubanks started out as the Piltdown Men a couple of years before they entered a battle of the bands at the Living Eye club in late 1966. Winning the contest, they succeeded the Lost And Found as the club's house band; one condition imposed by owner Jimmy Duncan however was that they change their name and become the Lemon Fog.

The Lemon Fog played regularly at the Living Eye throughout 1967, opening for the 13th Floor Elevators, Fever Tree and the Moving Sidewalks, as well as touring bands like Question Mark and the Mysterians and the Electric Prunes. With Jimmy Duncan acting as manager and producer, the Lemon Fog (now minus guitarist Keith Manlove) went into Doyle Jones studio during the summer vacation to record a selection of the original songs that featured in their club repertoire. Of these, two Jimmy Duncan compositions were chosen for their debut single: *Lemon Fog / Echoes in Time*, released on Ray McGinnis's Orbit Records in November 1967.

Lemon Fog was originally named *The Living Eye Theme*, but keyboard player Ted Eubanks remembers protesting the fact that Duncan named the song after his club rather than the band. The change may also have been to avoid confusion with the Lost And Found's *Living Eye*. Although he was an accomplished songwriter in the country and easy listening fields, it's apparent that the 40-year-old Duncan struggled to get to grips with psychedelic rock, despite Eubanks rearranging Duncan's songs to give them a more contemporary edge. He was however able to call in a favor from local TV star Larry Kane, who acted as an intermediary in passing the Lemon Fog recordings on to McGinnis; the Orbit label would release three singles from the band, who duly promoted them on the *Larry Kane Show*. On the first occasion they performed amidst dry ice and a yellowy filter over the camera, which presumably only worked if you already had color television in 1967.

Lemon Fog itself was a pacey but somewhat pedestrian folk-rocker, with lyrics that still obviously referred to Duncan's nightclub, the phrase "lemon fog" rather clumsily substituted for "living eye" throughout. Better was *Echoes of Time*, with Eubanks' phased Farfisa organ giving the song a genuinely psychedelic, mellotron-like sound. Both tracks are saved by the excellent yet weirdly detached performance by the young band, with Danny

Ogg's plunging, swooping basslines nodding to the jazz-influenced style of Pink Floyd's Roger Waters, and interacting brilliantly with Chris Lyons' manic yet disciplined drumming. *Echoes of Time* also features a neat guitar solo from Terry Horde, but most striking are Bill Simmons' understated, melancholy vocals, which give the Lemon Fog's records an unearthly, romantic atmosphere of lost youth and troubled introspection.

This is nowhere more evident than on the Lemon Fog's second single, *Summer*, which for obvious reasons was held back till June 1968. Written by Ted Eubanks in 1965 at the age of 15, it's probably the most quietly sorrowful summer song ever released. "I spend my Saturday nights alone," Simmons begins; "nothing to do, just sit at home." It may be summer, but "they've closed the dancing; I've seen the show." Over a circular, minor-key riff, highlighted by Eubanks' gently sympathetic organ, the song unwinds into a perfect miniature of quiet, lonely desperation, *The Catcher in the Rye* summarized in two minutes, forty-three seconds. Yet the teenage alienation, boredom and frustration is never overplayed; throughout, Simmons sounds resigned to his fate, and one recalls what Janis Joplin's father called "the Great Saturday Night Swindle." It seems that summer, as a time of immediate and accessible teenage fun, is equally a painfully false myth. "Summer: it's coming again; summer: with me and my friends," Simmons groans, with abject irony. "Summer: the date and the beach; summer: within my reach." Unfortunately, this lost classic was backed by Duncan's dire *Girl from the Wrong Side of Town*. Presumably a Fabian reject, its manufactured angst sounded even more melodramatic and inauthentic when played after the devastating A-side.

The Lemon Fog recorded their final single *Day By Day / The Prisoner* at Huey Meaux's studio, but by this time the band members had graduated from high school and were drifting apart. *Day By Day* was an enchanting mix of folk and jazz, penned by Ted Eubanks and featuring Simmons voicing reflective hippy philosophizing over a laid-back, sun-flecked groove clearly influenced by the Buffalo Springfield. At two and a half minutes it violently explodes into a fierce jazz-raga coda dominated by Eubanks' atonal, fuzzed-up Farfisa. *The Prisoner* is more upbeat, but equally dense both lyrically and musically.

Like Thursday's Children keyboard player Charles Helpinstill, Ted Eubanks had an interesting and successful afterlife. After the Lemon Fog he went on to work with Jimmy Duncan in the band Wichita, and then an Allen's Landing bar band named Sweet Peter, before going back to college and receiving a BA in journalism in 1978. His interest in environmental issues led to him founding the Austin-based Fermata Inc. in 1992, a holistic, private-sector conservation effort promoting sustainable nature tourism, environmentally friendly landscape solutions, restorative economic strategies and community development. Eubanks is also an acclaimed nature photographer.

If Thursday's Children and the Lemon Fog seemed behind the times in 1968, then the once-popular Neal Ford and the Fanatics must have come over as positively antediluvian, with their old-fashioned show-business values and choreographed stage show. Yet Ford's onstage athleticism was not a million miles from the sort of performance for which Iggy Pop would later be acclaimed; stage diving, executing splits and somersaults, climbing the walls and balancing on balcony railings. Moreover, the band was still capable of rocking hard when allowed, and Ford was a decent songwriter, not afraid to experiment with fuzz and other weird effects in the studio. But their more adventurous songs were too often left in the can, and the Fanatics' November 1967 album for Hickory was hamstrung by too many written-to-order bubblegum confections and middle-of-the-road ballads. In 1968 the clean-living Ford even turned down Mickey Newbury's *Just Dropped In (To See What Condition My Condition Was In)* because of its sly drug connotations, which didn't bother Kenny Rogers' First Edition, who turned the song into a soft psych-country classic.

The symbolic turning point came when Neal Ford and the Fanatics opened for Jimi Hendrix on two Texan dates of his spring 1968 US tour, and were all but booed off the stage. The first show, at San Antonio Municipal Auditorium (February 15th) apparently went down well, but the following night at Dallas Fair Park Music Hall the jeers from the audience got to the band. With their Hickory deal expired, they lost confidence and momentum and never really recovered; Ford quit in May 1969, and the Fanatics struggled on without him until mid-1970.

Hendrix's remaining two Texan dates were opened by the Ames Brothers' other big band, the Moving Sidewalks, and they too viewed the shows as a major turning point, though for different and more positive reasons. Drummer Dan Mitchell acted as an advance man for the Texas leg of the tour, meeting the Experience in San Antonio and showing them around, so the two groups were already friendly ahead of their dates together, at Fort Worth's Will Rogers Auditorium and the Houston Music Hall. Hendrix acknowledged the Sidewalks' spectacular performance during his own set in Fort Worth, and watched the band's set from the wings in Houston. They all hung out together after the shows, and Gibbons was invited to jam with Hendrix at a bizarre 3am session that also involved gallons of fluorescent paint being hurled at a giant white paper backdrop, action-painting style.

The 18-year-old Billy Gibbons was already a Hendrix fan, but the experience of actually playing with his hero was mind-blowing enough to provide a well of inspiration that would last his entire life. He upped his game as a fiercely psychedelic blues guitarist, and Hendrix covers like *Can You See Me* and *Red House* would become staples of Moving Sidewalks' shows. These also became known for their onstage explosions and flash bombs, strobe lights, smoke machines and Don Summers' self-built spinning Flying V bass guitar (he also made a fur-covered guitar for Gibbons). In fact, their over-exuberant use of flash bombs resulted in them being kicked off a potentially lucrative national tour opening for the Doors, when they accidentally set the headlining band's amplifiers on fire. It's possible too that Morrison's crew feared being upstaged by the wild young Texan quartet, after shows at Dallas Memorial Auditorium (9th July) and Houston Coliseum (10th) saw them receive a thunderous reception from their local audience.

In August 1968, the Moving Sidewalks released a new single on Tantara (having been dropped by Wand); a slow, heavy, feedback-riven take on the Beatles' *I Want To Hold Your Hand*, perhaps inspired by Hendrix's similarly drastic deconstruction of *Sergeant Pepper's Lonely Hearts Club Band* on stage (or, just as likely, Vanilla Fudge's sludge-psych hit version of *You Keep Me Hanging On*). The song was backed by *Joe Blues*, taken from the Moving Sidewalks' then-unreleased debut album, *Flash*.

The influence of Jimi Hendrix is all over *Flash*; indeed, the trademark sound of arguably the greatest rock guitarist of all time so dominates the album that the Moving Sidewalks' own unique sound struggles to get out from underneath. The teenage Billy Gibbons in particular seems to have almost completely sublimated his own playing style and personality into that of his idol. Though he would later assert himself and become a highly distinctive and influential guitarist in his own right, here Billy Gibbons is still suffering from a bad case of hero worship, and it shows.

The album starts well with the strutting, funky *Flashback*, the band grooving tightly together and Gibbons' soulful lead guitar tone weaving through layers of percussion and echoing chorus vocals. The song is actually in two parts, with the second section an eastern-tinged lament, featuring tabla-like drums and raga-ish acoustic guitar. *Scoun Da Be* is a choppy, hard funk-boogie workout rich with Hendrix-like licks and mannerisms; it fades into *You Make Me Shake*, essentially more of the same, broken up by a drum/organ solo and enlivened with spacey effects.

Tom Moore's brilliant *You Don't Know the Life* stands out as a sparse, soulful ballad, his warm descending Hammond chords providing the main musical accompaniment alongside tastefully restrained bass and percussion. Gibbons restricts himself to unobtrusive splashes of acoustic guitar, before the cod-Hendrixisms return with a vengeance on *Pluto Sept 31st*. The highlight of this song is a freaky, two-minute bad trip interlude of whispered, echoing voices, spooky laughter and backwards effects. It's apparent by this point that *Flash* is intended as an ambitious sonic collage rather than a collection of distinct songs; the tracks all run together, linked by feedback and studio effects, and most of the songs are divided into different sections, where the change in mood and tempo is often more dramatic than between the songs themselves.

A show-stopping cover of *No Good to Cry* by the obscure Connecticut band the Wildwoods rocks up the soulful original, and gives Gibbons the chance to unleash one of his most powerful solos, before the unremarkable *Crimson Witch* and *Joe Blues*, the latter a slow jam dragged out to over seven and a half minutes. The collage approach is taken to its furthest, absurdist extreme on *Eclipse / Reclipse*, which takes a Zappa-esque studio-as-toy approach, utilizing in-joke catchphrases, TV commercial parodies, reversed vocals, sped-up studio chatter and all manner of what would now be called samples, including gunshots, classical music and horror-movie effects. The resulting cut-up almost anticipates 1990s hip-hop scientists like Coldcut and DJ Shadow, except that underpinning it all is a red-hot blues-rock band. Ultimately *Flash* is never less than an enjoyable listen, and its addled stream-of-consciousness construction and liberal use of disorienting sonic effects make it a deeply psychedelic record. If you can get past the Hendrix pastiches there are many original ideas to hand, and certainly some stunning playing throughout. It's just that overlooking the Hendrix influence is so very difficult to do.

At the end of August the Catacombs club hosted the KNUZ Pop Festival, a major event and the biggest show ever held at the club, featuring the Mothers of Invention, Country Joe and the Fish and Canned Heat in a ten-hour show for just five bucks. The Moving Sidewalks, along with Neal Ford and the Fanatics and Matchbox, were to be the local support. But disgruntled with the way Ames Productions were handling their album the band decided, on the spur of the moment, to miss the gig and drive out to Los Angeles instead. They played Gazzarri's and The Galaxy on Sunset Strip minus organist Tom Moore, who assumed they were having him on and refused to get out of bed when they pulled up outside his house at midnight, trailer loaded with their equipment. He was left to explain the band's no-show to Steve Ames alone.

Things got worse soon after when Moore was drafted to fight in Vietnam; the Moving Sidewalks continued playing as a trio, but started to feel like they were chasing their own tail, going round in circles playing the same old club circuit, while their album release date was continuously put back. Following a performance at Spring Branch High School Senior Prom in May 1969, the Moving Sidewalks parted company with Ames Productions. By this time they already knew that *Flash* was dated in its psychedelic trickery, as well as being too in thrall to Hendrix, and the remaining trio were desperate to go back into the studio to record new material, which Ames refused to allow. The final straw came when Don Summers too was drafted, and on the 6th and 7th of June the Moving Sidewalks played their final shows at Love Street Light Circus. Against their wishes, *Flash* was finally released at the end of August.

Gibbons and drummer Dan Mitchell were determined to carry on however, and with Steve Ames out of the picture they signed a management contract with an ambitious Texan music impresario in his early thirties named Bill Ham. Ham had caught the

Moving Sidewalks opening for the Doors, and had introduced himself to the band afterwards. On the 4th of July, Gibbons and Mitchell were back onstage at Love Street, with former Fanatics keyboard player Lanier Greig playing organ and laying down bass parts with his foot pedals, while Bill Ham looked on approvingly. This new configuration of the Moving Sidewalks also had a new name: ZZ Top.

Chapter 23

If any band should have been in a position to ride the psychedelic wave as it carried an international audience into deeper waters, it was the 13th Floor Elevators. Yet their second album, *Easter Everywhere*, was doomed to commercial failure by International Artists' typical lack of promotion, and Stacy Sutherland's bail conditions meant that the band was unable to tour outside of Texas. On the bright side, the opening of the Vulcan Gas Company in Austin provided them with a perfect venue for their live comeback, a San Francisco-style psychedelic ballroom right there in their hometown.

The Elevators' headlined the Vulcan's second weekend, on November 3rd and 4th 1967, supported by the Conqueroo and Shiva's Headband, and promoted with Lieuen Adkins and Gilbert Shelton's famous Pooh Bear poster and handbill. Though elements of the Elevators' audience missed the old rhythm section and the band's earlier high energy sound, the shows were apparently a runaway success, with the band feeding off the chemically-enhanced energy of the crowd, who for the most part greeted them like returning heroes.

The Vulcan felt like a sanctuary for all the freaks, hippies and beatniks who'd been terrorized and marginalized by the local authorities for years. Suddenly they had a place that was theirs, with its pulsating lightshow, enlightened musical policy, and old Salvation Army booths converted into toilet cubicles. Typically eccentric and DIY was the fact that equipment was brought in backstage via an ancient, hand-powered wooden freight elevator. But most importantly, you knew that everyone else in the Vulcan was a like-minded soul; that you were all on the same trip, with nothing to hide or fear. The result was an unprecedented warmth and empathy, an atmosphere of love and joyous relief that soon gave way to ecstatic abandon when the bands came on stage. Every night was a celebration, and though the cops didn't much like it, they could find no reason to shut the place down. Besides, it was handy having all the freaks in one place, so you knew where to find them.

The Elevators returned to the Vulcan for an equally successful three-night run on December 8th, 9th and 10th, and were also playing regularly at Love Street Light Circus, both the original Houston club and a second venue of the same name that had opened in San Antonio. But the band's demons were on the attack again, with Roky's erratic performances the most obvious symptoms. On a bad night he would frequently forget his lyrics onstage, and had begun turning his guitar up far louder than anyone else and blasting out over the top of the group with waves of feedback and distortion, oblivious to whatever the other musicians were doing. The band responded by swapping his amplifier for the tiniest, quietest model they could find, and ignoring his attempts to steer songs in the direction he favored at the moment.

Some saw this as a symptom of Roky's mental illness; others recognized a commitment to improvisation and free playing that sought to create new music in the moment, rather than digging the band into a rut by playing the songs exactly as arranged on their records, night after night. The original band had often worked that way, but the new songs, with their dense, complex lyrics and arrangements, really needed to be played as they were written in order to come over. Roky didn't seem to get that, as Billy Miller remembers. "The Elevators, at their very best, could improvise, but it was kind of like pushing the whole thing uphill," he says. "I saw them right after *Easter Everywhere* came out and there was no improvisation; it was strictly sticking to the form, and those shows were really together. Although they weren't as powerful as some of the shows with John Ike, I would trade the raw sound for the more polished thing any day. But it wasn't getting them anywhere; it was getting them nothing but grief."

On the other hand, when Stacy Sutherland failed to turn up for a show, as he frequently did, Roky could really pull it out and play spontaneous, amazing lead guitar to cover. Stacy was capable of the same magical flights when Roky failed to show. The Elevators were still of one mind; it was just that the group mind was becoming increasingly schizophrenic. Tommy Hall was still insisting that they all drop acid before every show, and Stacy and bassist Danny Galindo were putting speed into the mix as well. At a gig at Love Street San Antonio, an hour after showtime, former Stoics/Laughing Kind drummer Sam Allen (who was then working as assistant manager of the club) found Roky hiding in a closet backstage, wearing a crash helmet and muttering fearfully about the FBI and the CIA. He refused to go on until Allen announced onstage that any CIA or FBI personnel should leave the building. Roky still spent the entirety of the Elevators' set cowering behind his amplifier, and Galindo decided that he'd had enough. He quit, and was replaced in the New Year by Wayne Earl 'Duke' Davis, a member of Houston's Starvation Army Band and the Grits.

The band also relocated to Houston, where Tommy Hall had been accepted as something of a psychedelic guru by the turned-on teenage set. With a new 15-year-old girlfriend, Gay Jones, also in town, Hall convinced the other Elevators that Houston was about to become the center of the American recording industry. So what if we can't tour, he argued; we'll simply stay put until the stars align, and the world will come to us. In a way Tommy was right; it would just take a whole lot longer than anyone anticipated.

International Artists refused to pay the band a wage, believing they'd only spend it on drugs, and instead gave them a tab at a local waffle shop, while coercing them back into the studio to work on a new album. But Roky was at the very least exhausted, alienated and justifiably paranoid, and in no fit state to work. By this time he'd taken to wearing a Band-Aid over his 'third eye,' and claimed that he was "communicating, but not receiving." Tommy on the other hand was having doubts about whether the band was still the best medium to spread his message. While his esoteric studies continued unabated, and his all-encompassing mystical-scientific philosophy maintained its onward evolution, he preferred to directly lecture audiences before shows, sometimes for up to an hour, rather than attempt to condense his ideas into lyrics for new songs. Accordingly he was happy for Stacy, who had a stockpile of his own material waiting, to take the reins on the next album. Tommy would resume control on the record after that, which he'd already provisionally titled *Beauty And The Beast*.

Stacy and drummer Danny Thomas were the only constant presences in Gold Star Studios, with first Danny Galindo and then Duke Davis also usually on hand. Tommy and Roky would contribute only intermittently; Tommy was more fired up by the lecture-workshop-revival meetings he was holding regularly at his large basement apartment on Louisiana Street, where Houston's hip intelligentsia would gather to smoke dope and DMT and hear him talking at length about his ideas, which increasingly drew on Christian Mysticism and Gnostic Heresies. This further alienated him from Stacy, who felt that specifically Christian imagery shouldn't be twisted and manipulated in the band's music. Tommy meanwhile detested Stacy's use of speed and, as the pressures from the record company and the law grew heavier, heroin.

At the last full Elevators shows, which mostly took place at Love Street Light Circus during March 1968, Tommy took to performing a bizarre song called *Jerusalem Supersonic Highway*. This was never recorded but was apparently just a lengthy drone piece over which Tommy would scream and moan "Jerusalem" over and over again. The song related to his idea that Texas was the new Holy Land, with Houston as the New Jerusalem; the "supersonic highway" referred to the city being the focal point for space exploration, and mankind's evolution off this planet and out into the universe.

On April 8th Roky bailed out of a major show at the San Antonio HemisFair and ended up back at his mother's, where he stayed in bed for three weeks, occasionally being dragged out into town by friends or hangers-on where he was inevitably plied with acid or other drugs by star-struck, well-meaning fans. Eventually he had a breakdown, screaming and speaking gibberish in the middle of the night, out by the family swimming pool his father had designed, and into which he'd dived and broken his leg as a child. Evelyn took him to Austin's Holy Cross Hospital, where he was sedated and kept under observation for a fortnight.

It was clear to most observers that the Elevators were over. Duke Davis wisely walked away from the mess, so Stacy and Danny Thomas convinced Ronnie Leatherman to return as a hired hand, in order to complete the band's third album. He moved in with Stacy and Danny at Funky Mansions, a Houston flophouse where International Artists paid the minimal rent. Everyone in the place was injecting speed and/or smack; Stacy may have been the one original Elevator who was still fiercely loyal to the idea of the band, but in such conditions his morale was swiftly sinking through the floorboards.

International Artists booked an Elevators comeback show at the Baytown Safari Club on July 12th. Ronnie Leatherman was playing bass, while Lost And Found drummer Steve Webb, who had demonstrated an impressive Roky scream on that band's album, was brought along as Roky's understudy. In fact it seems IA had no intention of having Roky perform that night, as the day before the show the label, in collusion with Evelyn Erickson, had Roky committed to Hedgecroft Private Mental Hospital in Houston. Moreover, at the end of the band's performance, which by all accounts went pretty well, the local police arrested Danny Thomas for supplying Roky with drugs.

Tommy Hall visited Roky in Hedgecroft and was appalled to find that he was being given electric shock treatment as well as being kept under heavy sedation. After consulting Evelyn, who had thought her son would just be given psychiatric counselling, Tommy enlisted the help of a couple of friends to spring Roky from the joint, and in August 1968 they both set off for San Francisco, with the hope of starting a new incarnation of the Elevators out there, away from International Artists' control and Stacy Sutherland's drug problems.

The Elevators' International Artists labelmates the Lost And Found and the Golden Dawn were also floundering in early 1968. They too were frustrated by the label's lack of promotion, lack of payment and refusal to either book them a proper tour or to allow them to solicit their own gigs. In the Golden Dawn's case, this was compounded by their deep anger and resentment against IA for holding back their album, recorded in July 1967, until after the release of The Elevators' *Easter Everywhere* in November of that year. As mentioned earlier, when *Power Plant* finally emerged early in 1968, with little or no promotion, the Golden Dawn were written off as Elevators copyists. Unable to secure shows, they splintered under the weight of hopeless frustration, bitterness and external pressure from the authorities. One of the last recorded instances of the band playing is a series of shows over Christmas and New Year 1967 at the Vulcan, alongside the Conqueroo, Shiva's Headband and Wali King's multi-racial, percussive jazz outfit Afro Caravan.

The beginning of 1968 found Golden Dawn drummer Bobby Rector back in Kerrville, playing in a Cream-influenced power trio alongside Ronnie Leatherman and guitarist Terry Penney, called Killer Chicken and the Dumplings. Dawn Guitarist Bill Hallmark joined the Rubayyat, the new band put together by Danny Galindo after his departure from the Elevators. This group also featured his brother Bob Galindo on guitar, plus two other old associates from the San Antonio scene, former Stoics members Al Acosta (vocals) and Sam Allen (drums). They took their name from popular hippy text *The Rubaiyat of Omar Khayyam*, but changed the spelling to avoid copyright issues; the only problem was that none of the band could remember what the correct spelling was meant to be. To make matters more confusing, during their short existence they were also sometimes billed as the Electric Rubaiyat.

The Rubayyat played regularly at Love Street Light Circus, and managed a dozen or so shows at the Vulcan Gas Company between February and April 1968. They lasted just long enough to release one single on International Artists, a cover of Tim Hardin's *If I Were a Carpenter*, backed by a Bobby Hallmark-Dan Galindo original, *Ever Ever Land*. Though apparently unrepresentative of their live set, the single is a minor gem, fusing Elevators/Golden Dawn-style garage rock with the acid-blasted, desperately utopian visions of some post-Dylan folk troubadour. There's something too of the more straightforward moments of the Red Crayola in the troubled, questing fragility of the performances, as well as the Velvet Underground's tough, wounded idealism. Hallmark's spiraling raga-tinged fuzz guitar is a highlight of *If I Were a Carpenter*, which also features backing vocals from Cassell Webb of the Mind's Eye, and later the Children.

The Rubayyat had broken up by the summer, with Dan Galindo moving on to form New Atlantis alongside legendary Austin guitarist Jim Mings, drummer Jay Meade and keyboardist Mike Reid. They played the Vulcan Gas Company at the end of July, and many times thereafter; a recording session with Sonobeat in October 1968 yielded half a dozen songs, but none were ever released. By 1969, Jim Mings and Mike Reid had been replaced by Bob Galindo and Roky Erickson's younger brother Mikel on lead guitar. The demise of the Golden Dawn was sealed when George Kinney and Tom Ramsey were busted on drugs charges in mid-1968; Ramsey joined the army to escape jail, while

Kinney fled to San Francisco and essentially spent the next couple of years living as a fugitive, passing in and out of Texas on a false ID.

The Lost And Found fared only slightly better. Their debut album was released in the fall of 1967, its title ambiguous; though it's now generally known as *Everybody's Here* (as printed in large letters on the rear sleeve), it's also been referred to as *Forever Lasting Plastic Words* (as printed in small letters on the front). The spine had no title at all, and no reviews were forthcoming to clarify the situation. A lack of shows outside the south and paltry sales compounded the aura of mystique around the band; too much mystique, as Spinal Tap may have said. Nevertheless, the Lost And Found played regularly at the Vulcan Gas Company during the first three months of 1968, and began recording a second album.

Alas, the only tracks to see the light of day emerged on a new single, though it was arguably the best thing the band ever recorded. Pete Black's *When Will You Come Through* was a pulverizing, swaggering beast of a song, bristling with fuzz and madness, while Black himself was the subject of James Harrell and George Banks' *Professor Black* on the B-side. Produced by International Artists' founder Fred Carroll, both tracks sound like the Yardbirds at their heaviest, but shot through with unmistakable Texas grit. The tragic irony is that, on the evidence of these tracks, the Lost And Found could have come through to the heavier musical climate of the late sixties and early seventies far better than most of their peers.

One other song emerged from the aborted album sessions, an unfinished-sounding but intriguing demo piece called *25 MPH*. Consisting mainly of a speeding rollercoaster bassline, barely audible acoustic guitar strums and percussion, and a curiously unsettled vocal that seems to be reporting from the darkness of a backstage closet in the midst of some overwhelming chemical trip, it's an enigmatic final dispatch from the Lost And Found. In the spring of 1968 the band were sent out on a 30-date tour of Texas, Louisiana and Alabama supporting Sean Bonniwell's black-clad LA garage-punks the Music Machine, still riding the slipstream of their sole hit, *Talk Talk*. When they returned IA informed them that not only should they not expect to see any money from the tour, or from their records, but that they were in fact deeply in debt to the record company. This was the final straw, and the Lost And Found split up, though they were still financially and legally obligated to work off their contract to IA.

It would appear from the evidence that, with both the 13th Floor Elevators and the Lost And Found falling apart at the seams, IA simply decided to merge the two bands. Thus, following the July 12th show at Baytown, at which Steve Webb stood in for Roky, an ersatz Elevators consisting of Steve Webb, Stacy Sutherland, Danny Thomas and Ronnie Leatherman played in Corpus Christi, San Antonio and Houston before all concerned realized it wasn't working out. The label's next plan was to pair Stacy and Danny with the Lost And Found's Pete Black and James Harrell, as "Stacy and the 13th Floor Elevators." Oddly, it appears that Pete Black took up the bass guitar, while Harrell played Roky, handling rhythm guitar and vocals, a reversal of their roles in the Lost And Found.

This line-up headlined three nights at the Vulcan Gas Company on the 29th, 30th and 31st of August, supported by New Atlantis; an event billed, appropriately, as "The Delightful Demoniacal Grackle Debacle." Gilbert Shelton's monochrome poster painted the event as some kind of blackly comical wake for the whole scene, for a whole era that was suddenly, obviously lost. The Grackle birds, like the bands and their fans, were still dancing on the edge of the abyss as their dreams caved in around them.

Stacy's Elevators played at most a dozen gigs, and those under extreme protest, promoting the 13th Floor Elevators *'Live'* album, which only added insult to injury. In lieu of any other new product, 'Live' was released by IA in August 1968, and consisted of old studio recordings (including some drawn from the original Contact demos) augmented with ridiculously dispro-portionate levels of fake applause, screams and cheers, appar-ently taken from the recording of a boxing match, and clumsily cut into the actual songs at random intervals, as well as between the tracks. There was even a corny introduction from an anonymous and highly inauthentic MC. Though such fake live albums were commonplace in the 1960s, and now have a certain kitsch appeal, the record seemed to mock the Elevators' once-solid reputation as a genuinely incredible live act. This had already been tarnished by their increasing unreliability, not to mention the fact that the real band had already broken up; now it was as though they were admitting that they could never cut it onstage, and had to resort to this obvious sham of a fake live LP.

At least the album made available some previously unreleased material, namely the early demo *You Can't Hurt Me Anymore*, Powell St John's plaintive *You Gotta Take That Girl*, and strong covers of *I'm Gonna Love You Too*, *Everybody Needs Somebody to Love* and Bo Diddley's *Before You Accuse Me*, origi-nally only available on the B-side of *Levitation*. Few considered this though, and in the summer of 1968 the 13th Floor Elevators reputation lay in tatters, their comrades in the sacred quest all fallen by the wayside as well. With its admittedly impressive, apocalyptic sleeve art, 'Live' might as well have been called 'Dead', so resoundingly did it sound this once great band's death knell. Danny Thomas later said that by the end of 1968 everyone was in jail, in a mental hospital or had run to California. And maybe it was in California that the Texan psychedelic movement would have its glorious last stand.

Chapter 24

Powell St John had arrived in San Francisco in December 1966. After leaving Austin in the wake of the Charles Whitman shootings, he'd spent some three months in Mexico, studying his beloved cacti and soaking up the scene, before hitching a ride with a carload of students from the American University in Mexico City. After two days and nights of travelling, Powell was deposited on the doorstep of a household of ex-pat Texans, with just $20 to his name. He survived for the next two months by collecting the deposits on discarded cans and bottles, overjoyed to be taking in the sights and sounds of the big city as the summer of love got underway. "Powell St John used to just get on the bus and ride all day in San Francisco," his Conqueroo buddy Charlie Prichard recalled to *Terrascope*. "Get on the bus, sit there with his little book and write weird shit out... The other guy that used to do that was Richard Brautigan. They'd run into each other on the bus."

Luckily, Powell St John had fallen in with the so-called 'Texan Mafia' already ensconced in the city, who had done their best to aid Janis Joplin and the Elevators, among others, in making a go of life on the California coast. For many Texans, San Francisco was a home from home, and indeed much that would be celebrated and mythologized about San Francisco in the late sixties would be created from the hard work, talent and innovation of these Lone Star State renegades. Probably the most influential was Chet Helms at the Avalon Ballroom, but second place must surely go to Travis Rivers, whose profile was not so high, but who nevertheless remained a crucial catalyst, making connections, facilitating meetings and nurturing talent. Rivers' importance in Janis Joplin's career, and to a lesser extent that of the Elevators, has already been outlined; now the Texan fixer would take a drifting Powell St John in hand, and introduce him to the musicians that would make up the initial iteration of perhaps the definitive 1960s Texacali rock band: Mother Earth. Travis had opened a second-hand bookstore in Haight-Ashbury in November 1966 that he immediately leased out to the Print Mint psychedelic poster gallery and shop. He also partitioned off the back section of the store and gave this over to the newly-launched *San Francisco Oracle*, the world's first psychedelic newspaper, thus effectively becoming the paper's publisher. Though often accused of romanticizing the Haight-Ashbury scene and glossing over the harsh reality of street life, the utopian, pro-acid, anti-heroin and anti-establishment *SF Oracle* was vital in disseminating the San Francisco psychedelic vision via its iconic artwork, essays, poetry, listings and music coverage. Many hippy kids also earned their only income by street-selling the *Oracle* during its approximately 18-month existence.

The *Oracle* further increased Travis's web of connections and contacts, and early in 1967 he introduced Powell St John to Ira Kamin, an organist newly arrived from Chicago and looking to put together a band. Kamin also knew a young blues singer from Madison, Wisconsin who was living in Berkeley, called Tracy Nelson, and the three of them decided to work together. After they'd added 18-year-old guitarist Herbie 'Five Pack' Thomas, Travis Rivers somehow convinced the then rhythm section of the Sir Douglas Quintet to quit and join up with this still untested new group. As a result, the first line-up of Mother Earth was completed by future Dr Hook bassist Jance Garfat, pianist Wayne Talbert and Texan drummer George Rains.

Rains had been a member of the original Wigs in Austin, alongside Boz Scaggs, who by this point was also plying his trade in San Francisco, having been reunited with his old Dallas schoolmate Steve Miller. Miller had been playing blues in Chicago with Barry Goldberg, before returning to Texas where he found a job as a janitor at Jack Maxon's recording studio in Fort Worth. A season of songwriting and studying recording techniques preceded his move to the West Coast, where he put together the Steve Miller Blues Band, soon dropping the 'blues' in deference to the more eclectic SF acid-rock styles he was starting to take on board. Scaggs meanwhile had been bumming around Europe following the dissolution of the Wigs, even recording a solo album for Polydor in Sweden. A postcard from Miller, strongly urging him to come to San Francisco to play guitar in the Steve Miller Band, arrived in timely fashion just as Scaggs' money was starting to run out. He duly accepted the offer, and joined the group in September 1967, just before they signed to Capitol Records for a ground-breaking $885,000 (to be paid out over five years).

Though all concerned would later drift into the middle of the road like sleep-deprived truckers, the first two Steve Miller Band albums, on which Scaggs shares guitar duties, vocals and to an extent songwriting, are overlooked gems of San Francisco psychedelic rock. Both from 1968, *Children Of The Future* was mostly written by Miller in Fort Worth, and vibrates with imagination and potential, while *Sailor* is rated by many as not only Miller's finest work, but among the very best albums of its era. Starting with a strong blues base, they extend into electronic effects and sound collages, jazz-inspired riffing, feedback manipulation, pulsating organ drones and spaced-out choral harmonies, and are prime examples of the acid-inspired fusion music that was at the cutting edge of late-sixties rock.

Mother Earth and the Steve Miller Band shared a close relationship; indeed, Tracy Nelson and Steve Miller had been an item for a while, and Nelson's heart-wrenching signature song, *Down So Low*, was written about their break-up. Ira Kamin knew Miller from his Chicago blues days, as well as future Electric Flag members Mike Bloomfield, Barry Goldberg and Nick Gravenites. When the Steve Miller Band had to pull out of a support slot for Donovan at the Winterland Auditorium at the last minute they told Mother Earth, who cut short their set at the Matrix in order to fulfil the engagement, a gig that greatly increased their profile.

Mother Earth played many benefits and free shows to build up their fan base, and soon became much-loved fixtures of the San Francisco scene. "Playing with Mother Earth was the fulfilment of a dream for me," Powell St John told *Terrascope*. "With a Hammond organ on one side of the stage, a piano on the other, guitar, bass and drums in between and two vocalists up front, the power was exhilarating." He noted too that in the early days the experienced rhythm section could fill in as a jazz trio when they ran out of songs.

Only a year after they formed, Mother Earth signed to Mercury Records and began work on their debut album. However the line-up had changed somewhat by this point, with founder Ira Kamin resigning and Wayne Talbert replaced by former Butterfield Blues Band pianist Mark Naftalin. Herbie Thomas and Jance Garfat were also out. "We had to replace the guitar and bass player from the original group, because they were lame assholes," Tracy Nelson told the *Austin Chronicle's* Bill Bentley in 2005. But with recording about to begin on their album, replacements were needed urgently. Boz Scaggs came up with the answer: Bob Arthur and John 'Toad' Andrews, who had completed the original Wigs line-up with him and George Rains, and who had later played with Powell St John in the Chelsea. Travis Rivers made the call, and the pair rocked up in SF and began work the next day.

Powell St John was never a full-time member of the Chelsea, but 'sat in' regularly, as did a number of other players. Among these was David 'Spider' Price, who for a time shadowed John Andrews as the Chelsea's rhythm guitarist, replacing his older brother by virtue of being able to play louder. Price had also been a college buddy of Mike Nesmith in San Antonio, and when Nesmith landed his part in the *Monkees* TV show in 1966 he invited Price to join him out in Hollywood. David Price went from being an unofficial member of the Chelsea to landing the job of Monkee Davy Jones's stand-in, and appeared as an extra in most episodes of the hugely popular program.

Nesmith was born in Houston and raised in Dallas, where his mother famously invented typewriter correction fluid, AKA liquid paper. Leaving school without any qualifications, he had enrolled in the Air Force and then attended San Antonio Community College, where he'd met David Price, and also formed a locally successful folk duo with John London, who would prove a long-term musical collaborator. In 1963 the pair moved to Los Angeles and started making waves in the city's folk clubs. By the time he auditioned to be one of "four insane boys" in *The Monkees*, Nesmith was not only already an experienced musician and songwriter, but a married man in his mid-twenties with a two-year-old son of his own.

As such, it was hardly surprising that Nesmith should strive to retain a life and a creative output outside of the hurricane of Monkeemania that he soon found himself at the center of. The Monkees' albums may have initially featured mostly session musicians and production-line pop, but Nesmith was able to get his own songs onto the LPs and into the shows from the beginning, also producing his own compositions. On the Monkees set he was known for surrounding himself with old friends, such as David Price, a coterie quickly dubbed the "San Antonio Mafia" by the cast and crew. And Nesmith also became friendly with a couple of LA singer-songwriter-musician-actors named Chris Ducey and Craig Smith.

Ducey and Smith had been cast in a pre-*Monkees* TV show called *The Happeners*, about a fictitious Greenwich Village folk trio. This was cancelled when *The Monkees* took off, and was never aired, but Smith had also auditioned, unsuccessfully, for *The Monkees*, and bonded with Nesmith over their shared background in the LA folk scene. In 1966 Ducey and Smith had recorded a couple of singles for Capitol as Chris and Craig before being dropped, but the following year Nesmith decided to help relaunch them as a psych-tinged folk-rock group called the Penny Arkade, with the line-up completed by bassist Don Glut and 19-year-old drummer Bobby Donaho, still reasonably fresh from his time with Corpus Christi's Bad Seeds.

Donaho had vaguely known Nesmith and his wife Phyllis back in Texas, and was in Los Angeles playing pick-up gigs with Rod Prince following the collapse of their New Seeds. Donaho met the other members of the Penny Arkade for the first time at Nesmith's palatial Hollywood home, where the woolly-hatted Monkee outlined his vision for the new group. They would be more positive and upbeat than most of the other heavy groups around, they would wear matching expensive blue suits, and they would all have their hair styled by Monkee barber Michael Graber. As well as having his waist-length blond locks shorn, Donaho was required to adopt the new nickname 'Dunny' (Don Glut, an avid comics collector, was renamed Captain Marvel, or just Marvel for short).

The Penny Arkade played their coming-out show at the Christmas 1967 party for Screen Gems, the Monkees' publishers, before a heavyweight industry audience. They were a decent band and recorded an album's worth of material, but for various reasons never secured a record deal. Craig Smith however was making money writing songs for other artists; his *Salesman* opened the fourth Monkees album, *Pisces, Aquarius, Capricorn and Jones*, and he also placed tracks with Glen Campbell and Andy Williams. He used this windfall to go travelling to India and Tibet, and returned with a shaven head, a prominent spider tattoo on his forehead and a radically changed outlook on life, under the name of Maitreya Kali.

With Smith/Maitreya now unanimously declared too weird to work with, the Penny Arkade struggled on as a trio, and briefly added lead guitarist Dave Turner. But by this time (early 1968) Nesmith had lost interest in the concept, and had a new musical vision he wanted to pursue. Chris Ducey, Don Glut and Bobby

Donaho were convinced by the Texan Monkee that they should fold the Penny Arkade into a new heavy country-blues-rock band, to be called Armadillo. The other members were to be David 'Spider' Price, plus his old Chelsea bandmates John 'Toad' Andrews and Bob Arthur.

"I got a call from my friend Spider Price," John Andrews told the *Austin Chronicle;* he had spent the intervening year or so playing the blues around Houston. "He'd been pals in San Antonio with Michael Nesmith, who hired him to work on *The Monkees* as a stand-in for Davy Jones. Spider said Nesmith wanted to put together a white Texas blues band called the Armadillo. I drove to LA and got Bob Arthur to meet me there. He was just getting out of the Army, where he'd been on the DMZ in Korea. We put the group together and would rehearse at Nesmith's big house up on Mulholland Drive. Then we played around the San Fernando Valley, and three months later the network didn't renew the Monkees' show, so the money dried up."

Armadillo never recorded and played hardly any shows (bassist Don Glut remembers just the one gig) before breaking up when the Monkees' TV show was cancelled. Glut would go on to a long career as a writer and film director, his work encompassing science fiction, fantasy and horror movies, TV and comic books. David Price joined Dewey Martin's New Buffalo Springfield, which eventually (minus Martin, but with Bobby Fuller's brother Randy) evolved into Blue Mountain Eagle, who recorded one flop LP for Atlantic in 1970. Bobby Donaho went back to Corpus Christi and formed Ginger Valley with John Kenney (who had briefly been a member of the Zakary Thaks). And John Andrews was in the midst of auditioning for Little Richard's band when he got the call from Travis for him and Bob Arthur to come to San Francisco and join Mother Earth.

Mother Earth's *Living With The Animals* is not a psychedelic record; it's a solid collection of American roots music, drawing on blues, R&B, soul, gospel and jazz, played in an electric rock band format, but never attempting to overwhelm the source material with bombast, feedback or unnecessary experimentation. Unlike the work of the Steve Miller Band or Big Brother and the Holding Company, *Living With The Animals* is not some acid-inspired extension of the blues, but an album that aspires to be as authentic and true to its sources as possible, without ever denying that it's been made by a bunch of young white folk in San Francisco in 1968.

Half the album's ten songs are respectfully performed covers; Memphis Slim's *Mother Earth, I Did My Part* and *Cry On* by Allen Toussaint, *It Won't Be Long*, written for Aretha Franklin, and Willie Dixon's *My Love Will Never Die*. Tracy Nelson sings the first four of these with just the right balance of power, subtlety and empathy, while the band vamp tastefully behind her; yet it's Powell St John's take on the Willie Dixon number that sticks in the memory, perhaps because he has to struggle harder to overcome his limitations as a vocalist. Kept back in the mix and swathed in reverb, Powell hits an eerie high yodel on the verses, battling to be heard against the piercing guitar licks (which may be John Andrews or guest Mike Bloomfield) and the sensual pounding of Naftalin's piano, grinding against the slowly swaying, heat-haze horn section.

Nelson's soulful original, *Down So Low*, is the album's center-piece, with its unusual time signatures and painfully raw lyrics, delivered in a bravura performance that is all hard-won dignity and control. Nelson also contributes *Goodnight Nelba Grebe, The Telephone Company Has Cut Us Off*, again utilizing some tricky timing on a striking jazz/R&B hybrid. This leaves Powell St John's three originals, all songs that surely no-one else could have written. *Marvel Group* ropes The Human Torch and Spider-Man into an old-timey lament, where Powell's harmonica jousts with the fiddle-playing of guest Spencer Perskin, and the Marvel superheroes are just an ironic backdrop to Powell's very human loneliness and frailty. The slow 12-bar blues *Living with the Animals*, also featuring Perskin, revisits the themes of Powell's earlier *Monkey Island*; the struggle to retain one's dignity, honor and humanity when the society around you seems determined to devolve to the level of dumb beasts. Though the album takes its title from the song, it has a more positive meaning in that the sleeve photo shows the band on the porch of a large wooden house in the company of several obviously much-loved dogs.

The album ends with Powell offering his own rendition of a song he wrote for the 13th Floor Elevators, and which became indelibly associated with them; *The Kingdom Of Heaven (Is Within You)*. Mother Earth's version is a revelation, swapping the valedictory acid-preaching of the Elevators' reading for an unmistakable sadness. Opening with an ominous click of muted, echoing strings and a dark, sliding bass, Powell moans through the lyrics over shimmering guitar and Naftalin's swamp-blues piano, before giving way to a gorgeous flute solo from Martin Fierro, where the instrument Powell was forced to give up as a child represents a glimpse of paradise lost. The song dances into a glorious jazz coda as Link Davis joins in on alto sax, achieving finally the sense of pure wonder and freedom that the earth-bound hard rock of the Elevators was ultimately unable to ascend to.

While Mercury Records sent Mother Earth off on tour to promote the album, Tommy Hall's vision of reforming the Elevators in San Francisco was doomed from the outset. He was aware that both Roky and Stacy were essential to the band's sound, but Roky was in a state of complete mental breakdown, unable to communicate coherently, much less rehearse or write songs, while Stacy remained both unwilling and unable to leave Texas. Tommy, Roky and a bunch of friends had set off in an old VW van that got as far as Big Springs, Texas before the engine exploded, forcing the group to separate and hitch the rest of the way to San Francisco. Eventually they arrived at Clementine

Hall's house where they lived off food stamps and what Tommy could raise through dealing drugs. Roky meanwhile claimed he was receiving radio transmissions through his teeth, alternately from the Russians or the Martians, and soon started abusing whatever drugs he could lay his hands on, including speed and heroin, which Tommy and Clementine had both done their best to keep him away from.

Neither was able to offer the full-time care Roky needed however, and when Dana Morris arrived in town looking for Roky, they effectively turned him over to her. Unfortunately, Roky and Dana together just sank deeper into drugs, and both contracted hepatitis from sharing a dirty needle. When George Kinney, himself on the lam from the law in SF, saw the state that his childhood friend and his ex-wife had gotten into, he insisted on taking Roky back to his family in Austin.

"Roky was an incredible person and had been a very close friend of mine," Kinney explained when I asked if he was ever tempted to just walk away from this guy who seemed to be intent on a path of self-destruction, with little regard for anyone around him. "Sure I was tempted, lots of times. But I could tell that many others involved with him were mainly interested in what he and his reputation as the lead singer for the Elevators could do for them. He was my boyhood friend and I had little taste for abandoning him. The inner circle loved Roky very much."

Even the fact that Roky was in a relationship with his wife didn't make Kinney bitter. "Dana always loved Roky, even when we were together," he now admits. "Roky never made aggressive moves to take Dana away. Dana and I were just kids who had a child together and never had a very solid marriage."

A nightmarish drive back to Austin ensued, with George and Roky hitching a ride with a bunch of old school friends, who were shocked at Roky's condition; barefoot, emaciated, dehydrated and incoherent. They were stopped by the police but talked their way out of the situation, even though the school friends had been in San Francisco to buy acid, and Roky helped himself to a fistful of tabs before going into an intense bad trip, pounding his arms and shouting to exorcise the demons from his body. When they arrived at El Paso, Kinney took Roky to another friend who gave him heroin in order to counter the speed and LSD and calm him down.

The Conqueroo also arrived in San Francisco in June 1968, now reduced to a trio of Ed Guinn, Charlie Prichard and Bob Brown. Before leaving Austin they'd released a single on Sonobeat, Guinn's dramatic, strangely elegant *I've Got Time* backed by Brown's blueswailing *1 to 3*. Both sides were recorded live at the Vulcan Gas Company, though not in front of an audience; Sonobeat recorded there after hours in lieu of a studio, despite the sonic limitations of the big empty space that caused many artists, including the Conqueroo, to be dissatisfied with the results. Darryl Rutherford had been briefly replaced on drums by Steve Petrovcick, before jazz player Gerry Storm (ex- Blue Crew) arrived in time for the single sessions.

In San Francisco the Conqueroo recorded three tracks at Pacific High studios with drummer Alvin Sykes, but these would remain unreleased until 1987, when the 5 Hours Back label compiled them on an album along with some genuinely live (i.e. on stage in front of an audience) material from the Vulcan Gas Company, including extended versions of the single tracks and a number of blues/soul covers. The sinuous, patchouli-scented *Banana and the Cat*, the propulsive, minor-key jazz-rock of *Passenger* and the slow blues *Words Are Not as Strange* suggest the Conqueroo could easily have held their own alongside the Dead or Jefferson Airplane. But in fact gigs in San Francisco were scarce, and Brown and Guinn eventually returned to Austin. They formed a new version of the Conqueroo that played on through the seventies as Texoid, with guitarist Danny Rhodes and Mother Earth drummer George Rains. Prichard stayed in

California, joining the band Cat Mother for one album and tour, before finally returning to Austin in the mid-seventies.

Artists Gilbert Shelton, Dave Moriarty, Jack Jackson and Fred Todd, all veterans of the *Texas Ranger* and the original Austin Ghetto scene, had also headed out west in 1968. Shelton had handed over the role of art director at the Vulcan Gas Company in Austin to his old buddy Jim Franklin, intending to produce psychedelic rock posters for the Avalon Ballroom, and maybe publish the odd comic book on the side. Unfortunately at the beginning of December 1968 Chet Helms' Family Dog lost their vital dance permit at the Avalon following a noise complaint, just as Shelton, Moriarty, Jackson and Todd had founded Rip-Off Press. They re-thought and quickly established themselves as a comic art studio, producing both books and original strips that were syndicated nationwide in the underground press. Though operating hand to mouth for many years, and set up by a bunch of hippies who were, as Jackson wrote in a comic strip for the press's 20th anniversary, "all trying to avoid anything that vaguely resembles work, perpetually stoned and totally without printing skills," Rip-Off Press would soon become a major publisher of underground comix, thanks in no small part to the success of Shelton's *Furry Freak Brothers*.

Janis Joplin too seemed to be riding high, as Big Brother And The Holding Company's brilliant breakthrough second album, *Cheap Thrills*, was released in August 1968 and sat at number one on the national charts for eight consecutive weeks. Behind the scenes however the singer was descending into her own private hell, her insecurities and loneliness intensified by the pressures of fame, success and the need to live up to an impossible image. Self-medicating with booze, heroin and speed, by the end of the year Janis had left Big Brother, the band playing its final show together back where it began, on December 1st as a benefit for Chet Helms' Family Dog at the Avalon Ballroom. Powell St John had seen his former lover and bandmate several times since he arrived in San Francisco, but knew that she was operating on another level from him now. He insisted however that she never changed: "She was genuine straight up front and very friendly always to me," he told biographer Ellis Amburn. But Janis, with her love for the warm insulating comforts of heavy downers, smack and strong liquor, was rapidly disappearing into a dark place where none of her old friends would be able to reach her.

Chapter 25

Back in Texas, Walt Andrus's Houston studio was becoming recognized as the place to go for a contemporary psychedelic rock sound. While other recording engineers still lived in mortal fear of distortion and feedback, Andrus and his partner Frank Davis encouraged experimentation, and the results were classic records by the 13th Floor Elevators, the Red Crayola, the Moving Sidewalks and more. But as early as 1966 Andrus had also established his own label, Cinema Records, and after releasing a couple of promo singles that were given a full release on International Artists, he scored a local hit in 1967 with Cinema's first proper release; a soft pop cover of the Elevators' *Splash 1* by Beaumont band the Clique.

Formerly the Roustabouts, and then the Sandpipers, the Clique were vocalist Randy Shaw, horn player David Dunham, guitarists Bill Black and Cooper Hawthorne, bassist Bruce Tinch, keyboard player Larry Lawson and drummer John Kanesaw. Like the Moving Sidewalks' *99th Floor* on Richard Ames' Tantara label, *Splash 1* was picked up for national distribution by New York's Scepter/Wand label, and reached number 113 nationally in October. Though not a big hit, the Clique single drew attention in Los Angeles for its similarity to that city's burgeoning 'Sunshine Pop' sound, built on the post-surf teenage symphonies of Brian Wilson and Gary Usher, and the deft close-harmony vocals of groups like the Association. This led to Walt Andrus connecting up with an enterprising if unlikely production company, Zax-Altfeld & Associates.

Steve Zax had actually grown up in Houston, graduating from the city's Baylor College of Medicine in 1964 before migrating to Los Angeles, where he met Don Altfeld studying at the California College of Medicine. Altfeld's college roommate was his close friend Jan Berry who, like Dean Torrence, his partner in legendary surf duo Jan & Dean, was able to combine a successful and demanding pop career with full-time higher education (Torrence majored in Advertising Design at USC). Don Altfeld had been co-writing and arranging songs with Berry since 1958; his credits included *The Little Old Lady from Pasadena* and *Bucket T* among others.

Zax and Altfeld both qualified as practicing doctors (Steve Zax became a successful plastic surgeon and in 2000 married Michelle Phillips of the Mamas and Papas), but also teamed up as a music business production and development company. Their "associates" included attorney Mickey Shapiro, on his way to becoming a heavyweight entertainment lawyer, manager, producer and a serious player in the West Coast music industry. Though Zax, Altfeld and Shapiro would eventually work with the Clique, the first Houston band to benefit from their connections and expertise was not one of Andrus' Cinema Records signings, but Scott Holtzman's Fever Tree.

The band's two Mainstream singles in early 1967 had been big enough local hits for the suave and cosmopolitan Holtzman to secure a production deal for Fever Tree with Zax-Altfeld, who in turn were able to sign Fever Tree to Uni Records, the music division of MCA-owned Universal Pictures. During the latter part of 1967, Scott and Vivian Holtzman produced Fever Tree's debut album at Andrus Studios, but with a far greater budget than the International Artists albums that had previously been recorded there. Strings and horns were added by in-demand orchestral arranger Gene Page, whose work for Motown, Phil Spector and Reprise Records put him at the peak of his field, and David Angel, fresh from his seminal work on Love's *Forever Changes* LP. The album was launched on March 27th 1968 with a preview party at Universal Studios in Hollywood, where the band were introduced on stage by actor Robert Wagner.

Fever Tree is an intriguing album, precariously balancing grand romantic balladeering with ambitious psychedelic rock and just about pulling it off. Every slip into Las Vegas show-tune affectation is countered by a blitz of feedback guitar and reversed tape effects, and at times the effect can be like flashing stroboscopically between Broadway and the Avalon Ballroom. Prone to classical quotations (Bach on the opening *Imitation Situation 1*, Ravel on *Where Do You Go?*) Fever Tree are nevertheless defined by the interplay between Dennis Keller's grandstanding, hyper-masculine vocals, Rob Landes' baroque arrangements of flute, harpsichord and clavinet, and Michael Knust's distinctive sustained, overdriven guitar tone. Apart from the three cover versions, Scott and Vivian Holtzman write all the lyrics, which are as consistently evocative and poetic as they are ultimately shallow and meaningless, contributing to the impression of Fever Tree as some assiduously cultivated hothouse confection; elegant, stylized, sometimes appealingly raw and aggressive, but never quite present in their own recordings, enigmatically lost in some endless labyrinth of mirrors.

The opening fragment, *Imitation Situation 1*, sets the scene: Rob Landes playing a snatch of Bach on his organ, a mariachi trumpet curling upwards, and Keller, like the bellowing, wounded Minotaur in the center of the maze, asking why they are all so lonely, in this imitation situation. Then, as though we are too close to the truth too soon, the track is abruptly curtailed, and Knust's piercing guitar feedback ushers in the murky fuzz-rock of *Where Do You Go?* A lengthy flute solo breaks up the garage band groove, and the song ends with a sharp tape edit into a well of feedback.

Next up is Fever Tree's signature song and sole hit single, *San Francisco Girls (Return of the Native)*. On the surface as romantically mythologizing as Scott McKenzie's *San Francisco (Be Sure to Wear Flowers in Your Hair)* and Eric Burdon's *San Franciscan Nights*, *San Francisco Girls* is perhaps unwittingly elegiac, the idyllic West Coast Utopia it hymns already corrupted and spoilt by 1968, if it ever truly existed. "Out there it's Summertime; milk and honey days," Keller croons, over Landes' flute and harpsichord introduction, "San Francisco Girls, with their San Francisco Ways." So far we're drifting among the gentle people of the city's early folk-rock era, as musically represented by the aforementioned McKenzie or the Mamas and Papas. But then the discordant, siren-like wail of Knust's guitar kicks in, with a hint of menace and foreboding, and something other; not just the disorientation of LSD, but perhaps the smell of old wooden houses going up in flames, and tear gas amid the pot smoke. The drums set a military, marching rhythm, the pace growing faster, until the song breaks into a descending three-chord rocker, Keller singing about how he's got to "get back to the bay" and his girl can do what she wants, but she's not going to stop him. The mood of confusion, anger and resentment at reality failing to live up to expectations breaks in a wave of vicious soloing from Knust, before returning to the yearning of the song's opening passage. But there's no going back to the innocent dream of flutes and harpsichords.

A grinding rock reading of Wilson Pickett's *Ninety-Nine And One Half* is followed by *Man Who Paints the Pictures*, Knust holding a single note of feedback through the relentless rhythm of the verses and wailing chromatically on the choruses, before hitting a dramatically gothic tone on the instrumental break. *Filigree and Shadow* is a bizarre and brilliant fusion of existential Broadway ballad and alienated psychedelic rock, in some ways anticipating later Scott Walker and David Bowie. Rolling drums are shadowed by electric organ for a cold, robotic feel, as themes of loneliness and unreality recur: "Masquerade the past, impersonate the real." An atonal coda of stabbing strings and pulsing bass swirls finally into madness.

The jazz-rock of *The Sun Also Rises* and a heavily orchestrated Beatles medley play a straighter bat, before a faithful reading of Neil Young's *Nowadays Clancy Can't Even Sing*, originally featured on the first Buffalo Springfield album. The spooky *Unlock My*

Door shows the softer side of Dennis Keller's voice, before the album closes with *Come with Me (Rainsong)*. This track was recorded during an actual rain storm, which Walt Andrus was able to capture on tape; arguably the most memorable feature of a number that definitely errs on the Broadway ballad side of Fever Tree's repertoire.

Around the same time as the album preview party, Fever Tree also played LA's Kaleidoscope club, opening for Jefferson Airplane and Canned Heat, before launching into a seemingly endless US tour, accompanied, for some members anyway, by the inevitable drug use. "We went on tour for probably a year, where we'd go out for six weeks, come back for two weeks," chief indulger Michael Knust told the website *Psychedelic Guitar*. "We toured probably every city in the United States." It's no wonder that many assumed Fever Tree were a new Californian band, as they hardly ever made it back to Texas, and promotion was focused on the industry cities of LA and San Francisco. Billboards and magazine ads had trailed the album's release, claiming simply "Fever Tree Is Coming." The LP peaked at #156 nationally, while the single *San Francisco Girls* rose to #91, though it was a much bigger hit in the city itself. A second album was recorded in various locations during 1968 while the band were touring, though much of the work was done in Sunset Sound Studios in Los Angeles. Sadly, although it fared better commercially, reaching #83, *Another Time, Another Place* (released in October 1968) isn't a patch on its predecessor, sounding understandably rushed and for the most part uninspired.

Opening with a slow, heavy metal re-working of a track from their debut album, itself barely six months old, is hardly promising, and *Man Who Paints the Pictures Part 2* is lacking in all the charm and innovation of the original, despite being nearly three times as long, coming off as a straight rip of Jim Morrison fronting Iron Butterfly. The jokey barrelhouse blues *What Time Did You Say It Was in Salt Lake City?* is plain embarrassing, and the cover of Peggy Lee's *Fever* is a bad idea poorly executed. The chest-beating rock of *Don't Come Crying to Me, Girl* and *Grand Candy Young Sweet* likewise have little to recommend them.

You also know things are desperate when over seven minutes of side two are taken up with a soporific supper club jazz instrumental, *Jokes Are for Sad People*. The best tracks on the album are the haunting, hallucinatory *I've Never Seen Evergreen*, which features Mike Knust singing over acoustic guitar and flute, like Donovan at his most meditative, and *Death Is The Dancer*, which was a partial return to the swirling, baroque style of the first album, and which featured on the soundtrack of Roger Corman's biker B-movie classic, *Angels Die Hard*.

Ironically, the lyrics to *I've Never Seen Evergreen* were transcribed by Vivian Holtzman from the mutterings of Mike Knust as he lay in a fever. This seems to symbolize too well the way that Fever Tree drifted semi-consciously through their own music, under the (mis)guidance of the Holtzmans. Scott Holtzman had by this time abandoned his former matinee idol look, grown his hair and a saturnine beard, and regularly affected a black cape, latterly adding the management of the Living Eye club and its house band the Lemon Fog to his interests.

In January 1969 Fever Tree came off the road and took stock. What they found wasn't good; their year of touring had left them $13,000 in debt after their road manager had made off with the cash float rather than pay the hotel and travel bills. The fiery Keller, who'd already clashed with Knust over the second album, decided that he'd had enough and quit. The rest of the band, exhausted and disillusioned, also drifted apart. Cream fan Michael Knust formed a heavy blues power trio called the Ark, with Lost And Found drummer Steve Webb and bassist Jerry Lightfoot; they signed to Polydor and recorded an album, but it was never released.

Meanwhile, in June 1968, Walt Andrus' Cinema label released

its sole album: *Rebirth* by the Children, the San Antonio band formerly known as the Mind's Eye and before that, the Argyles. When the Mind's Eye nightclub had closed down the previous summer, the band had headed out to Los Angeles, hoping to capitalize on a loose acquaintance with former San Antonio college student, Monkee Mike Nesmith. Nesmith was cordial but too busy to work with the group, possibly having his hands full managing the Penny Arkade. Instead he passed the Mind's Eye on to English Monkee Davy Jones, who renamed the combo the Children, and paid for them to record a single, *Picture Me / Enough of What I Need.*

Following a row with Jones, original Argyles bassist Benny Treiber was replaced by Mike Marechal, along with lead guitarist Bill Ash a former member of the Stoics, and the spitting fuzz-psych of *Enough of What I Need* was a remake of the Stoics' debut single. With the remaining Children consisting of singers Steve Perron and Cassell Webb, drummer Andy Zsuch and organ, piano and tuba player Louis Cabaza, *Picture Me* was a driving slice of off-center sunshine rock, Cassell Webb's vocal riding a tense, tightly-wound backing, metallic bells and reedy organ mixing in a proto-steampunk tapestry of clockwork folk-rock.

Unfortunately Davy Jones was ripped off by his personal manager and found he had no money left to promote the Children, so the single slipped out unnoticed on the tiny Laramie label in a limited run of 500 copies. The Children played regularly around LA over the summer, with Cassell Webb claiming they were taking six tabs of acid a day, mixing original songs in their set with covers of the Doors, Buffalo Springfield, the Stones and the Velvet Underground, and supporting the likes of the Seeds and Spirit. But by fall they were broke and back in Houston, where they were picked up by Zax-Altfeld and signed to Cinema. Production was actually handled by Lelan Rogers, who had recently split acrimoniously from International Artists.

With orchestral arrangements by the multi-talented Louis

Cabaza, and Steve Perron handling the bulk of the songwriting in collaboration with either Cabaza or Bill Ash, *Rebirth* is that rarest and strangest of things, a Texan acid-folk album. From the trilling flute and rolling drums of *Daybreak*, in which Cassell Webb sings of "Little children in the garden, gathering rainbows and falling stars" in an obvious 1960s generation-gap, freaks v straights analogy, to the jaunty yet acid-spooked *Maypole*, there's something curiously pagan and unusually anglophile about *Rebirth*. With its mixture of fuzz guitar and jazz piano, Steve Perron's strained, reverb-heavy vocals and odd time changes, the marvelous *Don't Ever Lose It* could have been conjured from the Canterbury prog scene, while the harpsichord-heavy *Beautiful* is just that; a stunning, melancholy ballad with Perron's vocals vapor-light over Cabaza's inspired string arrangements, sounding for all the world like the early solo work of Zombies singer Colin Blunstone.

By contrast, Cassell Webb tackles *Sitting on a Flower* with force and power, somewhere between Grace Slick and Julie Driscoll on another heavy jazz-rock gem that has an ambitious instrumental piano coda. She displays a softer singing style on *I'll Be Your Sunshine*, a gorgeous, feather-light ballad the group had origi-nally cut for Davy Jones. But then Steve Perron's fiddle-led satire *Military School* and the even dafter *I Got Involved* sound like the Fugs or the Holy Modal Rounders, cleansing the palate for the near-eight-minute *Pictorial*: a menacing psychedelic epic that starts out with isolated fuzz-blasts of doom guitar over a building organ-and-drum march that grows increasingly frantic, until the song settles into a steady, Jefferson Airplane-style groove. Heavy distorted guitars alternate with lighter acoustic passages and stinging bursts of lead playing from Bill Ash. The closing *Dreaming Slave* is a mature slice of jazz-soul, with an excellent vocal from Cassell Webb, and Cabaza on vibes at the song's conclusion.

Rebirth was picked up for national distribution by Atco, but failed to replicate its regional success. The Children continued to play live regularly, despite Steve Perron contracting hepatitis from shooting speed and having to leave the band for seven months to recover (Cassell Webb took over vocals). In May 1969 Bill Ash left for good, emigrating to Japan with his family after his Air Force colonel father had been transferred there. He was replaced by 14-year old Kenny Corday, while drummer Andy Zsuch was in a serious car crash and was replaced by Jim Newhouse. This line-up recorded a new single for Cinema in the summer of 1969, a great, Stonesy version of Bo Diddley's *Pills* (four years before it was recorded, in a similar style, by the New York Dolls), backed by the poignant *Once More*.

Apart from *Rebirth*, Cinema had continued as a singles-only label, and as early as its third release (*Losing Faith* by Susan Giles) it was declaring itself a division of Horizon Records Corporation, though the address was still Andrus Studio on 3204 Broadway, Houston. On the 7th December 1968, an announcement appeared in *Billboard* magazine that Horizon Records had merged with Zax, Altfeld & Shapiro Inc. to form Gulf Pacific Industries, "a record production company" (in fact, the Gulf Pacific identity seems to have been in use earlier, with a magazine ad for Fever Tree's *San Francisco Girls* on October 5th 1968 proclaiming the record "a Gulf Pacific production"). Walt Andrus was declared president, with Mickey Shapiro as vice-president, Don Altfeld production vice-president and Steve Zax director of special projects. It was noted that they incorporated the music publishing companies Filigree, Arianna, Peddler and How, and the bands they represented included Fever Tree, the Children and the Fun And Games.

The Fun And Games had started out as the Six Pents, the original 1964 house band at La Maison. They released three 45s under that name: *Good to You / I Didn't Start Living*, the proto-feminist garage classic *Your Girl Too* (with the lame *Good to You* recurring on the flip) and *Summer Girl*, backed by the much-compiled killer *She Lied*. They then changed their name slightly to the Sixpentz, and released two 1967 singles on Mainstream subsidiary Brent that already found them moving in more of a frothy pop direction: *Don't Say You're Sorry / Tinkle Talk* and a cover of Fever Tree's *Imitation Situation*, backed by *Please Come Home*. The transformation was complete when they became the Fun And Games Commission, releasing *Today-Tomorrow / Someone Must Have Lied* on Mainstream in October 1967, and finally winding up on Cinema at the beginning of 1968, with the undeniably swinging *It Must Have Been The Wind / Hold Me Back*.

The band were led by singer/guitarist Rock Romano, who had originally been in the Six Pents' La Maison rivals the Baroque Brothers, before switching to the more popular team (Romano was also a member of fellow Cinema signings the A440, who specialized in lightweight novelty pop). By the time they landed on Cinema, the other members were guitarist Paul Guillet, bassist John T Bonno, drummer Carson Graham, pianist DJ Greer and singer/flautist Sam Irwin. When Gulf Pacific signed the band to Uni as the Fun And Games, Rock's brother Joe was brought in on bass and Joe Dugan replaced DJ Greer on keys.

Don Altfeld knew West Coast producer, singer and songwriter Gary Zekley from when they had both worked with Jan & Dean. In 1967, Zekley hit number 25 in the charts with *Yellow Balloon*, a song he wrote, produced and sang, but credited to a fictitious band of the same name (an actual band was quickly manufactured around teen actor Don Grady and an album just as swiftly recorded). On the basis of this success, Altfeld invited Zekley up to Houston to meet both the Fun And Games and the Clique, with a view to working with both of them. With his white turtleneck and rose-colored shades, Zekley seemed the epitome of LA sunshine pop to the Houston rockers, and initially hooked up with Fun And Games, producing their 1968 Uni album *Elephant Candy*.

Elephant Candy was pure bubblegum, albeit rich with sugar-high harmonies, harpsichords and even a streak of drowsy melancholy on the likes of *Topanga Canyon Road*. Zekley wrote seven of the eleven tracks; an over-fizzed cover of the Beach Boys' *Don't Worry Baby* left room for the band's Cinema 45 and a song each from Joe and Rock Romano, the relatively sophisticated *Something I Wrote* and *The Way She Smiles*. More typical was the single, Zekley's insistently upbeat *The Grooviest Girl In The World*, a chunky, organ-led nugget that gave the likes of the 1910 Fruitgum Company and the Ohio Express a run for their money, or indeed the pocket money of the prepubescent audience that the late-sixties bubblegum fad was aimed at. And while the genre did produce some genuine pop classics (I point you in the direction of *Quick Joey Small* by the Kasenatz-Katz Singing Orchestral Circus), *Elephant Candy*, while certainly not without merits, is probably for serious gum gluttons only.

Zekley repeated the trick as producer, for Gulf Pacific Industries, of the Clique's *Sugar On Sunday* LP (White Whale, 1969). This was admittedly a better class of bubblegum, edging into the more refined neighborhood of sunshine pop. Zekley wrote over half the album, while Tommy James, of Tommy James and the Shondells fame, provided the title song, which was the Clique's biggest hit as a single (it reached #22). The B-side was Zekley's *Superman*, now the Clique's best-remembered song after it was covered by REM in 1986.

Though most of the album was recorded with session musicians backing vocalist Randy Shaw, *Superman* was one of the few songs the Clique did all play on. Only Shaw and guitarist Bill Black remained from the original line-up however, with the rest of the Clique having been summarily replaced by the members of another Houston band, the Lavender Hour: Sid Templeton (guitar), Tom Pena (bass) and Jerry Cope (drums), with Oscar Houchins also joining on keyboards. *Superman* is nevertheless a soft-psych classic, it's slurred, sliding hookline "I am Superman; I can do anything" refracted through a thousand paisley-colored looking glasses, suggesting that if it is indeed Clark Kent's alias singing, he should have stayed away from the brown Kryptonite.

Both the Fun And Games and the Clique had built-in obsolescence stamped all over them. The Clique hung on till 1972, when the bankruptcy of the White Whale label finally sunk them, but the Fun And Games disappeared sooner, after Sam Irwin allegedly insulted Uni Records staffers onstage at a major music industry showcase to launch their album. Rock Romano resurfaced as leader of Houston party band Dr Rockit in the late seventies, and has latterly maintained a career as respected post-impressionist painter R Francis Romano.

Both bands, and to a lesser extent Fever Tree, were victims of a trend in the late sixties towards restoring power to the music industry rather than the artists. Once more it would be the record companies, producers, staff songwriters and session musicians who determined product and marketing. One might say that this had never really changed, but the psychedelic moment had allowed a wild, unprecedented freedom in which everything was up for grabs, and self-determining musicians, artists, poets and visionaries could briefly dictate the terms of their creativity. As the leading lights of this unplanned revolution crashed and burned, the industry moved swiftly to re-assert control. Bubblegum music was only the most blatant example of obvious psychedelic tropes being co-opted, while any radical intellectual, spiritual or political content was dumbed down or simply dumped and discredited. The amateurs were ousted as the professionals once again took over, sidelining the young bands they feted while simultaneously siphoning their energy to feed the capitalist machine. Bubblegum music may not have been all bad aesthetically, but it was unavoidably reactionary, signaling the end of the psychedelic dream of freedom and the restoration of business as usual.

Chapter 26

Another band that would rue the advent of bubblegum music, purely for the unflattering associations it leant their name, was Bubble Puppy. Nevertheless, for a while in 1968 and 1969 they were flying high. Following their debut show opening for the Who in San Antonio the whole band moved together to a house in Austin with new drummer David Fore, the former Marauders/Riptides skin-basher who was kicked out just as the band changed their name to the Zakary Thaks, and who was an old motorcycling buddy of Rod Prince. They survived on little money and canned black-eyed peas, went swimming at Barton Springs in the afternoon, and rehearsed all night. They also played regularly at the Vulcan Gas Company, and by the fall had come to the attention of International Artists, who signed them and sent them into the studio with producer Ray Rush. Their debut single was to be a Rod Prince/Roy Cox song, *Lonely*, and for the B-side they worked up a fiery jam in the studio, built around a face-slapping Rod Prince guitar lick. Stuck for a lyric and a title, they borrowed an exclamation from that night's *Beverley Hillbillies* TV show: "Hot smoke and sassafras!"

The rest, as they say, is history. On the single's release in December 1968, Houston DJs began playing the B-side rather than the A, and in Spring 1969 *Hot Smoke And Sassafras* by Bubble Puppy ascended to number 14 in the Billboard national charts, giving International Artists their biggest hit single by far, and in fact their only chart success since *You're Gonna Miss Me* reached #55. The Bubble Puppy single could've got even higher (it was number one on many regional stations and was an international hit), but was allegedly kept off New York and Los Angeles radio stations by the Mafia, which demanded payola from International Artists and were turned away. The band recall three burly men in black suits pulling up in a black limousine while they were in the studio and going up to the company offices, then leaving looking even less jolly than when they arrived.

IA had no idea how to handle a hit. They vaguely realized that the band should tour in support, but were clueless about the logistics of organizing nationwide bookings. Instead they booked Bubble Puppy into a Holiday Inn in Chicago and had them play every tiny club and support slot within driving distance of the hotel for the next six weeks. Bubble Puppy were by all accounts a formidable live act that could blow most headliners offstage, but six weeks working bars in the Midwest do not a career make. Somehow their old Corpus Christi pal Carl Becker, of J-Beck and then Cee Bee Records, got a copy of *Hot Smoke and Sassafras* to Apple Records in London, who wanted to license the single in the UK; but IA, fearing losing control, turned the Beatles down.

Instead, in the band's absence, the label hurriedly mixed the songs Bubble Puppy had recorded with producer Ray Rush in Gold Star (now International Artists Recording Studios, since the label purchased it), and attempted to capitalize on the hit with an album. But on its release in May 1969, *A Gathering of Promises* only reached number 176, and a second single, *Beginning / If I Had a Reason*, also went nowhere. Unusually for International Artists, the album cover was a photo of the band, and perhaps it would've been better if they'd taken their usual enigmatic approach, as the photo screams hubris. The quartet are dressed somewhere between Regency dandies and medieval princes, Cox, Potter and Fore smiling uncertainly while the genial man-mountain Rod Prince towers above them, his oak-thick arms folded across some kind of plastic heraldic breastplate, grinning unreservedly through his lustrous black beard and mighty mane of hair; a Gathering of Promises indeed.

Riding in on a streak of feedback and a tense, stuttering intro, *Hot Smoke And Sassafras* explodes into powerful hard rock riffing from twin lead guitars, and the sound of a tight ensemble playing at the peak of its powers, before breaking down into the close-harmony, pseudo-mystical verses. A nimble, progressive instrumental break completes the impression of thrusting, Viking warrior prowess, and while the song is pure hokum lyrically, it remains a dexterously controlled exercise in perfect musical dynamics, as thrilling a blend of quiet-then-loud hard rock as Nirvana would hit upon with *Smells Like Teen Spirit* 23 years later.

Todd's Tune is an equally impressive technical showcase, building from a behind-the-beat shuffle to the kind of soaring harmonies and twin guitar action that Wishbone Ash would become famous for in the early 1970s. Likewise the near-eight minute *I've Got To Reach You* steps out of the psychedelic swamp of the 1960s and sets its sights on the yet-to-be-born progressive seventies, its late Beatles-esque melody extrapolated into intricate heavy metal jamming and choirboy vocals. The single-that-never-was, *Lonely*, belongs more closely to 1968, with echoes of the Yardbirds and Cream flitting melodramatically through its three minutes of six-string pyrotechnics.

The title track, co-written by Rod Prince and Mike Taylor back in Corpus Christi, contains suggestions of the Byrds gone High Church in its elegant folk-rock lament, while *Hurry Sundown* is exemplary acid-jazz-rock. The blazing progressive madrigal psych of *Elizabeth* should have been a single, and a version of *It's Safe To Say* by Austin guitarist Jim Mings (of New Atlantis) provides a mellow counter-argument to claims that Bubble Puppy are all bombast and dazzle. The final two songs, *The Road to Saint Stephen's* and *Beginning* seem to join the psychedelic folk-rock of Jefferson Airplane to the emerging heavy sound of Blue Oyster Cult and the flash and filigree of Yes.

Undoubtedly Bubble Puppy should have been an enduring major success, so in tune were they with the kind of sounds that would soon captivate teenagers across America and Europe, and draw the biggest audiences and record sales that rock music would ever know. In addition they were all incredible musicians, and still barely into their twenties. Whether their ultimate failure can be blamed on refusing to give in to Mob pressure or the notorious incompetence of the rapidly unravelling International Artists is hard to say. But after two further non-album singles (the upbeat neo-psychedelia of *Days Of Our Time* backed by *Thinkin' About Thinkin'*, which blatantly recycled the *Hot Smoke And Sassafras* riff in a more manic context, and the West Coast flavored hard rock of *What Do You See*, paired with *Hurry Sundown*), Bubble Puppy returned from touring with Steppenwolf to find IA claiming, as they had with the Lost And Found, that the band actually owed them money.

Lawsuits flew, and Bubble Puppy walked out on International Artists; walking all the way to Los Angeles in fact, where they hoped the Musician's Union and the California legal system would help them with their case. The Union however didn't want to know, possibly as a result of Bubble Puppy's LA blacklisting by the Mafia, so it was up to Steppenwolf bassist Nick St Nicholas to take them under his wing and secure Bubble Puppy a deal with Steppenwolf's label, ABC-Dunhill. Legally needing to change their name, they became Demian (like Steppenwolf, the title of a Herman Hesse novel), and recorded one hard-rocking, eponymous album in 1971 that traded the optimism and ambition of *A Gathering of Promises* for an altogether heavier, angrier feel.

Demian is Bubble Puppy redux, desperate to hang onto their careers and adrift in the cruel playground of Los Angeles. The mixture of intricacy and aggression on opening track *Face the Crowd* reflects the sound of *Hot Smoke and Sassafras*, but the lyrics speak of the band's justified anger at their treatment by IA; similarly, the jazzy *Windy City* contains harsh words surely inspired by Bubble Puppy's pointless Chicago residency and the rioting that occurred while they were there, even as the music anticipates the smooth crunch of Steely Dan. And if the gentle *Love People* bemoans the demise of sixties idealism, then *Coming* embraces the technical virtuosity and narcissism that would characterize much rock music of the next decade. When a tougher reworking of *Todd's Tune* is followed by *No More Tenderness*, the title seems to sum up the band's attitude at this time, but the loping, neo-ska strut of *Are You With Me Baby* vaults over Neil Young to anticipate the still-unhatched Eagles, while *Only a Loner* is classic cock rock, fusing the outlaw machismo of Steppenwolf's *Born to Be Wild* with the twin guitar flash of the Allman Brothers. Indeed, on its own terms, *Demian* is a prime slice of country-tinged hard rock, and should have been a contender; yet it sank without trace. A follow-up was demoed, but ABC-Dunhill suddenly withdrew their support, and the pressures of LA life plus frustration at the obstacles placed in their way led to Bubble Puppy/Demian splitting in 1972.

Back at the beginning of 1969 however Bubble Puppy were the prodigal sons, and International Artists lavished all of their attention on the band, to the detriment of the final 13th Floor Elevators album, *Bull Of The Woods*, released with even less pretense at promotion than was usual for the label. Just how low a priority the record was is indicated by the fact that the sleeve art was simply reproduced from the menu of a local steak house.

And in truth, *Bull Of The Woods* is something of a mess. Recorded in fits and starts, seven of its eleven tracks are performed by the trio of Stacy Sutherland (on guitar and vocals), Ronnie Leatherman and Danny Thomas. Only four songs feature Roky on vocals and guitar, with Duke Davis on bass alongside Sutherland and Thomas. Tommy Hall's trademark jug only appears on one song, *Never Another*, though he also wrote the lyrics to *Livin' On*, *Till Then* and *Dr Doom*. The remainder was solely composed by Stacy, with the exception of Ronnie Leatherman's *With You* and Roky's closing, elegiac *May the Circle Remain Unbroken* (which had been issued as a single in the summer of 1968). *Bull Of The Woods* is the sound of a great band in the throes of disintegration, but that's only one of the reasons it remains a powerful and enthralling listen.

Livin' On is the first track, and the only one to feature the whole band playing together in the studio. There is Roky's familiar, behind-the-beat acid-fuzz boogie and unmistakable if fragile-sounding vocal, topped with Stacy's shimmering, reverberating cosmic blues licks. Though he was in the room, Tommy declined to add jug in this instance, and instead the song is augmented with low-in-the-mix horn overdubs. The song seems a plea to hang on in there through the rough times that are coming; the "dead end kings" in "the ice age" and indeed "the space age and the yellow balloons" (possibly a put-down directed at Gary Zekley's Yellow Balloon, and the bubblegum music business machinations that were swallowing up other Texan bands with promises of short-lived success?). Like Prospero in Shakespeare's *The Tempest*, the alchemist Tommy Hall is speaking to us as he prepares to take his leave of this world; he's "bringing in his stocking" as "the times are tight"; yet he may return, to "plant some smoke stacks." In the meantime he reminds us: "good living leaves no tracks; what's ugly is wrong." It's a simple, holistic and ecological code to live by, and though we may miss his watching, Tommy assures us he'll never really be gone; the spirit of the Elevators will keep living on.

Before we can process the fact that Tommy has said goodbye in the album's first number, we're into the murky funk of Stacy's *Barnyard Blues*, which is almost the work of a different band. A down-home love song that separates into loose jamming, it threatens to fall apart at any moment, finally meandering aimlessly off into the fog. Fast-paced and with catchy backing vocals, *Till Then* at least sounds more focused, and was reworked from a song of Stacy's originally intended for a single, *Wait for my Love*. At the last moment however Tommy Hall contributed new lyrics, and Stacy added further overdubs, which only served to muddy the mix; in truth, *Wait for my Love* would have been better left as it was, and is a far superior, more direct and accessible track.

Roky returns on *Never Another*, accompanied by both Tommy's jug and a horn section who sound at a complete loss as to what is expected of them. No wonder, as the song shifts gear into frantic, almost free-jazz mode halfway through, Roky heading out over the edge with Stacy scrambling behind him. Lyrically, this is another of Tommy's cosmic love songs, with lines like "It's no chance the way we rhyme; our pulse happens right on time" and "Our two backs together makes one human."

The next four tracks are pure Stacy Sutherland numbers, and all have the rough spontaneity of uncertainly-jammed demos. Ghostly wailing backing vocals haunt the driving hard rock of *Rose and the Thorn* like the guitarist's own demons; *Down by the River* has potential, but this cracked boogie number proves to be a mere fragment, fading out after less than two minutes at the end of side one. By contrast, the eerily prophetic *Scarlet and Gold* and *Street Song* meander on for five minutes each, jammed-out sermons that only demonstrate just how special the Tommy Hall-Roky Erickson team was, to be able to make such a potentially dreary recipe sound vital and alive. Stacy was an essential part of all the great Elevators songs too, of course; but left to his own devices, struggling with depression and drugs, and with a rhythm section who sound like they're gamely plodding along behind him, he just isn't up to the task.

Tommy Hall apparently wrote *Dr Doom* as an answer to Bob Dylan's *The Ballad of Frankie Lee and Judas Priest*, which he took to be a critical riposte to his own *Slip Inside This House*. So when Roky sings "Dear Dr Doom, I read your recent letter," we should hear it as "Dear Bob Dylan, I heard your recent album," and go from there. Tommy doubles up on backing vocals when Roky seems to meander off message, possibly following the wandering horns on a folk-rocker that somewhat resembles the work of the LA band Love.

Ronnie Leatherman's fuzz-waltz *With You* leads into the album's final and most affecting track; *May the Circle Remain*

Unbroken, which Roky wrote and recorded single-handedly, playing an eerily whistling organ (shades of Joe Meek) and acoustic guitar before the rest of the band came in to add their own tastefully spare accompaniment the following day. Most effective is friend and Houston singer-songwriter John David Bartlett, clinking a chunky glass ashtray which Stacy then fed through his Echoplex. Bare and haunted, like a copse of leafless winter trees, the song is a far more fitting final epitaph for the 13th Floor Elevators than the morbid *'Live'* LP; here instead is a ghostly message from beyond the grave, from a band who are already gone, yet are never gone; mythic, supernatural, living on, the circle unbroken to the end.

At the beginning of 1969 Roky was back living with his mother, and cut a sorry figure when sighted on the streets of Austin; disheveled, confused, sometimes barefoot or with a syringe of speed protruding from his pocket. In the early hours of February 22nd 1969 he was arrested for possession of a small vial of marijuana, allegedly tossed out of a parked car on top of Mount Bonnell, though Roky suggests the police may have planted it. He was in the car of a young student, Steve Kennedy, who was bailed the next day and had all charges against him dropped. Roky though remained in jail and was advised by state attorney Phillip Sanders to plead insanity in order to avoid jail time, a decision that would have life-changing consequences for the 21-year-old singer. On March 12th he was sent to Austin State Hospital for psychiatric observation; the doctors there seem to have been divided as to whether Erickson was genuinely schizophrenic or merely faking it. In the meantime, Roky kept walking out of the hospital, which he was bound to remain in by court order. Well-meaning friends, including Dana Morris, would encourage and assist him to abscond; his equally well-meaning and perhaps more responsible family would take him back.

Roky lit out to Houston, where International Artists booked him into the former Gold Star studios to demo new songs, and even set him up with a handful of solo gigs at Love Street Light Circus over the summer. Playing in Austin was more risky, but on August 15th he made his hometown comeback, in a white suit and top hat, at a packed Action Club. After his first set Roky went out into the parking lot, only to be arrested as a fugitive by the Austin police; though not without some resistance from the local crowd, who saw Roky as a returning outlaw hero.

"That's something that most people don't understand about the Elevators; the rednecks didn't bother them, because they were dope addicts, and so they were bigger outlaws than the rednecks," remembers Billy Miller, who was in the audience that night. "They had long hair, but they were special, they were different. That night at the Action Club, two police cars were torn to bits by short-haired rednecks wearing cowboy hats, who weren't going to let the cops take Roky. But they got more cops. Roky's brother Donny, he told the cops, can I just ride in the police car with my brother? And they said yeah, you can ride in the police car, we'll take you to jail too if you don't get out of here!"

On October 8th, following a diagnosis of acute, undifferentiated schizophrenia exacerbated by "marijuana and/or other hallucinogenic drugs," Roky was sentenced indefinitely to Rusk Maximum Security Prison for the Criminally Insane. He would remain there, in the company of the worst kind of murderers and rapists, doped up with Thorazine and subjected to electric shock treatment, for the next three years.

Tommy Hall had remained in San Francisco, moving from one flophouse to the next, his utopian vision of a psychedelic rock 'n' roll band that would change the way people thought about the world finally crushed. He drifted down to Laguna Beach, a small town south of LA that was the base of the Brotherhood of Eternal Love. This was a so-called hippie mafia, dealing in marijuana and LSD, with close associations to Timothy Leary and ideals not dissimilar to Tommy's own;

utopian acid-evangelism mixed with a strong dose of materialistic pragmatism. How involved Tommy was with the Brotherhood, who were the biggest suppliers of LSD in the world at this point, is unknown; however, he lived for a while in a cave on Laguna Beach before being busted with a large amount of drugs at a festival, possibly the Seattle Pop Festival of July 25-27, 1969, at Woodinville, Washington. As a result, Hall would also be incarcerated for the next three years.

Stacy Sutherland tried to keep the Elevators going with various pick-up line-ups, while sinking deeper into the squalor of heroin addiction. He was still on parole, and it was only a matter of time before the authorities caught up with him. He was sentenced to two years in Huntsville Prison in January 1970, by which time his Kerrville buddy Ronnie Leatherman was fighting for his country and his life in Vietnam.

As the sixties ended, all three core members of the Elevators were incarcerated one way or another, and the band's name counted for less than nothing in their home state. From being near-messianic figures, the Elevators were now seen as an embarrassment, along with the whole psychedelic movement. In January 1969, Austin's Lyndon B Johnson had been replaced as President by the notorious Richard Nixon, who had the hippy counter-culture and the growing "drug problem" firmly in his sights. Janis Joplin and Johnny Winter may have played at Woodstock in August 1969, as well as the Texas International Pop Festival at Dallas Speedway a fortnight later, but this was also the summer of the Manson murders, with Altamont waiting in the wings. The dream was over. And one way or another, the Texan Psychedelicists had finally met their Alamo.

PART VII

YOU'RE GONNA MISS ME

Chapter 27

Sonobeat Records was founded by 45-year-old Bill Josey Sr. in 1967. Josey had spent the fifties working as an industrial psychologist, rooting out potential communists and left-wing sympathizers at companies with government contracts, using specially conceived personality tests. After the Red Scare died down, he became general and commercial manager for Austin radio station KAZZ-FM, where his son, Bill Josey Jr., was an afternoon DJ under the name of Rim Kelley. In those days FM stations generally played classical music, while Top 40 programming remained on the lower fidelity but more wide-reaching AM band. Josey Jr. convinced KAZZ to let him play rock music, and the station became one of the first in the country to play rock 'n' roll on FM.

Another innovative policy at KAZZ was to make live broadcasts of local jazz, rock and folk acts from Austin clubs, four nights a week. Janis Joplin, the 13th Floor Elevators and Townes Van Zandt were among those whose early performances went out live on the station. "Bill Josey was a real pioneer, he was a character," remembers Spencer Perskin of Shiva's Headband. "He was responsible for keeping a lot of stuff going and alive. He did a live radio show where he'd put a microphone in the middle of the dancefloor, and it sounded like a big bunch of elephants having a terrible mess over the radio, but at least something's happening, you know!"

Sonobeat Records was a direct and natural continuation of the KAZZ live broadcasts. The Josey father and son team had access to professional recording equipment at the station, and were well aware of the bubbling pool of local musical talent available to them. One thing they didn't have at first was access to a studio, so all Sonobeat recordings were made 'on location' in the nightclubs they'd established a relationship with through the live broadcasts, but after hours, either during the day or in the very

early morning. Initially a singles label, Sonobeat also distin-
guished itself by recording all of its 45s in stereo. In the sixties,
singles were almost universally cut in mono, for a punchier
sound on AM radio, but the Joseys were making their records
initially at least to be played on their own FM station. Sonobeat
singles also all carried picture sleeves as standard, adding up to
a distinctly boutique product.

In August 1967 the soulful, Farfisa-drenched rocker *A Picture
of Me* by popular local club band the Sweetarts was the label's
first release, backed by the bluesy *Without You*. Following 45s by
jazz band the Lee Arlano Trio and Club Seville crooner Don
Dean, the label returned to rock with the first release by the
Lavender Hill Express, a new local 'supergroup' formed by ex-
members of the Wig, the Babycakes and the Reasons Why. The
Wig rhythm section of Rusty Weir (drums) and Jess Yaryan (bass)
had teamed up with Babycakes guitarists Layton DePenning and
Leonard Arnold, plus Reasons Why organist Johnny Schwertner,
after the first Moby Grape album had inspired them to form a
psychedelic country-rock band with West Coast vocal harmonizing; the Byrds and Buffalo Springfield were other obvious
influences.

Released in time for Christmas 1967, Layton DePenning's
Visions was a slice of melodic, orchestrated pop baroque, with a
string quartet and a clavinet solo augmenting the Lavender Hill
Express's gentle, upbeat folk rock. Johnny Schwertner took lead
vocal on the B-side, a soulful ballad titled *Trying to Live a Life*.
They followed this with Rusty Weir's heavily-flanged psych-
rocker *Watch Out* in the spring of 1968, but it was the flip that
was to prove most prophetic and influential: Leonard Arnold's
Country Music's Here To Stay. A sincere, down-home paean to a
musical style that most longhairs then associated with
reactionary rednecks, or worse, their parents' generation, the
song went the whole country hog with plangent pedal steel,
bluegrass picking, hokey, straw-chewing vocals and a hoedown

two-step rhythm. "Give me more, more, more country music," Arnold sang. "If I ever get to where I'm good on this guitar, I reckon that's the music I will play." He would get his wish soon enough.

The single was released as a double A-side, with different picture sleeves so that it could be stocked in both the rock and country sections of record stores. Arnold had taken to wearing cowboy duds (boots, western shirt, ten-gallon hat) which at first aroused the mistrust of his bandmates, who were still trying to affect an anglophile mod image. Eventually however the look started to catch on, and the Lavender Hill Express would prove ahead of the curve regarding the imminent crossover of hippie rock and country music, one that would be crystallized six months later with the release of the Byrds' *Sweetheart of the Rodeo* album. By the end of the decade, for better or worse, 'progressive country' would be identified as the Austin sound, and dope-smoking, beer-chugging cosmic cowboys would subtly displace the peyote-eating psychedelic voyagers in the city's music clubs and open-air festivals.

The Lavender Hill Express's third and final single was Layton DePenning's *Outside My Window*, a driving hard-rock number featuring new keyboard player Gary P Nunn that was edited down from seven-and-a-half minutes to 3:45 for release. On the B-side, Rusty Weir's plaintive, questioning lament *Silly Rhymes* was basically a solo acoustic performance from the erstwhile drummer and vocalist, who would retain the song in his repertoire in a long and successful solo career as a singer-guitarist. Perhaps the quintessential Austin rock 'n' roll cowboy, after taking up the guitar Wier initially continued in a trio with Layton DePenning and John Inmon, as Rusty, Layton and John, before going solo and hitting paydirt with the song *Don't It Make You Wanna Dance?* as covered by Bonnie Raitt and many others. John Inmon and Gary P Nunn were also founder members of the Lost Gonzo Band, which initially made its name backing former

Circus Maximus vocalist Jerry Jeff Walker. Walker had returned to Austin to establish himself as a singer-songwriter with his own brand of progressive country that he styled 'cowjazz.'

Shiva's Headband also recorded a single for Sonobeat, but considered the results unsatisfactory, so *Kaleidoscoptic / There's No Tears* never went past the acetate stage. The songs were recorded in February 1968 at the Vulcan, as Spencer Perskin recalls. "We did the recording at the Vulcan at two in the morning and all of us had to wear gloves because it was so cold. It wasn't the best of circumstances whichever way you look at it." Perskin describes the resulting record as "scratchy and primitive... I just felt like it wasn't the way I wanted to come out." The single was cancelled and replaced with the Conqueroo's *I've Got Time*.

Shiva's re-recorded *Kaleidoscoptic* and released it on the one-off Ignite label later that year, backed by *Song for Peace*. Famously described in a *Rolling Stone* article by Chet Flippo as the most important recording in Austin music history, the single found the original line-up augmented by keyboard player Shawn Siegel, who would become Spencer Perskin's longest-standing sideman in the ever-evolving group. On *Kaleidoscoptic*, Perskin's reedy vocals float over Siegel's warm organ tones and a steady, crunching guitar groove before the fiddle kicks in after the first verse and bridge. The track is unique and indefinable; definitely psychedelic in subject matter and feel, but even the violin, the most confusing element for many listeners, vacillates between folk, country and classical styles from one bar to the next. "Back then most people in the world of rock didn't even know what instrument that was," Perskin says now of the violin. "They had no idea; 'what kind of guitar is that there?' The music we did was almost like progressive jazz, but coming from rock 'n' roll or actually folk type of roots, really." Featuring Perskin sawing elegiacally over Siegel's rolling piano cascades, the haunting *Song for Peace* is equally unclassifiable; a folk lament performed with the intensity of a rhythm and blues band, but also the deft elegance of young, well-educated white men brought up on the classics.

Along with the Conqueroo, Shiva's Headband were the official house band at the Vulcan Gas Company; early on, both groups had also established residencies at Ira Littlefield's IL Club in black East Austin, which had a sign outside boasting "Famous beatnik bands, nightly." Spencer Perskin's fiddle got backs up just as soon as he got it out of its case, with the instrument strongly associated in the south with redneck racists, and both the all-white Shiva's and the multi-racial Conqueroo initially had to adapt their sets for the IL Club's mostly black audience, leaning heavily into a soul, R&B style. Soon however both bands were accepted and were playing to mixed crowds, with Shiva's Headband holding down Monday and Tuesday nights, and the Conqueroo (who also had a residency out in San Antonio) claiming Wednesdays.

"Fans started bringing little Shiva and Buddha statues, photos that were psychedelic and other crazy stuff," Spencer Perskin later wrote. "Instead of mike stands we used two old floor lamps from our house. Each had three light sockets, so we put in colored bulbs and left them kinda loose so they blinked with the movement of the old wooden stage."

All went well until one evening when Ed Guinn from the Conqueroo and the band's soundman Sandy Lockett were watching Shiva's Headband play. Between sets, Guinn (a black man) mentioned to Lockett (who was white) that they really needed a new speaker cabinet built. Lockett's casually joking reply was "Why don't you get your nigger to do it?" meaning himself. This was an in-joke between close friends, but unfortunately the offending word was overheard by a waiter, who grabbed Lockett by the collar. Another musician laid into Guinn, and quickly precipitated a full-scale brawl. With chairs flying and even pistols drawn, most didn't know what the chaos was about, and the fighting apparently wasn't on racial lines: Guinn took more beatings than anyone in defending Lockett from all comers. Nevertheless, the famous beatnik bands were forced to withdraw from the IL after that night.

The Conqueroo relocated to San Francisco in the summer of 1968; Shiva's made a couple of attempts to do likewise, but ultimately stayed in Austin and remained the house band at the Vulcan throughout its existence. They would also be instrumental in continuing its legacy when the club closed due to financial difficulties in July 1970. "When you have a home, a place where you can keep playing a lot, people can get familiar with what you do, so it gets better," Perskin says, explaining the importance of the Vulcan to Shiva's Headband. "It's hard to just come into a town and give a concert and have that same feeling. But the local newspaper wouldn't even accept ads for the Vulcan. That was part of the purpose of the posters; that that was how they could advertise. They wouldn't carry advertisements for a long time, and the local music writer wouldn't have a thing to do with it."

Perskin had settled on Armadillo as the name he was going to use to self-release Shiva's second single, *Take Me to the Mountains / Lose the Blues* in 1969. "The Armadillo itself, the animal, we just always kind of associated with and everything, because it kind of related to the hippy thing and it was just the strangeness of the beast itself," he says. Texan writer Bud Shrake later pointed out the similarities between the armadillos and Texan hippies, saying that both were nocturnal and lived communally, were weird-looking but tougher than they seemed, and liked to keep their noses in the grass. More obsessed with the creatures than most was artist Jim Franklin, who had started drawing cartoons of them for *The Rag*, and who was ultimately left running the Vulcan Gas Company almost single-handed. "When I thought of it, I went down and I was going to ask Jim to make me a label," says Spencer. "I went down to ask him because I knew he was the expert. He even had one in the bathroom there that was clawing itself through the wall trying to escape. He actually went and got them and hung around with them and everything! There was a myth that you could get leprosy from handling armadillos, but he had little baby armadillos running around. Occasionally they'd fall out the window onto the sidewalk and he had to go get 'em."

When *Take Me to the Mountains* came out on the Armadillo label, with Jim Franklin's artwork, it was another pointer towards the country rock that would soon take over Austin. This was not entirely intentional, however. "When we did *Take Me to the Mountains* there's a song called *Lose the Blues* on the backside of it, which I thought was actually the main song," Perskin says. "When we put it out and people told me they were listening to it on the radio I assumed it was the other side, because we almost did the country song as a spoof. We didn't even tune the guitars up; it had to be as funky as possible! But I think it struck a chord for sure; it was another one of those unintended things. Even though I'd been using the violin, I wanted to be accepted as a rock band and not a country band. But somehow the country-ish songs we did are the ones that seem to have caught on and did the best."

The single was intended as a calling card to get Shiva's Headband a major label deal, and after several misfires, including offers from International Artists, Elektra and Columbia (who withdrew fearing Perskin would spend his entire advance on dope), Capitol Records came through and the band signed for a $27,000 advance. Against Capitol's express wishes, Perskin promptly invested the majority of this money in a venue to replace the dying Vulcan; the institution that would become known as the Armadillo World Headquarters.

"That never would have happened if the Vulcan had stayed open, but that all came apart and Jim tried to keep it open all by himself," Perskin remembers. "They wanted me to give them the money to take over the Vulcan, and they were pretty pissed off about it. But I wanted to get off Main Street there because a lot of negative stuff was starting to happen, a lot of bad element kids were hanging out, and it wasn't big enough necessarily for, anyway I wanted to start something totally new. And by default again, people go out to take a whiz behind this club in South Austin and behind this building where they piss a lot was this great big vacant place, and that became the Armadillo. It was actually a National Guard Armory before, and then it had been turned into a Federal Trade School actually. And then by sort of political manipulation we wound up getting it. They never would have let it to us, but the fellow that actually owned it was the superintendent of the school board, and he had sort of a wayward son that actually looked up to us and acted really respectful when he was around us, and got him to go ahead and let us get in there and rent that place. But the Armadillo in its whole entire ten year existence never had a lease. It was on a month to month rental for the entire ten years."

The man who had that initial vision of the Armadillo while taking a late-night leak was Shiva's manager Eddie Wilson; he and Jim Franklin were to be the main partners in the business. Wilson also claims to have named the club, but there's no doubt that the Armadillo was already a totem animal for the Texas freaks, a fetish or spirit guide just waiting for a body to move into and possess, so that it could lead its people to freedom. This may sound hyperbolic, but for many Austinites the Armadillo World Headquarters is the founding myth of old, weird Austin; the ur-hall where the hippies and the rednecks finally came together in post-psychedelic Valhalla after nearly a decade of conflict, swapping joints and beers to the unifying sounds of outlaw country music.

The Dillo, as it became known, had a capacity of 1500, most of whom sat on the floor openly smoking weed on stitched-together fragments of carpet. Legend has it that dope smoking was tolerated because by the early seventies it wasn't just the preserve of young hippies and blacks; that might just be an off-duty cop sat next to you, enjoying a fine hit of Acapulco Gold, and the Austin Police Department weren't going to risk busting their fellows. When Willie Nelson moved to Austin and re-invented himself as the dope-smoking outlaw country king in 1972 he adopted the Armadillo as his home base, and then there was no looking back; that Nelson was good friends with the Austin sheriff didn't hurt much either. Depending on your point of view, either the freaks had won over the redneck, conservative majority to their way of thinking, or the psychedelic movement had been co-opted and absorbed into a blander, less threatening hybrid monoculture. Either way, as Jim Franklin noted, the Dillo "was where the 'necks met the heads," and soon you couldn't tell one from the other.

As for Shiva's Headband, there was just one minor detail that Spencer Perskin had neglected to mention to Capitol; while waiting for the protracted negotiations to conclude, the band had effectively broken up. No matter, as Perskin was the contract's sole signatory, and from that point on Shiva's was essentially him plus whoever was available and sympathetic. For their debut album Perskin and his wife Susan persuaded bassist Kenny Parker and pianist Shawn Siegel to get back on board, and brought in Robert Gladwin on guitar and Richard Finnell on drums. Re-recorded versions of both sides of their debut single were joined by eight new tracks.

Released in 1970, *Take Me To The Mountains* is a unique take on what would become known as roots rock. Opening with the country-folk/R&B fusion of *My Baby*, Perskin's versatile, keening violin takes the place of a lead guitar, riffing against a solid, under-stated rhythm section. The title track, originally a spoof, remember, sets out their back-to-the-country philosophy in no uncertain terms, with Spencer singing "Take me to the land, it's the only thing I really understand" over a laid-back, honky-tonk two-step, before letting his fiddle most eloquently do the talking. The message is repeated by Susan Perskin on *Armadillo Homesick*

Blues: "I'm going to Texas, I'm going to stay awhile; I don't hate California, it just ain't my style."

Certainly, Shawn Siegel's *Ripple* perfectly captures the laid-back, live-and-let-live, what-me-worry atmosphere pervading early-seventies Austin. "I'm a wave upon the ocean, I'm a little ripple on the sea," he insists, over a stoned, meandering rock 'n' roll groove; "Don't you get no crazy notion, you know you're very much like me." A kazoo solo seals the deal: no pretensions, no arty ideas or aggression, no getting above your station or taking yourself too seriously. Just kick back, have a toke and enjoy the moment. It was all a far cry from the 13th Floor Elevators' and the Golden Dawn's shared vision of urgent psychedelic evolution, or the Red Crayola's abrasive, confrontational stance.

Yet for all his laid-back image, Perskin was one of the most politically engaged figures on the Austin scene, particularly when it came to campaigning against the Vietnam War, or in favor of universal civil rights, and this commitment always underscored his music. "Now they're willing to exploit music people and make money off of them, and pretend that all of that stuff arose out of people just frolicking and having fun," he says. "They want to discount the fact that there was a long and tedious and terrible war that actually brought all of that stuff to a head."

The howling, haunted gospel-blues of *Ebeneezer* betray the band's psychedelic roots, but *North Austin Strut* is a loose-limbed fusion of country, soul, rock and calypso, and *Come with Me* a melting-pot marriage of black R&B and honky hoedown. After this, the harpsichords and clipped harmonies of the stately *Good Time* seem like a throwback to the elegant mid-sixties chamber pop of *Ruby Tuesday* and *As Tears Go By* by way of Nico's first album, before a more layered and sophisticated take on *Kaleidoscoptic* closes the LP, sacrificing the spare toughness of the original for a more elegiac folk-rock version, with the Perskins sharing vocals.

Take Me To The Mountains represents Spencer Perskin's dream of music uniting disparate cultures and attitudes; black and white, redneck and freak, idealistic activist and daydreaming slacker. The Armadillo World Headquarters would make this dream a reality, proving that good music and good times in the moment can triumph over ingrained prejudices, imaginary resentments and past grudges. Yet there's a too-easy conservatism in the album's grooves too, that fails to capture the lengthy experimental improvisations the band were capable of live. Creating true World Music before the term existed, Shiva's Headband added plentiful primo-quality weed, acid and mescaline to wide musical knowledge and peerless technique on stage, and could take off on truly psychedelic raga-quests into complete freedom and rapture. Unfortunately, these could never be captured in the studio.

"We were a band that did new stuff; we actually had a work ethic that included learning a new song every week, and a policy of representing them," says Perskin, a man who considers both Leadbelly and Ravi Shankar as key musical influences. "We played the same little underground clubs all over the state; we had a place in Houston, Corpus, San Antonio and Dallas, you know, and when we came back to a place a month later, six weeks later, I didn't just want to play the same material. I wanted to have two or three or four new items to fill it out, and that was part of what kept us alive on that circuit for a couple of years or so. They could expect something new, and we went through 150 original pieces in a matter of a couple of years. Half of which got forgotten, but sixty or seventy developed into something. Our problem back then was we'd developed the songs into such long pieces of music that we wouldn't have time to play but maybe two or three songs per set, because our songs almost always went on for twelve, fifteen minutes, sometimes longer. We once did a two song set for two hours and forty-five minutes, which was kind of ridiculous. But that was in California."

Chapter 28

With the 13th Floor Elevators sundered, Roky locked away and Bubble Puppy not proving the cash cow they had hoped for, International Artists was floundering by 1970. It would finally file for bankruptcy in April 1971, but a year before that it released one final album, and one of the strangest in its strange, slim catalogue; *Thank You All Very Much*, by Endle St Cloud.

Originally named Endel St Cloud In The Rain (the spelling seemed to vary continually), this was the new venture of Pete Black (guitar) and James Harrell (bass) from the Lost And Found; still under contract to IA, but now freed of the obligation to act as ersatz Elevators. They teamed up with drummer Dave Potter from their old friends Euphoria, and the former bassist with Houston garage band the Iguanas, the enigmatic Alan Melinger, on vocals and piano, who adopted the stage name of the eponymous Endle St Cloud. Potter and Melinger had met during Euphoria's brief but memorable time as a Houston band, and after spending a couple of years out in California playing with the Lee Michaels Band (live and on the LP *Carnival of Life*) and the East Side Kids among others, Potter returned to Space City to start a writing partnership with the now ex-Iguana. Given the former close friendship between Euphoria and the Misfits/Lost And Found, Black and Harrell were obvious choices to join the new project.

Endel St Cloud In The Rain played their first show opening for Johnny Winter at the Vulcan Gas Company in September 1968, only a month after Black and Harrell had played there as part of "Stacy's 13th Floor Elevators" at the Grackle Debacle. Eager to move on from any Elevators associations, Endle nevertheless acted as Roky's backing band and support act during his initial solo shows, and were playing with him the night he was arrested at the Action Club in August 1969. By this time however IA had already released their debut single, *Tell Me One More Time*

(What's Happening to Our World) which, backed by *Quest for Beauty*, proved that Endle St Cloud had their own distinct sound. Over heavy, distended wah-wah guitar, Endle/Melinger declaims on the A-side like a hip priest making the groovy nature scene: "We ask you to pick a flower, feel the petal, feel the stem" and landing on just the right side of camp. *Quest for Beauty* is more genuinely affecting; a ghostly, freaked-out piano number with reverb-heavy whispered vocals that occasionally reveal the odd audible, intriguingly surreal phrase. Subtle guitar squeals antic-ipate the nightmarish glam-rock theater of Alice Cooper, and the song seems like a dramatic overture for the full production that was to come.

That arrived just over a year later, in a sleeve promising "an intoxicating mixture of sex and religion," yet which featured Melinger dressed as a candy-striped fairground hustler, peaking out of the album's title, and that superimposed over a forest scene in the midst of a mirror or porthole, itself set in Edwardian curlicues. In fact, *Thank You All Very Much* is something of a concept album or rock opera, with all the tracks linked by bizarre piano-and-spoken-vocal introductions. Indeed, the bludgeoning hard rock of *Street Corner Preacher* could have come straight from the Pretty Things' *SF Sorrow*, though Melinger's vocals also start to sound oddly like Bryan Ferry on the first Roxy Music album. The western vaudeville and yodeling of *Who Would You like to Be Today?* may seem schizophrenic on first listen, but fits with the notion of a Texan take on post-*Sergeant Pepper* rock theater, while the screaming organ and crunching guitars that subvert the slow ballad *This Is Love* once again evoke a strange, cusp-of-glam Pretty Things, though perhaps as led by Frank Zappa, with Melinger's delivery growing increasingly unhinged. A version of the Lost And Found's *Professor Black* meanwhile comes pretty close to the original (hardly surprising, given the players) but Melinger's vocals and additional lyrics give it a much more dramatic, theatrical feel, closer to Arthur Brown's Kingdom

Come than the Yardbirds.

After a shouted exhortation to "Turn the record over!" side two begins with a screaming maniac demanding that we "Smile! Smile! SMILE!" before heading into *Laughter*, an organ-led glam-psych epic with some soaring guitar from Pete Black. The bombastic slice-of-life that is *Jessica* throws in the kitchen sink and everything else, as "Jessica comes crumbling in for dinner," before Endle cover the other side of that final Lost And Found single, *When Will You Come Through*. Here the theatrical delivery and progressive arrangement detract from the raw power of the original, but arguably make it a better fit in the context of the album. The final number, *Like A Badge*, was plucked for another single, and could pass for a radio-friendly piece of operatic, heavy country-funk rock, at least until it collapses into the slow-motion black hole sound of a turntable winding down to a standstill.

By the time that last single was released however Endle St Cloud had already split, only for Melinger, Potter and Harrell to regroup in LA as Potter St Cloud, releasing one further album in 1971 on Nik Venet's Mediarts label. With an anti-Vietnam War theme, the album was a decent enough piece of work, but for the most part lacked the unhinged bombast and sheer wonderful ridiculousness of their debut. Endle St Cloud's *Thank You All Very Much* stands alone as a glorious folly, straddling the gap between the disturbed psychedelia of the Monkees' *Head*, the Who's early rock operas, and the heavy glam rock of Alice Cooper, Mott the Hoople etc. that was waiting in the wings. Behind the bombast and the excellent and innovative musicianship lie savagely satirical attacks on all manner of sacred cows; religion, psychiatry, education, family and even the idealized hippy principle of love itself. It seems oddly appropriate that Alan Melinger would eventually qualify as a psychiatrist; by the eighties he was a partner in a drug and alcohol rehab center in Denver and also worked with several other mental health faculties in Colorado, which led to him curating a privately-pressed album of music performed by the patients, titled *Art of the Gifted*, that also featured several of his own compositions. Sadly he died of a heart attack in 1987, at the tragically young age of 38.

Euphoria also released their sole album in 1969, though by this time the band was essentially an LA-based duo of founder member Wesley Watt and his old songwriting partner Bill Lincoln, who had returned to California after his marriage in Manchester, England broke down. After the Houston-based Euphoria Mark II had split, Watt had joined Dave Potter in the Lee Michaels Band and had also written some songs for his next group, the East Side Kids. While Potter formed Endle St Cloud in 1968, Watt and Lincoln began recording *A Gift From Euphoria* with top session musicians in Hollywood, Nashville and London. Released on Capitol in November 1969, also under the auspices of Nik Venet, *A Gift From Euphoria* hardly qualifies as a Texan album, but deserves a mention as an undervalued masterpiece with strong links to our story. This ambitious suite of songs, mixing orchestral soft pop, country, fuzzed-up hard rock and studio-based psychedelia (tape effects, sound collages) is well worth your time and rewards repeated listens. Sadly, when Venet was sacked from Capitol and subsequently set up Mediarts, the Euphoria album went unpromoted and sank without trace; supposedly the band toured with Blue Cheer, though given their studio-based nature and intricate compositions, this seems unlikely. Certainly Watt and Lincoln would both later play with the great Dory Previn (again thanks to Venet) before quitting the venal music industry to run a tree-felling business in Northern Minnesota.

Los Angeles in late 1969 also saw Fever Tree reforming after Uni Records demanded one further album. Scott and Vivian Holtzman once more wrote and produced for Don Altfeld and Walt Andrus's Gulf Pacific Industries, and *Creation* (released in

1970) was actually a slight improvement on the largely dire *Another Time, Another Place*. Opener *Woman, Woman* may have been mediocre, piano-led blues-rock, but *Love Makes The Sunrise*, extracted as a single-featured strings by Gene Page and a strong, melodic, but slightly sinister vocal performance from Keller. *Catcher in the Rye* is Fever Tree in show-tune mold, but it's a decent enough tune, and *Wild Woman Ways* is an effective country-tinged ballad. The mistitled *Fever Glue* (surely it should be *Fever Blues*) is pretty dull, as is the saccharine *Run Past My Window*. But the album does finally include the full-length version of *Imitation Situation*, with strings by David Angel, and two great closing numbers, the incense-scented *Time Is Now* and the bombastic, swirling, Gene Page-scored *The God Game*.

With *Creation* recorded both at Andrus Studio in Houston and Western Recorders in Hollywood, Fever Tree now included Kevin Kelley (formerly of the *Sweetheart of the Rodeo*-era Byrds) on drums, leading to live shows supporting the Flying Burrito Brothers (featuring Kelley's cousin, Chris Hillman). Billy Gibbons also made a guest appearance on *Creation*, adding some much-needed stinging guitar work to *Time Is Now*, and bringing the relationship between Fever Tree and Gibbons' Moving Sidewalks full circle. He was also covering for Michael Knust, who by this time was largely incapacitated by drug use, and whose once-distinctive guitar playing is largely sidelined on *Creation*.

Rob Landes remembers that he and Bud Wolfe, the non-drug-takers in the band, quit Fever Tree after the *Creation* tour because Knust was too out of it to play his guitar parts on stage; Knust for his part put the second split down to Keller suddenly deciding that he'd had enough, though this may well have been after Landes and Wolfe had already departed. Certainly it seems that one Grant Johnson played keys in the final Fever Tree line-up, but the group had already completely disintegrated when Ampex Records released the cobbled-together *For Sale* album in late 1970.

The Gulf Pacific production company had done a deal with the successful electronics firm, known for their state-of-the-art tape-recording equipment, guaranteeing tape rights to at least 36 albums over three years, in return for what Gulf Pacific's Mickey Shapiro described to *Billboard* magazine in April 1969 as "a substantial operating budget." Fever Tree were one of Gulf-Pacific's key properties; the fact that the band no longer existed was a minor detail, as there was enough material lying around on the studio floor that, when cleaned up a tad, could fill two sides of vinyl perfectly well. And, against all odds, the end result is decidedly listenable, including as it does Fever Tree's first two singles, *Hey Mister* and *Girl Don't Push Me* and assorted studio outtakes, embellished by top LA session musicians drawn from the legendary Wrecking Crew, and backing vocalists the Blackberries, featuring Gloria Jones. To top it all off, the sleeve is designed by Don Altfeld's old buddy Dean Torrence of Jan & Dean. The seven songs include one previously unissued S&V Holtzman composition, *You're Not The Same Baby*, and creditable covers of *I Put A Spell On You*, Arthur Lee's *She Comes In Colors*, and Sean Bonniwell's *Come On In*, though the 13-minute rendition of *Hey Joe* does rather outstay its welcome.

By the time of *For Sale*'s release however it seems that Gulf Pacific industries too was no more, as the record is described as a Prophesy Records production; Prophesy being the label founded by former Gulf Pacific partners Mickey Shapiro and Don Altfeld. Walt Andrus was out; he was still based in Houston and had set up a new label, Texas Revolution, which in 1970 released the first and only solo LP by the Red Crayola's Mayo Thompson: the brilliant *Corky's Debt To His Father*.

Aside from Thompson, the musicians on the album were all drawn from Andrus's old Cinema Records roster. Engineer/producer Frank Davis helped out on guitar and fiddle, while latterday Children drummer Jim Newhouse appeared alongside Roger 'Rock' Romano (who also co-produced), Joe Dugan, Mike Sumler and Carson Graham from the Fun And Games. *Corky's Debt...* couldn't be further removed from the bubblegum froth of *Elephant Candy*, yet compared to Thompson's work with the Red Crayola it's positively a pop album. Gentle, off-kilter melodies abound, and Thompson sings in a high, keening voice; at times off-key certainly, but always reasonably friendly on the ear. His lyrics deal in the earthy, universal truths of love and sex pretty much throughout, and there's plenty of humor, though Thompson's imagery is characteristically inventive and his story-telling resolutely non-linear. Comparisons could be made to the rambling acoustic blues of Kevin Ayers, the surrealist doo-wop of Brian Eno's *Here Come The Warm Jets* and associated singles, certain Velvet Underground songs, or John Cale's attempts to combine the avant-garde and mainstream folk-rock throughout his 1970s solo career. Ultimately though, and even within Mayo Thompson's own discography, *Corky's Debt To His Father* exists in a category all of its own.

The album could also almost be described as roots music, though certainly not in the fashion that the Armadillo crowd had in mind. It's an over-educated white man singing the end-of-the-sixties Texas blues, with a love and awareness of tradition but an equally strong sense of his own position outside of it. "I'm a student of human nature," Thompson begins, on the foot-stomping folk-blues of *The Lesson*. "I held your little breast in my hand, and I kept my eyes on your knee." A song of desire, loss and regret, but written with a carefully-observed detachment, it sets the tone for the rest of the album. *Oyster Thins* is a spare but complex multi-part rumination on the value of music as a healing and redemptive force in life: "One song in a million falling on our sleepy heads, in our sleepy beds: dreams were always meant to be like this."

The flamenco-rockabilly-lounge-jazz rhythms of *Horses*

contrast with some of Thompson's most charmingly out-of-tune singing; *Dear Betty Baby* is a gorgeous and heartbreaking romantic lament, underscored by LeAnne Romano's baritone saxophone. The romping *Venus in the Morning* is pre-punk in the vein of the Modern Lovers' still-to-come *Pablo Picasso*, while *To You* could be smooth chamber jazz if it weren't so jagged and lumpy. Joe Dugan's piano and Mike Sumler's slide guitar enliven the slow sunset descends of *Fortune*, before the spare and lonesome Rick Barthelme co-write *Black Legs*, which finds Thompson hesitantly accompanying himself on solo acoustic guitar. *Good Brisk Blues* is a full band performance, and could almost have been an alternative radio hit: a driving, lusty number given a nervous, wrong-footed edge by Carson Graham's oddly syncopated beat. Following the cubist foxtrot of *Around the Home*, the album ends with *Worried Worried*, in which Thompson yodels and Joe Dugan plays steel guitar over an off-kilter rhythm that anticipates the spindly, anti-macho of UK post-punk.

"I'm so worried, yes I am worried; I told you I was worried." The fragility and peculiar honesty of *Corky's...* is central to its appeal, particularly the openness about sexual desire coupled with an equally strong sense of confusion and insecurity, and a refreshing lack of bravado. Musically, it sits loosely with the early-seventies art rock that would often find a home on Chris Blackwell's Island Records, but also anticipates the scratchy DIY post-punk experiments that would turn up several years later on indie labels like Rough Trade, where Thompson would eventually find work as a producer. Needless to say it had absolutely no commercial impact at the time of its release, though this was at least partly down to the fact that, without the investment money of Shapiro and Altfeld and their various deals, Walt Andrus's Texas Revolution label collapsed almost as soon as it was launched.

Before that happened though Mayo Thompson also recorded a contemporaneous single in collaboration with Frank Davis,

Rick Barthelme, guitarist Brian Feehan and the Children's Cassell Webb under the name of Saddlesore. Davis sang lead on Thompson and Barthelme's weird western ballad *Old Tom Clark* and the near-Beefheart freak-folk of *Pig Ankle Strut*. Thompson and Barthelme continued playing together around Texas in a band called the Blue Diamonds (sometimes appended with either 'Mighty' or 'Rocking') that may also have featured Rock Romano. They never recorded. "I was making music, I was involved with a few people here and there, tried a few things, had a band in Texas for a while," Thompson told Richie Unterberger. "But nothing ever really coalesced, particularly in the way that I wanted it to. You could get a band together, they could play tunes, they'd be very competent, make wonderful arrangements and so on and it was kind of like [yawns]. I just wasn't that interested. I was always looking for the most radical position."

Rick Barthelme remembered that, in the Red Crayola, "We didn't really want to play well. Playing well was what we were against. It was what everybody else did. Much later, in the second (and little known) band that Mayo and I put together, the Rocking Blue Diamonds, playing well became an issue, so we solicited the talent; coerced it, is probably more accurate."

The Children story had one final act when they signed to Lou Adler's new label, Ode. In Houston for the filming of the movie *Brewster McCloud*, the legendary music mogul saw the band play an outdoor show in Memorial Park in July 1970. The Children were whisked back to California to record a new album, but only two singles saw the light of day: the orchestral soft pop of *From the Very Start* backed by *Such a Fine Light*, and *Hand of a Lady* with the excellent slow-churning hard rock of *Fire Ring* on the flip. Notable demos from this period included the dirty-ass, teen-lust boogie of *Francine*, written by Steve Perron and Kenny Cordray with Billy Gibbons, who recorded it in 1972 for ZZ Top's second album, *Rio Grande Mud*.

The Children were offered a brief tour alongside ZZ Top opening for BB King, and jumped at the chance; unfortunately, this meant having to pull out of a major gig at the Whisky in LA, which Lou Adler had organized as an industry showcase both for them and his new label. As Adler and Ode cooled on their new signings, the Children's drug use was escalating dramatically, and for Steve Perron it got out of hand; the BB King/ZZ Top tour ended with him checking into a mental hospital. Drug damaged and old before their time, the Children broke up shortly after, in May 1971.

Chapter 29

While the 'Armadillo effect' would see Austin celebrated around the world as a laid-back groover's paradise, not everyone was happy with the way things were going. "Austin was the absolute capital for the outlaw cowboy movement, and I actually like all those guys a lot; Willie and Waylon and the boys. But the local rock scene there was kind of disgusting," says Billy Miller, a teenage Elevators fan who saw the rot setting in from 1967 onwards, and felt totally out of place by the time the early seventies came around. "The bands that were popular locally, no-one will ever hear of again. They were just totally middle of the road. People who had been in a number of the underground bands, they got into this country rock type thing, and then they wanted to completely disavow that they were ever part of the psychedelic thing at all."

Billy Miller grew up obsessed with the strange, unique pop singles produced by tragic English genius Joe Meek. "During the British Invasion era people were either into the Beatles or the Rolling Stones," Miller says. "But my girlfriend and I, we were really into the Honeycombs. We thought the Rolling Stones were kid's stuff, and the Beatles. We didn't think that about the Honeycombs. And I knew that they were produced by the people who did *Telstar*." Miller and his girlfriend were pretty much Goths before the term was invented; black-clad, pale, nocturnal and anti-social. Mostly avoiding his peers, Miller preferred to spend his free time on projects like constructing a complete armored Dr Doom outfit (he only got as far as one glove). His other enthusiasm was for the large lizards that he kept as pets; on one occasion his tegu lizard ran away and was placed in a dog pound by the authorities, from which it promptly escaped once again.

Miller was also a dedicated peyote eater, and formed his own psychedelic punk band, Cauldron, who played one gig at a general strike/protest on the university campus before changing their name to Amethyst. For a while Amethyst featured former Spades/Misfits/Power Plant drummer John Kearney, alongside guitarist Tom Mcgarrigle and a variety of fly-by-night members. Miller's own instrument was the autoharp; a not-uncommon axe for folkies, but never played the way he played it, electrified and run through a fuzzbox to give a weird unearthly tone somewhere between Tommy Hall's amplified jug and Del Shannon and Max Crook's Musitron, or the weird, unearthly sound Joe Meek got from the Clavioline organ on records like *Telstar*.

Amethyst, who Miller claims "sounded almost like Nirvana," played Austin's IL Club and the church-run Jubilee Hall, but mostly gigged out of town in Houston and San Antonio. Huge Velvet Underground fans, Miller and Mcgarrigle ventured into the mistrusted Vulcan Gas Company to catch their heroes' October 1969 three-night stand at the club, which proved profoundly influential on their future development. At this time they were looking for a new rhythm section, and Miller met bassist Mike Waugh, who in turn knew former Elevators drummer John Ike Walton. Walton ultimately declined to join the band, but instead made a perhaps more valuable bequest, suggesting that Waugh introduce them to Bill Josey Sr. at Sonobeat, for whom Waugh had worked on occasion as a session player.

With a musician of John Ike's caliber vouching for him, Josey had Miller record a solo demo, and was enamored enough of his songs to sign him and his co-conspirators to a development deal, recording an album's worth of material that could be shopped to major labels. Though they still used the name Amethyst for occasional live shows, the new band was initially listed simply as the Bill Miller Group in the studio, with Miller, Mcgarrigle and Waugh eventually joined by one Hugh Patton on drums. Sonobeat now had its own basic recording studios, and the sessions lasted approximately six months, winding up in spring

1970; by the time the album was completed, the Sonobeat master tapes would list the band name as the Daily Planet and the album title as *Cold Sun*. Later, Cold Sun would become the name of the group, and the album would eventually gain a highly limited release in 1989 as *Dark Shadows*.

Dark Shadows is a proto-gothic masterpiece. Weird and lo-fi and minimal like the best Joe Meek-derived punk, but also steeped in a tense, brooding, liquid psychedelia that pulls you down into the deep undertow of its ever-shifting tide. Ahead of its time? With its utter disregard for conventional verse-chorus song structures or any kind of musical tradition, *Dark Shadows* stands outside of time, belonging no more to 1970 than 1980, 1960 or 2070. The slamming, discordant tones of Miller's mutated autoharp usher in *South Texas*, before Mcgarrigle's twisted fuzz guitar line kicks in, carrying us into deeply dark, Doors-like territory. "You have seen the eyes of the gecko," Miller half-sings, in agonized, peyote-haunted tones, closer to a particularly desperate and strung out Lou Reed than Jim Morrison's manly baritone. A melancholy-euphoric chord change and time slows like treacle; guitar lines cascade down like falling stars. "Behold the moon beaming through your third eye."

Twisted Flower again comes on like a neo-primitivist Doors, capturing all of that band's mystery and ghostly-galleon majesty, but substituting tottering freak-punk outsider art for the near-cabaret, whisky-bar boorish professionalism Morrison, Manzarek and company too often slipped into. As such, Miller comes closer to true, Mescali-whacked shamanism than Big Jim ever did, poet though he was, and *Here In The Year* finds him declaiming unblinking over Mcgarrigle's spiraling folk-rock arpeggios, as though both are stumbling forward with the sacred relics the Elevators dropped held outstretched before them. After two minutes the song segues into an ominous bridge: "It's Halloween; the early autumn winds raise a fog upon the room..." until at roughly 2:30 the song stops dead and the very gates of hell are opened. A shocking, pre-industrial cacophony of sci-fi noise breaks into a brief, Stacy Sutherland-esque guitar solo, and then Miller reaches through the mist, haltingly like a prophet transmitting messages from the other side: "And, uh, you can eat on television someday too; we shall sleep on television someday soon; and you can die on television someday soon; right there on television in the middle of the living room," describing a surreal, technological nightmare world that nevertheless within thirty years would more or less come to pass. The track stretches on to nearly nine minutes, trudging out on vapor trails of feedback, comparable only to the still-unborn mid-seventies Cleveland scene of Pere Ubu, Rocket From The Tombs and, especially, the still largely-unheard Mirrors.

For Ever staggers fetchingly like some impossible mutant crossbreed of the Seeds and Hawkwind or even Can, slowing down to a staring drool then accelerating madly, crashing through barriers of time and space to finally land in the post-punk future for which it was made. "Where does she come from? Where does he come from?" Miller repeats dumbly, over and over, surely echoing the confusion of every complacent cosmic cowboy unlucky enough to have his stoned equilibrium severely jangled by Cold Sun's appearance on an Austin stage. But then *See What You Cause* rides in on a fast boogie, with Mike Waugh taking over lead guitar, though the garbage-can beat and dentist-drill dissonance is closer to the Velvets than ZZ Top. Once again, Miller has his sights firmly set on unknown future consequences: "You may never see what you cause in your present plea; you can try to work free," while at the same time exercising (exorcising?) his best Lou Reed moves with frequent speed-tic asides and overseeing random antisocial blasts of distorted white noise.

Fall is a spitting, flailing outpouring of visions, Miller like a post-psychedelic Rimbaud straddling a monomaniacal garage band tunneling its way through to a parallel universe where music is holy terror and history can still be rewritten: "I'll never go to war; I've been there before." The album concludes with the eleven minutes, twenty seconds of *Ra-Ma*; a paranoid treatise on Egyptian/Lemurian mythology inspired by the writings of Colonel Jim Churchward, and extended to its final length in order to fit in with Bill Josey Sr.'s numerological superstitions (both *Dark Shadows* and Johnny Winter's *Progressive Blues Experiment* are exactly 43 minutes and 15 seconds long). It's a terrifying, mesmeric trip; a journey into Conrad's *Heart of Darkness*, following the black oily river snaking into the pitiless jungles of your soul via some mysterious concoction of powerful plant hallucinogens. If Tommy Hall's lyrics are multi-layered gnostic essays, then *Ra-Ma* sounds like an alchemical treatise, a hidden occult history of civilization no less, in a spontaneously-generated musical setting that represents the missing link between the garage-psych of the Seeds et al on one side and the visionary post-punk of Wire, the Blue Orchids and Magazine on the other.

Josey's intention was that the album could be shopped around major labels to secure the band a deal; the label had successfully achieved this with its most famous act, the great albino blues guitarist Johnny Winter. Born and raised in Beaumont, Johnny and his brother Edgar had been playing around Texas in various bands since the late fifties, but had never played Austin. The Vulcan crowd discovered him early in 1968 when he was booked alongside the Conqueroo at the Family Dog in Denver. Chet Helms had opened a second Family Dog venue there after deciding that a major earthquake could send San Francisco crumbling into the Pacific at any moment, and that if that happened then Denver would be the next major cultural center. He must have been in a similar frame of mind when he hired Billy Lee Brammer to manage the Denver Dog; by this time less a working writer and more a walking drugs laboratory.

Winter became a regular attraction at the Vulcan, and Sonobeat recorded an album with him there, using the club after hours as usual. Although he had occasionally flirted with psychedelic sounds early on, such as the single *Birds Can't Row Boats*, Winter's sound was strictly blues based. However, he wasn't above taking psychedelic drugs for inspiration, and his album, *Progressive Blues Experiment*, was recorded in the shifting colors and shapes of the full Vulcan lightshow, to get the correct mood. Spencer Perskin recalls giving the guitarist two hits of Mescaline Sulphate before his headlining set at the Texas International Pop Festival in 1969, assuming he'd share them with bassist Tommy Shannon and drummer 'Uncle' John Turner. Instead Winter, who'd already taken a tab of acid, had the whole lot to himself, and before taking the stage was kissed by a girl fan who passed another tab of acid into his mouth as she did so.

Josey pressed up 100 white-label copies of *Progressive Blues Experiment* to attract interest, and eventually sold the rights to Liberty Records. By this time however, Johnny had already signed a multi-million-dollar deal with Columbia, following a rave article in Rolling Stone that drew a record company feeding frenzy. By contrast, Cold Sun were unknown and unwanted, and although there was apparently some interest from Columbia, if they hoped for another Johnny Winter in Billy Miller they were looking in the wrong place. Moreover, *Dark Shadows* was circulated on tape, so no demo vinyl pressings even existed.

Cold Sun continued to write new material and play the occasional live show, even after the departure of bassist Mike Waugh. He was replaced by Mike Ritchey, and it was Ritchey who in 1973 had the sole vinyl acetate of *Dark Shadows* manufactured from the Sonobeat masters, just so that he would have a copy of the album to listen to at home. But by this point there were few people around Austin or elsewhere who wanted to listen to Cold Sun at all, as Miller recalls. "I couldn't have been more unpopular with the musical crowd that dominated the scene," he says. "If you speak to George Kinney, he's aware of how you didn't want to be caught dead saying you were psychedelic... though Cold Sun by the way, I never thought of it as psychedelic."

George Kinney was back in Austin and was trying to keep the spirit of the Elevators and the Golden Dawn alive by playing with a loose aggregation of musicians he named Headstone. "I stayed at large for a couple of years, dodging the FBI and looking over my shoulder," he says. "My second wife's father was an important man in Florida and helped me resolve my legal problems in Texas through his influence with the governor." Headstone featured Kinney and Elevators drummer Danny Thomas alongside Harry Buckholts and Terry Brown, and at various times John Kearney, Danny Galindo and Mikel Erickson. "I wanted to get back into the fray after the screw job handed to the Golden Dawn by International Artists," says Kinney. "So I did. We played a few gigs, rehearsed a lot, then faded into history, largely unknown."

Headstone played several benefit shows for Roky while he was incarcerated, and were crucial in making sure that he wasn't forgotten as the outlaw country movement superseded the now discredited psychedelic era. Naturally, Kinney also visited his old friend regularly. The Rusk Maximum Security Prison for the Criminally Insane housed highly dangerous criminals, murderers and rapists, and practiced a harsh prison regime. But in addition to the regular prison brutality, inmate-patients like Roky were given electro-shock treatment and prescribed heavy medication; in Roky's case, the powerful sedative and anti-psychotic Thorazine, which locked his muscles, caused his eyes to roll back and his tongue to stick to the top of his mouth. Essentially he was rendered a living zombie, in which condition he was expected to work on the prison farm like a regular convict.

At first when Kinney and others had brought him in guitars, Roky had given them away, but eventually he started writing songs again, finding ways to avoid taking his medication and, after attending classes to complete his high school education, studied the Bible to the extent that he qualified as a minister. He even formed a band in Rusk, which he called the Missing Links: the other members included guitarist John Walcott, who had murdered his own family while high on glue, bassist Charles Hefley, who raped a policeman's daughter then murdered her along with her two babies, and a motley selection of child murderers and rapists who came and went. They were eventually allowed to play out (under escort of course) at rodeos, galas and even a high school prom.

As Roky's new poems and lyrics amassed, George Kinney conceived a plan to sneak copies out of Rusk and publish them: *Openers* by "Rev. Roger Roky Kynard Erickson" came out in April 1972 on "Pyrimid [sic] Publishing Co., Austin, Texas." Wide-eyed and intense, *Openers* reads like an outsider art fusion of beat poetry and Christian mysticism, its language mixing archaic formalism with the casually contemporary, compulsive wordplay and constant references to love, peace and God, in roughly that order. The results are always poignant and moving, and the fact that the writing shifts easily from greetings-card blandness to strained desperation, to utter strangeness and the occasional genuinely visionary insight, only proves how much it's an utterly sincere and uncontrived reflection of Roky's troubled and questing but ultimately always loving and generous mind.

"There were two main motives for publishing the book," Kinney says. "The first was just the beauty of his words and the sincerity of the way he wrote them; that was the creative reason. The other was that according to the lawyers we had hired to handle his legal and mental situation he needed some form of gainful employment in order to ever be released. Publishing the book gave him something tangible to do when he got out; he could promote and sell the book. As for the actual smuggling, well, I came about it honest, being a natural outlaw and all. I got to know the guards and brought them stuff from the real world and they liked me, so they let me pass without severe searching. I smuggled the manuscript out in sections in my boots, written on paper towels and the backs of envelopes."

Roky was finally judged legally sane and released from Rusk into his mother's custody on November 27th 1972. By January 1973 he was rehearsing with a reformed 13th Floor Elevators, although he and John Ike Walton were the only original members, with Roky's brother Donnie on lead guitar, a bassist named John McGiver and one Johnny McAshan on keys. They played at the Armadillo World Headquarters before McGiver was replaced by Ronnie Leatherman (back from 'Nam) in time for 'The Last Bash on the Hill' at the Hill on the Moon, a huge free outdoor concert on Sunday 18th March 1973. The Hill on the Moon was a natural amphitheater on the way out to Lake Austin, and the location of a large house where various country-rock musicians lived and rehearsed, including former Lavender Hill Express members Rusty Wier, Layton DePenning, Leonard Arnold and Gary Nunn. The Last Bash marked the fact that the land was about to be sold, and even though the Elevators headlined, appearing over the Conqueroo, Storm (featuring Danny Galindo and Jimmie Vaughan), Tanglefoot and Freda and the Firedogs, they were playing in progressive country's ground zero. Indeed the event was overshadowed by the unbilled arrival of Willie Nelson, who played only his second show in Austin immediately before the Elevators went on, effectively stealing their thunder and pushing them well back into the night, by which time many people had already left or had passed out in their sleeping bags.

Donnie Erickson was replaced on guitar by Terry Penney, before John Ike cautiously allowed Stacy Sutherland to reclaim his place in the band. Stacy had been out of jail for some time, but was still struggling with heroin addiction and the authorities. Meanwhile, Roky was taking whatever drugs he could get hold of again, and a familiar pattern began to reassert itself. He began missing gigs, and when he did show up would sing every song in a perfect Mick Jagger impersonation, while thrashing his guitar at top volume, all feedback and distortion with no regard for what anyone else was playing. A final gig in Port Aransas on April 25th found Roky disheveled and disoriented, staggering around the stage and seemingly on another planet from the rest of the group. The whole reunion lasted for maybe a dozen shows, and when John Ike sacked Roky and Stacy his attempts to carry on the Elevators with a new singer were doomed from the start.

It was Tom Mcgarrigle's younger brother Patrick, a friend of Roky's younger brother Mikel, who first introduced Roky to Billy Miller. By 1973 Miller had already decided to call time on Cold Sun. "The night that I decided to forget about Cold Sun, it was the night I saw Lou Reed live in Memphis," he says. "Right after *Transformer* had come out, and it was really rock 'n' roll, I tell ya. More than usual. And then when I got home I read the *Rolling Stone* review of the *Nuggets* album, and I also read what they had to say about the Elevators. And I thought god, Cold Sun wouldn't even have made it to the *Nuggets* album, even if we'd have had a hit. And if they did, what would they say about us? And that was the night I decided to go in a more rock 'n' roll direction, but I had no idea what to do. I didn't write those type of songs. But pretty soon after that, within a month or two, I met someone who did, namely Roky Erickson."

The release of Lenny Kaye's seminal *Nuggets* compilation of 1960s pre-psychedelic obscurities and one-hit wonders effectively invented the genre of 'garage-punk,' reigniting interest in then-forgotten and uncared-for groups like the 13th Floor Elevators, whose *You're Gonna Miss Me* featured on the original album. *Nuggets* would prove hugely influential on the new punk rock movement a few years later, pioneered by among others the Patti Smith Group, featuring Lenny Kaye on guitar, and Television, who covered *Fire Engine* live. But at the time it also marked the moment that those 1960s bands were first fixed in history. 1966 was only six years ago, yet in 1972 the Elevators, along with the Standells, the Electric Prunes, the Strangeloves and others, were already fossilized as relics of a bygone age, to be recalled with fond nostalgia or held at arm's length and studied with critical historical detachment. No wonder *Nuggets* gave Billy Miller pause for thought.

The fact that Roky shared Miller's enthusiasm for Joe Meek sealed the deal. "I liked Roky's songs, but I didn't realize he was striving to be the next Screaming Lord Sutch," he says. "He wasn't doing psychedelic, he wasn't doing country... he wanted to be a new version of Screaming Lord Sutch. And when he started telling me about all that, that's when I really thought he was somebody special and important."

Chapter 30

Although it was Pat Mcgarrigle who suggested that Billy Miller collaborate musically with Roky Erickson, the two already had a connection through professional exorcist Winston 'Wink' Taylor. Taylor was the assistant to the Bishop of the local Liberal Catholic Church, a Christian splinter sect that was based at the Serpentarium, an abandoned snake farm on the outskirts of Austin that was converted into a religious commune. Taylor lived there along with the Bishop, Father Robert Williams, and a house band known as Alpha Centauri. For a while the congregation also included Cold Sun's original bassist Mike Waugh, and Roky's mother, Evelyn Erickson.

Winston Taylor's involvement with Cold Sun extended to a co-writing credit on the lyrics of their song *Fall*, and following Roky's release from Rusk Evelyn asked him to act as her son's spiritual advisor, bodyguard and, if necessary, exorcist. Roky often considered himself to be possessed by demons, and it seems that Evelyn took this possibility seriously. Knowing that Billy Miller was an Elevators fan and of good character, Taylor introduced him to Roky on a casual basis. Most memorably, Taylor asked Miller to call for Roky, who by this time was living in a communal house away from his mother, and take him to a restaurant where Taylor and others would be waiting. Miller arrived to find Roky sitting on a large, throne-like chair, smoking a large joint while a man in white robes washed his feet in a ceremonial, ritual manner, using a special cloth and water in a golden bowl. The whole scene was lit by a pile of wax candles that had melted into a shag carpet in the center of the room, the strands of the carpet becoming the wick of this one great misshapen candle.

Pat Mcgarrigle had similarly been assigned to look after Roky by Evelyn, and being musically inclined he had helped out at some of the ill-fated Elevators reunion shows. He eventually became one of Roky's closest and most trusted friends, and on leaving school at 16 moved into the singer's communal house on West 33rd Street. Although the Elevators reunion was not a success, Roky's condition seemed to be improving once again and Mcgarrigle thought that developing his own songs, with new collaborators away from any associations with the past, could only be therapeutically positive. Plus, they were undeniably amazing songs.

For his part, Billy Miller had thought of Roky Erickson as a great vocalist and performer, but not necessarily as a songwriter. That all changed when Roky played him the song *Interpreter* on an acoustic guitar, and told Miller he had roughly 400 more songs written, most of them dating from his time incarcerated in Rusk. Miller was floored by the song, and also by Roky's new musical metaphor: Horror Rock. This was a way for Roky to escape from all the by-then negative connotations of the 13th Floor Elevators and the psychedelic sixties, while still allowing him a lens through which to focus his insights and emotions, and to facilitate his gift for manic, metaphysical puns, word association and wild imagery. Roky of course had been a fan of horror movies and shocking, supernatural or science fiction themes since childhood, and as constant drug use and incipient schizophrenia began to affect his perception and thinking, these former escape valves seemed to become as accurate an explanation of his reality as anything else. This all climaxed during Roky's stay in Rusk; how else to make sense of this bizarre, senselessly cruel experience than to reflect that he was finally trapped in the horror movies he'd devoured as a kid? A college-educated intellectual might have written about Rusk in language drawing on Kafka or Beckett, but for Roky B-movie chillers like *I Walked With A Zombie* (RKO, 1943) and *The Creature With The Atom Brain* (Columbia, 1955) more than sufficed.

Incidentally, both films were the work of screenwriter Curt Siodmak, also responsible for the classic pulp sci-fi novel

Donovan's Brain (1942), about a scientist controlled by a disembodied brain. After publishing this novel, Siodmak was invited to join the OSS, the precursor of the CIA; much of Siodmak's work deals with mind control, and *The Creature With The Atom Brain* allegedly contained accurate references to the CIA's then-current MKULTRA project, possibly responsible for the LSD tests Tommy Hall participated in at UT in the early sixties. Roky apparently knew the film off by heart, and included large sections of dialogue in his song of the same name.

Roky's religious belief, strong since childhood, also came to the fore in Rusk as both a comfort and a means of salvation, culminating in his qualification as a reverend. Yet following his release Roky went through many of the song-poems he'd written inside, some of which were published in his book *Openers*, substituting Satan and Lucifer for God and Jesus in the lyrics. Roky explained that for him God and the Devil were two sides of the same coin, and that although in the Bible Lucifer is described as a fallen angel, he is still an angel, and could be an angel again if he chose. But his role in the universe is to be the Devil, the personification of evil. Roky's notion that he was in some way rewriting the Bible to fit his own personal situation and vision led him to the name of the new band he put together with Billy Miller in 1974: Bleib Alien (Bleib being an anagram of Bible).

Miller had been honing and arranging Roky's songs without necessarily intending to put a band together. "At first I was arranging the bass, and playing bass with Roky, on most of the songs," Miller says. "And I also played guitar with Roky, just to get him accustomed to sticking to really tight arrangements. We were really trying to rehabilitate him after his experience with the Elevators, who also needed rehabilitation at that point!" They took a break when Miller returned to Memphis for a couple of months, and it was during this hiatus that an enthusiastic Dana (who Roky had married in January 1974) booked them their first gig; the opening night of the Ritz, an old movie theater on

Austin's Sixth Street that the Armadillo's Jim Franklin had converted into a live music venue. The grand re-opening, on October 18th 1974, would also coincide more or less with the world premiere of *The Texas Chainsaw Massacre*: the already notorious, locally-filmed debut of UT film graduate Tobe Hooper. The only problem was there was no band, and Miller was forced to return from Memphis to put something together at short notice. The only musicians he could think to call on, and who he could trust not to dilute or interfere with Roky's new music, were the other members of Cold Sun.

"He kept telling me that he wanted to start a band and call it Bleib Alien," Miller says. "We were forced to put a band together, because I was in Memphis for a couple of months and at that point somebody talked Roky into committing to a gig. And it was a very big gig; it was the opening of the Ritz, and it was the opening of the Texas Film Festival, and we were the house band. And the featured artist was Tobe Hooper, with his new film *Texas Chainsaw Massacre*. So they couldn't have found a better local band than Bleib Alien to play at that! And when we began putting it together the only people that I could trust to not bring in the locals, who just didn't get it, were the two guys from Cold Sun, because I knew they wouldn't bring in other people. And Roky didn't want other people either. He liked what I was doing with him, and if I could be three people then that would be the band. And these other two guys were totally my confidants and musically never a problem, never questioning the direction or whatever. And I knew that with Roky they would not question the direction or the type of music."

Roky was adamant that he would be the sole guitarist, alongside Cold Sun's rhythm section of Mike Richey and Hugh Patton, and urged Miller to take up the autoharp again, to add that unearthly edge to Roky's sci-fi-inspired chillers. Pat Mcgarrigle was the unseen fifth member of Bleib Alien, taking care of Roky and facilitating his interactions with the rest of the world. While Miller frantically rehearsed the band, Mcgarrigle organized the technical details of the show, buying Roky a Gibson Les Paul on credit (the guitar that would require the least amount of tuning and technical maintenance onstage) and recording the 25-song performance on a reel-to-reel tape recorder, or at least as much as he could capture before he ran out of tape. Once the band were playing, Mcgarrigle stood behind Roky, ready to swap over guitars should he break a string, and reminding him what song they were doing next.

Jim Franklin came onstage on roller skates and dressed in bizarre 1974 disco sci-fi fancy dress (wig, spandex, giant shades) to introduce Bleib Alien, who played a raw and ragged but by all accounts brilliant and well-received set of all new material, with the exception of one old Elevators song, *She Lives*. "The very first gig we did, I didn't want to put too much of a load on the bass player, so reducing his workload by four songs seemed like the way to get things rolling, because we had a deadline," says Miller. "I didn't want him wasting time trying to have me teach him the basslines when I already knew them. So with a little practice I decided to play bass on those four songs at the first show. And so that's actually me playing bass on *Sweet Honey Pie* and I'm singing backup. But that's Mike Richey playing bass on *Song for Abe Lincoln*."

The three songs from the show that later appeared on the compilation *Gremlins Have Pictures* reveal Bleib Alien to have had a kind of new wave folk-rock sound, the music simple and direct beneath Roky's complex lyrics and tongue-twisting delivery. *Song for Abe Lincoln* and *Warning (Social and Social-Political Injustices)* were essentially protest songs, the latter sounding like early Dylan, the former mixing a criticism of Republican politics with a typically macabre grave-robbing theme. Other songs played included *I'm Hungry*, *Birds'd Crash*, *Red Temple Prayer (Two Headed Dog)*, *Don't Slander Me*, *Crazy Crazy Momma*, *The Wind And More* and *Stand For The Fire Demon*.

Bleib Alien also had a strong theatrical element, sometimes playing on Roky's history of mental instability and confinement, as when the band would dress in white coats like doctors and bring Roky out in a straitjacket to sing *You're Gonna Miss Me*. This might seem distasteful, but it should be noted that such ideas apparently came from Roky himself, whose humor onstage was often overlooked by those who preferred to see him as a victim. A return to the Ritz, on April 25th and 26th 1975, particularly impressed Doug Sahm, who was in the audience and went backstage to talk to Roky in typically irrepressible, Texas Tornado style.

Doug Sahm convinced Roky he needed to get out of Austin, a sentiment that Billy Miller agreed with, even if it meant the end of their band together. "Roky was more or less, nobody took him seriously, until we did that first gig," he says. "And then people started taking us seriously, and they wanted a piece of it, they wanted in on it. And it was fortunate that Roky left Austin when he did, because there was just nothing there for him. There were just people who wanted to water down what he was doing." Initially Sahm invited Roky out to Los Angeles to guest with the Sir Douglas Quintet, at a prestigious three-night stand at Hollywood's Palomino Club on 18-20th July 1975. Sahm's tour manager Craig Luckin was a big 13th Floor Elevators fan who well remembers the initial call from a charismatic, persuasive and lucid-sounding Roky, who wasn't going to take no for an answer.

"It all sounded plausible to me, and basically I agreed to everything Roky suggested," Luckin says. "I got him the round-trip air fare and reserved him a room where Doug and the band and I were staying, and it all turned out really well. Roky did amazingly well at all three nights, doing his four songs with Sir Douglas backing him up: *Two Headed Dog*, *You're Gonna Miss Me*, *Don't Shake Me Lucifer* and *Starry Eyes*. And not only was he able to perform good, he was wonderful backstage with all the celebrity guests, and more importantly with all the press people that were there. Quite a few hip underground rock newsletters and local small-press publications interviewed him, which kind of helped things later on for getting concert dates for Roky and the Aliens in the LA area."

After the shows Roky refused to go back to Austin, and instead travelled down to San Francisco with Luckin, Doug Sahm and his live guitarist at the time, the great John X Reed, who Roky knew of old. He stayed at Luckin's house for a week, and also reconnected with Tommy Hall, who was glad to see Roky and gave him his blessing, but insisted that he was no longer interested in making music. Roky was at his most charming during this period, and it seems his intention was to get Luckin to become his personal manager, in order to restart his career outside of Austin's limited confines.

"At that stage I was aware of his past and his incarceration in Rusk, and so also I was kind of getting advice from Doug," Luckin says. "Doug and I had some of the same music lawyers that we used, and so I decided well, before I do anything with Roky I want to have an agreement. And so basically it wound up, instead of being a management agreement I became a co-publisher with him on, not all of his material but all the material that I helped demo, or that he recorded on *The Evil One* and so on. And I wanted to make sure he had both his wife and an attorney of his choosing in Austin to come up with this agreement collectively. And so maybe a month or less after Roky moved back to Austin from San Francisco, I flew down there and actually stayed with Roky and his wife Dana, he had this big house there in Austin, and we had these meetings with Peggy Underwood, who was Roky's lawyer and one of the most well-known music lawyers in Austin at that time. And so they were very fair negotiations; I didn't get everything I wanted, but I got enough. And I think a big reason I was motivated to do this wasn't just that he was a great singer and a good rhythm guitar player and a good performer, but that he was just a brilliant songwriter, and so that was really the focus."

The contract they signed gave Luckin (via his company, Orb Productions) control of Roky's publishing and thirty per cent of his songwriting royalties. Luckin was undoubtedly aware that Roky's future as a performer and recording artist could be precarious, depending on his state of mind, but that he had already written a bunch of great songs that, properly handled, could continue to generate a significant income for all parties concerned. According to the memories of sound engineer John Ingle, it was in August 1975, after Roky's return from the West Coast, but possibly before the contract with Luckin was signed, that Doug Sahm financed and produced a four-hour session in the small demo room at Odyssey Sound studio in Austin. This was something of a reunion between Roky and Bleib Alien, and much of the short time allocated was spent smoking weed, hanging out and jamming, while Sahm encouraged Roky and built up his confidence. Eventually two tracks were cut, with Sahm joining Bleib Alien on wild, phase-shifting lead guitar: *Red Temple Prayer (Two Headed Dog)* and the more folky, Buddy Holly-esque *Starry Eyes*, which employed a variable speed oscillator on the choruses.

Sahm, an old-school hustler with a good heart, felt that Roky needed to have a single out in order to obtain bookings, and the two songs were duly released on the one-off Mars label. The name may reflect the fact that on 13th June 1975 Roky had Peggy Underwood draw up a document, counter-signed by the Travis County Public Notary, stating that "I, Roger (Roky) Erickson, do hereby declare that I am not a member of the human race (not an earthling) and am in fact an alien from a planet other than earth. I hope that this will prove to the person who is putting electrical shocks to my head that I am an alien. I am declaring this so that I am not in violation of any world or international laws of this earth as I am showing by this admission that I am in fact an alien."

Starry Eyes was a beautiful, classic love song that became a swift favorite on Austin's progressive country station KOKE-FM (which had taken over the KAZZ frequency and building). *Two Headed Dog* meanwhile was brutal and extreme enough to qualify as an outlier of the emerging punk movement. "The thing we recorded with Doug; that was so raw, when you listen to that now, *Two Headed Dog (Red Temple Prayer)*, it's very punk sounding," says Miller. "And Doug totally went along with that, he was very supportive of that. He totally directed that whole session, and I truly owe a whole lot of that to him. It was a wilder version of what we were doing live, for that song. We had other songs that were pretty wild. And in 1976 the very first mention of what would be new wave and punk was an article, a review, of two 45 singles that was published in *Rolling Stone*. It was the first time that Rolling Stone had ever reviewed a single, and it was a review of the Sex Pistols and Roky Erickson and Bleib Alien."

The original *Red Temple Prayer (Two Headed Dog)* is still astonishing: opening with the discordant, clashing tones of Miller's autoharp, before Sahm's overdriven but oddly flattened-out guitar crashes in, and Roky begins screaming himself raw in his most terrifying and unhinged manner over a stumbling, club-footed beat from Patton. The *NME*'s Nick Kent described it as "A vision of psychotic dread... a record of unique mood and power," and even now it sounds like the work of mescaline-bludgeoned, chainsaw-wielding hillbillies, while still somehow retaining a compelling melodic drive.

Miller claims that the song relates to the Vietnam War. "Roky saw a picture of a little girl that had been crucified by American GIs, and that's what inspired him to write that song," he says. "Roky had kind of a morbid sense of humor. Roky would go up to people in uniform, military people; if he saw a soldier, he loved to talk to soldiers. Sometimes he'd want to go talk to cops too, narcs, and that made me nervous! But they all liked him.

They didn't like me! Well, I don't know if they liked him, but they acted friendly. Not so much towards me. But Roky would go up to someone in uniform and say, 'Hey man, glad to meet ya, I'm Roky Erickson, I'm with the Soviet Union, and hey, I want you to know man, I'm with you all the way. If you ever get busted for atrocities, I've got a lawyer; he can get you off just like that.' He'd snap his fingers and say, 'This guy could get Lenny Bruce off, but Lenny Bruce is already dead.' And he'd go into this whole thing about how he has this big-deal lawyer that can get soldiers off the hook if they'd massacred people. And he used to really get a kick out of doing that, talking to those guys like that. And somehow he was so far out that they didn't even realize what he was or who he was or that he was putting them on. This one guy, he was some kind of a lieutenant; I think he was a marine, and he said 'Well, thank you, we really appreciate it when people respect us and want to help us. But no, I don't think I'm going to get arrested, I just play by the rules.' I still remember that guy."

Disaster struck when Roky lost all of the lyrics to his songs in a house fire; amazingly, he was able to mostly reconstruct them from memory. "I was with him, giving him moral support, and according to him, some kind of hypnotic support," Billy Miller says. "He would hypnotize me into hypnotizing him. I mean, that was the idea. And it was mainly to give him some sort of psychic support or hypnotic support. And he'd say, 'Now Bill is this right? Is this how it was?' And I mean, I didn't have those 400 songs memorized. I may be a smart guy, but not that smart! But I was with him the whole time and he absolutely reconstructed them all. And there were some that I did remember vividly, and I would notice slight little changes that seemed like improvements. He had trouble remembering them, remembering each song, but once he'd remembered the song itself, the title, then it would come back to him. Roky can access any part of his memory if he wants to. He is very amazing, like Harry Houdini or whatever, he really is. That was a tall order though, even for

Roky. I was determined that one way or another we were going to do it. I read somewhere that people thought I was sitting there transcribing stuff, and that's not true at all. I didn't write anything down. It wasn't my idea, I just thought oh my god, this stuff's lost, what are we going to do? But before I had a chance to talk to Roky he said 'I'm going to remember them all, and you'll help me, won't you Bill?' And for two weeks that's all he did. And I was there for him, but I didn't actually come up with even one word."

Soon after this the original Bleib Alien disbanded when Roky and Dana moved out to San Francisco. Craig Luckin found them a place to live and wasted no time in assembling a new band for Roky. Guitarist Duane Aslaksen, Doug Sahm's sound mixer and guitar tech, picked Roky up at the airport and by the end of the drive into town the pair had become fast friends. He was the natural choice for lead guitarist in Roky's new band, and Luckin also brought in bassist Steven Morgan Burgess and drummer Jeff Sutton. John X Reed, who Roky had judged to be a fellow Martian, took on the role of the singer's close confidante and facilitator, as well as producing and arranging some initial demos. But Roky still felt there was something missing.

"We'd done maybe five or six shows around the Bay Area," Luckin recalls, "and then one day Roky said, we've got to have Billy Miller."

Miller: "I was in Memphis, and he played one of the songs over the phone, and I was sold, right then. But my advice to them was they'd be crazy to get one more guy. They don't need me, they don't need an extra person; it sounds perfect the way it is. And they were actually determined to get one more person; a keyboard player or something, a horn player maybe, anything atrocious to ruin that perfect sound. So I thought well, if that's what they're going to do it should be me. And so eventually I think the band, I got a lot of attention, I think the band stood out because of me, but I'm still not sure that it wouldn't have been better without one more person."

Roky initially considered the group simply another incarnation of Bleib Alien, but Miller had always had reservations about the name. "Most disc jockeys by the mid-seventies, they were total assholes," he explains. "If they got something in the mail, it didn't matter who it was from, if it was a name that they couldn't pronounce, they'd toss it right in the trash. And if they thought it was psychedelic, they'd toss it right in the trash, because that was last year's thing. And these guys were hip; these guys were up and with it. And they were all just really sleazy, payola-taking, strip club-travelling sleazeballs. And I was afraid that we would never get any airplay if it was called Bleib Alien, because these guys are dicks. They're not going to play something if they don't know how to pronounce it."

Miller suggested the shorter, simpler and more new wave-sounding 'the Aliens.' Often in Austin Bleib Alien had been shortened to the Aliens anyway, and the name change reflected the fact that the new band would be playing a more direct, punchy and relatively commercial take on Roky's songs. Roky was clean, sober and mentally stable, away from Austin and surrounded by his fellow Aliens. A new chapter was surely beginning.

Chapter 31

John X Reed originally worked on Roky's songs at a warehouse rehearsal space he had access to in San Rafael, rehearsing and recording four-track demos, as much to copyright Roky's songs and arrangements and keep him busy as anything else, before bringing in the band. They then went into Bill Steele's San Anselmo recording studio, The Church, where Reed produced the single *Bermuda / The Interpreter*, crediting it to 91 Productions as for some reason he didn't want his name on the record (91 Joseph Court was the address of the rehearsal space they'd been using). Recorded in 1976, with Bobby Gorman replacing Morgan Burgess on bass, the fuzz-drenched *Bermuda* (a satanic celebration of "the devil's triangle," complete with jug-like burblings for all the old Elevators fans) became the third-ever release on Rhino Records, then just a side project for an LA record shop, early in 1977; in the UK, it was licensed to Richard Branson's Virgin Records. *The Interpreter*, with its complex chord sequences, doubled-up lead guitar (Sutton overdubbing on top of Aslaksen) and Miller's scything autoharp, had something of the feel of Thin Lizzy or the proto-new wave of Nick Lowe.

1977 also saw the release of a four-song EP on the French Sponge label, featuring a thumping, almost glam-rock version of *Mine Mine Mind*, the existential angst of *Click Your Fingers Applauding The Play*, a new take on *Two-Headed Dog* and the mystical *I Have Always Been Here Before*. While the last was Roky solo on acoustic guitar, the remaining three tracks featured an Aliens line-up of Sutton, Aslaksen, Miller and Chris Johnson, AKA Johnny Christian, on bass, and all were produced by drummer Jeff Sutton more or less live at 91 Joseph Court. Sponge was run by Phillipe Garnier, an American correspondent for France's Rock & Folk magazine, who was extremely hip to the still-underground California punk scene. Garnier originally licensed these tracks to release them as a freebie single for

Parisian record store Music Action; instead they gained a wider release, with import copies of the 7", in distinctive purple sleeve with lyric sheet insert, being much sought after among budding punks and psychedelic record collectors in America and the UK.

The singles proved that interest in Roky was stronger than ever, especially in Europe where not only the 13th Floor Elevators but the now-defunct International Artists label itself were gaining a cult following. One man aware of this was Lelan Rogers, who despite leaving the company acrimoniously managed to secure the rights to the IA name and back catalogue, as well as surviving master tapes. In 1978 he reissued all 12 International Artists albums in a vinyl box-set, and followed this in 1980 with the double-album compilation *Epitaph For A Legend*, that included previously unreleased material alongside a cross-section of IA album and single tracks. In the UK, Radar Records reissued the 13th Floor Elevators and Red Crayola albums, along with a new Red Crayola album, *Soldier Talk*, that found the now-UK resident Mayo Thompson working with Jesse Chamberlain, Lara Logic and fellow avant-garde ex-pats Pere Ubu. In this auspicious climate, Craig Luckin decided that the time was right to press ahead with an album, and sessions shifted to Cosmo's Factory, the rehearsal space owned by former Creedence Clearwater bassist Stu Cook.

Cook had played bass on Doug Sahm's 1974 album *Groover's Paradise*, alongside his Creedence rhythm buddy Doug Clifford, who produced and played drums. Though Clifford was the more experienced producer, Cook crucially was a fan of the Elevators who had seen them live in San Francisco back in the day, and was more than willing to take on the risks associated with working with Roky Erickson. Recording began promisingly at the Church at the end of 1977, with great live-in-the-studio versions of *Sputnik* and *Bloody Hammer*. Unfortunately Jeff Sutton quit the Aliens soon after; John Oxendine (AKA Fuzzy Furioso) took his place behind the drums, while Duane Aslaksen replaced him as *de facto* bandleader. New bassist John Maxwell also left after those two tracks, with Morgan Burgess returning for the rest of the sessions. "Without Jeffrey Sutton, the band just fell apart," Billy Miller says. "Jeffrey seemed to boss people around; he was kind of a bully. When Jeffrey was gone Duane more or less took over, and he wasn't an arranger. He was a natural born rock star, but only if someone else was in charge, telling him what to do. The original bass player though, who had written the original basslines, Morgan, he rejoined the band, and he was the best we could get. He was on a par with Jeff, but he wouldn't really bully people into keeping them tight. And without the bully, things were not as good. Not because John Oxendine wasn't a great drummer; he was, but Jeff was more than a drummer. He was a bully! No, he was a leader, and he knew that we needed leadership."

Roky's mental state also began to unravel again, as Craig Luckin recalls. "Roky had stopped taking his prescription medication, and I remember Duane and I were kind of supportive a little bit of Roky; I don't know if we should've been, but we were a little supportive of him not wanting to take that medication, because it seemed like it was really strong. When he started taking it, it seemed like he had no energy. He wasn't ever misbehaving, but also there were none of the fun, exciting performances. You know, in hindsight I don't know if we were wrong about that. But he did stop taking it, and then he seemed to be doing great."

Luckin also blames Roky's problems on the fact that once they started playing live shows regularly, fans would want to take drugs with the legendary singer. "It would be when we really started to do a lot of shows in the Bay Area that the problems happened," he says. "I can remember doing a show at the Long Branch Saloon, I think we were opening for Tom Fogerty, and we were to do two sets. Roky did a great first set, and then some fan intercepted him on the way back to the dressing room and gave him something, I don't know what. But he came out for the second set and I'd never seen him like this, before or since. His eyes were rolling back in his head, he could barely hold his guitar, let alone sing. So that became something that Duane and I especially became aware of, going forward. Because of the legend of the Elevators there were all these little fan boys that were into LSD or whatever that were like oh boy, I get to meet Roky Erickson, let's slip him something. And it wasn't always LSD either; it would be heroin, or sometimes he'd act like he was on speed or something, and in the end, even if it wouldn't necessarily ruin that performance, he wouldn't get any sleep the next night, and then he'd just be in a really bad mood. So that was the biggest problem; maybe well-intentioned but harmful interaction with the fans."

"My input was to take Roky's ideas and carve them into songs, with verses, choruses," says Stu Cook. "The hardest part was straightening out the lyric. I had to take a lot of liberties with Roky's songs from the lyric point of view, to put them into a cohesive story sometimes. Roky was starting to get a little more inconsistent as the process went along, and so as we got closer to the finish line it became more and more difficult to get there! Craig and I had to spend hours trying to piece together songs, in some cases, so that they made sense. They didn't always end up in the same order that Roky revealed them in. I just decided to run a tape all the time, because I never really knew when the magic was going to appear, when the Roky that I needed was going to be there. He was getting more and more distracted by things in his personal life, and it was getting sometimes very difficult to focus on the album. This was before digital editing, so I would have to wild sync in, and that was a tedious process; start one machine, start the other machine, hit record, do it again because it doesn't feel right, it doesn't have the swing on it. Some of the songs came together like that."

Towards the end of 1978 Roky grew so unmanageable and

impossible to work with that the Aliens quit; Roky's wife Dana also had a nervous breakdown and left him, taking their baby son Jegar with her, and Luckin was forced to send Roky back to his mother's in Austin. Before long he'd been forcibly hospitalized again.

"More than once, that happened," Luckin says. "It happened in San Francisco too, at least once, where it'd be the same kind of thing; the cops would get him late at night, and he'd be acting crazy, and they'd just give him immediate commitment. I think in California at the time it was a 30-day minimum, but in Texas it was more like 90 days. This was when we were still in the middle of recording *The Evil One*, and we'd pretty much got all the overdubs done, the solos and so on, and the basic tracks, but we didn't have good lead vocals from Roky on all of them. And he had been back in Austin and had gotten picked up at night for doing something weird at three in the morning walking around, and had got committed for 90 days. And so after he'd been there for maybe 60 days or something, I got another one of those phone calls, just like that first phone call when I first met him, it was from a pay phone again, only this time it was a pay phone in the mental hospital. And he said hey, Craig, why don't you and Stu bring the tapes down, I'm ready to do the rest of my vocals. And so we did, we flew down with 64 boxes of 16-track reel-to-reel. I don't so much blame Roky for any of this; it was just all part of who he was, and even the crazy parts are part of what makes him a great songwriter."

"I came down to Austin and put on a coat and a tie and went over to the institution where they had Roky locked up, and I would check him out," recalls Stu Cook. "And several of the other inmates, patients, they thought I was a doctor and they tried to get me to get them out. I would spring Roky and we would take him down to the studio and we would work on vocals. And when he would stop being productive I would be like, okay Roky, go have dinner and go back home, got to check you back in. See you tomorrow! We did that for a week. It was a very unusual project."

Luckin quickly struck a deal with the UK arm of CBS Records, via A&R man Howard Thompson, a former teenage acidhead in the North London suburbs who had developed a reputation by signing experimental but commercial post-punk acts like the Psychedelic Furs and Adam and the Ants. With a cover painting by Californian artist Captain Colourz, the untitled LP, often referred to as *TEO*, or Five Symbols, from the cryptic artwork, featured ten tracks from the sessions and came out in the UK in 1980. The promotional budget allowed for Roky and his new girlfriend, and future second wife, Holly Patton to fly to London for interviews, but not for the Aliens, who were no longer working with Roky in any case, to come over and play live shows. This policy proved to be a disaster, as prior to the first press day Roky and Holly visited Stonehenge, and the singer returned almost a different person. Whether someone had given him acid or more mysterious forces were at work, Roky varied between near-catatonia, incoherence and cryptic non-sequiturs during the interviews, most damagingly in a scathing *NME* profile by an unsympathetic Nick Kent.

The album was released in the US the following year by Howie Klein's San Francisco-based punk and new wave label 415 Records, under its original title of *The Evil One*, but with a different track-listing. *The Evil One* had five songs in common with *TEO*, but also had five exclusive tracks, to differentiate it from import copies of the CBS album and to attract buyers who had already bought the original version. Earlier tracks and outtakes were subjected to extra production work in Wally Heider Studios; in particular, Stu Cook overdubbed his own bass playing over John Maxwell on the Jeff Sutton recordings of *Sputnik* and *Bloody Hammer*.

By this time however Roky had already moved on, and was playing shows around Texas with Dallas punk band the

Nervebreakers, before hooking up with Austin hard-rockers the Explosives in 1979. Stu Cook confirms that *The Evil One* was completed in Roky's absence, and indeed that the singer never even heard the final arrangements of his songs until after the album was released. Nevertheless, Roky has repeatedly described *The Evil One* as his favorite among his solo albums, and there's no doubt that it remains the definitive Roky Erickson collection, particularly in the complete 15-song version released by Light In The Attic in 2013.

Miller's autoharp adds an unearthly edge to the Aliens' no-frills hard rock, which nevertheless is always sympathetic to Roky's performance, and surprisingly flexible. Witness the neo-doo-wop backing vocals on *I Walked with a Zombie*, or the way autoharp and Link Davis's Hammond organ combine in atmospheric fog beds beneath Duane Aslaksen's wailing guitar on *Night of the Vampire*. The real star of course though is Roky, whose deftly-controlled screams are as unmistakable as they are inimitable, the ringmaster in his own circus of terrors, sending delirious shivers down the spine whenever he throws his head back and howls. Highlights include the voodoo-choogle swamp rock of *It's A Cold Night For Alligators* and the driving, bubbling groove of *Sputnik*, driven along by Jeff Sutton's disco-tight, Clem Burke-like drumming, which Billy Miller claims is Roky's answer song to Joe Meek's *Telstar*.

Of course, Roky's traumatic time in Rusk is never far from the surface in his horror rock creations. *Night of the Vampire* may be named after the Moontrekkers' 1961 instrumental (produced by Joe Meek), but *I Walked with a Zombie* is surely a metaphor for the Thorazine shuffle, while the pounding *Creature With The Atom Brain* ("Why is he acting so strange?") resonates with institutionalized paranoia, lobotomies and electro-shock therapy. The amped-up rockabilly of *Don't Shake Me Lucifer* is a prayer for salvation after another tormented, sleepless night in a padded cell, made especially poignant by the fact that one of the side-effects of the anti-psychotic Fluphenazine, which Roky was prescribed, is uncontrollable shaking and tremors. Most chilling of all is *Bloody Hammer*, with its near-hypnotic flow of nightmarish imagery: doctors and psychiatrists, demons and vampires, a baby ghost from 1910 urging him to beat it with his chain, eyes rolling to the back of the head, and Roky repeatedly screaming "I never hammered my mind out; I never had the bloody hammer."

By the time of the album's release the Aliens too were doing their own thing, playing around the San Francisco punk clubs with Billy Miller on lead vocals. "We were doing songs written by me and Roky, and we did *Telstar*, and we also did a song called *Spectre Man* which is the theme song of a Japanese TV show," Miller says. "And one thing I was surprised about: locally, around the Bay Area, the Aliens were no less popular without Roky. We were just as popular. But then when Roky made the scene again later, his legend had grown even more, and that's still happening to this day. But the songs we played in the Aliens were songs that I wrote... Duane didn't want to have much input or leadership at all, and he didn't actually want to play much more than rhythm guitar. So I was totally in charge of that, and I was pretty much doing all the lead stuff with the harp, because he just liked to play rhythm and sing back-up. But we had a few songs like *Spectre Man* where Duane and I did a double lead vocal, and we had a song called *The Fly* that I had written. There was one song we did that was called *Africa* and John Oxendine, Duane and I all wrote lines. A friend of ours, a Mr. Taylor, who had written some of the Cold Sun lyrics, he contributed a line or two, and so that was a complete group effort."

John 'Fuzzy Furioso' Oxendine was replaced on drums first by Darren Peligro (who swiftly went on to join the Dead Kennedys) and then Paul Zahl, and in 1983 Craig Luckin managed to reunite the Aliens and Roky in the studio to record a second album for CBS. The Explosives had finally run out of patience with Roky's erratic behavior, but Luckin knew he just had to wait out the singer's cycle and then grab him quickly when he was ready to record. Sessions went relatively smoothly, with Jefferson Airplane bassist Jack Cassady replacing Morgan Burgess in the studio and Duane Aslaksen producing. Unfortunately, Muff Winwood at CBS was dissatisfied with the resulting album, originally titled *Burn The Flames*, and rejected it; it was eventually released as *Don't Slander Me* in 1986, on Pink Dust in the US and Demon Records in the UK.

Initially the album is a perhaps surprising return to Roky's rock 'n' roll roots, with rockabilly boogie rhythms, albeit played with a punk-metal heaviness, alternating with new wave-tinged ballads. Roky's percussive vocals on the title track are more right-eously aggressive than we've ever heard him before, but the trip-hammer fuzz blues of *Haunt* are punctuated by a smooth saxophone solo courtesy of the Sir Douglas Quintet's Martin Fierro. *Nothing In Return* finds Roky doing his best Buddy Holly impersonation, but the backing is closer to the Cars or Tom Petty's Heartbreakers. *You Drive Me Crazy* is at least a more authentic Crickets pastiche, Andre Lewis's dated synth sound notwithstanding.

Roky returns to horror rock with the theatrical *Burn the Flames*, but the genuine desperation and weirdness of his performances on *The Evil One* is absent, and the Aliens too fail to harness the edge and menace of the Stu Cook recordings. Remakes of *Bermuda* and *Starry Eyes* are worthwhile if only because the superior originals were, by 1986, decidedly hard to find; *Can't Be Brought Down* benefits from having Jeff Sutton back on drums, and for a few moments Roky and the Aliens almost get back into their old groove. It's also one of only four of the ten tracks to feature Billy Miller's autoharp at all. Best of all is a song that was bafflingly left off the original 1986 release, only being added to the 2005 CD reissue; *Realize You're Mine*, which is one of Roky's sweetest and most genuine love songs, with the catchy simplicity of a timeless classic.

After playing with the Resurrectionists and Evil Hook Wildlife, Roky joined a disastrous and mercifully brief 13th Floor Elevators reunion in the summer of 1984; once again, the only other original member was John Ike Walton, although Ronnie Leatherman returned for one show. He was then taken under the wing of Austin bassist and producer Speedy Sparks. With John X Reed, guitarist Harry Hess and drummer Ernie Durawa, Sparks put together a five-song EP for the French New Rose label in 1985 that featured two new songs, the plaintive *Clear Night For Love* and the classic Byrdsian folk-rock of *You Don't Love Me Yet*, alongside tasteful versions of *Haunt, Starry Eyes* and *Don't Slander Me*. But Roky's condition was worsening, even as a new generation of supporters emerged to sing his praises. These included San Antonio band the Butthole Surfers, who were surely the post-punk equivalent of the 13th Floor Elevators; an unhinged, surreal and nightmarish fusion of hardcore noise, folk-rock and heavy Texan psychedelia, whose live shows were nothing short of legendary. They even had a song called *Roky*.

The Buttholes opened for Roky Erickson when he returned to the place where his solo career began: the Ritz Theater in Austin, on February 21st 1987. This was Roky's first major live appearance since the ill-fated Elevators reunion, more than two years previous; aside from his mental fragility, Roky's absence from both the stage and the studio was explained as a protest against the fact that he never seemed to see any money from his work. By the late eighties, there was quite a torrent of Elevators and Roky Erickson compilations, reissues and live recordings, of usually dubious quality and legality. Inevitably, an album of the Ritz show would join this deluge, based on an audience recording made by Roky's mother. Listening to it now, an initially enthusiastic Roky seems to grow increasingly disinterested as the band (Will Sexton, Chris Holyhaus and Explosives drummer Freddie Krc) extend the songs into tedious, over-long jams, illustrating the risks, as Billy Miller knew, of letting capital-M Musicians loose on Roky's work. As another endless, blues-based guitar solo fills the vinyl, Roky seems to disappear, becoming a ghost in his own songs. It would be his last live show for eighteen years.

PART VIII

IMITATION SITUATION

Chapter 32

In July 1970 Janis Joplin quietly returned to Austin for Kenneth Threadgill's birthday celebrations, at the party barn in Oak Hill. Janis sang solo renditions of *Sunday Morning Coming Down* and *Me and Bobby McGee* at the event, before presenting Threadgill with a wreath of flowers she'd brought back from Hawaii. "I bought him one thing I knew he'd like," she said; "a good lei." Janis was modest and self-effacing, declining to publicize her visit and doing her best not to steal the limelight from Threadgill himself. Very different, in August, was her Port Arthur high school reunion. Janis insisted on attending against the advice of many of her friends, and it became a widely-publicized media event, with Janis arriving 'in character,' complete with feathers and beads and hippy-showbiz entourage. In one sense, this was intended as a form of revenge upon her school and hometown; to prove that she was successful, sexually desirable, and not still the misfit ugly duckling that they'd said she was and that, not too far from the surface, she still felt herself to be. In another sense, Janis still desperately craved acceptance and approval from Port Arthur. Inevitably, there was no resolution or reconciliation; Janis rowed with her parents, endured a painful and humiliating press conference, was scorned by her deliberately unimpressed peers, and ended up going to watch Jerry Lee Lewis at the Pelican Club, where she got into a fight with the veteran rocker, who punched Janis in the face. This was her last visit home; six weeks later, in the early hours of October 4th, 1970, Janis Joplin died of an accidental heroin overdose. She was 27 years old, and had recorded two albums with Big Brother and the Holding Company, and two under her own name, that had already sealed her place as one of the all-time greats of rock music history.

Less noticed was the death of Steve Perron, singer with the Children. On August 8th 1973 he also died of an accidental overdose, in his case of prescription pain killers. Unlike Janis, he never received the acclaim and success he deserved, and his band was still barely remembered outside their immediate circle when Children guitarist Bill Ash succumbed to a fatal heart attack in 2001.

By 1973, Mayo Thompson was more focused on art than music, though a move to New York and an ongoing collaboration with the conceptual art group Art & Language would see him return to recording and performing. In 1977 he moved to England and worked as a producer and A&R man as the UK indie music scene erupted out of punk, with many of the bands involved referring back to his own pioneering sixties work. His production credits, first for Rough Trade and then for Creation Records, would include seminal records by the Monochrome Set, the Raincoats, Cabaret Voltaire, the Fall, Stiff Little Fingers, the Blue Orchids, the Shop Assistants, Felt and Primal Scream.

Beginning with 1979's *Soldier Talk*, the reactivated Red Crayola would be one of the very few bands to be even more acclaimed as a post-punk act than they were during the psychedelic era. Now essentially a vehicle for Thompson and a rotating cast of collaborators, they became the Red Krayola once again when Thompson returned to the States and began recording for Chicago indie label Drag City. Nineties post-rockers like David Grubbs, John McEntire and Jim O'Rourke were the crew of the good ship Red Krayola as she sailed into a remarkable third act, and thirty-odd years on they had lost none of their power to shock, baffle and dismay even the most supposedly broad-minded of music critics. Their 1999 album *Fingerpainting*, in which Thompson and his current collaborators reworked unreleased material by the original 1960s line-up, so upset Pitchfork's Nick Mirov he wrote an entire review explaining how the album was essentially unreviewable, giving it 3.7 out of 10 and spluttering that the record was "Avant crap... fucking stupid... nothing to do with entertainment, or even art."

Frederick Barthelme left music, avant-garde or otherwise, and received a Masters in Fiction Writing from John Hopkins University, going on to teach writing at the University of Southern Mississippi. An extremely successful novelist and short story writer, as well as the editor of the literary magazine *Mississippi Review*, Barthelme would be recognized as one of the key American minimalist-realist writers who emerged during the 1980s and after. His reputation rose in contrast to that of the once-celebrated Billy Lee Brammer. Despite beginning a rock 'n' roll novel based on the life of Doug Sahm, to be called *Rock of Aegis*, Brammer never completed another book after *The Gay Place*. He died of cardiac arrest on February 11th, 1978, his health ruined by years of abuse. He was just 48 years old.

The most successful act to emerge from the Texan psychedelic underground was surely ZZ Top. After releasing the single *Salt Lick / Miller's Farm* in 1970, Lanier Greig and Dan Mitchell left the band to be replaced by Dusty Hill and Frank Beard, from Dallas psych-rockers the American Blues. ZZ Top broke through with their third album, 1973's *Tres Hombres*, setting a template that would sustain them through a long and deservedly successful career of blues, beards and boogie, cannily steered (till 1996) by manager Bill Ham. Even after 1983's synthesizer-and-drum-machine-driven *Eliminator* album sent them into the upper echelons of pop music worldwide, Billy Gibbons never forgot his roots, and championed the likes of the 13th Floor Elevators at every opportunity. In 2013 he reformed the original line-up of the Moving Sidewalks for a series of sold-out live performances; sadly Lanier Greig died in February that same year.

The original Elevators proved less lucky than their former opening act. After his release from prison in 1970, Stacy Sutherland formed Raincrow, a covers band specializing in blues and country rock, with Ronnie Leatherman, Bobby Rector and Elevators roadie Cecil Morris. Unfortunately Stacy returned to heroin and was forced to leave town, drifting around Tennessee before returning briefly to take part in the 1973 Elevators reunion. In his absence, Raincrow evolved into Travis, with Leatherman, Rector and Morris joined by singers Paul Tennison and Barry Below. An unemployed, overweight ex-con, destitute and struggling with depression and alcoholism, Stacy eventually settled in Houston with his new wife Bunni. On August 24th 1978, he embarked on an all-day drinking session with former Fever Tree guitarist Mike Knust, himself still struggling with drink and drugs. That evening Stacy returned home and resumed rowing with Bunni; the argument ended with her accidentally shooting Stacy in the stomach with his own rifle. 32 years old, he was dead by the time the ambulance arrived.

Tommy Hall remained in San Francisco, working as a kindergarten janitor before deciding to concentrate entirely on his Great Work. This no longer involved creating or performing music, although he remains a keen and voracious listener, particularly of jazz, and still occasionally ventures out to see potentially interesting bands live. He moved into a cheap hotel room in the city's Tenderloin district, where he remains to this day: surrounded by mountains of CDs, cassettes and videotapes, sat meditating on his bed between the stereo and the giant flatscreen TV. Hall retains his enthusiasm for LSD and marijuana, but refrains from alcohol and other body drugs; mostly though he continues to pursue his grand design with an astonishing focus. Based in higher mathematics, it encompasses quantum science, art, religion, mysticism, yoga, and is in fact all-encompassing, uniting and incorporating all other disciplines. Hall frequently claims that the work is near completion, though apparently he has yet to write any of it down.

Clementine Hall worked for 37 years as a legal secretary while bringing up her children; she now lives alone in quiet retirement in California. She and her son Roland are still in touch with Tommy, and they remain good friends. John Ike Walton, Ronnie Leatherman and Danny Thomas all remain alive and well and living in Texas at the time of writing; Danny Galindo died of liver failure in 2001, and Benny Thurman passed in 2008.

Fever Tree reformed in 1974 to support Billy Joel at Houston Music Hall, and Michael Knust and Dennis Keller resurrected the name once again in 1978, touring around Texas, Louisiana and Mississippi. Their final show was recorded for an album, *Live At Lake Charles 1978*, but by this time Knust had sacked Keller, and new keyboard player Pat Brennan took over vocals. Knust briefly revived the Fever Tree name again in the early nineties, before moving back to Austin and the inevitable succession of blues-rock bar bands. He died on September 15th, 2003, aged 54. Scott and Vivian Holtzman both died in the 1990s; there were no notices or obituaries to mark their passing, not even in the *Houston Post* where Scott Holtzman's 'Now Sounds' column tirelessly documented the now legendary local music scene.

Rod Prince, Todd Potter and David Fore reformed Bubble Puppy in 1977 and opened for Fever Tree at a few shows, but when Fore left they changed their name to Sirius, and released one album of country-tinged hard rock in 1979, *Fusion*. Fore formed new wave band D-Day, co-writing their 1979 semi-hit, the controversial Blondie-meets-Runaways underage sex anthem *Too Young to Date*. Meanwhile Rod Prince's old *compadre* Mike Taylor was working as a recording engineer in San Antonio, and produced the first records by the Butthole Surfers (who, unaware of his past history, nicknamed him 'Trombone' Taylor). A full Bubble Puppy reunion (including Roy Cox) followed in the mid-eighties, resulting in a new LP, 1986's *Wheels Go Round*, which included re-recordings of old material. They were dormant again until Prince, Potter and Fore revived the Bubble Puppy name (aided by Mark Miller and Jimmy Umstattd) in 2011. Greg Stegall replaced Todd Potter in 2013, and the band continues to perform regularly, while Potter remains lead guitarist in Austin covers band the Fabulous Chevelles and his own Todd Potter band. Roy Cox formed the Bluesknights in the late nineties, and after a long struggle with alcohol died on April 3rd 2013, at the age of 64.

In June 1969, Thorne Dreyer of *The Rag* founded a similar left-wing underground paper in Houston, called first *Space City News*, then just *Space City*. This ran until August 1972, and was instrumental in uniting the disparate strands of Houston's early-seventies counterculture. For its pains, it was subjected to frequent drive-by shootings and bomb attacks upon its offices; the Houston police seemed only minimally interested in finding out who was responsible, though the local Ku Klux Klan had issued written threats to the paper. *The Rag* published its final issue in 1977, but a 2005 reunion of veteran staffers led to the founding of the online Rag Blog, and Rag Radio, both still overseen by Thorne Dreyer and embracing social activism, good music and countercultural activity.

The Armadillo World Headquarters finally closed its doors on New Year's Day 1981, following an all-night concert featuring Asleep At The Wheel and Commander Cody and his Lost Planet Airmen. During its ten-year run it hosted legendary shows by Frank Zappa, Bruce Springsteen, AC/DC and the Clash among many others. Though the building was razed and replaced by high-rise flats, the success of the Armadillo was instrumental in creating Austin's current reputation as the live music capital of the world. The renowned PBS music program *Austin City Limits*, which started in 1976, was directly inspired by the Armadillo; in 2002 it launched the annual Austin City Limits Music Festival in Zilker Park, site of the sixties love-ins pioneered by the Vulcan Gas Company. The legendary South By South-West city-wide music festival, which began in Austin in 1987 and is now one of the most important events in the global music industry calendar, would also have arguably never happened if the Armadillo, and before that the Vulcan, had not put Austin on the musical map.

Interest in Texan psychedelic music, and the 13th Floor Elevators in particular, grew steadily throughout the 1980s. In 1986 there was a seemingly unrelated flurry of cover versions by English underground bands, with Spacemen 3 covering

Rollercoaster on their debut album, the Shamen recording *Fire Engine*, and most prominently Julian Cope placing *Levitation* on the B-side of his biggest hit, *World Shut Your Mouth*. The following year it was the turn of the Red Crayola to be feted, as Spacemen 3's *Transparent Radiation* and Alien Sex Fiend's *Hurricane Fighter Plane* (following a bootlegged live version by The Cramps in 1984) were both released as singles to substantial press and radio attention.

In 1990 Julian Cope, ZZ Top, the Butthole Surfers, Doug Sahm, REM, the Jesus And Mary Chain, Primal Scream and many others contributed to *Where The Pyramid Meets The Eye*, a fund-raising Roky Erickson tribute album assembled for Sire Records by long-time Elevators advocate Bill Bentley. The following year, Primal Scream included their version of *Slip Inside This House* (retitled *Trip Inside This House*, and making the connection to the ecstasy-fuelled psychedelic experience of the rave and acid house generation) on their breakthrough album *Screamadelica*, arguably the highest profile cover of an Elevators song.

But as his reputation grew, in 1988 Roky Erickson moved into a government housing project and withdrew into seclusion. To drown out the voices in his head he played several radios and televisions at full volume constantly, creating an unintelligible babble of noise that served a similar function to the guitar feedback he once generated onstage with the Elevators. He stopped taking medication, stopped washing, stopped taking care of himself. His hair grew into a filthy clumpy mass, and as his teeth fell out he developed an abscess that would be life-threatening if untreated. His interaction with his neighbors was limited to collecting their mail and delivering it for them, but as people moved out of the projects Roky simply kept their letters, allowing it to pile up around him or pinning it to the walls in what almost seemed like a strange art project. Eventually Roky was arrested and charged with mail theft, a federal offence that landed him in jail. Tary Owens, by then a drug and alcohol counsellor after his own battles with substance abuse, set up a trust fund to pay Roky's legal costs, which prompted not only *Where The Pyramid Meets The Eye* but Julian Cope's 1990 album *Droolian*, originally conceived as a Texas-only limited edition to help pay Roky's legal fees.

Friends and family still sought Roky out, but his mother, as his legal guardian, supported her son's decision to stay off medication and trust in God's will. In the early nineties the role of carer, confidant and facilitator fell jointly to Casey Monahan and King Coffey, drummer with the Butthole Surfers. Coffey managed to get Roky back into the studio, and released a new album, 1995's *All That May Do My Rhyme*, on his own Trance Syndicate label in 1995. This included all five songs from the 1984 *Clear Night for Love* EP, alongside six new recordings in a similarly tasteful folk-rock style. Lou Ann Barton dueted with Roky on a new version of *Starry Eyes*, while Butthole Surfers guitarist Paul Leary was surprisingly understated, alongside John X Reed, Speedy Sparks, Charlie Sexton, drummer Barry Smith and Sumner Erickson on tuba, on a selection of mostly sorrowful love songs like *I'm Gonna Free Her*, *We Are Never Talking* and *For You*. The poignant *Please Judge* meanwhile reflected a lifetime of persecution from the authorities, for crimes that were only borne of extreme innocence. Although more than ten years of trauma separated the recording sessions, *All That May Do My Rhyme* is a remarkably consistent and accomplished body of work.

Concurrent with the album's release was the publication of a book of Roky's lyrics, *Openers II*, by Henry Rollins' 2.13.61 imprint. "I think it was King Coffey from the Butthole Surfers who contacted me, and asked if we would be interested in putting out Roky's lyric book," Rollins says. "We jumped at the chance to work with the guy. No one writes like Roky. The lyrics are so sincere and at the same time so brilliantly nuts."

Rollins is a massive fan of the 13th Floor Elevators and Roky's solo work, citing *The Evil One* as his favorite, and Roky's voice as the defining quality. "There's really nothing like it," he says. "I think this happens with a lot of people; they hear him and they immediately connect in some way. He is really coming from a different place." Nevertheless, Rollins was dismayed to see the state that Roky was in by the mid-nineties. "When I met him he was not fully in charge of his thoughts and it was quite intense to be around him in such a paranoid state. I reckoned he had a good support team, people like King, who really cared about him. I was always curious about the mother; that seemed like a strange relationship. It seemed like Roky needed some real medical assessment, not just the care of good friends and family. That can only go so far."

Rollins remembers that Roky was not in any condition to promote his book, or really even take much interest in it. "I remember showing him a copy and he just laughed and stared at it. I don't think he was all that interested in checking it out. We did have a book signing at SXSW when the book came out. That did not go very well as Roky was not in a state of mind to handle a line of people who wanted to meet him."

In 2001, after Sumner Erickson went to court to wrest legal guardianship of Roky from their mother, Henry Rollins paid for Roky to have life-saving dental surgery and a set of dentures, the beginning of a long process of recovery for the singer. In 2002 the first Roky Erickson Psychedelic Ice Cream Social took place at Threadgill's World Headquarters (a venue owned by Eddie Wilson, near the site of the Armadillo), jointly organized by three charities; the Roky Erickson Trust, the Coalition for the Abolition of Electroshock in Texas, and Families who Rock. The event was intended to support not just Roky, but electroshock survivors across the state, particularly creative artists, such as Jim Franklin and Townes Van Zandt, who had been incarcerated and forced into damaging electroshock treatment against their will. At the March 2005 event, backed once again by the Explosives, Roky returned to the stage for the first time since the 1987 Ritz show, bar an aborted set at SXSW in 1993. In 2007 Sumner was able to resign his guardianship when a medication-free Roky had his legal rights fully restored, an extremely rare occurrence for anyone judged to be as mentally ill as he was. Later that year, he played his first ever UK show, at the Jarvis Cocker-curated Meltdown Festival in London.

George Kinney resurfaced in 2001, releasing a solo album, *After The Fall*, that featured Jerry Lightfoot and Jud Newcomb on guitars. A tough but vulnerable country-rock album that compared favorably with *Desire*-era Dylan, it included the standout ballad *How Could I Ever Say Goodbye*, which was heart-breaking in its simple purity. The following year, Kinney and Jimmy Bird reformed the Golden Dawn to play *Power Plant* in its entirety, first in Austin and then on a self-booked national tour, which also saw Bill Hallmark and Tom Ramsey rejoining the band. These shows were documented in a 2004 live album, *The Legend Of The Dawn*, and in 2006 an album of new material was released, credited to George Kinney and the New Riders of the Golden Dawn. *Texas Medicine* featured Bill Hallmark on bass and Charlie Prichard on guitar, and showcased a similar mix of blues-rock and country ballads to *After The Fall*. Unable to make the reunion, original drummer Bobby Rector died in 2007, and Jimmy Bird also passed in 2008.

Kinney has self-published two novels, *The Bandit King* (2003) and *Brave New Texas* (2013), and obtained a Master's degree in Traditional Chinese Medicine and Acupuncture. He still respects Tommy Hall as one of the great philosophers of our time, and continues to develop his own studies in what might be termed New Age philosophy. A believer in limitless human potential and the immanence of species-wide psychic evolution, his is an odd and perhaps characteristically Texan combination of universal eco-consciousness, love-based spirituality and armed, power to the people anti-authoritarianism. In the early eighties he contracted hepatitis C after a blood transfusion, and despite suffering no particular ill effects underwent experimental treatment in 2010 that left him with liver cancer. The music community rallied round to help pay for his medical costs, and in 2011 George underwent a successful liver transplant. George Kinney still writes, performs and thinks out loud, and remains a genuine southern gentleman and a True Believer in The Quest.

The influence of 1960s Texan psychedelic rock reached its apogee with the Black Angels, a Texan band who moved to Austin precisely because of its illustrious history. They were formed in 2004 by guitarist Christian Bland, bassist Nate Ryan, singer Alex Maas and drummer Stephanie Bailey, and released their debut album *Passover* the following year. Songs like *The First Vietnam War* and *The Sniper at the Gates of Heaven* showed the band to be bastard children of the Elevators and the Velvet Underground, albeit filtered through a bloodline that includes the Jesus And Mary Chain, Spacemen 3, the Brian Jonestown Massacre and Black Rebel Motorcycle Club.

"The first people that were coming to our shows were record store owners in their fifties and sixties," recalls singer Alex Maas. "And it was that way for a long time. And just recently, very recently we're like wow, there's younger people!" The Black Angels would eventually form a bridge between Austin's psychedelic past and its 21st Century hipster community. "There are people at our shows that were hanging out with the 13th Floor Elevators, that were shooting photos of them, and they'll come up to us after the show and say look at these photos that I took of the 13th Floor Elevators and Roky Erickson in 1965, and they'll tell us their stories. These elaborate amazing stories from people who were there, they were living that, they were a part of that scene, they saw that scene happening. And so they do feel that something might be happening again. And whenever those people come to our shows it's like, wow, maybe we're doing something on the right path."

In 2007 Christian Bland and Alex Maas founded the Reverberation Appreciation Society with Rob Fitzpatrick and Oswald James, initially in order to help promote like-minded bands and the artists that had influenced them. The following year, the first Austin Psych Fest was staged as an offshoot of SXSW, a one day event at the Red Barn featuring nine contemporary psych bands, plus the Black Angels headlining. With Roky Erickson returning to live work, it was inevitable that the two acts would cross paths, and later in 2008 the Black Angels toured as Roky's backing band.

"He came to our house," Maas recalls of working with Erickson. "We're all living with each other, and we sat down and we re-taught him these songs that he wrote, when he was 16, 17 years old. We re-taught him the lyrics and the guitar parts. It was fascinating; it was like, you wrote this song in 1965; can you tell me about it? And he was like; I don't really remember writing that song. And then we'd play it for him, and Christian would play his part for him on the guitar, and it would start to come back to him. And then all of a sudden he'd remember more and more of the song, and by the end of the session he'd remember the entire song, when he wrote it, and what he was thinking about. But in the beginning he didn't really remember any of that.

"Music really cleared his mind up a lot, and really made him more focused. If we were hanging out with him before we were making music he would just be kind of looking off into the distance. He was there, but he was distant. But once you started playing music, he became more alive. It was feeding his soul; you could see it in his eyes. And he'd clear up and start communicating more, and he'd start smiling and it was truly like this therapeutic thing that I noticed, it was amazing, it was beautiful. I don't know why he plays music, I don't know why at all. If I was him, at his age, I might not even play music, or want to go back to that spot either. But he did agree to go on tour with us and it was very fun. It wasn't easy. I'd kind of compare it to riding an unbroken horse, while being chased by a vampire bat, in the dark. And there's no saddle, and you're just holding on to the mane, and trying to stay completely connected to that beast, and help guide it and just live through that whole experience and get out safe! I remember there were a couple of times when we just kind of looked at each other on stage and we were all just kind of lost in a way. Sometimes Roky would play a verse a couple of times not how we had practiced it, and we just had to go with it, which made us better musicians."

While backing Roky, Maas would play the jug on any Elevators songs they attempted, and in San Francisco word reached him that Tommy Hall was going to be in the audience. "I knew he was going to come to the show, to see Roky. But it was really kind of interesting: here I am, on stage playing the electric jug, and Tommy Hall is out there. Like, what was he thinking? What was he thinking about that? Did he notice, did he care? Did he think that I was doing a good job? I was trying to recreate the sound that he created, you know."

Maas's experience of playing the jug led him to reflect on how it was almost trance-inducing, using circular breathing techniques that could be related to Gurdjieff's theories of self-transcendence. "There's something about doing that, it's kind of euphoric, actually. If you think about breathing for thirty minutes, like really heavy breathing, imagine just doing that anyway, it becomes like this euphoric kind of thing."

Maas also had an audience with Tommy after the show. "He talked about existentialism and where the world is going, and his theories for this equation that he's been working on, that is like the key of life equation," he says. "Higher Maths. He was really into that. And speaking to me, his eyes were closed the entire time. He was very focused on this higher math, and very intent on describing it to me. And all the conversation, it wasn't a very long one, it wasn't short by any means either, but that was what our conversation consisted of. I didn't quiz him, I didn't ask him tons of questions; I just let him talk. He had a big beard, and he was kind of unrecognizable as Tommy Hall, but he had the same eyes. The eyes never change. And every once in a while, his eyes were closed but they would flutter, you know when really intelligent people are talking and they close their eyes because they're thinking about what they're talking about, or not just really hyper-intelligent people, but also savants, and whether he became this way after drugs or whether that's just the way that he is, I don't know, because I've never met him before. But his eyes would kind of flutter, kind of like a butterfly, open and close really quickly as he was talking about this, his eyes would move out of rhythm with his voice, very quickly, in almost like a savant-type way. And every once in a while he'd open his eyes and look me right in the eye very clearly, like everything had stopped. Like the whole world had stopped. He looked at me, and he'd say, 'you know what I mean? You understand what I'm saying?' And then he'd close his eyes and go right back into it, and continue talking about higher maths and his equations. I don't pass any judgment on him; I try not to pass any judgment on anybody, but you can describe how somebody was, and that's kind of how he was. But he seemed a little bit sad. I don't want to step on anybody's toes, but it was a little difficult to have a full conversation with him, put it that way."

It seemed possible that Roky would record with the Black Angels, but in 2011 he released a new album, *True Love Cast out All Evil*, in collaboration with Will Sheff and Okkervil River. The album opened with a solo recording of *Devotional Number One* by Roky that was actually made by Evelyn Erickson on a reel-to-reel tape recorder while the singer was incarcerated in Rusk Maximum Security Prison in 1972. Indeed, the album focused on songs Roky wrote during or about his time in Rusk, and just a list of the titles tells a heartbreaking story: *Ain't Blues Too Sad*, *Goodbye Sweet Dreams*, *Be And Bring Me Home*, *Bring Back The Past*,

Please Judge, John Lawman, Birds'd Crash, God Is Everywhere. Sheff's alternative country/post-rock settings brought out the full poignancy of the lyrics, while Roky's vocal performance had the grizzled, careworn quality of an old cowboy, a Texan outlaw who has seen too much of life; at times accepting and melancholy, at others raging almost ecstatically against the dying of the light.

"I thought the album he did with them was the best thing he's done since the Aliens, and I rate it as equal to the Aliens, at least," says Billy Miller. "Because it was really a concept album, and what they had to work with, they were not really inside of so much. So they made it kind of a tribute to him with him in it. And I thought they did really great."

Powell St John left Mother Earth after they recorded their second album, *Make A Joyful Noise*, in Nashville. He returned to San Francisco and claimed unemployment benefit while looking for a job in music. The Angel Band, with Tary Owens and Charlie Prichard, lasted until a chapter of Hell's Angels came to a show and demanded that they change the name with immediate effect. Depending on whom you believe, they either became the Leapin' Lizards or Free Chicken, but split soon after.

In 1976 Powell took a job as a costume jewelry fabricator that lasted until 1990, when he retrained as a computer tech, a job he held until he was able to retire in 2005. That year he joined Roky, John Ike Walton, Benny Thurman and Ronnie Leatherman at SXSW, as the 13th Floor Elevators were inducted into the Texas Music Hall of Fame. "The town I had fled almost 40 years before had transformed dramatically," he told *It's Psychedelic Baby*. "Instead of viewing musicians with suspicion and disdain, musicians and their music were now embraced. The town's bad boys were now heroes and the subject of a panel discussion. Austin was calling itself the live music capital of the world. What the fuck?"

Powell cut a new album, *Right Track Now*, backed by an assortment of top Austin musicians only too happy to work with him, before hooking up with the Aliens (Billy Miller and Duane Aslaksen) for a second CD, *On My Way To Houston*, and an ongoing series of live performances. He continues to work on jewelry designs, songwriting and his remarkable artwork and paintings, while tending to his collection of cacti.

In 2009 the Austin Psych Fest expanded to a three-day event, and featured the Golden Dawn performing *Power Plant* in its entirety, alongside the Black Angels, Sky Saxon, Wooden Shjips, A Place To Bury Strangers, the Warlocks, Dead Meadow and dozens of other bands. The 2011 line-up was topped by Roky Erickson, with a reformed Cold Sun also performing. The Golden Dawn returned in 2012, and 2013 saw Roky Erickson and the Moving Sidewalks co-headlining as the festival moved to Carson Creek Ranch on the Colorado River and expanded over three stages, with outdoor camping and warm-up events in Austin's bars and clubs for festival-goers arriving from all over the world.

As Powell St John noted, Austin now celebrates its psychedelic heritage, and the artists it once persecuted are now heroes whose music is celebrated and imitated worldwide. It would seem as if the battle has finally been won; but at what cost? The casualty list alone is striking; and of those musicians who still survive, few have ever reaped the just benefits of creating music that remains profoundly influential on succeeding generations. This, perhaps, is the fate of all trailblazers; to be lost in the wilderness you are mapping, and to never truly feel accepted by the settlements you help found.

The 1960s in Texas saw a true gathering of promises, when social upheaval and artistic ferment took root among people known for their fierce independence and their questing, frontier spirit. Yet it would be a brave few who would take a stand against a prevailing climate of proud conservatism and a heavy-handed implementation of law and order. Young people all over America and the world were fighting the same battles, but in Texas neither side was prepared to back down. It was also, in a sense, a religious struggle, for Texas has always been a deeply religious state. Where the established church had grown corrupt and complacent, a clutch of wild-eyed heretics trusted to their own gnostic experience of the godhead, and fought for what was, in a way, an impassioned religious revival. In the end, it was the spirit of commerce that would defeat this impulse, as the music was first brutally suppressed, then re-packaged and sold back as mere entertainment, a souvenir of a supposedly more naive and innocent time. The message of this music remains, however; as striking and as relevant as it ever was, for all those who will take the time to listen.

Bibliography

Amburn, Ellis, *Pearl: The Obsessions and Passions of Janis Joplin*. New York: Warner Books, 1992.

Barthelme, Donald, *Unspeakable Practices, Unnatural Acts*. New York: Farrar, Strauss and Giroux, 1968.

Bowart, Walter, *Operation Mind Control*. London: Fontana Books, 1978.

Brammer, Billy Lee, *The Gay Place*. Boston: Houghton Mifflin, 1961.

Castaneda, Carlos, *The Teachings of Don Juan: A Yaqui Way of Knowledge*. Oakland: University of California Press, 1968.

Churton, Tobias, *The Gnostics*. London: Weidenfeld & Nicolson, 1987.

Cooper, Kim and David Smay, ed., *Bubblegum Music is the Naked Truth: The Dark History of Prepubescent Pop, from the Banana Splits to Britney Spears*. Los Angeles: Feral House, 2001.

Cope, Julian, *Copendium: An Expedition into the Rock 'n' Roll Underworld*. London: Faber and Faber, 2012.

Davis, Stephen L, *Texas Literary Outlaws: Six Writers in the Sixties and Beyond*. Fort Worth: Texas Christian University Press, 2004.

Didion, Joan, *Slouching Towards Bethlehem*. New York: Farrar, Strauss and Giroux, 1968.

Doggett, Peter, *There's a Riot Going On: Revolutionaries, Rock Stars and the Rise and Fall of '60s Counter-Culture*. Edinburgh: Canongate Books, 2007.

Drummond, Paul, *Eye Mind: The Saga of Roky Erickson and the 13th Floor Elevators*. Los Angeles: Process Media, 2007.

Echols, Alice, *Scars of Sweet Paradise: The Life and Times of Janis Joplin*. London: Virago Press, 2000.

Erickson, Roky, *Openers*. Austin: Pyrimid Press, 1972.

Friedman, Myra, *Buried Alive: a Biography of Janis Joplin*. London: W.H. Allen, 1974.

Huxley, Aldous, *Brave New World*. London: Chatto & Windus, 1932.

—— *The Doors of Perception*. London: Chatto & Windus, 1954.

Joplin, Laura, *Love, Janis*. London: Bloomsbury Publishing, 1992.

Kent, Nick, *The Dark Stuff*. London: Penguin, 1994.

Koster, Rick, *Texas Music*. New York: St. Martin's Press, 1998.

Lieberman, Robbie, *Prairie Power: Voices of 1960s Midwestern Student Protest*. Columbia: University of Missouri Press, 2004.

Long, Joshua, *Weird City: Sense of Place and Creative Resistance in Austin, Texas*. Austin: University of Texas Press, 2010.

Lowenthal, Steve, *Dance of Death: The Life of John Fahey, American Guitarist*. Chicago: Chicago Review Press, 2014.

Lydon, Michael, *Rock Folk: Portraits from the Rock 'n' Roll Pantheon*. New York: Dial Press, 1971.

McMillian, John, *Smoking Typewriters: the Sixties Underground Press and the Rise of Alternative Media in America*. Oxford: Oxford University Press, 2011.

Peck, Abe, *Uncovering the Sixties: The Life & Times of the Underground Press*. New York: Pantheon Books, 1985.

Perry, Charles, *The Haight-Ashbury: A History*. New York: Random House, 1984.

Slick, Grace with Andrea Cagan, *Somebody to Love? A Rock-and-Roll Memoir*. New York: Warner Books, 1998.

Stein, Ricky, *Sonobeat Records: Pioneering the Austin Sound in the '60s*. Charleston: The History Press, 2014.

Tendler, Stewart and David May, *The Brotherhood of Eternal Love: from Flower Power to Hippie Mafia, the Story of the LSD Counterculture*. London: Cyan Books, 2007.

Turner, Jeffrey A., *Sitting In and Speaking Out: Student Movements in the American South, 1960-1970*. Athens: University of Georgia Press, 2010.

Vorda, Allan, *Psychedelic Psounds: Interviews from A to Z with 60s Psychedelic and Garage Bands*. Telford: Borderline Productions, 1994.

Wilson, Colin, *Aleister Crowley: The Nature of the Beast.* Wellingborough: The Aquarian Press, 1987.

Wilson, Robert Anton, *Cosmic Trigger: Final Secret of the Illuminati.* New York: Simon & Schuster, 1977.

Wolfe, Tom, *The Electric Kool-Aid Acid Test.* New York: Farrar, Strauss and Giroux, 1968.

Other sources consulted (by chapter in which first referred to):

Chapter 1

Bentley, Bill, 'The Kingdom of Heaven: Psychedelic Pioneer Powell St John on the Right Track Now,' *The Austin Chronicle*, Friday December 22nd 2006.

Breznikar, Klemen (2011), 'Powell St John Interview,' *It's Psychedelic Baby* [online]. Available from www.psychedelic baby.blogspot.com/2011/07/powell-st-john-interview.html

Burr, Beverly (1988), *History of Student Activism at the University of Texas at Austin (1960-1988)* [online]. Available from www.campusactivism.org/server-new/uploads/burrthesis.pdf

Crutcher, Carlton (2009), 'Powell St John Interview,' *Terrascope* [online]. Available from www.terrascope.co.uk/Features/Powell%20St%20John&20interview.htm

Marley, Brent, 'Powell St John,' *Psych Trail Mix issue 4* [online]. Available from www.helioschrome.com/psychtrailmix.html

http://texasghetto.org/GhettoHistory.htm

Chapter 3

Maerz, Jennifer, 'A Long Strange Trip,' *SF Weekly*, Wednesday February 18th 2009.

Marley, Brent, 'The Neon in Your Eyes is Splashing into Mine: Clementine Hall,' *Psych Trail Mix issue 4* [online]. Available from www.helioschrome/psychtrailmix.html

Moser, Margaret, 'She Lives: the Clementine Hall Interview,' *The

Austin Chronicle, Friday August 20th 2004.

Trybyszewski, Joe, 'Where the Pyramid meets the High: Founding Elevator Tommy Hall and his Horizontal Thinking,' *The Austin Chronicle*, Friday August 13th 2004.

Chapter 5

Brown, Andrew (2003), 'An Interview with Spades drummer John Kearney' [online]. Available from www.scarletdukes.com/st/tm_spadesint.html

'Dr Rock' (2009), 'Getting to Grips with Roky Erickson: A Dr Rock Interview,' *The Quietus* [online]. Available from www.thequietus.com/articles/02536-getting-to-grips-with-roky-erickson-a-dr-rock-interview

Kinney, George (2006), 'The Austin Music Scene: 1969-1970,' *Texas Psychedelic Ranch* [online]. Available from www.texaspsychranch.com/history.htm

The Mal Thursday Show #35: Texas Tyme Machine Vol. 5 The Golden Dawn Story (2010), radio podcast, Austin. Available from www.malthursday.podomatic.com/entry/2014-04-16T20_30_01-07_00

Chapter 6

Bucholz, Brad, 'Tary's Tale,' *Austin-American Statesman*, Sunday March 26th 2000.

Reid, Jan, 'Return to the Gay Place,' *Texas Monthly*, March 2001.

Reinert, Al, 'Billy Lee,' *Texas Monthly*, February 1979.

Chapter 7

Ash, Cliff, 'Billy Royce Rolls into The Limelight,' *Dark Star* issue 9, June 1977.

Bentley, Bill, 'Mr Toad's Wild Ride,' *The Austin Chronicle*, Friday October 28th 2005.

The Mal Thursday Show #49: Texas Tyme Machine Vol. 14 The Wig Story (2013), radio podcast, Austin. Available from www.malt

hursday.podomatic.com/entry/2013-0929T11_56_03-07_00

Chapter 8

Crutcher, Carlton (2006), 'The Charlie Prichard Interview,' *Terrascope* [online]. Available from www.terrascope.co.uk/Features/Conqueroo_interview.htm

Langdon, Jim, 'Unique Elevators Shine With Psychedelic Rock,' *Austin Statesman*, Thursday February 10th 1966.

Chapter 9

Unknown author (1977), 'Stacy Sutherland Interview' [online]. Available from www.slidemachine.livejournal.com/1136.html

Chapter 10

Macleod, Marlee (2014), 'Charles Whitman: The Texas Bell Tower Sniper,' *Crime Library* [online]. Available from www.crimelibrary.com/notorious_murders/mass/Whitman/index_1.html

Chapter 13

Buesnel, Peter, 'The Zakary Thaks,' *The Sherwood Forest Gang* [online]. Available from www.sfgsite.org/Thaks.htm

Long, Pat, 'Thak's Entertainment,' *Shindig!* Volume 2, issue 7, November 2008.

Uncredited sleevenotes (2011) to *Revolution! Teen Time in Corpus Christi (1965-1970)*, various artists CD on Cicadelic Records, Tucson.

Chapter 14

Bentley, Bill (2012), sleevenotes to *The Complete Collection*, Moving Sidewalks anthology CD on Big Beat Records, London.

Bishop, Chris (2008), 'The Baroque Brothers,' *Garage Hangover* [online]. Available from www.garagehangover.com/baroquebrothers

Kit, Charles (2007), 'Lost And Found,' *Garage Hangover* [online]. Available from www.garagehangover.com/lostandfound

Forster, Tim (2003), sleevenotes to *A Gift from Euphoria* by Euphoria, CD reissue on Rev-Ola Records, London.

Gangl, Bert & 'Ken from Colorado' (updated 2014), *ZZ Top Tour Dates* [online]. Available from www.comcast.net/~mrrandom/tourzz.htm

Holtzman, Scott, 'What is Psychedelic? Well Uh...,' *Houston Post*, Sunday February 12th 1967.

Mole (2009), sleevenotes to *Everybody's Here* by the Lost And Found, expanded CD reissue on Charly Records, London.

Palao, Alex, (2013), sleevenotes to *Good Men*, Neal Ford and the Fanatics anthology CD on Big Beat Records, London.

Unterberger, Richie (1996), 'Mayo Thompson of the Red Krayola' [online]. Available from www.richieunterberger.com/mayo.html

'1960s Texas Music: Houston Live Music Venues,' *Scarlet Dukes* [online]. Available from www.scarletdukes.com/st/tmhou_venues1.html

'1960s Texas Music: Stephen Hamilton Interview' (2003), *Scarlet Dukes* [online]. Available from www.scarletdukes.com/st/tmhou_hammondint.html

'Tests Set on Pills seized by Officers,' *Brownwood Bulletin*, Wednesday November 30th, 1966.

Chapter 15

Dreyer, Thorne (2013), 'Rag Mama Rag,' *The Rag Blog* [online]. Available from www.theragblog.com/rag-history

Hickey, Dennis (2004), *The Complete Illustrated List of Vulcan Gas Company Posters and Handbills* [online]. Available from www.people.missouristate.edu/DennisHickey/vulcan.htm

Lerner, Mitchell (2010), 'Erwin, Frank Craig Jr.,' *Handbook of Texas Online* [online]. Available from www.tshaonline.org/handbook/online/articles/fer08

Ratcliffe, Martin (2010), 'An Interview with George Kinney' from the sleevenotes to *Power Plant* by the Golden Dawn, CD reissue on Charly Records, London.

Smith, Cheryl, 'Everything Old is New Again,' *The Austin Chronicle*, Friday September 2nd 2005.

Chapter 16

Barthelme, Frederick (2014), 'The Red Krayola,' *Frederick barthelme.com* [online]. Available from www.frederick barthelme.com/notes-comments/the-red-crayola

Campbell, Rick (2008), 'Fever Tree was Here,' *40 Years After/The Houston Chronicle* [online]. Available from www.blog.chron .com/40yearsafter/2008/04/fever-tree-was-here

Curran, Pat, 'Return of the Natives,' *Shindig!* Volume 2, issue 7, November 2008.

Holtzman, Scott, 'Coming: Frisco Art, Love-Ins,' *Houston Post*, Sunday April 9th 1967.

Holtzman, Scott, 'Grove-In Coming,' *Houston Post*, Sunday April 16th 1967.

Savage, Jon (1979), 'Lelan Rogers Interview' from the sleevenotes to *Epitaph for a Legend*, compilation album on International Artists Records, Houston; also included in the booklet for the 2008 3-CD IA box set *Never Ever Land*, Charly Records, London.

'Webmaster Scott' (2003), 'Former Fever Tree guitarist Michael Knust,' *Psychedelic Guitar* [online]. Available from www. psychedelicguitar.com/knust.htm

The Story So Far of the Red Crayola and the Red Krayola, A Biography, Drag City Records press release, 2004.

Chapter 17

Goldstein, Richard, 'WOR and the Future,' *Village Voice*, October 5th 1967.

McDevitt, Molly, 'An Interview with the Late, Lamented Murray the K,' *FM Guide*, April 1968.

Chapter 18

Bruno, Bob, 'The Circus Experiment,' *Inside the Box/Test Site* [online]. Available from www.insidethebox.yolasite.com/the-circus-experiment.php

Uncredited sleevenotes (2006) to *Take Me To The Mountains… Plus* by Shiva's Headband, expanded CD reissue on Akarma Records, Italy.

'The Thingies,' *Sonobeat Records* [online]. Available from www.sonobeatrecords.com/sonobeatartists1.html#thingies

'The Thingies: from Topeka to Miami to Austin!,' *Cicadelic Records* [online]. Available from www.cicadelicrecords.com/thingies.htm

Chapter 19

Fornatale, Mike, 'Holy Smoke,' *Shindig!* Volume 2, issue 7, November 2008.

Prince, Rod, 'The Tale of Bubble Puppy 1966-1972,' *Official Bubble Puppy Website* [online]. Available from www.bubblepuppy.com/bubblepuppy_016.htm

'The Who Tour Archive: 1968,' *The Who Concert Guide* [online]. Available from www.thewholive.net/tour-list/index.php?GroupID=1&Year=1968.

Chapter 20

Helsing, Lenny, 'The Stoics,' *Shindig!* Volume 2, issue 7, November 2008.

James, David (2002), 'The Children,' sleevenotes to *Rebirth* by the Children, expanded CD reissue on Gear Fab Records, Orlando.

Moser, Margaret, 'Returning to when San Antonio ruled South Texas,' *San Antonio Current*, Wednesday August 31st 2011.

Robbit, Peter, 'Drab It Ain't… Color Bomb Mar 10th,' *San Antonio*

Express and News, Saturday March 4th 1967.

Stieb, Matt, 'Trippin' Out in TX: A Journey Through Texas' Psychedelic Music Scene,' *San Antonio Current*, Wednesday April 30th 2014.

Chapter 21

Heller, Jason (2014), 'Starter: John Fahey,' *Pitchfork* [online]. Available from www.pitchfork.com/features/starter/9314-john-fahey

Chapter 22

Rowland, Hubert, 'Static,' *Houston Press*, Thursday November 21st 1996.

Uncredited sleevenotes (2011) to *The Psychedelic Sound of Summer* by the Lemon Fog, compilation CD on Cicadelic Records, Tucson.

The Mal Thursday Show #32: Texas Tyme Machine Vol. 4 The Thursday's Children Story (2010), radio podcast, Austin. Available from www.malthursday.podomatic.com/entry/20 14-04-16T20_47_50-07_00

Chapter 23

'New Atlantis,' *Sonobeat Records* [online]. Available from www.sonobeatrecords.com/unreleasedmaterial1968.html#atl antis

Chapter 24

Breznikar, Klemen (2012), 'Blue Mountain Eagle interview,' *It's Psychedelic Baby* [online]. Available from www.psyche-delicbaby.blogspot.co.uk/2012/12/blue-mountain-eagle-inter view.html

Glut, Donald (2004), 'The Penny Arkade Story,' *donaldfglut.com* [online]. Available from www.donaldfglut.com/PENNY.htm

Jackson, Jack, 'Rip Off Press in the Golden Era,' *Rip Off Comix* number 21, Winter 1988.

Todd, Fred, 'The Real Story according to Fred Todd,' *Rip Off Comix* number 21, Winter 1988.

Chapter 25

Cress, Sara (2008), 'The Clique, a Hit in the '60s, reunites for Hall of Fame Show,' *Handstamp / the Houston Chronicle* [online]. Available from www.blog.chron.com/handstamp/2008/01/the-clique-a-hit-in-the-60s-reunites-for-hall-of-fame-show

Dansby, Andrew (2013), 'Superman soared for the Clique in 1969,' *Houston Chronicle* [online]. Available from www.blog.chron.com/entertainment/music/article/Superman-soared-for-the-Clique-in-1969-4595957.php

'Disk, 2 Prod. & 7 Pub. Firms Invade LA,' *Billboard* magazine, December 7th 1968.

Chapter 27

Perskin, Spencer 'The IL Club Brawl,' *Shiva's Headband/Spencer Perskin's Rock 'n' Roll Stories* [online]. Available from www.texaschainsawmassacre.net/perskin/story/brawl.html

Perskin, Spencer 'The Texas Connect,' *Shiva's Headband/Spencer Perskin's Rock 'n' Roll Stories* [online]. Available from www.texaschainsawmassacre.net/perskin/story/connect.html

'History,' *Sonobeat Records* [online]. Available from www.sonobeatrecords.com/history1.html

'Lavender Hill Express,' *Sonobeat Records* [online]. Available from www.sonobeatrecords.com/lavenderhillexpress.html

'Shiva's Headband,' *Sonobeat Records* [online]. Available from www.sonobeatrecords.com/unreleasedmaterial1968.html#shivas

Chapter 28

Lundborg, Patrick (2007, updated 2011), 'Art of the Gifted,' *Waxidermy* [online]. Available from www.waxidermy.com/art-of the-gifted

Potter, David, 'Endle St Cloud,' *David Potter Musician* [online]. Available from www.davidpottermusician.com/?page_id=169

'Biography,' *David Potter Musician* [online]. Available from www.davidpottermusician.com/?page_id=179

'Gulf Pacific Produces 13 Groups in Record-Tape Tie,' *Billboard* magazine, April 12th 1969.

Chapter 29

Breznikar, Klemen (2012), 'Cold Sun Interview with Billy Bill Miller,' *It's Psychedelic Baby* [online]. Available from www.psychedelicbaby.blogspot.co.uk/2012/10/cold-sun-interview-with-billy-bill.html

Lundborg, Patrick (2003, updated 2011), 'Cold Sun: Austin's Lost Psychedelic Visionaries,' *Lama Workshop* [online]. Available from www.lysergia.com/LamaWorkshop/lamaColdSun.htm

Miller, Billy, sleevenotes from *Dark Shadows* by Cold Sun, 2008 expanded CD reissue on World in Sound, Schwetzingen.

Powell, Austin, 'Dark Shadows: Billy Miller on the return of Cold Sun at Austin Psych Fest,' *The Austin Chronicle*, Friday April 29th 2011.

'Bill Miller Group (Cold Sun),' *Sonobeat Records* [online]. Available from www.sonobeatrecords.com/unreleasedmaterial1971.html#miller

Chapter 30

Ingle, John (2008), 'Roky Erickson and Doug Sahm Remembrance' *Perfect Sound Forever* [online]. Available from www.furious.com/perfect/roky2.html

Patowski, Joe Nick, sleevenotes from *The Evil One, Don't Slander Me* and *Gremlins Have Pictures* by Roky Erickson, 2013 CD reissues on Light in the Attic Records, Seattle.

Chapter 32

Lynskey, Dorian, 'The Man Who Went Too High,' *The Guardian*, Friday June 8th 2007.

Moser, Margaret, 'Starry Eyes: Roky Erickson is Back,' *The Austin Chronicle*, Friday December 30th 2005.

Sheff, Will (2010), sleevenotes for *True Love Cast Out All Evil* by Roky Erickson, Chemikal Underground Records, Glasgow.

Press Release, Roky Erickson Ice Cream Social, 2007.

Contemporary culture has eliminated both the concept of the public and the figure of the intellectual. Former public spaces – both physical and cultural – are now either derelict or colonized by advertising. A cretinous anti-intellectualism presides, cheerled by expensively educated hacks in the pay of multinational corporations who reassure their bored readers that there is no need to rouse themselves from their interpassive stupor. The informal censorship internalized and propagated by the cultural workers of late capitalism generates a banal conformity that the propaganda chiefs of Stalinism could only ever have dreamt of imposing. Zer0 Books knows that another kind of discourse – intellectual without being academic, popular without being populist – is not only possible: it is already flourishing, in the regions beyond the striplit malls of so-called mass media and the neurotically bureaucratic halls of the academy. Zer0 is committed to the idea of publishing as a making public of the intellectual. It is convinced that in the unthinking, blandly consensual culture in which we live, critical and engaged theoretical reflection is more important than ever before.

ZERO BOOKS

Weird Realism Lovecraft and Philosophy
Graham Harman
As Hölderlin was to Martin Heidegger and Mallarmé to Jacques
Derrida, so is H.P. Lovecraft to the Speculative Realist philoso-
phers.
Paperback: September 28, 2012 978-1-78099-252-5 $24.95 £14.99.
eBook: September 28, 2012 978-1-78099-907-4 $9.99 £6.99.

Sweetening the Pill or How We Got Hooked on Hormonal Birth
Control
Holly Grigg-Spall
Is it really true? Has contraception liberated or oppressed
women?
Paperback: September 27, 2013 978-1-78099-607-3 $22.95 £12.99.
eBook: September 27, 2013 978-1-78099-608-0 $9.99 £6.99.

Why Are We The Good Guys? Reclaiming Your Mind From The
Delusions Of Propaganda
David Cromwell
A provocative challenge to the standard ideology that Western
power is a benevolent force in the world.
Paperback: September 28, 2012 978-1-78099-365-2 $26.95 £15.99.
eBook: September 28, 2012 978-1-78099-366-9 $9.99 £6.99.

The Truth about Art Reclaiming quality
Patrick Doorly
The book traces the multiple meanings of art to their various
sources, and equips the reader to choose between them.
Paperback: August 30, 2013 978-1-78099-841-1 $32.95 £19.99.

Bells and Whistles More Speculative Realism
Graham Harman
In this diverse collection of sixteen essays, lectures, and inter-
views Graham Harman lucidly explains the principles of

Speculative Realism, including his own object-oriented philosophy.
Paperback: November 29, 2013 978-1-78279-038-9 $26.95 £15.99.
eBook: November 29, 2013 978-1-78279-037-2 $9.99 £6.99.

Towards Speculative Realism: Essays and Lectures Essays and Lectures
Graham Harman
These writings chart Harman's rise from Chicago sportswriter to co founder of one of Europe's most promising philosophical movements: Speculative Realism.
Paperback: November 26, 2010 978-1-84694-394-2 $16.95 £9.99.
eBook: January 1, 1970 978-1-84694-603-5 $9.99 £6.99.

Meat Market Female flesh under capitalism
Laurie Penny
A feminist dissection of women's bodies as the fleshy fulcrum of capitalist cannibalism, whereby women are both consumers and consumed.
Paperback: April 29, 2011 978-1-84694-521-2 $12.95 £6.99.
eBook: May 21, 2012 978-1-84694-782-7 $9.99 £6.99.

Translating Anarchy The Anarchism of Occupy Wall Street
Mark Bray
An insider's account of the anarchists who ignited Occupy Wall Street.
Paperback: September 27, 2013 978-1-78279-126-3 $26.95 £15.99.
eBook: September 27, 2013 978-1-78279-125-6 $6.99 £4.99.

One Dimensional Woman
Nina Power
Exposes the dark heart of contemporary cultural life by examining pornography, consumer capitalism and the ideology of women's work.

Paperback: November 27, 2009 978-1-84694-241-9 $14.95 £7.99.
eBook: July 1, 2012 978-1-78099-737-7 $9.99 £6.99.

Dead Man Working

Carl Cederstrom, Peter Fleming

An analysis of the dead man working and the way in which capital is now colonizing life itself.
Paperback: May 25, 2012 978-1-78099-156-6 $14.95 £9.99.
eBook: June 27, 2012 978-1-78099-157-3 $9.99 £6.99.

Unpatriotic History of the Second World War

James Heartfield

The Second World War was not the Good War of legend. James Heartfield explains that both Allies and Axis powers fought for the same goals - territory, markets and natural resources.
Paperback: September 28, 2012 978-1-78099-378-2 $42.95 £23.99.
eBook: September 28, 2012 978-1-78099-379-9 $9.99 £6.99.

Find more titles at www.zero-books.net